SPAIN'S
LONG SHADOW

SPAIN'S LONG SHADOW

*The Black Legend, Off-Whiteness, and
Anglo-American Empire*

MARÍA DEGUZMÁN

UNIVERSITY OF MINNESOTA PRESS

MINNEAPOLIS • LONDON

Portions of chapter 3 first appeared in "Consolidating Anglo-American Imperial Identity around the Spanish-American War (1898)," in *Race and the Production of Modern American Nationalism,* ed. Reynolds J. Scott-Childress (New York: Taylor & Francis Books, 1999), 97–126. Copyright 1999. Reproduced by permission of Routledge/Taylor & Francis Books, Inc.

Portions of chapter 6 first appeared in "Terrorism as Terrorific Mimesis in Floyd Salas's *State of Emergency* (1966)," in *Fear Itself: Enemies Real and Imagined in American Culture,* ed. Nancy Lusignan Schultz (West Lafayette, IN: Purdue University Press, 1999), 237–49. Reprinted with permission.

Published by the University of Minnesota Press
111 Third Avenue South, Suite 290
Minneapolis, MN 55401-2520
http://www.upress.umn.edu

Library of Congress Cataloging-in-Publication Data

DeGuzmán, María.
Spain's long shadow : the black legend, off-whiteness,
and Anglo-American empire / María DeGuzmán.
p. cm.
Includes bibliographical references and index.
ISBN 0-8166-4527-2 (alk. paper)—ISBN 0-8166-4528-0 (pbk. : alk. paper)
1. American literature—Spanish influences. 2. United States—Civilization—Spanish influences.
3. Literature, Comparative—American and Spanish. 4. Literature, Comparative—Spanish and American. 5. American literature—History and criticism. 6. Spain—Foreign public opinion, American. 7. United States—Relations—Spain. 8. Spain—Relations—United States.
9. Imperialism in literature. 10. Spaniards in literature. 11. Ethnicity in literature.
12. Spain—In literature. 13. Race in literature. I. Title.
PS159.S7D44 2005
810.9—dc22
2005000808

Printed in the United States of America on acid-free paper

The University of Minnesota is an equal-opportunity educator and employer.

12 11 10 09 08 07 06 05   10 9 8 7 6 5 4 3 2 1

For Elizabeth and Luis

CONTENTS

ACKNOWLEDGMENTS

I would like to thank Daniel Aaron, José Amor y Vázquez, Lawrence Buell, Jill Casid, Karen Encarnación, Margarita Estévez Abe, Marjorie Garber, Mary Gaylord, Roland Greene, Graham Huggan, Debbie López, Roxana Pagés-Rangel, Geoffrey Ribbans, Rennie Scott-Childress, Doris Sommer, Jack Trumpbour, and the members across the years of the American Doctoral Colloquium (English Department, Harvard University), all of whom read or listened to initial and later portions of this manuscript and whose comments and suggestions I have tried to integrate into the present work. I would like to express my many thanks to Sacvan Bercovitch for his abiding belief in this project and to Luis Fernández-Cifuentes for his insightful readings of the chapters. I am very appreciative of the University Research Council, the Institute for the Arts and Humanities, and especially the English Department at the University of North Carolina, Chapel Hill for granting me research and study leave as well as financial support to prepare this manuscript, among other things. In particular, for their sound advice, I would like to thank Linda Wagner-Martin and William L. Andrews. I am grateful for the archival and curatorial assistance of Jennifer Brathovde, Becky Cape, Erika Dowell, Laura A. Foster, Jennifer Hughes, Mary Ison, Ruth Janson, Claudia Jew, Francis Lapka, Danielle Mann, Daniel Moulton, Lois Oglesby, Kristin Parker, Mario Pereira, Vaughn Thibodeau, Donna VanLeer, Tessa Veazey, Nicholas Wharton, and Danielle Zahaba. I would like to acknowledge the University of Minnesota Press, notably Doug Armato, Gretchen Asmussen, Adam Grafa,

Emily Hamilton, Dan Leary, Mary Poggione, Nancy Sauro, Mike Stoffel, David Thorstad, and Laura Westlund, as well as the anonymous readers of the original manuscript. I am profoundly grateful to Dominique Fisher, Patricia Juliana Smith, Mary Slayter, Margaret Diane Stetz, and Rashmi Varma for their life-sustaining friendship and to my parents Elizabeth and Luis de Guzmán for their love and encouragement.

INTRODUCTION

Out of that old entire European debris . . . A glimpse as of thy Mother's face
Columbia . . .

—WALT WHITMAN, "Spain, 1873–74"

Since the early 1980s, American literary and cultural studies have been
seeking new approaches to the subject of American literature and culture within the framework of "multiculturalism."[1] Although the new
approaches have yielded much impressive and exciting scholarship, particularly with regard to ethnicity and race, the focus of these enterprises
has been, until quite recently, on the United States not as the United
States of the Americas, but as "American."[2] Despite the shift from American studies to Americas studies, even within American studies the move
to give a more multicultural dimension to English departments, curricula,
and scholarship generally under the rubric "ethnic" has often meant the
supplementation, frequently tokenist, of the study of American literature
with something called ethnic literature(s), leaving relatively intact the traditional, mostly Anglo canon of U.S. literature as "American," and "American," by extension, as not only "white" but also "nonethnic."[3] Ethnicity has
been attributed to practically all non-Anglo-Americans, and particularly,
in the confusion of ethnicity with race and in the lingering nineteenth-
century positivist and self-perpetuatingly race-ist approach to the concept
of "race," to those designated as "people of color." Of course, these tendencies vary from institution to institution and region to region in the practice
of English and American literature departments and American studies.
For example, the widespread presence of Chicana/o studies in schools of
the Southwest borderlands has managed to challenge deeply what might

be called the Anglo canon and tokenist multicultural supplementations. And Chicana/o studies, as well as Chicana/o cultural production, learned a great deal from the African American Civil Rights movement and the gradual institutionalization of African American and African Diaspora studies both within and alongside English departments and American studies programs and departments. Nor must we overlook the curricular and critical changes effected by Native American studies, Asian American studies, and Latina/o studies more generally on the practice of English and American literary and cultural studies and American studies.

Ironically, the often limited inclusivity of a multiculturalist rubric has obscured the existence of a hegemonic ethnic group in the United States— what I designate in this book as "Anglo-American." The hegemony of this ethnic group is not so much numerical—although on a temporally and geographically local level it may have been and may continue to be so— as socioeconomic, political, and ideological. This ethnic group, through warfare, land grabbing, slavery, educational institutions reproducing the sociocultural order, and rhetorical reiteration of stories (historically based and otherwise) favorable to themselves, managed to extend their English language, their varieties of Protestantism, and their ethos, systems of belief, and representation over a large part of North America and finally other parts of the world, assimilating other peoples in their homogenizing image while demonizing difference. I contend that no multicultural or ethnic studies approach will succeed in a deep-structure questioning of American culture *without* recognizing the existence of such a hegemony and the manner of its self-construction not as an ethnicity but as transcendentally or transparently "American."

The fundamental claim of this book is that the construction of Anglo-American identity as "American" has been dependent on figures of Spain. Figures of Spain have been central to the dominant fictions of "American" exceptionalism, revolution, manifest destiny, and birth/rebirth; to Anglo-America's articulation of its empire as antiempire (the "good" empire that is not one); and to its fears of racial contamination and hybridity. Figures of Spain have been indispensable to the constitution, elaboration, and even interrogation of these dominant fictions. I use the term "figure" to mean historical personage as well as image and rhetorical device. From colonial times to the present, figures of Spain and Spaniards have occupied, in the process of "American" identity formation, a position as important as that of Britain or France. The figuration of Spain and Spaniards, produced by the relation between ideology and identification, is not always intentional. Nevertheless, it is possible to analyze these textual and visual productions for the ideological implications of certain semiotic formations. Figures of Spain and Spaniards occupy a position somewhat similar to those of the "American Indian" and the mythic "old South" inasmuch as these were used to constitute an "American" identity through a double movement of *repulsion* (in the former case through genocide) and *romancing*—that is, the "Native" spirit deemed integral to the American continent or the postbellum nostalgia for a romantic South of magnolias and moonlight. With regard to U.S. and what I would call *Anglo-American* obsession with depicting Native Americans, particularly Indian ghosts or spectral Indians, through what I would term a double movement, Renée L. Bergland has published a book on precisely this subject titled *The National Uncanny: Indian Ghosts and American Subjects.* A similar double movement of romancing and repulsion at the heart of appropriative identification has been charted at length in Eric Wertheimer's *Imagined Empires: Incas, Aztecs, and the New World of American Literature, 1771–1876.* This study examines the investments, simultaneously postcolonial and imperial, in Columbus, the Black Legend, against Spain vis-à-vis the treatment of the Indians (Incas and Aztecs) and empires (both Native and Spanish) in South America in the writings of Philip Freneau, Joel Barlow, William H. Prescott, Herman Melville, and Walt Whitman. His study seeks to chart the creation of a form of Anglo-American identity that "uses the frontier [southward] to formulate hybrid identities that enable the national imagination of empire."[4] His study and mine converge upon the recognition of the uses of the Other Americans in the consolidation of Anglo-American imperial identity. His book concentrates on a North–South axis, the so-called New World hemisphere, and on representations by Anglo-Americans of the Incas and Aztecs and, following the work of David Shields on the Black Legend, only secondarily on Spanish empire taken as an antitype, of course, to supposedly democratic, libertarian Anglo-American empire in formation.[5] My book, in contrast, is dedicated to an in-depth examination of Anglo-American and, more generally, U.S. representations of Spain and Spaniards. This story has not been told, particularly along a West–East axis with important implications for the North–South axis that the new American studies has begun to probe.

For the most part, the importance of figures of Spain has been un-recognized in "American" literary and cultural studies conducted within the self-protective walls of U.S. academia frequently acting as part of the "citadel culture" described by O. K. Werckmeister.[6] The one book, a two-volume study, dedicated to the importance of Spain for "American literature" per se is Stanley Williams's *The Spanish Background of American Literature* published by Yale University Press in 1955 and in the making for almost twenty years. It is not exhaustive, but it is impressively extensive. It draws on material manuscripts, unpublished documents, and the direct aid of twentieth-century U.S. Hispanophiles such as John Dos Passos and Waldo Frank. In its investigation of the immense historical and cultural influence on Anglophone American literature of Spain, Mexico, and the presence in the Southwest of the Spanish borderlands, it stretches from Cotton Mather and other Puritan divines to the late-nineteenth-century social critic and writer William Dean Howells. The strength of Williams's study resides in his elucidation of the influence of the presence of Spain, New Spain (Mexico), and the Spanish borderlands on Anglophone American letters generally in the form of transatlantic and trans-American literary influences. As such, his work exemplifies a particular handling of the topic of Spain and Spanishness in Anglo-American culture, namely, that of the influence of one or more cultures and literatures on another.

The historical swath of my study is similar, except that I start in the late eighteenth century and end in the late twentieth rather than begin in the seventeenth century and end in the early twentieth century, and my focus differs considerably from *The Spanish Background of American Literature*. It is not about the influence of Spain on American letters, but rather about the uses of representations of Spain in the creation of an Anglo-American identity. The emphasis is on the representations of one culture by another, not the influence of one on another. As such, my study does not treat Spain as a "background" but, more psychoanalytically, as a collectively incorporated and projected historical and contemporaneous object within and of Anglo-American culture. At stake is not the truth or presence of Spain so much as the ideological valences of its figuration. I argue that figures of Spain in Anglo-American culture also have a transhistorical (as well as transnational) status of totemic symbols, marked by the ambivalence toward totems swinging between taboo and totem. Furthermore, this "also" is not characterized by a mere parallelism with representations of

Native Americans, but instead actually overlaps with and includes such representations, as I shall demonstrate. Suffice it to say for the moment that if spectral Indians function through the logic of ambivalent totemism (simultaneously dispossessed and conjured up, the object of disavowal and identification), so do Spain and Spaniards, but with the major *difference* of being geopolitically located in a more parallel and therefore intensely rivalrous relationship with Anglo-American subjects themselves, thus granting them the status of alter ego/*imago* as well as totem.

Sigmund Freud in *Totem and Taboo* (1913) posits that generally the totem animal is an entity that represents the "common ancestor of the clan."[7] Within a patriarchal system, the "common ancestor" translates into the ancestral father or forefather who usually, Freud claims, has met a violent death at the hands of a rebelling band of brothers vying for the father's power. In the wake of the murder and driven by guilt, the brothers consecrate an animal to symbolize the murdered father, that is, create a totem to cover for and expiate their guilt. As such, the totem is actually the result of and is marked by deep emotional, social, and political ambivalence. For instance, prohibition (taboo) may exist against killing the totem animal, but, just as often, the totem animal is killed. This killing functions as a repetition or reenactment of the action of murdering the common ancestor for whom the totem entity stands in symbolic embodiment. When I claim that Spain and Spaniards fulfill a totemic function in Anglo-American culture, I am signaling a historical relation that is represented through generational difference. "Spain" in these cases is figured as an influential parental figure that inspires a certain degree of awe and also provokes anxiety of influence and mixed responses of respectful memorialization and rebellion, similar to those elicited by England but more pronounced on account of cultural differences deemed threatening (Roman Catholicism, for instance). At the same time, for reasons belonging, in terms of psychoanalytic object relations, to "external" historical reality, Spain and Spaniards could not be confined to merely totemic status. After all, Spain was in the Americas, and in North America itself in New Spain/Mexico and the Spanish borderlands. "Spanish" America was and still is the territorially and demographically larger portion of the Americas. Herein lies the difference between Spain as totem and Spain as alter ego/*imago*. The totemic function implies both generational remove and ambivalent consecration shadowed by an act of vanquishment. The alter ego/*imago* function entails rivalrous contest and possible equivalence in the present, that is, in the present of a designated time period. Of course, in some cases, Spain and Spaniards are figured in such a way as to occupy all these positions and roles. They are not mutually exclusive. Many scholars have observed the confusion of roles in depictions of the relation between England and the American republic. Obscured in this concentration on the importance of England are similar, but in many ways more potent, dynamics between Spain and the United States that extend into a drama of imperial identity. Ironically, it has taken U.S. writers of many different ethnicities, often not academics, to both unwittingly and deliberately highlight the marginalized or eccentric centrality of Spain and Spaniards. Consider, for example, Jewish-American poet Allen Ginsberg's incisive verses from his famous epic poem "Howl" (1956): "I saw the best minds of my generation destroyed by madness . . . who . . . *followed the brilliant Spaniard to converse about America and Eternity, a hopeless task,* and so took ship to Africa ."[8] Or, consider the lines from Chicana writer Ana Castillo's novel *Peel My Love Like an Onion* (1999): "Spain remained for me a make-believe place where nothing and no one was real and everything sparkled like a jewel necklace" and "To me Spain was a myth."[9]

Phrases such as "the . . . Spaniard," "America," "Eternity," "make-believe," and "myth" speak to another fundamental claim of this study. "Spain" and "Spaniards" are abstracting unifications for people and places historically heterogeneous, nonunitary, and constantly changing. In 1917, U.S. writer John Dos Passos recognized that "Spain" was not one:

> [T]here are many Spains. Indeed every village hidden in the folds of the great barren hills, or shadowed by its massive church in the middle of one of the upland plains, every *huerta* of the seacoast is a Spain.[10]

Dos Passos spoke of the many cultures, different languages of the Peninsula—Gallego-Portuguese, Basque, Castilian, and Catalan—and of the "immense variety of topography."[11] However, the vast majority of the works I examine—by people who both were and were never in any part of the Peninsula—conceive of it not only as unified but as uniform, even when they acknowledge variety or difference from region to region. The uniformity constructed by most of these representations denies the categorical disorder of material conditions. It passes out of the messiness of history into an almost Platonic realm of unchanging essential forms. "Spain," much like "Eternity," and, of course, the reified ideal "America," is hypostasized. In other words, "Spain" is a concept or an idea treated as a metaphysical, transhistorical reality underlying or overarching all possible disparate manifestations of "itself." Specifically, in relation to Anglo-American culture, Spain functions as a virtual or mirror image in front of which, in a libidinal dynamic of identification and disavowal, Anglo-American culture, despite its fragmentation and initial fragility, ascends toward a seemingly unified and coherent imperial identity, its Ideal-I. Spain as symbol has operated for Anglo-American culture the way the *imago*—the internalized image in the mirror—does for the developing human infant, according to psychoanalyst Jacques Lacan.[12] This *imago* provides none other than the illusion of a whole autonomous, but nevertheless potentially expansive, self.

The increase in the symbolic power of Spain, as with other symbolized signs, corresponds to its decline in actual economic, military, and territorial power, revealing an inverse relationship between historical realities and symbol making. The life of the symbol depends on the death of the thing. The actual influence of Spain was greatest in the Americas, especially in what is now the United States, from the sixteenth to the last quarter of the eighteenth century. However, the image of Spain grew more pervasive in the first half of the nineteenth century after Spain's loss of many of its colonies in the wake of revolutionary/independence movements in Latin America. It became especially powerful in the early to mid-twentieth century, after the loss of the last of Spain's colonies in the Spanish-Cuban-American War (1898). To call this phenomenon simply and exclusively a symptom and a continuation of an earlier nineteenth-century romanticization of Spain or part and parcel of the legacy of the construct "Romantic Spain," often taken for an actuality, as some scholars have done, is to miss the implicit (and sometimes very explicit) cultural and political work that figures of Spain perform—that is, their function as alter egos in the development of "American" imperial identity.[13] If the Lacanian *imago* involves the misrecognition of one's mortal, ephemeral, and vulnerable body as the idealized whole body in the mirror, then figures of Spain as alter egos constitute an *imago,* the image in the mirror, as a *rival* idealized and therefore demonic body. In fact, feminist psychoanalytic critic Jane Gallop, in her commentary on Lacan's work—interestingly, she refers to Lacan as "the

American other," signaling his difference with American ego psychoanalysis or *difference* within a context of similarity—points up precisely this double effect of the *imago*, that it elicits both identification and aggression: "For Lacan, aggression is produced in response to the mirror image. There is a rivalry over which is the self and which is the other, which is the ego and which is the replica" or alter-ego, if you wish.[14] A Spanish *imago* as alter ego is the image in the mirror experienced as external threat rather than internalized reassurance. Nowhere is the logic of the *imago* as alter ego more succinctly expressed than in Protestant minister and Yale professor of political economy William Graham Sumner's 1899 essay "The Conquest of the United States by Spain," written shortly after the official termination of the Spanish-Cuban-American War of 1898. His is a criticism of and a series of warnings about the transformation of the United States as nation-state into a world empire not only modeled on the methods and breadth of Spain's empire but actually composed of its former possessions, sharing in the very substance (not to mention image) of that Spanish Empire:

> During the last year the public has been familiarized with descriptions of Spain and of Spanish methods of doing things until the name of Spain has become a symbol for a certain well-defined set of notions and policies. On the other hand, the name of the United States has always been, for all of us, a symbol for a state of things, a set of ideas and traditions, a group of views about social and political affairs. Spain was the first, for a long time the greatest, of the modern imperialistic states. The United States, by its historical origin, its traditions, and its principles, is the chief representative of the revolt and reaction against that kind of a state. I intend to show that, by the line of action now proposed to us, which we call expansionism and imperialism, we are throwing away some of the most important elements of the American symbol and are adopting some of the most important elements of the Spanish symbol. We have beaten Spain in a military conflict, but we are submitting to be conquered by her on the field of ideas and policies. Expansionism and imperialism are nothing but the old philosophies of national prosperity which have brought Spain to where she now is ["poor," "decrepit," and "bankrupt"].[15]

Though a social Darwinist, unlike many of his contemporaries, and certainly those who shared his credo, Sumner was not in favor of the transformation of an Anglo-supremacist United States into an empire. However, his words articulate the deepest fascinations and fears of both imperialists and anti-imperialists (and many in between) with Spain and Spaniards, encapsulated in the concisely stated logic of the *imago* as alter ego. This ambivalent, dialectic dynamic had begun long before 1898 and is evident in numerous Anglo-Puritan tracts, treatises, sermons, poems, and diaries written in the "howling wilderness," notably, for instance, in John Wilson's "Song of Deliverance" from *Lasting Remembrance of God's Wonderful Works* (1680), Cotton Mather's *La Fe del Christiano* (1699), supposedly the first book written in Spanish in the North American British colonies, as well as in his *Magnalia Christi Americana* (1702), and Samuel Sewall's *Phaenomena Quaedam Apocalyptica* (1697). At that point in time, however, the *imago* as rival alter ego outweighed the *imago* as reassuring idealization (though some of this latter is apparent). The English Puritans and Pilgrims greatly feared Spanish power in both the New and Old Worlds. Spanish power was still waxing, not waning, in the Americas. The more confident post-Revolution epic poem by Joel Barlow, *The Vision of Columbus* (1779), tips the scales the other way in favor of the Spanish image as reassuring ego idealization, but mainly through claiming the discoverer Columbus, in service of the Spanish crown, to be a true "American," in contrast to the Spanish king Ferdinand, who is portrayed as the betrayer of Columbus's distinctly "American" vision. The point is that there is a continual oscillation between *imago* as reassuring ideal and *imago* as fearful alter ego. The two are rarely entirely separable, and Barlow's poem attempts to cut that Gordian knot by severing Columbus from Spain in myriad ways. The poem itself is even dedicated to the king of France, a snub to the king of Spain, for Louis XVI's help with the American Revolution.

The story that unfolds in my study is that of one imperialist shadowing another. In the aftermath of the "American" Revolution of 1776, actually aided by Spain in the form of money, muskets, medical supplies, and clothing, Anglos appropriated the name "America" from Spain. Ironically, when Spaniards used the word, they meant the lands of the New World *not* inclusive of North America. As Edgar Allan Poe observed, what "America" denoted was not the United States but South America. Nevertheless, the Anglos took it, officially dropping the rival name "Columbia," which, ironically, was equally tied to Spain by way of its Spanish-sponsored

Genoese navigator. This foundational act of symbolic appropriation was then obscured by the construction "American independence." During the seventeenth and eighteenth centuries, territorial and cultural battles over the Atlantic, the Caribbean, and the mainland of the Americas were waged between three contending imperial powers: England, France, and Spain. In North America, much of the actual fighting took place between the English and the French. Meanwhile, in addition to the extensive Spanish explorations (long before the Puritans and Pilgrims set foot on "American" soil) of what became the Southeastern coast of the United States from Florida to Virginia, Texas, New Mexico, and California, the Spanish crown had claimed practically all the land west of the Mississippi.[16] In 1776, with the financial support of France and Spain and help from soldiers of several countries, the rebelling English colonists won their "independence" from Britain and formed the Anglo-dominated United States. In 1800, under the covert Treaty of San Ildefonso, Spain gave the Louisiana territory back to France (France had originally ceded the territory to Spain in 1762 under the Treaty of Fontainebleau) in exchange for land in Italy. In 1803, the French, weakened by slave revolt in their Caribbean colonies, sold the extensive Louisiana territory (in the form of the Louisiana Purchase) to the United States. Thus, France, even more than Britain with its continued foothold in Canada, stepped out of the struggle for hegemony in North America. Although various wars of independence appeared to separate the "New World" from the "Old," this "New World" was already divided. Of the three imperial powers, Spain and Spaniards remained the truly galling Ur-sign of the "Other America." Here I borrow from the Venezuelan novelist, politician, and journalist Arturo Uslar Pietri the translation of the remarkably loaded phrase "la otra América," which he used to title an article published in August 1974 in Caracas (birthplace of Simón Bolívar) in the Spanish exile philosopher Ortega y Gasset's well-known journal *Revista de Occidente.* The phrase has continuing and accruing reverberations through the decades as the growing number of Latinas/os in the United States presses upon the consciousness (and the unconscious) of those who would deny the presence and legitimacy of that Other America and its descendants. Arturo Uslar Pietri's phrase "la otra América" translated in English as "the Other America" should not be confused with the Cuban activist, essayist, and poet José Martí's phrase "nuestra América," translated and so widely circulated in the United States as "Our America" within scholarly communities. Take, for instance, the 1999 collection of essays *José Martí's "Our America": From National to Hemispheric Cultural Studies,* edited by Jeffrey Belnap and Raúl Fernández. Like Pietri, Martí was concerned, among other things, with the imperial designs of the United States on the rest of the Americas. But his rhetorical response to the problem of the power imbalance in the Americas, and not that of Pietri, has been the one to gain currency in English. Many interpretations of this fact are possible, among them the reading that such a phrase was and still is more amenable to a U.S. perspective than that of "the Other America," which would seem to confront, to challenge with a reminder of a resistant difference, with a reminder that there is more than one way of being "American" and that "America" is a divided and contested, not a unitary or shared (as in "our"), entity or assemblage of entities.[17] This Other America or "Spanish" America was and still is, territorially and demographically, the larger half of the Americas. Within the geographic bounds of the United States, the ideology of "American independence" was articulated through an Anglo-American attempt to forge an independent identity out of a triangulated set of dependencies. This myth of "American independence," requiring and courting a persistent agon with Spain and things "Spanish," masked the facts of domestic crises and international conflict and dependence. The drama of the repulsion of and attraction to figures of Spain has evolved to include Latinas/os and the Spanish language itself.

This study concentrates on the part of the drama that has to do with Spain and Spaniards. The texts and visual works I consider refer either to the "Old World" country or simultaneously to the "Old World" and "the New," never exclusively to "the New." When analyzing texts that situate their stories in the New World, I do not take the adjective *Spanish,* or even *Spaniard,* to signify peninsular "Spain" or the presence of Spain in the Americas unless other signs add up to the formation of a trope that, through associational links, specifically implicates Spain. In the early nineteenth century, with incipient revolts and independence movements in various parts of Spain's New World empire, and in the wake of the Monroe Doctrine of 1823, the United States representationally homogenized Latin America, subsuming difference between former parts of the Spanish Empire into one unified threat or opportunity for its own step-by-step expansion. However, that threat/opportunity south of the U.S.

border was still symbolically constructed as a subset of an overarching concern with Spain's empire in the Old and New World. Only after the Spanish-Cuban-American War (1898) does one find a definitive split between Spain and Latin America, notwithstanding the increasingly contested term "Hispanic," which, contingent on context and situation, may or may not include the inhabitants and cultures of both Peninsular Spain and Latin America.

For the most part in the United States, those who incorporate Peninsular Spain, Latin America, and U.S.-born Latinos/as under the rubric "Hispanic" tend to be Anglos, not Latinas/os, if for no other reason than that the word itself is not only English-language based, unlike the term *hispano,* but ethnocentrically conceived in a way that distinguishes "Hispanic" from what is deemed "American." If Latinas/os use "Hispanic" to describe themselves, they are often (though not always) more politically conservative and thus more likely to accommodate what has come to be regarded as the *official* U.S. governmental label, a label that, according to Jorge J. E. Gracia, citing the work of David E. Hayes-Bautista and Jorge Chapa, had cultural currency beyond and, more important, before the U.S. census bureaucracy's use of it in the 1970s.[18] This tendency to accept the label "Hispanic" is double-edged and ironic. In *Ethnic Labels, Latino Lives: Identity and the Politics of (Re)presentation in the United States* (1995), Suzanne Oboler argues that in the United States the term "Hispanic" evolved as part of the systematic exclusion of nonwhite, non-Anglo-Saxons from being considered "American." In other words, the label "Hispanic" has functioned generally as an ideological construct to deem those of Latin American descent foreign, Other, un-American.[19] Fascinating subject matter for another book might be the manifold ways in which the category "Hispanic" has been deployed in Anglo-American culture precisely to replace, and yet replicate with a difference, the identity-reinforcing contest with Spain in the "American" hemisphere, a contest that came to an abrupt end on this side of the Atlantic with the termination of the Spanish-Cuban-American War, scripted as the expulsion of the Spaniard from the Americas. The racial term "Hispanic" created by Anglo-America to mark all those U.S. citizens with Spanish descent of any kind, as well as anyone from Latin America, refuses to differentiate between generations, language groups, cultures, identities, and identifications. This conjured phantasm of homogenized racial and cultural threat from south of the

U.S. border and of "Hispanic" un-Americanness within the United States may be understood as the second wave of the vengeful fantasy of the United States as independent, isolated, as simply "America."[20] Although this is a story for another book, I would like to suggest that, on the one hand, "Hispanic" as radically Other has come to replace the earlier cultural dependence of Anglo-America on its agon with Spain and Spanish Empire for the reproduction of itself as an antiempire. In this sense, the construction "Hispanic" has effected a further erasure of this dependence and of any current awareness of the presence of Spanish empire in what is now the United States, as well as of the history of cultural and political conflict with Spain. On the other hand, "Hispanic" has been taken up by conservative sociologists such as Lawrence E. Harrison as the continuation of the supposed underdevelopment and backwardness of Spain's "Ibero-Catholic culture," in contrast to "Anglo-Protestant" achievement and ongoing advancement.[21] According to models such as Harrison's, "Hispanic" immigration is made into the dangerous intrusion of antientrepreneurial, antimodernizing, and essentially backward Ibero-Catholic values that threaten to undermine what is constructed as the "coherence" of Anglo-Protestant "American" culture. Substituting the term "Latina/o" for "Hispanic," however, is unlikely to transform the content of such models, as has already been demonstrated by continuing mass-media associations of Latinas/os with underachievers who lack the motivation, ambition, and skills to take full advantage of the "land of opportunity" now known as "America." That is to say, a recognition of the limitations of terminology per se to effect social change is advisable. In fact, even with regard to social description, not to mention change, Jorge Gracia reminds his readers of compelling arguments against the use of *either* term ("Hispanic" or "Latino") on the grounds that it is colonialist, overgeneralizing, and therefore not usefully descriptive in relation to a host of particular factors.[22]

At the turn of the century the wealthy Mexican elites of New Mexico— *los ricos*—began to refer to themselves as *hispanos* in response to the Anglo category "Hispanic" and Anglo racial ranking of themselves, on the basis of a supposed racial purity, as the most superior, while equating "Hispanics" with an inferior "breed." Oboler writes that "in adopting the term *hispano,* they were emphasizing not their miscegenated, mestizo origins, but rather their specific class-based descent from original 'pure-blooded' Spanish conquistadores who settled in New Mexico."[23] Similarly, several centuries earlier, the fiction of the hidalgo with *sangre pura* (pure blood), untainted by the blood of *moros* (Moors) or *judíos* (Jews), evolved in the Iberian Peninsula to deny the vast amount of intermixing that had occurred over the centuries during the seven hundred years of Muslim conquest and since the Jews started arriving in the second century AD. The elitist "fantasy heritage" of racial purity among the Mexican *ricos* in the United States originated in Spain.[24] This racial discourse was modified and used by the Anglos to do "the Spaniards" one better in a game of one-upmanship. Anglo-Americans created a fantasy of racial purity through the representation of Spaniards as figures of morally blackened alien whiteness or *off-whiteness* and doomed hybridity. Much of this book's more than two-hundred-year-old story of dependence on figures of Spain necessarily concerns itself with the various kinds of racializations of Spain and Spaniards evident in the works, textual and visual, that I examine. I consider how those racializations "signify" within and for the dominant fictions of "American" exceptionalism, revolution, manifest destiny, and birth/rebirth, what rhetorical discourse preceded a blatantly racist one, and at what points persistent racializations were transmuted into or redirected to other modes of cultural comparison and differentiation that, though perhaps no less imaginatively colonizing, generated forms of empathetic identification and even incorporation.

By examining representations of Spain and Spaniards, one main objective of this study is to turn the lenses of "ethnic and critical race studies" and "postcolonial studies" on Anglo-American culture. *Spain's Long Shadow* turns the ethnic and critical race-studies lens on Anglo-American culture to show that what had previously been taken as simply "American" is as ethnically inflected as the cultural production of what is habitually marked "ethnics" or "others." I theorize Anglo-American culture as a discursive system produced and reproduced in the interests of Anglos, English-speaking, generally Protestant, self-declared "white" people of British, and particularly English, descent. With the term "Anglo-American culture," however, I wish to place the emphasis not so much on people or a group of people with a particular skin color, religious tradition, or place of origin as on hegemony in its material and symbolic senses and on the far-reaching effects of culture as ideology. Thus, to avoid the twin traps of essentialism and monolithization that obscure an appreciation of both the constructedness of culture and its capacity to construct subjectivity according to its dictates, when in fact it has managed to marginalize serious internal critique, I also examine the works of some non-Anglo-Americans who assimilated according to and/or in tension with the ethos and discourse of the dominant culture.

Within the rubric of postcolonial studies, this book demonstrates how figures of Spain and Spaniards operate as a third term or bridge between historically constructed subject/object positions, that is, between colonizer and colonized. It examines the ways Anglo-American works (verbal and visual) have Orientalized, racialized, and primitivized Spain, not in some historically "objective" fashion but as a vanquished imperialist over and around whose abjected body the Anglo-American empire might be erected. The truly noteworthy wrinkle in this operation is the ideological construction of Anglo-American empire as an antiempire, innocent of the barbarities of the Spanish Empire. This study also investigates the ways in which certain works resurrect the figure of defeated Spain according to a double dynamic of identification and displacement, at once postcolonial and pre-postcolonial, both challenging Anglo-American imperial ideology and reproducing parts of its discursive system of representation. The unearthing of Spain as a historical and symbolic contestant in the formation and fissuring of Anglo-American cultural identity argues for moving through and beyond the frequently isolationist and binaristic model of classic American studies (e.g., Old versus New World, white versus black) in the currently unfolding practice of the new Americas studies. Furthermore, this work is not without its important implications for Latina/o studies. In fact, I consider it a kind of Latina/o critique, where "Latina/o" functions as a perspective, a subjectivity, rather than a sociological object of study. Informed by this kind of Latina/o critique, this book interrupts dualistic and self-contained notions of what constitutes "American."

Thinking of the role played by representations of Spain in the creation of U.S. culture may seem like an unlikely and risky topic for Latina/o studies, as, understandably, there is a long tradition of simply viewing Spain as the European colonizer: white, Catholic-Christian, and so on. The rise of empire or imperial studies within new American studies in the 1990s has not significantly altered approaches to the representation of the presence of Spain on either side of the Atlantic. Spain is generally treated as a fixed entity with a more or less unambiguous identity—that of white Catholic-Christian conquistador and colonizer. Thus, complex and significant oscillations in representations of Spain within culture (Anglo, Latina/o, or otherwise) have been overlooked in favor of consideration of representations of "Latinos" (deemed other than "white") from the mid-nineteenth century onward (and even that is a relatively new endeavor) or "Spanish-Americans," but only with a New World and not a transatlantic focus. This book looks at the overlooked in Anglo-American culture—representations of Spain and "Spanishness" inasmuch as these representations point both back to the Old World and forward to the so-called New World and inasmuch as a study of these representations radically questions binaries of "white" versus "other." Representations of Spain and "Spanishness," to the extent that these are both assumed and proclaimed components of the histories, cultures, and identities of most Latinas/os, beckon to be examined in order to flesh out the ways in which a hitherto dominant Anglo culture has constructed or framed Latinas/os and *latinidad* in relation to *Spanish, Spic,* and *Hispanic.* Consider, for example, New York–based Puerto Rican writer Edward Rivera's satirical stories *Family Installments: Memories of Growing Up Hispanic* (1982), which show how the main protagonist, Santos Malánguez, is made to feel ashamed of being Puerto Rican and Hispanic through the history lessons he receives in school that equate southern Europeans, Spaniards in particular, and their descendants (full or partial) with barbarism. Likewise, Chicana writer Ana Castillo's novel *Peel My Love like an Onion* (1999), with its revisionary casting of Carmen (the Spanish Jewish Gypsy woman of the Mérimée story and Bizet opera) as a Chicana one-legged flamenco dancer who leaves the United States for Spain, calls our attention to the interest Latinas have not only in intervening in Anglo representations of Spain and Spaniards but also in drawing on that history to create a little *jaleo*—turning the "great Hispanic panic" into a source of celebration. In light of this impetus, consider Chicano poet Jimmy Santiago Baca's extended poem "Thirteen Mexicans," composed of elegiac vignettes in which, among other things, he inquires, "Why not erect a statue of a mestizo Chicano poet / who doesn't deny his Spanish or Native American ancestry / but builds on both?"[25] This study provides a context for understanding such work by Latina/o writers. The story it tells may be considered as one possible extension of Latina/o studies, as well as one possible precursor, a trajectory that has remained largely unexamined because of the lingering effects of the Black Legend against Spain in both Anglo-American and Latina/o criticism, a legend with substantial historical referents that nevertheless has functioned as a blinding white smoke screen, preventing scholars from venturing to raise certain questions about the formation of cultural identities and ethnicities in the United States. If anyone ever wondered whether Latina/o studies belonged in American studies (classic or new), or vice versa, I hope that this book will serve to swing the door open to a model of transnational and transcultural studies that recognizes the interdependence of American studies and Latina/o studies.

The primary aim of this book is to foreground "Anglo-American" as an ethnicity, an ethnicity historically very much dependent on both an antagonistic and exoticizing relation with Spain and "Spanishness." This study can be read as an investigation of "whiteness" and the construction of "the right kind" of whiteness in contradistinction to figures of alien whiteness, or, if you will, *off-whiteness,* to be abjected from the ideal body politic. Although my investigation of the construction of "Anglo-American" as an ethnicity and a racial identification in the United States takes me back to the end of the eighteenth century and forward to the present time, this book is by no means a survey, despite its scope. Each chapter poses a central question that leads into the next chapter in an unfolding narrative about the evolution of a specifically Anglo-American imperial identity in the United States. This narrative unfolds through case studies of canonical as well as seemingly "marginal" or overlooked literary and visual works, including paintings, photographs, cartoons, and films. To borrow the central image and narrative vehicle of Dos Passos's trilogy *U.S.A.* (first collected and published in 1938), this study may be compared to a camera eye, panoramic in its sweep but with plenty of close-ups on which to concentrate. These close-ups aim to make the theoretical contributions of the book clear, concrete, and vivid. The combination of panoramic and close-up treatment is crucial for demonstrating and qualifying the general historical and theoretical contentions through attention to aesthetics, to how these texts and images work, to how they may affect their readers and spectators.

Chapter 1, "The Shadow of the Black Legend," demonstrates how the infamous Black Legend against Spain lent a determining shape to the historical, cultural, and racial specificities of what Harry Levin and other critics have termed "the power of blackness" in four works of fiction written between 1798 and 1855, that is, between the foundational years of the union as a new nation to just before the Civil War: Charles Brockden Brown's *Wieland* (1798), Edgar Allan Poe's "William Wilson" (1839) and "The Pit and the Pendulum" (1843), and Herman Melville's "Benito Cereno" (1855) by way of Poe's "The Facts in the Case of M. Valdemar" (1845). I argue that the darkness and blackness assigned to the figure of the Spaniard was not only a religious, ethical, and historical evaluation, but increasingly became a racial typology as well. My contribution to studies of race in these writers, and more generally in Gothic "American" fiction, is to show how these fictions' (in)famous typologization of black versus white defines both poles of this binary, a binary that has characterized scholarly analysis as much as the fictions themselves, against a critically unacknowledged third position or figure, that of the not-right-white or the off-white, the figure of "the Spaniard." Overall, this chapter demonstrates how the Black Legend against Spain, a legend manifesting itself in terms of moralized and racialized mappings of "black" and "white" (or an off-whiteness) onto Spain, played a primal role in the construction of Anglo-American identity as "American."

Chapter 2, "Imperial Visions: Moor, Gypsy, and Indian," foregrounds the issue of race. Over the course of the nineteenth century, the Spaniard went from a figure of moral blackness and alien whiteness to a figure of dangerous, implosive "racial" mixture as a justification for further aggression and expansion on the part of the United States. Rather than a celebration of ethnic and cultural fusion, Anglo-American imperial discourse took the Moors, Gypsies, and Jews that the Spanish Empire had endeavored to expel from the Iberian Peninsula and Native Americans and Africans whom the Spaniards in the Americas had enslaved and used as labor, including sexual, and inscribed them under the skin of or transformed them into physical marks on the imagined body of the Spaniard. Far from reflecting mixture (as if there were such a thing as purity!) as an ongoing process among world populations, this representational practice projected Anglo-Americans' own fears and fantasies about miscegenation as national and, moreover, imperial degeneration onto the Spanish Empire in the New World and the Old. I examine a number of allegorical works, novels, and paintings that retell history, U.S. and Spanish, construct racial types, and, in the process, transform typology into implied or overtly stated fate standing in contrast to a posited Anglo-American destiny. The chapter focuses on three romances of this Anglo-American destiny—

William Gilmore Simm's *The Yemassee* (1835), Nathaniel Hawthorne's *The Scarlet Letter* (1850), and Oliver Wendell Holmes's *Elsie Venner* (1861)—and John Singer Sargent's painting *El Jaleo* (1882). I consider the way in which admiring exoticization of type reinforces typology as national and imperial destiny.

Chapter 3, "Consolidating Anglo-American Imperial Identity around the Spanish-American War," concentrates on how Spain and Spaniards figured in late-nineteenth-century U.S. popular consciousness, not merely in canonical narratives of "American" self-definition. Representations of Spain during and around the Spanish-Cuban-American War, a war fomented on one Caribbean island, Cuba, but that soon encompassed many other locations (and developed into the 1899–1901 war for control of the Philippines), were one of the chief means by which a sense of national social cohesion cutting across class and gender lines was promoted.[26] Furthermore, Orientalist representations of Spain and Spaniards tied together with strands of the Black Legend were shaped by, and in turn reinforced, a racially encoded imperial vision of manifest destiny that served to transform the rival colonizer (Spain) into the colonized and the Anglo colonizer-imperialist into the self-proclaimed "superior race" and "civilizer." The Spanish-Cuban-American War marked the definitive material transition of the United States from nation to imperial power equal to that of the British Empire. If this war is an often downplayed phase of U.S. history, even more so is the key role that figurations of Spain and Spaniards enacted in an Anglo-American repertoire of written and visual images in this transition, a move to an empire that was as much ideological as material.

Chapter 4, "Sacred Bulls of Modernism," explores transmutations of an Anglo-American imperial ideology among certain cardinal U.S. modernist expatriate figures. Expatriate U.S. modernist interest in Spain from the early 1920s to the late 1950s did not latch onto Spain as a well-charted colony but as a last frontier, a land to be discovered, totemic ground after the sacrificial defeat of the last of the Spanish Empire in the Spanish-Cuban-American War. Unlike writers of the nineteenth century obsessed with racial origins and the physiognomic aspects of race, U.S. expatriate modernist writers shifted away from racial typing of the inhabitants of Spain in favor of figuring them in relation to their country as land and of defining the purported essence of Spain through appeals to its land and landscapes. For the modernists, Spain doubled both as symbol for and destination of the writer-discoverer-and-creator of new worlds, of the avant-garde. Spaniards were represented as peasants, villagers, workers, bullfighters, dancers, and guerrilla soldiers, representatives of a primal, authentic, even boldly discontinuous relationship to the land. This chapter focuses on works about Spain by three U.S. modernist expatriates— Gertrude Stein, Ernest Hemingway, and Richard Wright, one Jewish American, one Anglo-American, and one African American. Whereas both Stein and Hemingway viewed Spain as a "wonderful country" and associated it with a generative primitivism (defined very differently by each), Wright identified what he considered Spain's primitiveness with a dangerously irrational paganism visible in the very landscape itself. Stein and Hemingway treated Spain as their sacred bull, as well as the vehicle by which they could make themselves into sacred bulls of modernism. For Wright, on the other hand, Spain became the abject scapegoat on which he heaped the sins of both "Western" and "non-Western" history, and the ancient beast against which he defined himself as an African American, modern and civilized. The chapter elucidates the ways in which all three of these writers' portrayals and uses of Spain fall inside, outside, or between Anglo-American conventions about Spain and the dictates of Anglo-American imperial ideology and the implications of these portrayals in the negotiation of ethnic identity within the framework of this ideology. This and subsequent chapters introduce relevant work by non-Anglos as well as Anglos to investigate an Anglo-American ideology that traverses ethnicities, and that was not simply confined to or exhibited by the cultural productions of Anglo-American ethnics.

Chapter 5, "(Post)Modern Denaturalizations of Nationality," evaluates modernist and postmodern attempts to represent Spain and Spaniards in a postnational manner. It discusses the work of writers (Felipe Alfau, Jenny Ballou, and Kathy Acker) and visual artists (Xurxo Lobato, Manuel Sendón, and Fernando Colomo)—the work of people from the United States (Anglo and otherwise) and Spain—that denaturalizes the conceptual categories "American" and "Spanish" and the notion of essential differences between "Spaniards" and "Americans." Examination of textual and visual works produced by variously located artists is a strategy employed to question the assumed natural basis for grouping artists or artifacts together under a national rubric. This strategy aims to reposition "nationality" and the notion of a "national" literature or visual field, as well as periodicity itself (modernism/postmodernism, old/new), as constructs and, therefore, as theoretical problems inescapably linked, in this case, to the historical and imaginative relations between Spain and the United States, relations both inherited from the nineteenth century by modernists and inherited from modernism by postmodernism.

The works I examine pertain to two ostensibly different and potentially incommensurable literary and cultural periods: the middle 1930s to the late 1940s, on the one hand, and the early 1980s to the early 1990s, on the other hand. However, the works from the modernist period presage or adumbrate a postmodern sensibility toward issues of identity. Conversely, the postmodern texts, films, and photographs I examine return to and reinvent the preoccupations of noncanonical modernist texts such as Jenny Ballou's novel *Spanish Prelude* and Felipe Alfau's novels *Locos* (written in short stories) and *Chromos*. The modernist texts examined here, unlike those examined in chapter 4, did not and have not received the critical attention and academic canonization that works by Stein, Hemingway, and Wright have, though Wright's *Pagan Spain* has certainly fared far less favorably than work about Spain by Stein and Hemingway. Alfau's novels were almost entirely neglected until the Dalkey Archive Press rehabilitated them in the late 1980s and early 1990s. Jenny Ballou's *Spanish Prelude* languishes on library shelves, barely checked out. I consider these noncanonical modernist writers in relation to particular postmodernist writers, filmmakers, and photographers figuring or dis-figuring nationality ("American" and "Spanish") to question assumptions about the newness of postmodern techniques of defamiliarization and disorientation, but also to argue that the pairing of late-1930s–1940s artifacts with those of the 1980s–1990s raises questions about the aesthetic and historic limits of denaturalizations of nationality and of postnationalism as a critical strategy to confront the ethnocentrism and cultural chauvinism typically associated with nationalism, and particularly a nationalism with imperial ambitions and dimensions. In retrospect, for instance, and speaking historically, these artifacts' iconoclasm about nationality is framed ominously in both instances by virulent returns of the fantasies of nationality and nationalism a few years after and sometimes in tandem with their production and publication.

Aesthetically speaking (and I contend that aesthetics cannot be divorced from ideology or vice versa), these works, from the 1930s–1940s and the 1980s–1990s are, for all their resistance, simultaneously encoded by power relations at work in the formation and maintenance of national identity, particularly a national identity or, more appropriately to the later works, a postnational identity co-opted by the imperial designs of espionage and global corporatism. At issue in this chapter are the aesthetic and ethical implications for cultural identity—in the face of the boundary-eroding strategies of empire—of attempts to destabilize conventions of identity and to denaturalize or "postnationalize" nationality. While acknowledging the power of techniques of ironic distantiation, subversive mimicry or "imposture," and the embrace of marginalization and abjection, this chapter also explores the limits of resistance to entrenched cultural modes, ways of seeing and being, Anglo-American imperial ideology being one of these. This seemingly out of step comparison between verbal and visual "Spanish" and "American" cultural artifacts of different time periods celebrates those works that were out of step with the conventional trappings of Anglo-American imperial ideology and its figurative dependence on Spain and also with the visionary colonialism of canonized modernists. And yet, at the same time, it explores the ways in which their out-of-stepness is dogged, like the detours of the female knight in Kathy Acker's *Don Quixote*, by the culturally encoded terms of their resistance.

Chapter 6, "Afterlives of Empire," performs double duty as a summation and a continuation into the mid-1990s of the analysis hitherto presented. It summarizes the twists and turns of the story of the long-term captivation of Anglo-American culture with figures of Spain, from the late eighteenth century where I begin this story to the late twentieth century where I end it. Having determined that the long-term fascination with Spain among Anglos has extended toward the horizon of newer obsessions—Asia, Hispanics or Latinos, "illegal" and extraterrestrial aliens, microorganisms and microchips, Arab terrorism, terrorism in general—this chapter also briefly examines relatively new trajectories of "American" dependence on figures of Spain initiated by certain non-Anglo writers—Afro-Latinas, African Americans, Chicanos, Puerto Ricans, Jewish Argentinians living in the United States. Finally, it explores the recycling of tropes and the relation of nostalgia for Spain as a familiar "pain" to Anglo-American imperialism in three works from the mid-1990s: Anglo-American director Whit Stillman's film *Barcelona* (1994), Jewish American novelist Dorien Ross's short novel *Returning to A* (1995), and Mexican American Floyd Salas's novel *State of Emergency* (1996). The chapter delves into three more cases to show that U.S. dependence on figures of Spain has hardly disappeared beneath the horizon line of other obsessions, though many other obsessions exist claiming seemingly more central significance. In fact, the continued appearance of Spain in the cultural imaginary functions, among other things, as a kind of screen, in the psychoanalytic sense, for many of these other preoccupations. This is evident in Stillman's *Barcelona* and Salas's *State of Emergency,* and it combines the analysis of paradigms of national reconstruction and regeneration manifest in studies such as Marsha Kinder's *Blood Cinema* (1993) about Spanish cinema and Richard Slotkin's well-known study of the mythology of the American frontier *Regeneration through Violence* (1974).[27] As for Spain as a return to a familiar pain (regeneration through pain, if not violence), through the final three case studies in this concluding chapter, I consider the branching permutations, the subtle imbrications of emotion/affect and ideology, characterizing the trajectory of dependence on figures of Spain in the United States within the context of a continuing Anglo-American imperial ideology.

A genuine multicultural focus must question "American" not only by accounting for the diversity within what we designate as the borders of U.S. culture but also by understanding the already dependent, fractured condition of "American" as a story of international, and moreover imperial, cultural conflict. This topic is the "repressed" within the discipline of American literary studies and even historical and cultural studies. From its beginnings, American literary studies especially has been concerned with establishing independence from the Old World (Spain being considered quintessentially "Old World" in the antimodern, primitivizing senses of this phrase). The expansion of classic American studies coincided largely with the Franco dictatorship and the Cold War. Closed-circuit literary and cultural histories have served as masks for imperial conflicts on the continent of North America and as screens against the memory of having to share the name and substance of "America" with the "Other" America to the south chronically emblematized, despite revolutions of independence, by the father and/or mother country to the east. The origins of "the (Anglo)-American self" have been said to have arisen not merely from reading the Bible through a Puritan and middle-class Protestant Reformation looking glass or from some "New World" baptismal experience. This study argues that Anglo-American identity was constituted through alter ego/*imago* imperial conflict with, and later totemic appropriation of, Spain as "Other."

chapter 1

THE SHADOW OF
THE BLACK LEGEND

The underlying claim of this chapter is that in the literature of what F. O. Matthiessen refered to as "the American Renaissance" the historical, cultural, and racial specificities of what Harry Levin and other critics, following suit, have termed "the power of blackness" have been largely overlooked beyond the black/white binary of U.S race relations, a binary challenged in much recent scholarship emerging from Latina/o studies and critical race theory/ethnic studies.[1] This chapter attempts to reorient the reader away from the horizon of a Manichaean dualism of "black and white" in the analytic discourse of much of American studies (particularly studies with a nineteenth-century focus) through readings of the blackened figure of alien whiteness, the Spaniard, in Charles Brockden Brown's *Wieland* (1798), Edgar Allan Poe's "William Wilson" (1839) and "The Pit and the Pendulum" (1843), and Herman Melville's "Benito Cereno" (1855).

The examination of American literature along the lines of good versus evil has made it possible to add on "black and white" as racial coordinates without having to rethink the binaristic logic of the ways in which these categories are understood and played out in the game of academic disciplines.[2] The racial categories of "black" and "white" are as nondescriptive and hazardously abstract as the metaphysical categories of "good" and "evil" for which in Euro-American culture(s) these very colors have been made to stand historically. Notably, in her book on reading "race" in antebellum U.S. literature, *The Word in Black and White*, Dana Nelson refers to "white" and "black," along with "red," as "perceptually invalid racial markers" (ix). They are conceptual traps or conundrums (part of a power-ful discursive apparatus that is "race") in that their invocation to describe people contributes to their seeming validity and descriptive force, when in fact they are anything but descriptive. Rather, they partake of and pro-duce fiction, metaphor. Following Henry Louis Gates Jr.'s analysis of race as a discourse, Nelson adds, to guard against the charge of diminishing the social effects of race as such, "To acknowledge this fictional dimen-sion is not to discredit actual, material effects of 'race' in society . . . but to highlight its arbitrary constructedness" (ibid). Its constructedness seems anything but arbitrary to me. I would argue that it derives from a Manichaean allegorical structure of good and evil inherited from both Judaism and Christianity, and probably derived from the Persian cosmol-ogies of Zoroastrianism as well as Manichaeism that taught a stark dual-ism of good and evil metaphysically grounded in the cosmic powers of Light and Darkness. One could pursue an archaeology of the metaphysics of white and black in relation to good and evil through a psychoanalytic and anthropological semiosis of the development of such a binding—one could say, enslaving—chain of signifiers and signifieds. Such a study would be quite daunting as the question remains how such a symbolization arose in the first place. Postmodernist thought would counsel against any such investigation into origins because the investigation itself would probably yield another misleading master narrative. But I wager that the symbol-ization has much to do with the division of planetary time into night and day and with the association of life with the sunlight and death with the literal organic "blackening" that occurs in processes of putrefaction. Black in alchemical lore, for instance, is almost always linked with putrefaction. It is referred to as *nigredo* and contrasted with the desired product of dis-tillation and purification termed *albedo* or the whitening. I also claim, though the argument cannot be developed here, that a writer such as Toni Morrison (in works such as *Jazz* and *Playing in the Dark*) challenges pre-cisely this constellation of associations forming an integral part of Persian Gnostic religions and influencing both Judaism and Christianity.

Although, given this philosophical and religious history, binary racial-ization is far from arbitrary in its Manichaean constructedness, the histor-ical application of this binary to persons and bodies has not been as fixed and stable as the critical translation of black and white into African/African American and European/Anglo would lead us to believe. I argue that "black" and "white" phenotypically map more than "African"/"African American" versus "European" or "Anglo." These markers migrate and are transposed according to their logic of hierarchical symbolic opposition. To assume that all "Europeans" are or have been considered "white" is as inaccurate as to claim that "black" actually describes "Africans"/"African Americans" or has always and everywhere been associated solely with certain human beings and not others. To miss the transposition of "black" and "white" onto other peoples beyond the Anglo/African binary in the way that much scholarship in American literary and cultural studies has done is symptomatic of the hold or power of the black/white binary despite attempted critical deconstruction of it. It would seem that criticism, as much as the literature that is the object of its analysis, has been inexorably drawn, until quite recently, toward this binary in ways that almost—but not quite—shake down deep-structure assumptions behind it.

Shaking down assumptions about the cultural behavior of the binary does not translate into the neutralization of the binary in the texts to be examined. One cannot *critically* wish its traces away or ameliorate them by showing how "complex" they are or how stratified beyond a two-tiered strata. When "white" and "black" are transposed to other peoples and places—as is the case with the representation of "Spain" and "Spaniards" in the tales I am about the examine—the elision of the metaphysical categories of good versus evil, fundamental to racism in the "Western" world, remains operative. In other words, the transposition of the binary onto other ethnicities and nationalities—even the transposition of both terms of the binary ("blackness" and "whiteness") onto a single figure, a "Spaniard—does not neutralize the effects of the binary and generally results in the pejorative (rather than merely descriptive) "blackening" of the Spanish character in order to maintain the threatened "whiteness" of the Anglo characters. As for this "blackening" or "whitening," the elision between moral and racial categories manifests itself in the physical darkening or blackening of morally dubious or ill-fated characters. Although not every physical darkening implies a racial stigmatization—for example, villains may wear black but otherwise not differ from heroes and heroines—frequently it implicates more than sartorial details.

In European and Euro-American Gothic fiction, black generally connotes evil or moral inferiority and white connotes good or moral superiority. In the so-called Gothic fictions of *Wieland* (1798), "William Wilson"

(1839), "The Pit and the Pendulum" (1843), and "Benito Cereno" (1855), black and blackness denote a color and also signify a mood or atmosphere and a metaphysical menace. However self-consciously employed, these attributions are, moreover, part and parcel not only of the moral *denigration* (from the Latin "to make black") of particular characters, but also of their stigmatization in cultural and ultimately racial terms. The latter type of denigration manifests itself in instances where the chromatic darkening of a character's physical features or bodily appearance occurs in tandem with an imputation of evil, unethical behavior, or moral defectiveness—that is, in tandem with the deployment of the character as an embodiment of sin or a fall from grace.

This chapter begins with the period just before what has generally been understood as the "American Renaissance." These four works of what has been classified as Gothic fiction cover the time period from 1798 to 1855, that is, from the foundational years of the union as a new nation to shortly before the Civil War. By tracing and analyzing the perhaps somewhat *unexpected* specificities of "the power of blackness" in these texts from the late-eighteenth to the mid-nineteenth century, I set in relief how the "power of blackness" by which these fictions are characterized depends on the use as a device not or not only of the African American, but also—or rather—of the figure of the Spaniard embedded within the rhetoric of the "Black Legend." My contribution to studies of race, ethnicity, and culture in these writers and, more generally, in Gothic "American" fiction is to show how these fictions' (in)famous typologization of black versus white defines both poles of this binary—a binary that has characterized scholarly analysis as much as the fictions themselves—against a critically unacknowledged third position or figure, that of the not-right-white or the *off-white*, the figure of "the Spaniard." Furthermore, I claim that this third position or figure plays a primal role in the construction of Anglo-American identity as "American" and in the reinforcement of that identity, which needs the shadow of the Black Legend against Spain for definition.

Promulgated by Spain's religious and economic rivals in the sixteenth and seventeenth centuries—primarily England and the Netherlands, but also France, Italy, Portugal, and Germany—the Black Legend or *la leyenda negra* elaborated a story or legend about the essential character of Spain around the historical facts of Spain's imperial sway, Inquisition, and treatment of indigenous peoples of the Americas.[3] In this legend, "the

Spaniard" became a typological emblem of religious and political intolerance, tyranny, misrule, conspiracy, cruelty, barbarity, bloodthirstiness, backwardness, slothfulness, and degeneracy. However fragmented, this "historical" story—the Black Legend with its culturally and racially stigmatizing implications—gives a determining shape to the power of blackness haunting these four "American" fictions.

Focusing on the particular ways in which the Black Legend is conjured by these fictions and set to work demonstrates not the historical actuality of U.S. inheritance of economic rivalry with Spain (though it does some of that in passing), but rather how the Black Legend had become separate enough to be used as effect, a highly effective effect in the construction of Anglo-American identity in contradistinction to what is posited as the essence of Spanish identity. Reading these fictions as case studies produces a story of how, over time, the Black Legend has been intimately involved with the construction of Anglo-American identity as "American" identity. Although since the sixteenth century the Black Legend has tended to fix characteristics that constitute an ethnic as well as national myth of essential temperament, the shadowy vestige of the Black Legend from the late eighteenth century to the mid-nineteenth century becomes increasingly imbricated with discourses of racialization. The Puritan association of Spaniards with the powers of "blackness of darkness" (Jude, verse 13) and the Southern colonists' characterization of all Spaniards as pirates and plunderers, as legitimate possessors of nothing but "dark" motives, became increasingly racialized as did the revolutionary trope of the tyrant and slave. "Darkness" and frequently the color black began to pertain as attributes not only to clothing or costume, but also to bodily features such as eyes, hair, and skin tone. The presumed blackguardism of the Spaniards was simultaneously externalized and internalized as an innate and thus indelible mark of "the Spaniard."

The "darkness" and even "blackness" of the Spaniard became not only a religious, ethical, and historical issue, but a racial one as well in which the body bore the stigma of its culture at the same time that it functioned as the main determinant of that culture. As such, it is crucial that this "blackening" and/or darkening of "the Spaniard" be distinguished from the notion of some objective or impartial representation of the historical fact that "Spaniards," despite the expulsion of the Muslims and the Jews in the late fifteenth century, are descended from Arabs, Jews, Berbers,

Romans, Vandals, Visigoths, Phoenicians, Celts, Greeks, and Carthaginians, and others, or that there have been and are Spaniards with a wide diversity of skin tones. About the historical ethnoracial and cultural hybridity in Spain, Jorge J. E. Gracia observes:

> The inhabitants of the Iberian peninsula are perhaps one of the most mixed people in Europe. Apart from the Celts, Iberians, Basques, Greeks, Phoenicians, Carthaginians, Berbers, Romans, Vandals, Suebi, and Visigoths, the peninsula had a large infusion of Moors beginning in the eighth century and Jews at various points in its history, and descendants of Amerindians have often moved to it and lived and mixed with other members of the population.[4]

However, from the late eighteenth to the mid-nineteenth century, the uses of the Black Legend began to shape a racialized typology of "the Spaniard" that fixed temper and character to outward physical signs of skin, physiognomy, and physical demeanor. By using the term "racialized" I mean to point out that a "racially" based system of classification is inextricably bound up in an ideology of race. After the Civil War, this racialized typology became an important part of the ideology of race on which Anglo-American expansionist policies depended for justification.

What unites the fictions analyzed here is the construction of Anglo-American identity as "American" identity through a one-to-one largely psychological conflict or challenging encounter between an Anglo-American character and "the Spaniard" descriptively blackened and marked as different in the terms of the Black Legend. These fictions retell encounter between Old and New World as a story of reassurance and possible regeneration in which the reader goes through a crisis of dependence and emerges with ego boundaries reinforced. *Wieland* stages the conflictual encounter as a rhetorical seduction in which "the Spaniard" as male seducer and purveyor of "dark motives" endangers the virtuous independence of the newly "united" states. The new union is figured as the initially felicitous friendship and trust between a community of four, that is, between Clara Wieland, Theodore Wieland, Catherine Pleyel, and Henry Pleyel, two sets of sisters and brothers, sealing with the endogamous blood ties of family the familiarity among them, a familiarity that turns into domestic tragedy under the supposed influence of the Spanish-converted

Carwin. From among that foursome, the Anglo-German American woman Clara Wieland bears the symbolic weight of an Enlightenment-era Lady Liberty whose Kantian torchlight of understanding is knocked out of her hand by her own fascination with a deceiver, the "Spanish"—or, more accurately, Spanish-like—Carwin.

"William Wilson" is a persecution narrative between rival equals, like twin brothers, in which the narrative "I," in the concluding masquerade sequence, takes on the guise (the "Spanish cloak of blue velvet . . . and mask of black silk") that distinguishes the Anglo-American's Spanish double. The lack of distinction leads to death: in killing the Other, the story suggests, the narrator kills himself. However, the narrator seems to remain cognizant beyond the grave, somehow having survived his encounter with "the Spaniard." "The Pit and the Pendulum," published four years after "William Wilson," marks a confidence greater than that reflected in the posthumous survival of the skirmish with "the Spaniard." Unlike *Wieland* and "William Wilson," which fatally insinuate the figure of the Spaniard as seducer and persecutor, "The Pit and the Pendulum" concludes with the rescue of the narrator and the defeat of the Inquisition. The narrator's persecutorial Other is more concretely and minutely distinguished and Orientalized as not only Spanish and Catholic but as Saracenic. "Benito Cereno" figures the conflict in the form of scenes between members of a maritime fraternity, two sea captains, the Spaniard Benito Cereno and the Anglo-American Amasa Delano. Although it may be and has been interpreted that the brothers share the same original sin, a deep complicity in slavery, it is the Spaniard over whom the rebellious slave Babo casts a shadow that becomes not only a curse but an indelible racial stain.

From *Wieland* or the end of the eighteenth century with its concerns about the viability of the new postrevolutionary union, its affiliations, and the consequences of those affiliations for its dimensions and future, this chapter skips ahead to the late 1830s/early 1840s and then again to the mid-1850s to examine the pivotal, though seemingly minor, role played by "Spaniards" and clusters of references to Spain in selected stories by Poe and in Melville's long tale "Benito Cereno." This chapter does not dedicate itself to those U.S. narratives that readers of "American" literature might be trained to expect to find in a section focusing on the end of the eighteenth century to the middle of the nineteenth—national romance narratives involving Spaniards or about Spain such as James Fenimore Cooper's *The Prairie* (1827) with its Doña Inez de Certavallos or the chronicles and historical romances of "Hispanophiles" such as Washington Irving and William H. Prescott. The reason for this trajectory is my interest in demonstrating the crucial role that Spanish characters and patterns of references to Spain play in tales that have been taken primarily for psychological thrillers and secondarily in relation to history. I reserve chapter 2 for the examination of more obvious historical allegory both verbal and visual. Of the works examined here, however, "Benito Cereno" serves as a transitional object between these two chapters as it has been read as much as a retelling of a historical event as a psychological thriller in the Gothic mode. In the next chapter, Nathaniel Hawthorne's *The Scarlet Letter* occupies a similar liminal position between Gothic tale and historical romance of Anglo-American destiny. This chiasmic structure or overlap between chapters 1 and 2 highlights the fact that while the relation of content to form or mode constitutes part of my thesis of the kind of work that a semiosis of Spain and Spaniards performs for an Anglo-American imaginary, it is not entirely determining of it. There is a larger question at stake not to be confused with an opposition between a Gothic mode and historical allegory or between the Gothic and history. Such a distinction is spurious, as Teresa A. Goddu has argued convincingly in *Gothic America: Narrative, History, and Nation* (1997). Citing Maggie Kilgour's *The Rise of the Gothic Novel* (1995), Goddu stresses the impurity of *gothic* as a mode or form, suggests that another term for it might well be *dark romance* (including historical), and, most important, stresses the extent to which whatever is deemed as "gothic" or "dark romance" is haunted by history and, in particular, social concerns with race.[5] With regard to questions of race, Goddu's focus is white–black and white–Native American relations, with most of the emphasis being on the former. Not a single mention is made of Spain or Spaniards, which brings me back to the larger question. I would like to stress that this larger question is not the opposition between Gothicism and historicity or the continuity between the two (I take the latter to be a first principle that I illustrate in my own readings). The larger question is the primacy of the psychological symbolization of historical residue over overt historical reference in the formation of Anglo-American identity. Hence, I have begun this book with an analysis of so-called Gothic tales or *dark* romances told at an obscure *remove* from the narration of history (and subsequently read in a historical vacuum) before moving to an analysis of more obvious historical retellings or what have been labeled less equivocally (except, perhaps, in the case of *The Scarlet Letter*) *historical* romances. Chapter 1 comes before chapter 2 not merely on account of chronology—that is, not merely because *Wieland* precedes William Gilmore Simms's *The Yemassee*, for instance. This sequencing is designed to emphasize how these Gothic tales' narratival remove from historical events and the literal geography of Spanish presence in the Americas (even "Benito Cereno" is set offshore, mostly at sea)—that is, their shifting of the terrain of national identity formation to the equivocal realm of literary signs and aesthetic effects—works powerfully to conscript an implied readership through the re-presentation of a far from resolved conflict between Anglo and Spaniard.

THE "SPANIARD" IN THE CLOSET:
CHARLES BROCKDEN BROWN'S *WIELAND* (1798)

Through the figure of Carwin, who "had adopted Spain for his country, and had intimated a design to spend his days there, yet now was an inhabitant of this [American] district,"[6] *Wieland* insinuates a fissure in the foundations of Anglo-American ideology: faith in America's providential exemption from "Old" World tyranny or enforced dependency and belief in the success of the 1776 Revolution. The Germanic name "Wieland," title of the novel and Theo and Clara's last name, does not detract from the argument about this work's Anglo-American concerns. No distinction is made anywhere in the text between the Anglo and Germanic characters. Rather, they are represented as unproblematically allied or coterminous with each other. The concept of a superior Anglo-Saxon race with Germanic origins and ideally endowed to govern themselves and the world had been developing since the early seventeenth century.[7]

In 1795, three years before the publication of *Wieland*, relations between the newly constituted United States and Spain were strained. The dispute with Spain was, on one level, straightforwardly economic and territorial; it involved the use and control of the Mississippi, the settlement of the boundaries of East and West Florida, and Spain's encouragement of settlers beyond the Appalachians to secede from the Union. Thomas Pinckney, the U.S. minister to Great Britain, negotiated a treaty with Spain that favored the economic and territorial interests of the United States. This treaty determined the use of the Mississippi. Most important, it contained the threat of secession on the part of the territories between the Appalachian Mountains and the Mississippi by making livelihood from commercial trade dependent on membership in the Union.

On another level, the dispute with Spain was not so easily or materially dismissed. By raising both the actual possibility and the lingering specter of secession, it marked an ideological fissure in the nation's image of union. Comprising this ideological fissure was not only the threat of the fragmentation of the Union and its imagined identity through internal factionalism, but also the threat posed to the newly constituted "United States of America" by the existence of other "American" unions or alliances—namely, the vast empire of Spanish America. Mid-seventeenth-century texts such as Anne Bradstreet's extended poem "The Four Elements" with its reference to "Spain's Americans" to Edgar Allan Poe's mid-nineteenth-century marginalia betray an insistent anxiety about the historical and symbolic power of an Other America.[8] As a passage from Poe's work reads:

> We may legislate as much as we please, and assume for our country whatever name we think right—but to us it will be no name, to any purpose for which a name is needed, unless we can take it away from the regions which employ it at present. South America is "America," and will insist upon remaining so.[9]

The dream of a post–Monroe Doctrine (1823) extension of a Southern U.S. empire aside, these remarks highlight the generally unwilling recognition that embedded within European notions of an original American identity was a very literal contradiction against Anglo-American sovereignty. At the end of the eighteenth century and into the first quarter of the nineteenth century, it was feared that territories of the recently *united* states (for example, parts of Kentucky, Tennessee, what became the states of Alabama and Ohio, and even sections of Georgia, one of the original thirteen) were not securely settled. The fear was that these territories might be "seduced" into what was wishfully viewed as an exogamous relationship with Spain and other "foreign" powers rather than alternately persuaded and coerced to remain in a supposedly endogamous one as part of the dominion of the United States. This fear was especially shared by the Federalists, who were concerned, to the point of veritable paranoia, that internal discontent such as was demonstrated by the New England farmers during Shay's Rebellion would find inspiration in the ideas of "foreign" powers and would result in the formation of regional alliances with those "alien" nations more than eager to court dissatisfaction in return for economic and territorial access and even annexation. In 1796, before George Washington, a Federalist president, left office, he warned the "American" people to uphold the Union by avoiding political engagements and alliances with foreign nations:

> The nation which indulges toward another an habitual hatred or an habitual fondness is in some degree a slave . . . passionate attachment of one nation for another produces a variety of evils . . . If we remain one people, under an efficient government, the period is not far off when we may defy material injury from external annoyance.[10]

Perversely and one might say almost obscenely, like an early-modern curiosity cabinet, *Wieland*, the novel, demonstrates how the paradoxes and paroxysms "engendered" by this fear may have the equivalent effect of that "habitual fondness" implied by Washington.[11] I contend that through the figure of Carwin with his associations to Spain the novel dramatizes Federalists' fears of "enslaving" foreign influences.

Chapter 3 of *Wieland* would seem to offer a picture of that society of self-reliance and self-absorbed felicity that corresponds not only to the Federalist prescription for the state of the nation, but also to the utopia of the Democratic-Republican-soon-to-be-Jeffersonian party's Enlightenment idealism. The little society formed by Clara and Theodore Wieland and Catharine and Henry Pleyel is set up as a true federation of coequal parties each concerned with the other's life, liberty, and pursuit of happiness. They are a "federation" not in the particular sense of a political party, but rather in the general sense of the Enlightenment ideal of social relations between individuals or states, which rested on good faith. The concrete symbol of this federation between the Wielands and the Pleyels is the temple on Clara Wieland's property. Rather than a place of private worship, the temple is the gathering place of the foursome, the site of their conversation pieces, scenes of private joy with a public aspect:

> Here we sung, and talked, and read, and occasionally banqueted. Every joy-
> ous and tender scene most dear to my memory is connected with this edi-
> fice . . . a thousand conversations, pregnant with delight and improvement,
> took place . . . the social affections were accustomed to expand, and the tear
> of delicious sympathy to be shed. (32)

Moreover, the placement by Clara's brother of a bust of Cicero in the temple serves to associate this structure with public action or civic vocation
and suggests that the foursome have, according to eighteenth-century dictates of virtue, balanced private interest and public responsibility.

In other respects, the society of Theo, Clara, Catharine, and Henry con-
forms to neither Jeffersonian nor Federalist ideals. Mere signs or appearances prevail over actual referents or substance. For example, although "it
was determined" that Theo's profession should be that of agriculture (29),
seemingly in keeping with the Jeffersonian ideal of the yeoman farmer, it
becomes apparent that "[t]he task to be performed by him was nothing
more than superintendence. The skill that was demanded by this was
merely theoretical, and was furnished by casual inspection, or by closet
study" (ibid.). Similarly, as much as each of the foursome exemplifies some
of the major attributes that the Federalists desired in civic leaders (wealth,
breeding, education, and talent), none of the four gives much thought to
her or his individual or collective security, to protecting herself or himself
from "danger," a theme at the center of the rhetoric of the Federalists ever
apprehensive about national security and property. Rather, the foursome
are represented as living a charmed, carefree existence with all danger and
misery kept in distant perspective:

> The sound of war had been heard, but it was at such a distance as to en-
> hance our enjoyment by affording objects of comparison. The Indians were
> repulsed on the one side, and Canada was conquered on the other. Revo-
> lutions and battles, however calamitous to those who occupied the scene,
> contributed in some sort to our happiness, by agitating our minds with
> curiosity and furnishing causes of patriotic exultation. (34)

The implication is that they are more interested in patriotic sentiment
than in patriotic duty. In many respects, their behaviors and actions correspond to the form, but not the content, of certain eighteenth-century

notions of virtue. The emblem of this passion for style is the bust of Cicero placed in the temple on Clara's estate by her brother Theo, whose "passion for Roman eloquence" is shared by Henry Pleyel. Unlike the prototypical Temple of Ancient Virtue in the Augustan garden at Stowe (England) dedicated to *civitas* and public life and presided over by busts representing the ancient paragons of philosophy, poetry, law, and military leadership,[12] the edifice associated for Clara with "every joyous and tender scene most dear to my memory" is the site of performance presided over by the ancient figure of elegant oratory, Cicero.

Oratory as a series of "revolutionary speech acts" both constituted the Union and was of concern to the framers of the Constitution as a threat against the unity of the "United States." In *Wieland* the conversation piece federation described through the narrative voice of Clara in chapter 3 is physically removed from the political action of the revolutionary conflict and analytically removed from the political problems of oratory. Just as patriotic exultation or sentiment replaces patriotic duty for this community, Clara and Theo Wieland confuse their careful study and minute anatomization of the effects of oratory on the senses with an immunity to its effects or "dangers." It is precisely their veneration of the power of oratory—a love of its devices and effects—that makes them susceptible to the influence of Carwin, whom Clara presents as in possession of an extraordinary voice capable of imparting "an emotion altogether *involuntary* and *incontrollable*" (63; my emphasis). The involuntary and uncontrollable effect of Carwin's voice is a violation of the very ideals for which the American Revolution was supposedly fought—*voluntary* obedience and self-governance.

The critical temptation is to imitate Clara's speculative captivation and fall into the trap of the conceit of the disembodied voice, the ventriloquist's art. Instead, I wish to examine the details of the construction of the character associated with that voice, which is imputed to have been, at the very least, the indirect motivator of the other characters' actions. The source of the voice is uncertain, even after all has presumably been divulged; doubts remain as to whether the voices were not, in fact, figments of the other characters' unhinged imaginations. However, there *is* a particular ventriloquist conjurer figure at the center of novel—Carwin. On the one hand, he frequently appears as an insubstantially described and circumscribed body. When present, he is often elsewhere—behind "the edge of the bank" (61), in "a copse at a small distance" (62), with his countenance half-averted (ibid.), a shadowy outline in a dark closet (104), a "human figure standing on the edge of the bank" (117), a "head thrust and drawn back [suggesting] that a form ordinarily invisible had been unshrouded" (170), a shape hunched on the floor with his knees drawn up and his face "buried in his hands" (221), and an "imp of mischief" (143) continually entering and departing from various spaces, lingering in Clara's house (262) and gliding out the door (257) like a phantasmal visitant. Conversely, more concrete description physically depicts Carwin than any other character in the novel. Whereas the other characters are allowed to occupy positions of transparency as representatives of the norm, Carwin is materially marked as being outside this norm. Some information is given about "his stature, hair, complexion, the extraordinary position and arrangement of his features, his awkward and disproportionate form, [and] his gesture and gait" (150). Nevertheless, perhaps because in the novel Clara repeatedly regards him as an apparition, readers and critics themselves have treated him as a kind of blank cipher, supernaturalized and then demonized. The problem with this ahistorical reading of Carwin as a prankster trickster made over in the mind of Clara into an imp, incubus, or devil is that it does not account for the specificity of the albeit sketchy map that shapes the figure of Carwin, nor does it explain his ideological significance. Even such history-conscious readers as Jay Fliegelman, Bill Christophersen, and Steven Watts do not trace the significant particulars of Carwin's coordinates. Fliegelman views him as first and foremost a practitioner of mesmerism, "a profane embodiment of Locke's principle of the inner voice and Rousseau's of the hidden hand."[13] Curiously, Christophersen characterizes the young Carwin of Brown's fiction *Memoirs of Carwin, the Biloquist*, the first sequences of which were completed, Christophersen claims, just before the publication of *Wieland*, as "the prototypical American revolutionary."[14] In his subsequent analysis of *Wieland*, he sums Carwin up as an "Old World villain."[15] Steven Watts describes him as a "mercurial Irish immigrant" "of disheveled appearance, personal allure, and unknown character, who slowly ingratiates himself into the Wieland circle."[16] His adjective *mercurial* is a telling one and could be read as synonymous with "chameleon-like," an adjective he employs later in his book.[17] It betrays an uncertainty about Carwin's cultural and geographic coordinates. It suggests that they mutate, change, shape-shift—

like mercury. The fact is that the Carwin of *Wieland* is variously identified with England, Spain, and, halfway through the narrative, Ireland— or, rather, with a criminal "escaped from Newgate prison in Dublin" (149). Watts does not attempt to explain in cultural or ideological terms this association with Ireland beyond reading it as an indicator of Carwin's immigrant and, it may be inferred in contrast to "the Wieland circle," *outsider* status. To return to Christophersen's readings, he does not attempt to reconcile his competing interpretations of Carwin, though such divergence cries out for some reconciliation or, at the very least, acknowledgment. If Carwin is viewed as an impersonation of the Other American, the Spanish American, then the divergence begins to make cultural sense. It is not so much that he is the "prototypical American revolutionary," but rather the head-spinning figure of an alternate order of things in the Americas, a Spanish order and all the fear and fascination that conjures in his fictional cohorts (Clara, mainly) and in Brown's readers of the time.

Carwin is a traveling confidence man borrowing from here and there, converting the external into the internal and vice versa, a representative in his person of the boundary-transgressing qualities of his own projected voice. Specifically, I argue, he is represented in *Wieland* as primarily a transnational traveler in Spain and, upon his return to the American strand, an ambassador of the "habits" of that country, as understood by Brown and his contemporaries. Clara declares:

> In answer to my inquiries he informed me that three years before, he was a traveller in Spain. He had made an excursion from Valencia to Murviedro, with a view to inspect the remains of Roman magnificence scattered in the environs of that town . . . His garb, aspect, and deportment were wholly Spanish. A residence of three years in the country, . . . attention to the language, and a studious conformity with the customs of the people, had made him indistinguishable from a native when he chose to assume that character . . . He had embraced the Catholic religion, and adopted a Spanish name instead of his own, which was Carwin, and devoted himself to the literature and religion of his new country . . . On topics of religion and of his own history, previous to *his transformation into a Spaniard*, he was invariably silent. (80–81)

It becomes difficult to dismiss this figure as an uncircumscribed sign of the devil or sinister temptations if one reads the following passage alongside the characterization of Carwin as Spanish, Catholic, and having a penchant for grand ruins:

> His cheeks were pallid and lank, his eyes ["lustrously black"] sunken . . . his teeth large and irregular, though sound and brilliantly white, and his chin discoloured by a tetter. His skin was of coarse grain and sallow hue. Every feature was wide of beauty, and the outline of his face reminded you of an inverted cone. (65)

Carwin is a particular type of demon based on a specific figure of the devil, Philip II, described according to the version of the Black Legend disseminated predominantly by the British and the Dutch. Philip II was often portrayed sitting on his throne in the monumental Escorial with pale skin, sunken eyes, a prominent chin, and a long, thin face. The mention of the tetter on Carwin's chin can be interpreted as an allusion to Philip II's well-known ulcerous condition during the last years of his life. Furthermore, in the unfinished sequel to *Wieland*, the *Memoirs of Carwin the Biloquist*, Carwin, now the narrator, describes how, through "[c]onverse with books, and natives of Spain" he learned to "efface all differences between [himself] and a Castilian with respect to speech." Carwin continues: "Personal habits, were interchangeable, by the same means," while the "religion of Spain," the final obstacle to his becoming "Spanish," was confronted in the "convent of the Escurial" or Escorial, the palace of Philip II where Carwin feigns the "Romish faith."[18] The "cone" shape of Carwin's face is also remindful of the miters worn by Roman Catholic prelates, the hats worn by Spanish flagellants during Holy Week processions, and also of the tall, cone-shaped cap worn by victims of the Inquisition such as the Jews. Thus, as a "devil," Carwin recalls both the Counter-Reformation imperial Spaniard, King Philip, symbol of tyranny, and the suspiciously regarded Jew or "Oriental" Spaniard associated with sallow skin, dark eyes, and, moreover, concealment and simulated faith. Clara's observation that "[i]t was not easy to reconcile his conversion to the Romish faith with those proofs of knowledge and capacity that were exhibited by him on different occasions. A suspicion was sometimes admitted that his belief was *counterfeited* for some political purpose" (81; my emphasis) further associates Carwin with anti-Semitic representations of Jews as false converts, *marranos*, as well as participants in international conspiracy.[19]

Most critics read *Wieland* through Brown's *The Biloquist*, published first in 1803 in *The Literary Magazine* and then posthumously in book form in 1822.[20] They therefore unhesitatingly identify the Carwin of *Wieland* as an Irish immigrant, even though in *Wieland* itself there is only the briefest mention of Ireland, merely the words that Clara narrates from a newspaper column: "escaped from Newgate prison in Dublin" (149). Whether these words actually apply to the Carwin that Clara knows rather than to another Carwin (Francis Carwin), a taunting double, is subsequently thrown into question by her uncle: "Have I not said . . . that the performance [of the crimes for which the agent was imprisoned] was another's? Carwin, perhaps, . . . prompted the murderer; but Carwin is unknown. The actual performer has long since been called to judgment and convicted" (185). The only explanation of Carwin's identity that is not put into question is Clara's more preliminary one: "Carwin was an adherent to the Romanish faith, yet was an Englishman by birth, and perhaps, a Protestant by education" (82). The "dangerous" power of Carwin's oratory is represented as transforming this hybridity—a not necessarily un-American union of "Romanish," Spanish, English, and Protestant—into a counterrevolutionary alliance. Clara's characterization works to associate the figure of the Spaniard Carwin with Spain and imperial command of the Holy Roman Empire (under Charles V) and of the dominant economic and political empire encompassing the Iberian Peninsula, Flanders, Artois, the Franche-Comté, and possessions in Italy, North Africa, and the Americas (under Philip II, husband to, among other wives, Mary Tudor). In an argument between Carwin and Henry Pleyel about the assumed "incongruousness between the religion and habits of a Spaniard with those of a native of Britain" (85), Carwin asserts that

> Britons and Spaniards . . . are votaries of the same Deity, and square their faith by the same precepts; their ideas are drawn from the same fountains of literature, and they speak dialects of the same tongue; their governments and laws have more resemblances than differences; they were formerly provinces of the same civil, and, till lately, of the same religious, empire. (86)

Thus Carwin is shown reconstituting the alliance between England and Spain as parts of one religious, economic, and political empire. This self-made Spaniard uses his oratory to reverse history and thus undo a succession of revolutions on which late-eighteenth-century "Americans" depended in order to claim both the existence and the success of their own revolution. If England never broke with Rome and with Spain, and if the Puritan Protestants never successfully separated from the "popish" Church of England, the question arises as to whether the thirteen colonies can be said to have separated from any of these three preceding empires—the Holy Roman, the Spanish, or the British.

If Carwin represents the remaking of identity, he more significantly represents the undoing of it, especially that of his listeners. For them, identity and unity have rested on good faith, on trust in each other, and on a certitude about their security. This trust and certitude Carwin undermines with a ventriloquist's tricks, leading Clara to the impression that murderers are plotting in her closet, encouraging Pleyel to think that his German sweetheart has died and later on that Clara has lost her "honor and virtue," and deluding Theo into believing that God has commanded him to kill his wife Catharine and his children. The characters are represented, according to the conventions of the sentimental novel and the Gothic romance, as experiencing this seduction on a personal, intimate level. However, the consequences of Carwin's seductions involve a change of geographical/national abode—a parting with the "patria," the United States. The two surviving members of the foursome, Clara and Henry, both give up their estates in America and move to Europe, to southern France. This parting implies a lack of any suprapersonal ties to "one's country." Patriotism or national duty, principles so paramount to the "American" revolutionaries, seem to be defunct in Clara and Henry. Like Carwin, who ultimately professes to have been born in America (226), they move—and more to the point, give themselves over to "wanderings" (269)—for what appear to be purely personal motives.

Paradoxically, Clara's fascination with and fear of Carwin cause her to seek him out ever more frequently. The substitution of the conversation pieces in the temple among the foursome for "closet dialogues" (112) with Carwin is of particular importance in understanding the ideological valences of Clara's transformation from a person of seeming equanimity and clarity (as her name denotes) to one of melancholy and "madness"— visited by suicidal and homicidal thoughts (114–15). Clara's transformation under the influence of his ventriloquist tricks is represented as a type of conversion in which the closet near her bed ("the door . . . was not more than eight inches from my pillow" [70]) and veiled by curtains functions both as an external symbol of the camera obscura of her mind and as a kind of confessional. It is in the closet that Carwin acts as a confessor, that he learns the secrets of Clara's soul by reading her journal, which is written in "characters which essentially agreed with a short-hand system which [he] learned from a *Jesuit missionary*" (233; my emphasis).

In *Wieland*, the role of confessor is portrayed through the filter of Protestant anti-Catholic and particularly anti-Jesuit prejudice. According to Barbara Stafford, "after the Counter-Reformation, it was the Jesuits— politically controversial since their founding in the sixteenth century— who were specifically denounced by rigorist Protestant and reform-minded Jansenists alike." The Jesuits, widely believed to be associated with Papist conspiracies, were accused in the eighteenth century of dressing up vice in "showy garb" and "ostentatious rhetoric" by French philosophes such as Rousseau, Helvétius, and d'Alembert and were expelled from France in 1764 by Louis XV.[21] *Wieland* deploys the same trope of the conspiratorial Jesuit who subverts the spiritual and political order that led to the expulsion of the Jesuits from France and, in 1767 under Charles III, from Spain itself. Carwin, as Jesuitical confessor figure, acts not as a helpful minister to the progress of Clara's soul, but as a seducer, unhinging the mind of his victim by "transform[ing] shadows into monsters and plunging [it] into . . . deplorable error" (123). Rather than enlightening Clara about the true nature of the voices, Carwin is represented as trespassing repeatedly onto her property and into the innermost sanctum of her privacy, a violation that in a "pornographically" chaste way suggests a rape, if not of her body, then of her mind. The novel—via Clara's narrative voice—suggests that these "interviews" or "midnight meetings" between Clara and Carwin contribute to the turning of her "clear" mind full of light into a camera obscura that, polluted with images impressed upon its surfaces during these interviews, becomes the theater or chamber of what critic John Seelye has identified as her personal Reign of Terror.[22] Down to closet scenes and what might be termed the "French connection," parallels may be drawn between the Carwin–Clara plot of *Wieland* and the Lovelace–Clarissa plot of Samuel Richardson's mid-eighteenth-century novel *Clarissa*. However, in Richardson's novel, Lovelace is merely a Frenchified rake and his role as incubus does not carry the same portentous political valence as does Carwin's in *Wieland* with its Edmund Burkean demonization of France and its revolution, only in this instance through the figure of the self-made "Spaniard."

Clara's contact and obsession with Carwin, unlike Clarissa's victimization by Lovelace, purportedly sets in motion a revolution in her mind—the antithesis of the order and stability that seemed to characterize the federation of the foursome—that results in a confused and frenzied state devoid of "order" (109), a condition that some critics have interpreted as a metaphorical reference to what Federalists in particular feared were the Terror-producing excesses of Jacobinism. The same critics, however, have neglected to pose the question why, if Carwin's treacheries may be viewed in light of a fear of the anarchy associated with Jacobinism and the Reign of Terror in France, he is characterized as a self-made Spaniard and not the obvious, a Frenchman. The answer lies in the potential for unequivocal demonization allowed by the association with Spain. In 1789, when the French Revolution began, many Americans were sympathetic to France because they regarded this revolution as one patterned after their own. During the 1790s, Democratic-Republicans, unlike Federalists, continued to favor strong ties with the French, despite their Catholic and Jesuit traditions. A French Carwin might, therefore, have won the sympathies of Brown's readership, whereas few readers would have had much fraternal feeling toward Spain.

Wieland makes the French "Spanish" in more ways than one. The French is displaced over the geographic and imaginative border between France and Spain or placed near enough to it to render what might have seemed familiar dangerous. When Clara moves to France with her uncle, they set up temporary residence in Avignon. Significantly, this city had strong historical links with the region of Aragon in the northeast of Spain, and, more important, was under the jurisdiction of the pope until 1792. Thus, it is possible to read this setting as yet another indication that Clara, though she claims to be free of Carwin, "the double-tongued deceiver" (276), has merely changed places with him. While he hides himself "in a remote district of Pennsylvania . . . probably engaged in the harmless pursuits of agriculture" (270), she wanders around popish and Spanish-like parts of France, places that lie within the "empire" (99) that Clara attributes to Carwin.[23]

Clara is not only "perversely drawn" to Carwin, as critics have noted;[24] she is possessed by him even more than Henry Pleyel, who "contracts" an affection for him (82). Her descriptions of her reactions to Carwin are loaded with sexual innuendo: "O most . . . potent of mankind; in what terms shall I describe thee? . . . Let me keep down the flood of passion that would render me precipitate or powerless" (61). The Clara–Carwin bond is not just the stock relation—the "immoral" moral tale—of Gothic romance; rather, it may also be interpreted as political allegory, as many critics have pointed out, though missing the mark and markings of Carwin's self-made Spanishness. If the various sensationalistic elements of the novel can be analogized to eye-riveting curiosities in a cabinet or, more appropriately, a closet, the objects in this cabinet/closet are not without their specifications (historical, geographic, ethnoracial, sexual, etc.), are not without their cultural "materiality." The weakness of the unprepared Wieland–Pleyel federation or union is displaced onto a woman's body and mind. The cracked foundation of "American" independence and union is emblematized by Clara Wieland's dark dependence on "the Spaniard" in the closet. The tale functions to warn Americans—and specifically, it would seem, Germanic and Anglo compatriots—of the dangers of seduction by "foreign powers" at the same time that it safely distances the consequences of paranoia which Washington cautioned his fellow country*men* to guard against in his farewell address of 1796.

The dangers of seduction by "foreign powers" are overwhelmingly illustrated through Clara's relationship to Carwin and through the person and habits of Carwin himself. So many critics have paid attention to the chief instrument by which Carwin supposedly seduces—his ventriloquist voice—that they have overlooked what material substance Charles Brockden Brown gave to his fascinating prankster and agent (whether direct or circumstantial) of the Wieland–Pleyel confederation's social and psychological demise. In a sense, scholars who have overlooked the physical and cultural characterizations of Carwin have taken one cue—the cue of the trick of the seemingly disembodied voices—and ignored other cues. My analysis returns to those other cues. However equivocating, Carwin's Spanish-like performance really does prevail over other signs of his Englishness or his Irishness and, in fact, subsumes them, as he himself suggests when he declares that "Britons and Spaniards . . . are votaries of the same Deity" and religious empire, presumably the Holy Roman Empire presided over not by a British monarch, but by a Spanish one.

Wieland; or, the Transformation: An American Tale associates Carwin, its prankster villain, with "the powers of blackness," but not only in a general way, as a Jesuitical schemer with uncanny abilities to sway and control, a type that perfectly corresponds to representations of Spaniards through the lenses of the Black Legend. Moreover, the words or phrases that Clara uses to describe Carwin's actions insistently impress on the reader the association of Carwin with darkness and blackness, though not necessarily in a legibly "racial" way: "night" (66), "deepest darkness" (75), "blackest of crimes" (137), "midnight" (145), "darkness rests upon the designs of the man" (206), and "black catalogue of strategems" (239). The overall effect is to conjure Carwin according to the typical Manichaean dualism of Gothic fictions where the villain is darkness and the Gothic heroine is light struggling not to be snuffed out. But, in *Wieland* these "powers of darkness" take on dimensions that complicate the black/white binary either in morally symbolic terms or in racial/cultural terms. The complication, however, does not exactly dismantle the binary: darkness connotes evil, and light, virtue. But, a third position is constructed that destabilizes the usually more or less fixed values of both poles of this binary. Carwin represents that third position at the same time that he bears the burden of "the powers of blackness." In morally symbolic terms, Carwin is guilty more by association than anything else and this indirect guilt already destabilizes a black/white binary. He is never proven beyond reasonable doubt to be the direct agent of the demise of the Wieland–Pleyel confederation or of Clara's emotional and intellectual breakdown, though she insists he is. Within Clara's first-person narration about Carwin he is a villain, a blackguard. But her own actions (which she also recounts to her readers) suggest that she is as much implicated in the collective downfall as Carwin, if for no other reason than by being moved and misled by his projected voices. Nevertheless, in terms of the way in which late-eighteenth-century Anglo Protestant readers would have received overall impressions of Clara and Carwin, his dubious moral guilt is established, however uncertain, by his association with Spain and the Romanish faith. Thus, in moral terms Carwin is, at the very least, ambiguous, and this moral ambiguity comprises a disturbing third position between the certainties of good and evil.

This moral ambiguity is figured as well as "established" or almost legalistically "proven" through cultural and physical ambiguities. In cultural and physical terms, Carwin is represented as occupying a very dubious third position. Neither really American nor really British, he is Spanish-like. It is this Spanishness, a third and perhaps, for some scholars, unexpected transcultural acculturation that, paradoxically, links him with "the powers of blackness." And yet, this blackness is not transparently legible in racial terms according to a black/white binary. All the adjectives that Clara uses to describe Carwin's physical features suggest racial and ethnic ambiguity—"sallow hue" combined with her simultaneous focus on Carwin's "eyes lustrously black" and his "brilliantly white" teeth (65). Black and white, when they are physiognomically invoked, occur together, as a composite "black/white" or "white-black." Black and white both characterize Carwin and do not, for his skin is "sallow," an adjective that connotes discoloration and dirt and a tonality rather than a specific color. That tonality usually ranges from yellow to brown, from the off-white to the not-black. The Black Legend that follows him, both Clara's about him and the one about the country Spain whose habits and habiliments he has assumed, is coded into his person as anemic sallowness, not distinctly legible in racial terms, yet vaguely racializing nonetheless. He is a "Spaniard" as *off-white*, not the right kind of Pleyel–Wieland whiteness. Carwin's vague racialization synthesizes the black/white binary, moral and physical, of so much Gothic fiction, but it does not dismantle it. In fact, it gives it new life by sustaining it while confusing and confounding.

In a similar vein, I argue that the ambiguities of *Wieland; or, the Transformation* do not dispel the Black Legend against Spain or the function of the narrative as a warning to "good" Anglo-Teutonic citizens of the new republic of what to avoid—conniving spies and tricksters like Carwin, possibly in the service of the Spanish Empire, preying on the vulnerability of reason and common sense to their opposites, irrationality and impracticality.

As mentioned earlier, this fiction retells encounter between Old and New World as a story of reassurance and possible regeneration in which the reader goes through a crisis of dependence and emerges with ego boundaries potentially reinforced, if in no other way than through a negative object lesson—do as Clara does not do and should have done. In other words, do not open your doors to Spanish deceivers. Instead, be on the alert and defend yourself. Having said this, I must point out a tendency in Charles Brockden Brown scholarship to translate "ambiguity" into irony and parody that eschews particular political or cultural positions beyond, perhaps, a critique of the excesses of Calvinism or the optimism of the Enlightenment. The concluding chapters of Steven Watts's study *The Romance of Real Life* suggest something more. Watts sees Brown's work as reflections and expressions of the contradictions of bourgeois liberalism, an interesting thesis that, in my opinion, implicates some of the scholarship on Brown and certainly on U.S. nation, and later, empire formation. But, it is not the argument about bourgeois liberalism per se that caught my attention. Rather, it is two bits of biographical material that Watts furnishes, one near the beginning of his book and the other toward the end. The first reads:

> Around his sixteenth year . . . Brown concocted a grand scheme for three epic poems on the early history of the New World: one on Columbus' voyage of discovery, one on Pizarro's expedition to Peru, and one on Cortez's conquest of Mexico.[25]

The second reads:

> Brown's *An Address to the Government of the United States on the Cession of Louisiana* (1803) appeared amidst the American uproar over the Spanish transfer of the Louisiana Territory to France. His *Monroe's Embassy; or, The Conduct of the Government in Relation to Our Claims to the Navigation of the Mississippi* (1803), published a few months later, urged a vigorous policy of American expansion into the trans-Mississippi west.[26]

Watts goes on to clarify that "Brown's political writing of the early 1800s ultimately envisioned an American imperial republic."[27] Taken together, the two passages just quoted suggest that his imperial interests had long roots back to boyhood and, furthermore, were predicated on an emulation of and rivalry with Spanish conquistadores and with the purview of Spanish empire both west of the Mississippi and southward. The words "Monroe's Embassy" in an article on the United States' divinely and naturally sanctioned claim to former Spanish lands seem to forespeak the Monroe Doctrine of 1823 by which the United States more or less arrogated to itself the right to arbitrate the affairs of the Americas as a hemisphere. In light of Brown's interests in accessing Spanish power and power over Spain, *Wieland*'s introduction of a third term between black and white—the morally ambiguous, off-white "Spaniard" in Clara's closet—

cannot be seen as an anti-imperial challenge to the black/white binary of Gothic fiction. Rather, it seems more like an attempt to widen the realm of those "cast" into darkness at the same time that it serves the purpose of giving voice to fears of being undermined from within (and not clearly from outside) by one's own fascination with those outsiders capable of passing for insiders and, above all, with Spanish-like mesmerists.

THE EGOISTIC SUBLIME AND THE SPANISH INQUISITION: EDGAR ALLAN POE'S "WILLIAM WILSON" (1839) AND "THE PIT AND THE PENDULUM" (1843)

Until the 1980s, scant attention had been paid to the specific racialized figures, motifs, and topographies employed in the fabrication of horror and the sublime in Poe's short fiction, that is, scant attention considering the staggering proliferation of racialized figures all over the stories and their saturation in ethnic and racial discourse. Poe's short fiction has had a long history of being regarded merely as tales of the bizarre and the supernatural. In a more serious vein, his tales have received critical attention for their engagement with aesthetics and what should be qualified as European and Euro-American philosophical premises about the nature of reality, "fables of the mind," to quote the title of Joan Dayan's 1987 study of Poe, before she turned to her self-acknowledged controversial investigations of Poe's stories, poems, and reviews in relation to "the ideology of Southern honor" and its dependence "upon fantasies of black degradation" and a "rhetoric of the natural servility" of women and Africans, as well as African Americans.[28]

More than Charles Brockden Brown's *Wieland*, Poe's stories have been treated largely as private psychological/philosophical dramas—as tales of the sinister contradictions of the human heart and mind, not in relation to "the real" or "the historical," and not as political fables or as engaged with fragments of history turned into legend or emblem. Besides denial endemic as much to the academy as to other parts of society about the pervasiveness of racializing colonial and imperial discourses, the tendency to treat Poe's tales as studies of the human heart's private recesses and the mind's dark chambers has been fueled, in part, by their being "short" stories (if not exactly short stories in the contemporary sense) and not novels. The same might be said about his *lyric* poetry. Had it been epic poetry, it would have been scrutinized earlier for its imbrications with discourses of race and slavery. In fact, there might not have been much need for scrutiny as its classification as "epic" poetry would have likely invited studies of national and regional identity formation including, one would hope but cannot assume, central factors such as slavery. For instance, critics have been hard-pressed to ignore the obsession with race and slavery in Poe's only novel, *The Narrative of Arthur Gordon Pym* (1838). In fact, Dana Nelson reminds us that with regard to *Pym* critics have been addressing these issues since at least the 1960s, and her own scholarship contributes to an examination of "the racist dimension of Poe's work" though that examination leads her to conclude, among other things, that in and through *Pym* Poe exposes the self-interested limitations of white "colonial knowledge."[29] Toni Morrison's 1990 William E. Massey Lectures in the History of American Civilization, one of which was dedicated to explicating the centrality of Poe to "American Africanism" (white writers' ego-reinforcing dependence on imagining Africans as Other), added a powerful voice to this history of scholarship on *Pym* and provided a much-needed incentive for other critics to follow in her footsteps and take up this question *across* Poe's genres. For example, the edited volume of essays *Romancing the Shadow: Poe and Race*, in its very use of Morrison's phrase for its title, directly engages with her central, rather than peripheral, placement of Poe in an Anglo-American national canon.

The essays in *Romancing the Shadow* not only consider and debate the imbrication of his work with "Southern views on slavery, as he pictures a universe colored in black and white."[30] Some of them, in particular John Carlos Rowe's "Edgar Allan Poe's Imperial Fantasy and the American Frontier," also touch on the correspondences between Poe's fantasies and antebellum U.S. genocidal expansionist projects against Native Americans, as well as Anglo-U.S. identifications with the imperialist exploits of the British in India, Ireland, Africa, and the Pacific. Taken together, essays such as Dayan's and Rowe's would seem to clinch Poe's demonstrable "enthusiasm" for the inseparable trio of racism, colonialism, and, imperialism. One of the essayists, Terence Whalen, complains that Dayan's and Rowe's essays, the first through purported misattribution (of the Paulding–Drayton pro-slavery review to Poe) and the second through overgeneralization, condemn Poe somewhat a priori as a Southerner and therefore a

Southern pro-slavery racist and expansionist. Although not one of the essays in *Romancing the Shadow* mentions Spain or the Black Legend, Whalen might as well have said that he thinks Dayan's and Rowe's essays construct a "Black Legend" about Poe, denigrating him for crimes that are not his. According to Whalen, as well as J. Gerald Kennedy, one of the editors of *Romancing the Shadow*, though neither Whalen nor Kennedy makes this analogy, essays such as these have "stigmatized" Poe as a Southerner with something equivalent to the Black Legend about Spanish cruelty that at least two of his well-known tales engage and underscore.[31] This is a truly ironic state of affairs—historically, culturally, critically, professionally. Evidently, the Black Legend is contagious and keeps migrating from country, to text, to author, to critic, and so on. No one wants its shadow to touch the artifact of their more sympathetic readings, and yet its shadow falls everywhere between the letter and its interpretation. The fact is that the Black Legend against Spain was not without its truths, and the same goes, one might conclude, for the supposed Black Legend against Poe.

I cannot here untangle the complexities of these claims and counterclaims with regard to the possible cultural investments and identifications of the critics involved. Suffice it to say that I am persuaded by many of Dayan's and Rowe's arguments, not so much about Poe per se, but about his texts' and his readers' complicity in colonial and imperial racial discourses—both the white versus black kind and the white versus "people of color" sort that Rowe points up in his discussion of the "prevailing ideology of 'white' as designating the U.S. 'citizen' and a wide range of peoples of color constituting the 'opposite of white.'"[32] However, in moving on, I would like to turn back to Dayan's work on Poe as a whole—from her 1987 *Fables of the Mind* to her 1990s scholarship on Poe, women, and slavery. Rather than divide Dayan's work into two distinct phases and irreconcilable approaches, the philosophical-formalist approach and the race and legal-studies approach, I suggest that the two approaches must be integrated—the one that emphasizes Poe's stylistics and mechanics (consider, for example, Dayan's focus on the "analytic of the dash" and the ellipsis) with the later approach foregrounding the historical and legal contexts for his images of "black and white" and "bondage." Dayan's earlier work sees Poe as a philosophical writer using "method" to expose the limitations of knowledge and power, whereas her later work reverses its stance and views him as a pro-slavery Southern gentleman keenly aware of the kind of power trip that white Southern pro-slavery gentlemen took—the trip of loyalty unto death and fear of the reprisals awaiting their excesses of "mastery"—and yet taking that power trip himself through his fiction. So, what might it look like to put the philosophical-formalist reading of Poe or the Poe of limitation together with the Poe of expansion of the self at the expense of the limitation, the veritable bondage, of the Other or another?

I would argue that it is the nature of Poe's writing—his technique(s)—that provides material for the ongoing controversy about the relation (or not) of his work to colonial and imperial discourses. Beyond the undecidability and indeterminacy of the text that deconstruction reminds us of (though undecidability should not be mistaken for infinite possibility or "anything goes"), Poe's passion for plotting, the strategic gamelike nature of his texts, both short and longer, leaves many readers feeling foolish to press on those works the "earnestness" of, the commitment to, a particular ideological formation. And, if they do, other critics accuse these critics of wantonly affixing labels and bad words such as *colonialism*, *racism*, and *imperialism* on Poe's work and the author himself. I would like to take a close look at Poe's narrative strategies and semiotic codes or sign clusters, the vehicles of his *impressment* of his readership, in "William Wilson" and "The Pit and the Pendulum." I use the term "impressment" in a multiple sense meaning to apply pressure, to produce a lasting effect, and to conscript into the service of some cause. Such an investigation reveals that both stories, like Charles Brockden Brown's *Wieland*, are fictions dependent on political and racial allegory of an ultimately usurping, self-congratulating, "inquisitively" imperializing sort and that they lead their readership to occupy an imperious, imperializing position by catching them in the pressure-cooker pleasure of a thrilling hoax through the vehicle of the narrating "I" who more than survives, either posthumously or in life.

As I shall demonstrate, this "imperializing" tricks the black/white binary that has informed most of U.S. Poe scholarship—it even tricks the more recent black-and-white critical complications of that binary, but, in my reading, the trick does not necessarily undercut the "imperializing." Confounding shadowy figures of "the Spaniard" projected through the dark lenses of the Black Legend run through and give shape to the stories, like the ghostly Arab in William Rimmer's best-known painting *Flight and*

Pursuit (1871). The main difference between Charles Brockden Brown's novel and Poe's stories is that in the latter the crisis of dubious identity that these enslaving or persecuting Spanish pursuers supposedly enact for the non-Spanish narrator (with whom the readership is implicitly asked to identify) is transmitted through the vehicle of a theatrical hoax, not that of the cabinet of bizarre curiosities transformed into a closet full of nightmares. The "parodic" application of a formula rather than the eye-riveting sensationalism of Brown's text functions less as a warning and more as a joke, with all the attendant implications of this distinction. The relation of the parodic application of a formula to achieve a calculated effect—so suitable, as Poe himself wrote in "The Philosophy of Composition," to short fiction—*and* what I call Anglo-American imperial ideology has been a hitherto obliquely addressed topic in scholarship on Poe's work. Please note my emphasis on Anglo-American imperial ideology, for I am not trying to claim that critics have entirely ignored this question in relation to racism and slavery, components of that ideology, but still very much within the assumptions of a black/white binary, meaning "African/African American" versus "white" planters and abolitionists, or "people of color" versus "white people." Joan Dayan's many readings of Poe taken together begin to lift that coffin lid, if you wish, but I would like to unite her early and later approaches to Poe's work in a third that seems not to be much condoned by the essayists of *Romancing the Shadow* and that is a more psychoanalytic reader-response one. And, I would like to distinguish my approach from the one essay in the book that does attempt a synthesis with an eye to what it calls Poe's depiction of a white racist psychology—Leland S. Person's "Poe's Philosophy of Amalgamation: Reading Racism in the Tales."

The strongest critique of either a Lacanian psychoanalytic or more generally a deconstructive psychorhetorical approach to Poe's work appears in Rowe's essay "Edgar Allan Poe's Imperial Fantasy and the American Frontier":

Lacanian and other poststructuralist interpretations of Poe's writings have interpreted them ingeniously as narratives that anticipate modern psychoanalytic accounts of the linguistic differences essential to psychic experience. Yet these same critics miss the ideological consequences of the psychic and linguistic origins Poe has offered us . . . Poe played with the gendered and racialized "bodies" he believed were effects of the language of which he was master.[33]

Rowe's objection to Poe's cleverness is, more or less, that he had no right to play with the bodies of "people of color" for the sake of proving himself master of linguistic play, and Rowe faults specifically Lacanian and other poststructuralist readings for colluding with this unethical "play." Person's essay, placed toward the end of *Romancing the Shadow*, picks up the question of "Poe's racial content . . . with both his playful, deconstructive impulse and his exploitation of first-person psychological romance" and stakes as its central claim that "first-person psychological romance in the Gothic or sensational mode represented an ideal vehicle for representing and destabilizing the psychological constructs of white male racism."[34] Drawing on some of Dana Nelson's arguments in *The Word in Black and White* about slippages and oscillations in the deployment of *black* and *white*, Person's essay explores the emplotting of this amalgamation, of black-and-white coding, of color and racial confusion, within the perspectival frame of first-person narration. Person's essay argues that Poe "understood the [socially] symbolic value of color, and clearly embedded dramas of color in his psychological romances . . . In the process . . . Poe ingeniously represented the workings of white racist psychology."[35] The essay seeks to demonstrate that through an encoding of amalgamation in a first-person account Poe exposed "the roots of white racist fears" about nondifferentiation between black and white, slave and master. Person concludes: "Without speculating on Poe's intentions, I think these tales reveal complicated patterns of racism and antiracist sympathy."[36]

Despite Person's final insistence that his essay does not appeal to notions about the author's intentions, phrases such as "Poe understood" and "these tales reveal . . . antiracist *sympathy*" (my emphasis) shift the focus to Poe the man and away from his texts as texts or away from his readers (either his contemporaries or our contemporaries). In fact, such phrases bespeak a strong identification of the critic (Person, in this case) with the writer such that although the essay does not quite clear Poe of the charge of racism, it does insist on the humanity of his critical awareness of his and others' racism and this awareness is conscripted into an argument, once again, about Poe's ingenious complexity. In Person's version of Poe, the latter becomes the self-appointed enactor and expiator of white male racists' sins. I would like to suspend that identification of critic with author—that transference. I am not interested in either rescuing or condemning Poe. Rather, I wish to usher in an investigation of the relation between Poe's parody and an Anglo-American imperial ideology by concentrating on the "psychodynamics" of the two well-known and widely read tales "William Wilson" and "The Pit and the Pendulum." I am interested in them precisely because they do not so readily lend themselves to the historical master–slave narrative of the "white man" versus an "African" or "an African American." In not lending themselves so easily to this mapping of social relations (or lack thereof), it becomes harder for the critic to play the role of either heroic denouncer or sophisticated apologist, or a subtle mixture of the two. How many U.S. critics would feel compelled to condemn Poe or apologize for his blackening of presumably white Spaniards into figures of alien whiteness? What is the connection between these tales and other works with more "domestic" references, be they frontier or not? How do these tales necessitate a different horizon line beyond that of Poe's disputed awareness? How does the focus of critical analysis change? How do these tales become less about Poe and more about his implied readers (mostly Anglo-American and British)?

Both tales are set in Europe. "William Wilson" (1839) is set in England ("a misty-looking village of England,"[37] Eton, and Oxford) and later Rome, with passing references to Paris, Naples, and Egypt that recall the Grand Tour on which a leisured man of Britain or the United States was expected to embark as part of his education. There are also fleeting mentions of Vienna, Berlin, and Moscow. "The Pit and the Pendulum" (1843) takes place in Toledo, Spain, first in a tribunal room of the Spanish Inquisition and then entirely in a dungeon. Let me summarize each story, though such summaries have the unfortunate effect of reducing Poe's myriad fantastic effects to plodding plot. "William Wilson" is a story about a boy turned a man (who grows up base and vicious, not by "degrees" but all at once) and his tormenting double, who may or may not be his own conscience, in Freudian language, his superego admonishing his ego ("Wilson," 626). The narrator relates this story, he tells his readers, because, as he speaks beyond the grave in a kind of purgatory, he wants sympathy, perhaps to soften his spiritual sentence: "I would fain have them [his readers or his spiritual judges?] believe that I have been, in some measure, the slave of circumstances beyond human control" (ibid.). The narrator wishes to convince his audience that he has fallen prey to some inevitable fate—to fatality. That fatality is conjured in the shape of a William Wilson No. 2, dressed first in a white morning frock and then in a "Spanish cloak of blue velvet" (640), who dogs William Wilson No. 1 wherever he goes, and yet whom the latter outlives. One of the most mysterious statements in the story is, "I am the descendent of a race whose imaginative and easily excitable temperament has at all times rendered them remarkable" (626). The account associates this "race" with willfulness, "wildest caprices," "ungovernable passions," "weak-minded-ness," and "constitutional infirmities" (626–27). If the Spanish-garbed William Wilson is a reflection of the original William Wilson, then it would seem that the English Eton- and Oxford-educated William Wilson identifies this potentially Spanish heritage as the cause of his later viciousness. It is as if in "William Wilson" we are given Carwin confessing against Carwin on the basis of that troublesome "Spanish" element. However, in Poe's story the Spanish imp is banished when the narrator stabs William Wilson 2, his potential mirror image ("mine own image" [641]) and yet survives, cursed by the dying double who, however, admits defeat. It is a Pyrrhic victory, to be sure, but a victory nonetheless.

The later "Pit and the Pendulum" is narrated from the point of view of a captive of the Spanish Inquisition who is tried by tall, black-robed judges (remindful of Dominicans), found guilty, and borne down to a deep dungeon in Toledo, Spain. In the dungeon he is surrounded by the "blackness of eternal night," and the intensity of "darkness" oppresses and stifles him.[38] In this darkness, the thought that dawns on him is that he has been condemned to death, to perish in an auto-da-fé ("Pit," 248). He is tortured not only by these thoughts, but by fatigue and hunger, and by the physical features of the dungeon—its shifting dimensions, the abysmal pit in the middle of it, the dankness, the extremes of temperature, and so forth. Initially able to move around, he explores the dungeon, which at first seems large. Then, after falling asleep and waking to find himself strapped to a wooden bed, the dungeon appears small, a claustrophobic iron vault with hideous forms on its walls and a painted figure of Time on the ceiling. To the narrator, the painted figure of Time appears to be holding a painted pendulum. However, this pendulum turns out to be not a two-dimensional representation, but a three-dimensional, slowly descending torture instrument, a crescent-shaped scythe designed to cut the bound narrator into pieces of flesh that will be devoured by the dungeon's rats. Through some sleight of hand with the remains of his food dish, the narrator induces the rats to eat the cloth restraints that strap him to the wooden bed and he escapes death by the swinging razor-like pendulum. He escapes death only to realize that he is still "in the grasp of the Inquisition" (255) and that the walls of his prison are heating up like four irons and closing in upon him. Just as he is forced to the brink of the abysmal pit in the center of the dungeon to avoid being burned to death, deus ex machina the walls stop closing in and the outstretched arm of General Lasalle saves the narrator from the pit. The last lines of the story read, "The French army had entered Toledo. The Inquisition was in the hands of its enemies" (257). The ending is much more triumphal than that of "William Wilson" with its tenuous and somewhat equivocal victory over what has been symbolized as the dark side of the self.

Let me begin with a word on colors in Poe's work. Black, white, and red appear repeatedly, not only in these two stories but throughout his writings. In fact, one might say that these writings exploit extreme contrasts and the shock of the color of blood as it issues from the body, red. But, in other stories an amalgamation of *black and white* in contrast to black versus white is the primary technique, for instance, in "The Black Cat." In yet other stories amalgamation of this sort is employed quite clearly in the context of physical descriptions of nationality, ethnicity, and "race." Such is the case in the two stories I am examining here, as well as "Ligeia," *The Narrative of Arthur Gordon Pym*, and "The Facts in the Case of M. Valdemar." Of the latter I will speak later in this chapter, but for now let me quickly sketch amalgamation as it occurs in the two stories in question. For instance, "William Wilson" codes Wilson's Spanish-garbed double or seeming "twin" brother ("Wilson," 630) as it codes its narrator in both *white* ("a white kerseymere morning frock" [635] and *black* ("A mask of black silk entirely covered his face" [640]). After William Wilson 1 stabs Wilson 2, both Wilsons appear with "features all pale and dabbled in blood" (641), suggesting a mixture of light and dark, though not necessarily white and black. In "The Pit and the Pendulum," the Spanish "black-robed judges" are given writing lips that appear "whiter" than the sheet of paper on which the narrator writes ("Pit," 246). This description suggests a kind of blackface, not with the exaggeratedly thick lips stereotypically assigned to Africans and African Americans, but rather with the thin ones conventionally associated with "whites."

Thus, in both stories, Spanishness is portrayed through a blackened whiteness or a whitened blackness, but, I argue, this amalgamation does not really confound and question racial stereotypes the way Person claims. Rather, it creates figures of alien whiteness or whiteness morally and physically blackened by the Black Legend against Spain. Or, another way of seeing these instances of amalgamation is that they create a "blackness" blanched from servility to despotism according to the same legend. In other words, to draw out the implications of these observations does not so much entail the recognition of hybridity (cultural, "racial," etc.) as the inscription of a phobia of an agent with potentially greater power than the narrator—the Spanish double, in one case, and the Spanish tormentors, in the other. And the phobia does not transmute into paternalistic sympathy with the oppressed because, in both these cases, unlike that of "The Black Cat," the narrators insist that they are victims, even slaves, not of a slave in revolt but of a Spanish-like imp ("William Wilson") and Spanish despots (the inquisitors in "The Pit and the Pendulum"). Poe's implied readership would likely have taken his narrators at their words, if for no other reason than that they have little choice but to see—to envision— through the narrators' eyes. Furthermore, supposing readers found themselves questioning their narrators—certainly the narrator of "William Wilson" hardly presents himself as a moral exemplum and the narrator of "The Pit and the Pendulum" is half delirious—readers of the time would have been particularly primed to view the amalgamated Spaniards of those tales as proper stage villains, regardless of how they were assessing the veracity of the account. These Spaniards would hardly have been the object of antiracist sympathy, but instead of fascinated phobia (for where there is phobia there is also fascination) and pleasurable anxiety, which was made all the more pleasurable upon these figures' vanquishment. The presence of these figures of alien whiteness in a first-person narrative about their difficult but eventual vanquishment suggests that Poe's tales were fulfilling another function besides giving expression to racism and antiracism, pro-slavery and antislavery positions. They were appealing to the thrill of losing cultural identity in the face of a growing confidence about that very identity defined against those vanquished figures of Spain. And the vanquishment can be enjoyed guilt-free as readers are constantly reminded of how much the narrator has suffered at the hands of these Spanish amalgamations. This observation brings me back to the question of the psychodynamics of these tales.

By "psychodynamics" I am not referring to the individual and/or personal reading experience with which so much of reader-response criticism has been preoccupied, nor that of the ahistorical, unspecified, and idealized Stanley Fishian "community of readers." Instead, I mean the ways in which these tales trap their implied readership, connecting readers through ideology. On the most general level, the readership traps of these tales are effected by the technique of conveying all associations via a first-person narrator. In *The Rustle of Language*, Roland Barthes reminds readers, citing the work of Émile Benveniste on subjectivity in language, that the grammatical category of person organizes subjectivity into a basic polarity, that of person (I or you) in opposition to the nonperson (he, she, or it). Barthes amends Benveniste by observing that language creates three oppositions,—the I to the you, the I to the she, he, or it, and the I/you dyad (the positions of which are convertible one to the other)— against the he, she, or it.[39] But, whether two or three oppositions, the basic point remains the same. The first-person narration as an unwavering technique in Poe's stories leaves readers nowhere else to go but to follow the psychological states and physical sensations of a seemingly interiorized subjectivity conjured up by the continual repetition of the pronoun *I*. Despite the emotional and psychological agitation of each of the tales' narrators, the first-person voice is rendered credible and authoritative rather than merely monomaniacal through its reiterated appeals to a perceptualist ontology—"I saw," "I felt" ("Pit," 246)—functioning not as a creed of belief to be contested, but of presumably evidential sensation, as well as through descriptive passages that appeal to a positivistic empiricist epistemology of quantification and measurement: "The house . . . was old and irregular. The grounds were extensive, and a high and solid brick wall, topped with a bed of mortar and broken glass, encompassed the whole. This prison-like rampart formed the limit of our domain" ("Wilson," 627). The tales as traps constituting a united readership may be said to function as hermeneutic domains that wall in their readership. The *immurement* within the narrator's *hermeneutic domain* of the implied readership's potential for interpreting things differently from the narrator is further sealed by the declarative mode. Although readers may have had or have doubts, they are compelled to follow what is presented as a meticulous reconstruction of events that requires their increasingly rapt absorption.

The equation of a recounted field of signs to be interpreted with a domain, a territory, or realm governed over by a single ruler, master, or lord (the narrator) and the acts of reading and interpreting with a submission to an increasing enclosure and an escalating compression are actually suggested by other Poe stories, such as "The Black Cat" and "The Cask of Amontillado." In "William Wilson" and "The Pit and the Pendulum," the notion of composition and reading as captivation, torture, and submission is more fully worked out. These stories operate as if to guard against failure to force an effect on the readership. As Poe claimed in "Twice-Told Tales," "the simple truth . . . that the writer who aims at impressing the people is always wrong when *he fails in forcing* that people to receive the impression."[40] In contrast to "The Black Cat" and "The Cask of Amontillado," in which the first-person narrator offers his readership the perhaps uneasily incorporated fantasy of imagining themselves to be torturers, these two stories furnish a first-person narrator who insists that he was or is the persecuted and tortured outcast. The main difference between "William Wilson" and "The Pit and the Pendulum" is that in the former, published four years before the latter, the narrator *explicitly* describes himself, in highly equivocal terms, as ambitious, vengeful, passionate, and avaricious—as simultaneously imperious and abject, victimizer and victim, master and slave, conqueror and conquered, torturer and tortured. Unlike that of the swooning narrator and his tall, "black-robed judges" in "The Pit and the Pendulum" ("Pit," 246), the relationship between the narrator and his supposed antagonist in "William Wilson" exists on a horizontal axis—it is one of rival equals, brothers, twins: "[I]f we had been brothers we must have been twins" ("Wilson," 630). Despite plot details and elements of characterization that suggest the narrator's complicity with his own torments, the narration is dedicated primarily to continual and minute persuasion that the narrator is being persecuted. Therefore, both tales ultimately have the effect of impressing upon their readership a more tasteful fantasy, that of being the tortured, where the reward of empathy, forced as it may be by the first-person narration, is the thrill (conventionally coded as sublime) of feeling, while not actually being, persecuted and terrified.

What distinguishes the subjectivity effect of these tales from that imparted by the poems of Wordsworth and Whitman or the essays of Emerson is that it does not involve the usual Romantic reverie-like communion between "self" and Nature, but rather the intensification—through a contrived isolation—of the experience of "self," the defense of which in Freudian discourse might be termed the embattled "ego's boundaries." In both tales, the willful "I" could be described as the ego attempting to survive its unbounding represented by the external world of people, things, and circumstances that threaten to objectify it, to render it not only ordinary but inconsequential: "when they at length unbound me and I was permitted to sit, I felt that my senses were leaving me" ("Pit," 246). I use the term "egoistic sublime" to define the heightening of all the ego's external and internal perceptions, particularly the unpleasant ones, the effects of which become *primae causae*, compelling the ego to *strain* itself until it overreaches its own limits of "reason and common sense." This overreaching, however, is a form of ego magnification, an enlargement of the ego's domain. Paradoxically, at the very same time that the ego is carried away by the id's "superior strength"[41] of the passions/instincts, the ego binds this strength to itself and ex-presses that energy in the form of a minutely described "madness" or delirium: "I felt every fibre in my frame thrill *as if I had touched the wire of a galvanic battery*" (ibid.; my emphasis). The narrative "I" is like—to quote from Freud's essay "The Ego and the Id"—"the ego . . . in the habit of transforming the id's will into action as if it were its own."[42]

Wilson's inquisitorial double caught at the conclusion of the tale in "a Spanish cloak of blue velvet . . . and a mask of black silk" ("Wilson," 640) in "William Wilson" and the "mill-wheel" ("Pit," 246) of the Spanish Inquisition in "The Pit and the Pendulum" function as superegos persecuting the narrative "I." The narrative "I" of these tales as the beleaguered ego acts paradoxically, trying to avoid yet courting the effects of these "superegos." The narrative logic for such bizarre courtship lies in the stories' connections of a personification of Spanish dominion seen through the lenses of the Black Legend in "William Wilson" and the Spanish Inquisition in "The Pit and the Pendulum" to the provocation of sublime emotions such as terror, hatred, and the death wish that the narrative "I" or ego seeks to tap in order to magnify itself.[43] These two Poe tales are analogues to Freud's claim that the "super-ego is always close to the id and can act as its representative vis-à-vis the ego. It reaches deep down into the id."[44]

I read these stories in relation to Freud's schema of the psyche (ego, id, and superego) to demonstrate the tales' mechanistic production of emotion. What is revealed is the extent to which these types of persecution (writ large) operate as devices, contraptions, by means of which the excesses of the narrative "I" are forcibly justified. To find the justification for the persecution or "Inquisition complex" gimmicky—a kind of *"diabolus" ex machina*—is part and parcel of experiencing the perverse effects of stories that are enactments of a parodic style simultaneously disguising and mirroring readerly resistance. The egoistic sublime is both the text's enactment and parody of a central trope of Romantic subjectivity, the expression of personal feeling as a confirmation of the feeling subject's extra-ordinariness or idealized individualism. Furthermore, these tales parody the benign organicism of the Romantic model—prevalent in the works of the U.S. transcendentalists and in the sentimental novel—of an empathetic union between ideal reader and textual subjectivity. Substituted for any such salutary organicism is a sadomasochistic mechanism; the text pulls its implied readership by "the tackle for scene-shifting"—to quote from Poe's essay "The Philosophy of Composition"[45]—toward a conversion, if not to the narrator's point of view, then along his tormenting chain of associations leading to his dark dungeon or solitary antechamber of sensational (as in both lurid and exciting) ideas.

Readers follow in the narrator's footsteps because there is nowhere else to go and, also, because this nowhere else is perversely fascinating, however gimmicky it may seem. The vicarious experience proffered by the stories is a complex one in that not only do the stories lend themselves as the perfect substitute for actual torture with the satisfactory ending of survival in extremis, but they appeal in their language, in practically their every word, to the desire and curiosity for going to extremes, to dangerous lengths, whether gimmicky or not. The stories successfully operate on the premise that with sufficient encouragement of imaginative engagement (and Poe's language is always chosen for effect) readers will be induced to suspend disbelief and enjoy the scary gimmick as an altered reality, more than adequately "real." The enjoyment of scary gimmicks that simulate near-death situations (the nearer the better, and there is none better than survival in some afterlife, however twilight-like) is the central topic, after all, of one of Poe's best-known, yet understudied, essay stories—"The Imp of the Perverse" (1845). Perversity or perverseness is defined as the strong tendency to "act for the reason that we should not," to act contrary to "our welfare" individually and collectively.[46] Through several examples about unwanted digression in speech, procrastination in action, and the sickening and dizzying appeal of standing on the edge of a precipice, and, most surprisingly, the desire to confess to a crime and thus be sentenced to the gallows ("Imp," 283–84), the essay story underscores how the tendency toward perversity converts from impulse to wish to desire to uncontrollable longing to later "regret and mortification" (281–82).

"William Wilson" and "The Pit and the Pendulum" both lead their readers to the edge of the precipice in agons with Spanish imps and inquisitors. However, they take the edge off "regret and mortification" for approaching an inquisitorial pit by allowing the narrators—and readers living vicariously through these narrators—to survive. Furthermore, the evil Spaniards, these figures of alien whiteness to an Anglo-American readership, are conjured to press the narrative ego into a tight spot and then release him like a genie from a bottle, all the more potent for having been corked up into what at first looked like certain annihilation. The operation accomplished can be summed up in a perfect inversion of the phrase Poe playfully deploys in "The Imp of the Perverse": "will-I, nill-I" (280). These stories nill the I to will the I! And, along with the narrator, the readership is invited to experience, genie-like, a thrilling escape from close encounters with a snuffing out at the hands of these Spanish figures. Thus, the figures serve ultimately to reinforce the narrators' egos, and most probably those of the identifying readers.

The principle of perversity outlined in "The Imp of the Perverse" easily corresponds to Freud's description of the death wish. But in these stories the death wish is placed in the service of near-death survival—the reconstitution, at the eleventh hour, of the imago of the ego even from beyond the grave, as in "William Wilson." Thus, the death wish ultimately effects a sublime exultation of the narratorial and readerly egos, surviving either directly or vicariously in extremis. This thrilling sublimation not of the wish for death (for that is there, all right!) but of death itself is accomplished thanks to these Spanish characters, ludicrously stock in their representation and yet indispensable. If they are imps in the service of the principle of the perverse—that desire to brush with death—then they are first and foremost historical imps of the perverse, one of the most formerly formidable enemies an Anglo, either English or Anglo-American, could pick, none other than reminders and remainders of an imperial (the pun "imp-erial" is just too tempting to avoid) rival for power in the Old and New Worlds. Yet, in these stories, this imperial rival, this historical imp is turned into a *diabolus ex machina*, a typecast figure in Poe's machinery of terror manufacturing the egoistic sublime.

Rhetoric repeatedly employed from the sixteenth century onward in British and Anglo-American accounts furthering the Black Legend is used in "William Wilson" to characterize the narrator and his double as "despot[ic]," "tyrann[ical]," "imperious," "impertinent," "arbitrary," and "enslaved." "The Pit and the Pendulum," set in Toledo, describes the trial, the judges, the sable draperies, the sentence, the tortures, the dungeon, and the swinging scimitar or "destroying crescent" ("Pit," 254) as all part of the horrors of the Spanish Inquisition. These rhetorical descriptions comprise more than just the trappings, the specific contents, of these tales' formal traps. The allusions to a tyrannical legacy or shadow and the Spanish Inquisition, corresponding to the well-known tropes of the Black Legend, function as an allegory of the way these texts work as traps for the readership. The relation of these stories to at least a nascent Anglo-American imperial ideology lies in their offering of the Spanish Inquisition and its Black Legend as the *obvious* instruments for, as well as types of, the textual persecution and immurement of the readership by which these tales work.

The question is whether this relation in "William Wilson" and "The Pit and the Pendulum" can be summed up as the reproduction and production of the dominant ideology. By dominant ideology I mean, with reference to Anglo-American imperialism, a general assumption of superiority or mastery (on any number of counts—moral, cultural, racial, and so forth) over that deemed or represented as "Other." Two aspects of both stories would seem to discourage the argument that they do reproduce or lend themselves to the production of such an ideology: first, the narrator, whose associations the implied readership is more or less forced to incorporate, maintains that he is in an inferior or disadvantaged position to his rival/enemy (even when the relation is twin-like); and second, the stories are elaborate contraptions, hoaxes, or parodic applications of a formula and thus, the reasoning might go, cannot be taken to task in this way as their ironic stance invalidates, or at least greatly disarms, certain questions.

The elaboration of the narrator's position as inferior is neither constant nor irreversible. Rather, both tales end with the narrator's victory or survival, however Pyrrhic or ambiguous. Among the final lines of "William Wilson" is "It was my antagonist—it was Wilson, who then stood before me in the agonies of his dissolution" ("Wilson," 641). Of course, the victory in this story is much more fraught as it involves a kind of self-murder or suicide. Yet, because the narrator as the teller of the tale seems to remain cognizant beyond the grave, the final impression is that he has survived his double who was dressed "altogether similarly" to himself, but with a difference.[47] The double, rather than donning "a fur cloak" (630), is in a "Spanish cloak of blue velvet" with a "mask of black silk entirely covering his face" (640). "The Pit and the Pendulum" concludes with the rescue of the narrator and the defeat of the Inquisition characterized all along as consummately Other—Spanish, Catholic, and Saracenic: "An outstretched arm caught my own as I fell . . . It was that of General Lasalle. The French army had entered Toledo. The Inquisition was in the hands of its enemies" ("Pit," 257). Thus, in both stories, the narrators' "egos" outlast, if not exactly triumph over, their Spanish, Catholic, and Saracenic Others.

The setting in motion of a claptrap contraption, of what Poe himself described as "the wheels and pinions—the tackle for scene-shifting—the step-ladders and demon-traps—the cock's feathers, the red paint and the black patches,"[48] all to achieve an effect—raises the question of whether the *functionality* of the descriptions and allusions to the Spanish Inquisition and the Black Legend as devices neutralizes their use. As part of the parodic application of a formula, these descriptions and allusions may be said to have the status of jokes. Despite current critical exoneration of irony, the play of these jokes does not preclude ideological investment and impression in that these jokes assert discursive control over their elements, allowing the readership to share in the spoils. The Spanish Inquisition and its Black Legend, though associated with terror in "The Pit and the Pendulum," have been reduced to a series of stage props such as black robes, thin white lips, a circular pit, enormous rats, a crescent-bladed pendulum, "oily and spicy" ("Pit," 255) pieces of meat, a wooden bed, a burning iron, a low whisper, a Spanish cloak, a crimson belt with rapier, a mask of black silk, and a large mirror—fetish objects for generating horror in "tales of the grotesque and the arabesque." On the other hand,

the Spanish Inquisition and the Black Legend are robbed of their historical coordinates and rendered nebulous and pervasive as "one dreamy inde-
terminate hum" ("Pit," 246) or "echo" ("Wilson," 632). They are made
to belong, as the narrator intimates, to "a thousand vague rumors of the
horrors of Toledo . . . strange things narrated . . . fables" ("Pit," 249), to
the province—turned empire—of discourse. The joke, the tall tale, the
parodic application already implies and further engenders psychological
distance from a sense of actual threat or danger.

These stories were written in the late 1830s and early 1840s at a time
when the United States had acquired a significant degree of clout and
confidence domestically and internationally (the Monroe Doctrine of
1823, the extension of various frontiers, the elaboration of the doctrine
of manifest destiny) and was about to annex more territory through the
war with Mexico (1846–48). The dominions alluded to in the stories—
England, Spain, the Ottoman Empire, and Venice—have several things
in common: they are situated safely across the Atlantic Ocean; they were,
even in Poe's time, defeated powers, powers in decline, or representationally associated with decadence and decay. Thus, as territories and powers,
they were understood as being "of the past"—like the year when French
troops occupied Spain (1808) relative to the composition and publication
dates of these tales (1839, 1843).

The degree to which Spain and things Spanish are allowed to terrify is
the measure of burgeoning Anglo-American imperial confidence in the
face of Spain's loss of actual economic, military, and territorial power. Furthermore, not only are these tales a gauge or reflection of Anglo-American
imperial confidence; they are also productive of an ideology of superiority and mastery to the extent that they use historical elements (such as
the Inquisition) to timeless effect, as types of evil. In so doing, the tales
continue the project of turning history into myth—the Inquisition into
the damning legend against Spain. By turning history into myth, the tales
turn themselves into handy contraptions for the conversion of a private
experience of the egoistic sublime into a national one with expanding
ambitions.

Myth does not always announce itself as a tale demanding or courting
the readership's belief system, but may even more deviously operate, as
in these tales, as a mantle (a *sanbenito*, if you will) of well-worn associations of Spain and things Spanish with evil, persecution, and, to quote the

narrator in "William Wilson," with an insult to "natural rights of self-agency" ("Wilson," 639). This set of associations forms a kind of theatrical con artist's compression chamber into which the readership may step for the thrill of danger, for the metamorphosis of pain into an occasion for egoistic sublimity. The implied readership is compelled along the narrative to emerge as a survivor of the Spanish Inquisition in "The Pit and the Pendulum" and of its threatening image as a Spaniard in "William Wilson." Aspects of these tall tales play to readerly resistance. However, these suspect, even ludicrous, accounts nevertheless impel the readership to indulge the imperious pleasures and pains of the texts' sadomasochistic contraptions. Despite irony, or what I prefer to call parodic tenor, the stories "wind up" doing the mill-wheel work of culture—impressing the readership in a *uniting* Inquisition complex.

This uniting inquisition complex between narrators and readers revolves around the notion of outliving and surviving inquisitorial Spanish imps and fiends who are presented as amalgamated figures of alien whiteness or blackened whiteness. Curiously, in both "William Wilson" and "The Pit and the Pendulum" much of this blackening and the general amalgamation of black and white takes place on a sartorial level, save for the writhing white lips of the black-robed judges. I say sartorial level rather than phenotypic level. This would seem to put these works more in the camp of the moral rather than the specifically racial blackening of Spain and Spaniards. In fact, these texts would seem to follow in the footsteps of Charles Brockden Brown's *Wieland* where, though physical darkening is imputed to Carwin, what is underscored again and again is his garb and behavior. However, as one nears mid-century, racializations of those deemed "Spanish" become increasingly apparent. It is the body of the Spaniard, not just the clothes and behavior, that is darkened and, if amalgamated, done in such a way as to stress the *off*-whiteness of the Spaniard's body. Even among Poe's tales involving Spaniards or "Spanish" characters one can see this trend of blackened whiteness: "William Wilson" (1839) is sartorial, and "The Pit and the Pendulum" is both sartorial and physical—recall the inverse blackface of the thin, writhing white lips.

In "The Facts in the Case of M. Valdemar," published in 1845, two years after "The Pit and the Pendulum," however, the amalgamation is undeniably physical and racializing. Although it is yet another tale about dubious deeds all around, the blackening of whiteness falls especially on the character living in Harlem, New York, a man with a Galician-Portuguese or northwestern Spanish name "Valdemar" who becomes the "patient" of the mesmerist-narrator, and not on the presumably Anglo mesmerist himself or on anyone else. In fact, this racialized blackening compounded with the blackening of putrefaction at the end makes this "Spaniard" an unequivocally abject person, to be distinguished from the more menacing versions in the earlier tales. Valdemar is not an inquisitor; rather, he is a zombie (an already racialized figure if one considers the origin of the notion of a zombie), mesmerized before his death by the narrator and outliving his allotted life in a putrid hypnotic trance. When readers are introduced to him, they learn that he has white whiskers and very black hair.[49] Then he is described as being of "a leaden hue" ("Valdemar," 97), that is, gray, and later on as cadaverously white as "white paper" (100) save for the "swollen and blackened tongue" (101). By the end of the story, however, Valdemar has become "a nearly liquid mass of loathsome—of detestable putrescence" (103). Although a color is not given, such a state of advanced decomposition would most likely be black. The unnatural whiteness resolves into the blackness of putrescence.

So great is M. Valdemar's abjection that he is threatening only to the extent that he presents a picture of *living death*, of death that lives as organic putrefaction—in this regard, he does present a horrible sight, in some ways far worse than any pose of William Wilson 2 or of the black-robed judges with the writhing white lips. But, catatonic, mesmerized by a narrator who remains ethnically unmarked except for his own comparison of Valdemar's lower limbs to those of John Randolph (96)—suggesting an Anglo-American image-repertoire—Valdemar has no active powers of persecution.[50] He is entirely at the mercy of the mesmerist and neither the mesmerist nor his doctors can save him from a death that manifests itself as continuous decomposition instead of peaceful cessation of existence. Whereas the other Spanish characters actively torment the narrator-protagonists, this character is introduced as "my friend" (ibid.), evidently a piteous one whom the mesmerist-narrator has decided to use as a guinea pig to test whether the "encroachments of Death might be arrested by the process" of mesmerism (ibid.). Unlike in the earlier tales, an able-bodied narrator is in a position of power in relation to a small, frail, infirm Valdemar who has a confirmed case of "phthisis" (archaic term for pulmonary consumption). The chief points of Valdemar's resistance to the narrator's power are presented to readers as *involuntary*—on the one hand, temperamental, and, on the other hand, situational. Temperamentally, Valdemar is very nervous, therefore not an easy candidate to mesmerize. Situationally, Valdemar's will, supposedly the essence of the voluntary, is "at no period positively, or thoroughly" (97) under the narrator's control, but neither can it be said to be under Valdemar's control when he is hypnotized. Thus, even his will is rendered involuntarily willful rather than voluntarily so—a paradox that contributes to the overall characterization of Valdemar as powerless, at times powerfully so.

At first glance, the usual tropes of the Black Legend seem to lack force in this story. Rather than an inquisitorial Spaniard, readers are given a consumptive one on his deathbed who spends two-thirds of the story dying (and then dead!) in a mesmeric trance. In life Valdemar was a reclusive and hardworking compiler and translator who, as a translator worked under a Polish-Jewish nom de plume—Issachar Marx. He is not presented as an Old World Spaniard as are the black-robed judges in "The Pit and the Pendulum" or even William Wilson 2 to the extent that he haunts Europe. Instead, Valdemar resides in Harlem—possibly what came to be known as Spanish Harlem, though such specificity is not confirmed. Readers are told that "he had no relatives in America" (ibid.) which suggests a possible Old World country of origin. Whatever the case, the Black Legend would seem to be muted in this story despite Valdemar's physical blackening.

I contend, however, that the Black Legend has morphed and this morphing deserves attention because it occurs again in this fashion in the text that I will examine next—Herman Melville's "Benito Cereno" (1855). "The Facts in the Case of M. Valdemar" does not give us the expected image of the evil conquistador or inquisitorial Spaniard torturing some hapless victim. There are no clanking chains or long black Dominican robes here. Nor is there bloodthirstiness or cruelty on the part of M. Valdemar. He is presented as a relatively inoffensive fellow, that is, until he is becomes a stinking mass of putrefaction. But therein lies the evidence for the Black Legend in another guise. Deadliness and corruption so much part and parcel of Spain and Spaniards framed by the discourse of the legend are literally internalized by the body of Valdemar. If the Black Legend against Spain associated that country, its culture(s), and its inhabitants with bloody deeds, bad government, and a grand historical death drive, and if, from the late eighteenth century through the nineteenth century, that legend increasingly traded in racialized figures, then the consumptive, death-ridden amalgamated Valdemar who repeatedly utters two lines after being mesmerized—"I am dying" and then "I am dead" (100–101)—can be read as an example of that legend thoroughly corporealized.

The threat of death or a scene of death lies at the center of most, if not every one, of Poe's tales. However, of all possible objects chosen to represent death in its most scandalous and offensive, its least idealized, form, the story offers to its readers M. Valdemar, a tiny man with a Galician-Portuguese name meaning literally "valley of the sea," who has "no relatives in America" (97), and who sometimes writes under a Polish-Jewish nom de plume. It is Valdemar and not "John Randolph," of whose lower limbs Valdemar's are remindful, who is cast not merely as a death mask, but death's body, "a nearly liquid mass of loathsome—of detestable putrescence" (103), blackened for sure. This casting of Valdemar as death's body anticipates Herman Melville's representation of Benito Cereno as marked by doom and fatality in the 1855 tale "Benito Cereno" with which I conclude this chapter on the Black Legend and Spaniards as figures of a morally and physically blackened whiteness. If a feature of the Black Legend against Spain was a generally pejoratively valorized association of Spaniards with the very peoples (Arabs and Jews) expelled by the Spanish Inquisition, not only is Valdemar an abjectly Semiticized Spaniard as is Benito Cereno (as I will show), he is also a man of the sea. He is a man of the sea not by profession like the Spanish captain, but via his name—Val-de-mar, "valley of the sea." In fact, the central image of Valdemar on his deathbed is that of him "evidently sinking fast" (98). His final dissolution suggests a drowning of his own body in its very own fluids. In Poe's poems and stories, the sea is often associated with the realm of the dead, a fact that further reinforces the association of Valdemar with death. Furthermore, the sea is, historically speaking, the medium of empire, particularly of seaborne empires as the Spanish Empire was and the United States was becoming by the mid-nineteenth century. But this "sea" is not the medium of power for Valdemar, who lies on his deathbed as if full fathom five, suffering a sea change that involves his nearly complete decomposition. Although the ending of the tale is hardly triumphant for the mesmerist-narrator, whose experiment in mesmerism has not managed to prevent Valdemar's death (rather, it seems to have prolonged it agonizingly and then, at the last, to hasten it), he at least lives to learn the limits of his steering powers as a mesmerist (somewhat like Amasa Delano, the "American" captain in "Benito Cereno" who learns the limitations of his domain as a sea captain). Meanwhile, the Spaniard suffers in his very body the unfathomable shame of the Black Legend. The Anglo-American remains afloat; the Spaniard sinks into the shadow of death but does not die—that is, does not die as a figure, a stereotype. True to the workings of the Black Legend, immortality for this Spaniard is as a stereotype of death or, if "stereo-" means solid in Greek, as a solid (even when gelatinous!) type (as in both sign and embodiment) of death.

Not surprisingly, though uncannily to me when I chanced upon the reference in Roland Barthes's *The Pleasure of the Text* (*Le plaisir du texte*, 1973), Poe's story of M. Valdemar was for Barthes an illustration of stereotype as that which refuses to die, to pass away. Barthes wrote, "In Poe's story, M. Valdemar, hypnotized and moribund, is kept alive in a cataleptic state by the repetition of the questions put to him ('Are you asleep, M. Valdemar?') . . . The stereotype is this nauseating impossibility of dying."[51] It is conceivable that Poe was aware of deploying stereotype and was doing so deliberately and, moreover, parodically—creating M. Valdemar as another instance of a parodic application of a formula. In fact, the story as a whole hinges on a stereotyped idea—that of a similitude between trances, sleep, and death, and the attempt to fight fire with fire, so to speak, to entrance someone out of dying. The clichéd experiment fails and the mesmerist is left with a gelatinous puddle of putrefaction. But, by the same token, despite these postulations of ironic awareness and parody, what remains, what will not pass away, is, as Barthes points out, the stereotype that refuses to die—the Spaniard according to the Black Legend and the legendary (as in long-lived) blackening of the Spaniard.

TABLEAU OF MASTER AND SLAVE: HERMAN MELVILLE'S "BENITO CERENO" (1855)

Some of the most salient and yet generally overlooked deployments of Spaniards and Spain as blackened figures of alien whiteness with and against which to create an Anglo-American identity as "American" destiny occur in Herman Melville's long story or novella "Benito Cereno" published in

1855, seven years after the termination of the Mexican-American War of 1846–48, in which the United States annexed what is known as the Southwest, and a mere six years before the outbreak of the U.S. Civil War between the Union and the Confederacy. Given the publication date of the story and its subject matter—a slave mutiny in 1799 aboard a Spanish ship off the coast of Chile and the subsequent intervention of a U.S. ship resulting in the suppression of a second mutiny, the ambiguous rescue of the Spanish captain, and the capture of the rebel slaves and a trial in Lima, Peru—scholars have concentrated on the story in terms of the historical facts of the slave trade and slave rebellion in the New World and in terms of the black/white binary of race and black–white relations as imagined by Herman Melville. All the questions raised about Poe's *The Narrative of Arthur Gordon Pym*, his tales, poems, essays, and reviews have been raised about Melville's work in spades. For the most part, *Moby Dick* and "Benito Cereno" have been at the center of that volley of scholarship. With respect to "Benito Cereno," for instance, Dana Nelson writes, "Reading 'race' in 'Benito Cereno' has a history as fraught with contention as the debates over the meaning of 'race' in the works of Edgar Allan Poe."[52] I would say even more so. She continues: "Scholars have for decades been concerned with how 'Benito Cereno' reflects on Melville's own political stance." (109). Most of the arguments, as Nelson reminds us, have revolved around the question of whether "Benito Cereno" is or is not a racist text. I would add that the preoccupation with race has been in terms of black and white in which black refers to Africans and African Americans and white to Euro-Americans and those categorized as Europeans. Nelson's essay "'For the Gaze of the Whites': The Crisis of the Subject in 'Benito Cereno'" does not much deviate from a consideration of the racial dynamics of the story in these terms, though, to its credit and that of Emory Elliot's essay on the story from which Nelson's essay draws for this point, it does speak briefly of Benito Cereno's Spanishness as an "unstable marker, semiotically balancing between light/fellow Westerner and dark/Other" (112). However, that observation is a sidelight in an essay with the main objective of tracing "countervailing tendencies"—racist and antiracist—in "Benito Cereno" and how it is that the story "subverts" but is not free from the white versus black (and also dominant white versus poor white and people of color) "Manichaean binarity [dualism] which undergirds the colonialist conceptual structure" (111).

Nelson's essay posits different levels of consciousness in the story—Delano's, the narrator's, and that conveyed through Benito Cereno's court deposition. Another way of putting this would be to say that the story is a classic frame tale of perspective in which perspectives are nested within each other and function to impose representational limitations on one another. Hence, readers view the narrator viewing Delano viewing the scene before him. The scene before him breaks up into frames that frame each other—Benito Cereno's actions and accounts at sea versus on land during the trial, Babo's actions and his comments to his master Don Benito and to Captain Amasa Delano, and so forth. But, to return to Nelson's argument, she contends that the narrator's perspectival frame offers a critique of "the [masculinist, classist, rank-and-file white supremacist] colonialist system that is epistemologically imposed by Delano" and that serves to prop up his sense of subjecthood (versus abject objecthood) (110). Her essay analyzes in detail the U.S. Captain Delano's "perceptual strategies" or, to borrow John Berger's phrase, ways of seeing. In the process of analyzing Delano's ways of seeing, Nelson's essay gives numerous examples of the narrator's rendition of those ways of seeing as "complacent reading[s] of black and white" (or better yet, black versus white), readings steeped in a racist Manichaean dualism (111). Where Delano sees white versus black, the narrator introduces shades of gray—in fact, did so from the beginning of the tale with the phrase in the third paragraph of the story, "everything [was] gray."[53] However, Nelson's essay cautions perceptively, "'Black' and 'white' may be artificial and even dangerous conceptual constructs, but grey is not a positive alternative in this text. It functions only as a state of irresolution, of uncertainty, an antecedent to the necessity of black and white interpretation" (127). Grayness, of course, connotes equivocation and ambiguity and where Delano seeks certainty about his position and mission in relation to the Spanish captain and his slave ship through his racist, sexist, and gendered classifications, the narrator proffers doubt and uncertainty, suggesting that Delano's certainty is a form of willful blindness, the most blinding act being, according to Nelson's essay, his denial of subjectivity to the rebelling slaves, to Babo especially (112). But, according to Nelson, epistemological amalgamation into the ambiguity of grayness represents a failure of the imagination, a capitulation to "the imaginative economy that he [the narrator] satirizes through Delano" (128). The last two sections of her essay are dedicated to demonstrating how the

narrator reproduces the terms of the Manichaean binarisms of white versus black with regard to Babo and how the narrator's "level of consciousness" participates in Babo's death sentence by objectifying him through
what she terms "legal" and "aesthetic" discourse. Nelson writes:

> The narrative [of the narrator] perpetuates the same structured exclusivity
> of white male subjectivity in its own necessarily limited portrayal of Babo's
> motives and goals, and ultimate humanity. This perspective can present
> Babo only as a *type*. (130; my emphasis)

Concentrating in particular on the last scene of the tale that presents the
spectacle of Babo's severed head impaled on a pike for all to see in the plaza
of Lima, Peru, the essay elaborates, among other things, how the narrator
dehumanizingly turns Babo into an art object, an artifact. I would like
to call attention to Nelson's use of the word *type*, which occurs only once
along with *archetypally, arrested, paralyzes,* and *paralysis* (130, 119, 110, 127).
Curiously, given the composition and publication date of the story, the
mid-nineteenth century, she associates this paralysis of type with photography—first with a general "snapshot" and then with a particular series
of horrifying, deliberately composed, *relatively contemporary* photographs
of the torture and death at the hands of Dutch South Africans of a black
South African named Thomas Kasire, a case that she borrows from Susanne
Kappeler's *The Pornography of Representation* (1986) (126). I understand the
connection between two kinds of apartheid systems and the political
impetus of "updating" the implications of "Benito Cereno's" strategies
and I am in agreement with the argument about Babo's objectification.
However, I hesitate at the elision of "type" in Melville's story with photography, and contemporary photography at that, without the mention of the
precedent (for much of early photography itself) of painting, historical
tableau in particular.

I would argue that the idea of "type" and "typing" deserves central bill-
ing in an analysis of Melville's "Benito Cereno." Each character—Babo,
Benito Cereno, Amasa Delano, Alexandro Aranda, Atufal, and so on—is
a type; that is, although each one appears to have an individual individu-
alizing name, they are all described in ways that erode that individuality
very quickly and conform their existence to a formula in the overall drama
of masters and slaves and Americans and Spaniards. This formulation is

evident in the language of the constitutive descriptions of these characters. For instance, Babo, the "body servant" (169), is repeatedly termed simply "the black" (194); Benito Cereno, "the Spaniard" (167); Amasa Delano, "the American" (ibid.); and Atufal, "the chained negro" (202). Many characters, more descriptive elements than characters, have no names at all, but this hardly excludes them from the allegorical functions of type; quite the contrary. One of the most salient examples of this nameless typing occurs in the following description:

> His [Delano's] attention had been drawn to a slumbering negress, partly disclosed through the lace-work of some rigging, lying, with youthful limbs carelessly disposed, under the lee of the bulwarks, like a doe in the shade of a woodland rock. Sprawling at her lapped breasts, was her wide-awake fawn, stark naked, its black little body half lifted from the deck, crosswise with its dam's; its hands, like two paws, clambering upon her; its mouth and nose ineffectually rooting to get at the mark; and meantime giving a vexatious half-grunt, blending with the composed snore of the negress. (198)

This description converts an unnamed enslaved African woman and her child into a picture of primitive happiness and animal affection so often associated by Europeans and Euro-Americans with Africans under the rubric of a favorite type from plantation ideology—the type of the "happy darkie."

The passage describing the African woman and her child illustrates a further feature of the text "Benito Cereno." It demonstrates not only that characters occur as types, but, moreover, that typing arises in tandem with—or rather, as part of—a whole scene. The story does not type single characters in isolation. Rather, it types all characters and places them in particular relations to one another—in certain configurations that create a scene often frozen by the description either before or after it has been activated by narration. In fact, a special interplay exists between stilling through verbal description and movement through narration. Ultimately, movement is subordinated to stilling, if for no other reason than because what movement exists is engineered toward a predetermined end, the reestablishment of an Anglo-American order despite the possibility of another order—movement is in the service of teleology, not mutation, open-ended change, or mutiny, if you will. In "Benito Cereno" the office of "typing" (pun intended) is to create a tableau, a depiction of a scene usually presented onstage by silent and stilled costumed participants in imitation of a painting as in *tableau vivant*. "Tableau" refers to painting itself that presents usually allegorized characters, as with history painting in particular. In terms of form and genre, not only content but the arrangement of content, "Benito Cereno" verbally simulates a tableau of history painting. As such, though all the characters are typed and though typing functions throughout to produce this tableau of history painting, the overall "scene" (composed of many scenes) the words "paint" is weighted in a particular direction and not another with respect to the configuration of "the black," "the Spaniard," and "the American," as I will demonstrate. The fact that all the characters are typed (and most definitely in a racializing, if not overtly racist, manner) and that the typing is configured in such a way as to turn history itself into a typological drama that, despite ambiguities and equivocations, leads to not only re-cognizable but pre-cognizable doom for certain characters and, if not salvation, then survival for others constitutes the real cul-de-sac or dead end of the story. This dead-end effect overrides with fatal determinacy the intricate play of the different narrative levels discussed earlier and any serious critique of "the colonialist system that is epistemologically imposed by Delano," to cite Nelson (110). The story's manner of typing and the dramatic configurations it creates, including the last scene of Babo's head impaled on a pike in the Lima plaza and of Don Benito's death to "follow his leader" (Babo) in contrast to the jovial (however shallow and hoodwinked) survival of Captain Amasa Delano, bespeak a deep-structure, perhaps fatalistic, acceptance, if not investment, in the manifest destiny of whiteness over blackness and off-whiteness despite a keen sense of the inhumanity of monomaniacal whiteness. Consider the tension between *Moby Dick* and *White Jacket* in this regard, or simply the enshrinement of the white, blue-eyed Billy Budd, picture of innocence and virtue. A similar figure is offered for contemplation in the course of one of Delano's strolls along the deck of the *San Dominick*. His eyes fall on a sailor occupied in tarring some part of the deck. The description reads:

> The mean employment of the man was in contrast with something superior in his figure. His hand, black with continually thrusting it into the tar-pot held for him by a negro, seemed not naturally allied to his face, a face which

would have been a very fine one but for its haggardness. Whether this haggardness had aught to do with criminality, could not be determined; since, as
intense heat and cold, though unlike, produce like sensations, so innocence
and guilt, when, through casual association with mental pain, stamping any
visible impress, use one seal—a hacked one.

Not again that this reflection occurred to Captain Delano at the time,
charitable man as he was. (196)

The sailor's whiteness is confirmed through figures of opposition—chiefly,
the black contents of the tar pot against which his face is contrasted and
the subservient presence of "a negro" holding the tar pot as if it were an
extension of himself, but not of the sailor thrusting his hand into it.
The passage clearly indicates that the white sailor's tarred hand seemed
"not naturally allied to his face," a face marked as noble despite his "mean
employment." This passage marks itself off from Delano's perspective with
the "not again that this reflection occurred to Captain Delano" and could
be said to fall squarely into the narrator's perspective. But I would argue
that it is representative of more than the narrator's perspective. Rather, it
symptomizes a certain racialized typology as tableau or history turned into
teleology that runs thoughout Melville's work. What follows is an analysis of "Benito Cereno" as one of its most salient expressions.

If *Wieland* works as an object-lesson warning from the cabinet or closet,
and Poe's tales like a theatrical hoax or "confidence" trick in its parodic
application of a formula revolving around the deployment of one particularly symbolic character or object (a masked figure, an instrument of torture, a femme fatale, a black cat, a Spaniard), Melville's "Benito Cereno"
is a configured tableau as much as any piece of writing may approximate
this traditionally visual form that was and still is painterly first and, in
imitation of painting, theatrical or performative as well. The tale is an
intricately, deliberately, and ultimately totalizingly plotted tableau (composed of multiple tableaux) of triangulated master–slave relations between
two sea captains—one Spanish, his ship being the *San Dominick*, and the
other a white Yankee from Duxbury, Massachusetts, his ship being the
Bachelor's Delight[54]—and the central provocation of their unease, the black
slave Babo who, in Benito's deposition, is named the alleged "plotter" of
the slave mutiny aboard the Spanish ship. Like history painting, the signs
composing the tableau of triangulated master–slave relations point up out

of their surface depth to the "real." "Benito Cereno" unveils itself, quite openly for all its mystifications, as an allegorical history painting about the historical relations of the imperial powers of Spain and the United States and their respective involvement with slavery. The tableau tale turns history into telos, the "import" or intent of which remains highly problematic because its "silent [written] signs" (189) are so heavily "cargoed," festooned with nineteenth-century Anglo-American typologies of race and nationality.

Critics have analyzed "Benito Cereno" in many ways—as a mystery, a riddle, a Gothic horror tale, a fable, a legal fiction, a pantomime, a masquerade, and a morality play.[55] Aspects of the tale do indeed correlate to each of these formal descriptions. In particular, references to the theater are scattered throughout the story, terms such as "the part" (189, 248), "posture" (173), "scene" (176, 183), "gesture" (181), "act" (189), and "expression" (189, 192). Many of these terms also apply to painting—especially repeated ones such as "scene," "figure," "spectacle," "gesture," and "silent signs." The form "tableau," associated historically and critically with both theater and painting from the early modern period onward, depends on all of these elements for the construction of its allegorical message. To understand "Benito Cereno" is to see the allegorical means by which it is constructed: tableau. The story is like theater in its succession of tableaux, its series of symbolically replete still arrangements or placed "scenes," each in synecdochical relation to the narrative as a whole, just as the galleries and galleys of the San Dominick are structured in relation to the ship in its entirety. Reviewers at the time and critics since have remarked on "Benito Cereno" as a very finely crafted story. As a story it is, to quote Roland Barthes quoting Diderot on tableau, "a well-composed picture [tableau] . . . a whole contained under a single point of view, in which the parts work together to one end and form by their mutual correspondence a unity as real as that of the members of the body of an animal."[56] An early passage of "Benito Cereno"—in the scene-setting introductory section of the narrative—compares a ship and its crew to a "tableau," actually offering this formal category, and not another, as a significant hermeneutic clue to the reader:

> [I]n the case of the ship . . . the living spectacle it contains, upon its sudden and complete disclosure, has, in contrast with the blank ocean which

zones it, something of the effect of enchantment. The ship seems unreal;
these strange costumes, gestures, and faces, but *a shadowy tableau just
emerged from the deep* which directly must receive back what it gave. (166;
my emphasis)

Words such as *spectacle, sudden, enchantment, unreal, strange,* and *shadowy*
may have encouraged responses like that of William Ellery Channing Jr.
(1856 review of "Benito Cereno"): "Melville is a kind of wizard; he writes
strange and mysterious things that belong to other worlds beyond this
time and place."[57] Even contemporary critics doing painstakingly detailed
contextual readings of the story tend to treat its form, its medium, as a
transparent window to somewhere else.[58] However, "Benito Cereno" does
instruct readers how to read its message. The descriptive mise-en-scène of
the ship as "a shadowy tableau" is a *mise en abîme* of the story's form and
the exegetic levels of its allegory. The descriptive elements of the mise-en-
scène coincide with Barthes's description of "tableau":

> The tableau (pictorial, theatrical, literary) is a pure cut-out segment with
> clearly defined edges, irreversible and incorruptible; everything that sur-
> rounds it is banished into nothingness, remains unnamed, while everything
> that it admits within its field is promoted into essence, into light, into view.
> Such demiurgic discrimination implies high quality of thought: the tableau
> is intellectual, it has something to say (something moral, social) . . . a
> fetishist subject is required to cut out the tableau. This point of meaning is
> always the Law: law of society, law of struggle, law of meaning."[59]

The phrase from "Benito Cereno" "just emerged from the deep" marks
an upward movement that compels a vertical reading of correspondences
between the scene or arrangement of objects, ideas about the objects or
interpretations of them, the perceived meaning of the whole, and its relation to history that lies beyond the tableau and to which the tableau
points. Barthes writes that through the work of tableau "history becomes
both intelligible and desirable" as something that can be reduced to and
cut out as an encapsulating scene or what he calls a "pregnant moment":
"Necessarily total, this instant will be artificial (unreal; this is not a realist
art), a hieroglyph in which can be read at a single glance . . . the present,
the past, and the future; that is, the historical meaning of the represented

action."[60] For example, what I call the scene of the knot is one such hiero-glyph in which symbolic objects, gestures, and historical referents are arranged in such a way that not only are present, past, and future illumi-nated at one swift glance but the mise-en-scène is so cargoed with mean-ing that the scene may be cut out without losing its significance. The scene of the knot is located at the approximate center of "Benito Cereno" and is clearly placed there as an allegory of reading (the story). Captain Delano, walking across the deck of the *San Dominick*, comes upon an old man tying an intricate knot who mutters when asked why he is tying such a knot, "For some one else to undo," and then throws it at Delano saying, "Undo it, cut it, quick" (202). A few sentences later, the text reads:

> For a moment, knot in hand, and knot in head, Captain Delano stood mute; while, without further heeding him, the old man was now intent upon other ropes. Presently there was a slight stir behind Captain Delano. Turning, he saw the chained negro, Atufal, standing quietly there. (Ibid.)

These symbolic objects—presented in such rapid succession that, to quote a later line in the tale, "past, present, and future seemed one" (232)—are carefully arranged as an allegory of interpretation. The spatial arrangement suggests none other than a vertical reading of correspondences: the "knot in hand" or the text below; the "knot in head" or the thought above; and the "chained negro . . . standing" vertical and "behind." The "chained negro" may be viewed as the signifier that points up and "behind" or beyond the text and the act of interpretation toward history, to the historical fact of slavery in the New World, in a typological manner—"chained negro."

What I call the scene of the salver suggests that the "faithful" repro-duction (not realistically, but through careful artifice) of the recogniz-ably "historical" is teleological, that is, about "original" causes and "final" destinations:

> From opposite sides, there were . . . two approaches to the cabin [of Don Benito] . . . Captain Delano, taking the nighest entrance . . . hurried on his way . . . With words of his intended business upon his lips, he entered. As he advanced toward the seated Spaniard, he heard another footstep, keeping time with his. *From the opposite door, a salver in hand, the servant was likewise advancing.* (225; my emphasis)

The words "advanced" and "advancing" in conjunction with the phrase "footstep, keeping time" imply both the passage and the progress of time. History is not merely passing phenomena, but a linear process with a goal or destination. Not only is history presented as a series of objects and gestures for interpretation as in the scene of the knot, but, furthermore, it is rendered teleological, its two conditions—as symbolic and teleological—being inseparable. This tableau or scene of master and slave relations is "pregnant with meaning" from which there is no retreat, only advancement toward a still point—the "seated Spaniard," typed as he is by the tropes of the Black Legend—that Amasa Delano, the "American" Captain, desires to set in motion again toward his (Benito's) intended destination according to his (Delano's) creed of salvific progress. As a "brother captain" (169) on his heroic errand into the wilderness of the *San Dominick*'s Old World ruin and decay (164) to save the "dejected" (169), "hypochondriac" (ibid.), "sour," "gloomy," "reserved," "proud," "moody" (170), "invalid" (171), "cadaverous" (178), "morbid" (184), "capricious" (206), "sullen" (218), "sinister" (229), and "ill-fated" (238) Spanish captain, Delano is faced, however, with a "black" counterposing mirror image of his errand—Babo, the slave mutineer posing as loyal servant, bearing a "salver in hand." Babo, preempts the "words . . . upon [Delano's] lips" with his own, "Don Benito . . . I give you joy; the breeze will hold, and will increase" (225), inserting his perfectly simulated announcement of "salvation" in place of Delano's. The objective correlative to this verbal message is the tray or salver, which functions as such a beautifully "bland satirical touch" that it offers "no handle for retort" (ibid.). A salver is a tray for serving food originally used for protective foretasting; the servant would taste the master's food to test whether it had been poisoned. If it had, the servant might very well die to save (*salvar*) the master's life. Babo's words and actions all seem to indicate his loyalty and submission to Don Benito, but the salver, borne toward Benito, is a Damoclean sword reminding him of the doom that hangs over his head at the hands of his mutinous slaves. Moreover, as the tray from which poisoned food may be ingested, it betokens Benito's physically internalized doom—his death under the permanent "shadow" (or stain) of "the negro," presumably a result of the guilt he carries for his involvement with slavery. Thus, the scene of the salver and the story as a whole checkmate the trajectory of advancement as "progress" with gestures of doom. History as tableau in

"Benito Cereno" is telos laid out along a blade-like axis of the absolutes of salvation/damnation. Who is on top in this triangulated relation of master and slave and how the typologies cut remains obscure until the final tableau.

The barber's scene, in contrast to the other scenes I have discussed, is characterized by the phrase "the similitude was heightened" (211). This tableau, in which Babo (the black slave) shaves his master Don Benito while Captain Delano looks on, is lightly arranged as a genre scene or scene of everyday life along the lines of a George Caleb Bingham painting. Concretely and minutely represented as a slice of the quotidian, of the real, the scene works to suspend the heavy-handed telos of the tableaux of the doomed Spaniard, the mutinous and ultimately doomed African, and the resilient white Yankee survivor. That this scene interrupts with a different order of things is signaled by the description of Don Benito's reaction to the reminder that "shaving-time" has come: "'Ah—yes,' answered the Spaniard, starting, as from dreams into *realities*" (210; my emphasis). The barber's scene, which alone occupies a tenth of the tale, functions both as relief from the relentlessness of the story and as a suspension that heightens the suspense of impending violence and doom. The setting is the ship's cuddy, according to Delano "a sort of dormitory, sitting room, sail-loft, chapel, armory, and private closet all together" (212). In this heterogeneous space of familiar activities, the American, the Spaniard, and the African mutineer share close quarters and the master–slave distinction is given several whirls. Babo, the mutineer unknown as such to Captain Delano, proposes the cozy arrangement of persons: "Why not let Don Amasa sit by master in the cuddy, and master can talk, and Don Amasa can listen, while Babo here lathers and strops" (210).

Following the loosening of Don Benito's collar and cravat, the narrative intermingles and implicates these three figures—Delano, Benito, and Babo—in a series of homoerotically charged configurations with Babo as the catalyst. Benito Cereno is compared to "Johnson and Byron," who "took to their hearts, almost to the exclusion of the entire white race, their serving men, the negroes" (212). Captain Delano, the reader is told, "took to negroes, not philanthropically, but genially just as other men to New-foundland dogs . . . seeing the colored servant . . . so debonair about his master, in a business so familiar as that of shaving, too, all his old weakness for negroes returned" (213). Babo, meanwhile, presses his master's head "gently further back into the crotch of the chair" (214) to keep him from shuddering as he shaves him. At one point, the narrative provocatively describes Delano as imagining that "master and man, for some unknown purpose, were acting out, both in word and deed, nay, to the very tremor of Don Benito's limbs, some juggling play before him" (217). Despite sprinkled hints of an impending execution ("black headsman . . . white at the block"), the genre-scene form suspends these three figures from their respective "destinies" in a semi-convivial relation of sympathy with homoerotic overtones. The scene is reminiscent of the mood in the "A Squeeze of the Hand" episode in Melville's earlier work *Moby Dick* (1851). This kind of homoerotic suspension in the narrative drive toward catastrophe or apocalypse is characteristic of a loosening of narrative tension in many of his works. But this antiapocalyptic homoeroticism is swiftly followed up by its opposite, in *Moby Dick*, for instance, by the ominous Spanish "Doubloon" chapter with its intimations of cannibalistic warfare among men out of greedy desperation for gold. It would seem that the narrative polices its own homoerotic desires; *Billy Budd*, of course, epitomizes this tendency, as many critics have pointed out.

Similarly, the semiconvivial relational knot among the men in "Benito Cereno" is suddenly cut apart when Babo's razor draws blood from Benito, whose terrified aspect is compared, in the former teleological manner, to that of the "timid King," James the First of England (215). The "cut" plunges Don Benito from a state of somewhat comical abjection at the hands of his servant back into the typological grave of the Black Legend characterizing "the Spaniard" in this tale: "neither sweet waters, nor shampooing, nor fidelity, nor sociality, delighted the Spaniard. Seeing him relapsing into forbidding gloom, and still remaining seated, Captain Delano . . . withdrew" (218). In the wake of the shaving scene, the figure of Don Benito is further inscribed into the typology of the Black Legend. When Captain Delano catches a glimpse of Babo with a bleeding cheek, Babo claims that Don Benito has cut him in *cruel* retaliation for the shaving "accident": "[W]hen will master get better from his sickness . . . cutting Babo with the razor, because, only by accident, Babo had given master one little scratch" (218). The shaving scene portrays each of the figures in a somewhat dubious light—Babo as a pretend Sambo, Delano as a paternalistic racist, and Benito as a coward. Nevertheless, the tail end of this scene brings down the full weight of the teleological blade on only two of the three figures. The Spaniard and the African mutineer each receive their cuts. They are "marked" men—men marked for doom—while "the American" walks away scot-free to continue his grand tour of the strange spectacles on the *San Dominick*.

Despite "the American"'s liberty, "Benito Cereno," written after the Toussaint, Dessalines, Nat Turner, Cinque, and Mure revolts and shortly before the Civil War, has been read, and justifiably so, as a warning about both the human costs of slave revolt and the evils of slavery as an institution.[61] A tableau of history, "Benito Cereno" functions as an apocalyptic warning—somewhat like Washington Allston's *Belshazzar's Feast*—calling naive "Americans," perhaps the "folks . . . in Duxbury, Massachusetts" (206), to wake up and keep watch lest they too, on account of their silent complicity with slavery, court doom like Benito Cereno, the "invalid courtier" (177), who, draped during his shave in the "castle and lion" flag (214), represents the Spanish Empire. Critics such as Carolyn L. Karcher have argued that although Melville does not countenance rebellion (which is why all his rebels, including Babo, are severely punished), his work is not racist or racializing, as Nelson would claim later, but the very condemnation of the type of discourse (the discourse of type) in Josiah Nott and George R. Gliddon's *Types of Mankind* disseminated at the time "Benito Cereno" was published.[62] She writes:

> Because "Benito Cereno" relies on the device of presenting all incidents both concurrently and in retrospect, through the eyes of obtuse observers, the central critical problem the story poses is that of distinguishing between Melville's interpretations of the events . . . and the interpretations he ascribes to his chief protagonists, the Yankee captain Amasa Delano and the Spaniard . . . Broadly speaking, we can identify the body of the narrative as Captain Delano's version of the *San Dominick*'s ordeal, the deposition as Benito Cereno's, and the few pages of narrative at the end . . . as Melville's.[63]

I contend that, although the story may be divided into three parts, and perhaps more if one counts the barber's scene, incidents are generally viewed through and limited to Amasa Delano's continuous "glances" and not those of another character. Even Benito Cereno's deposition or captivity narrative comes across as if through the reading eyes of Delano in accordance with the governing form of tableau—"a whole contained under a single point of view." The reader "looks" and reads from the vantage point of the Anglo-American Delano, which is not to say that the reader must adopt his perspective permanently or that Delano's point of view can be equated with that of the narrator or with the ever-elusive author "Melville," though separating them has been the task of at least several critics, which in itself is significant.

Simply put, I wish to redefine "the problem" of "Benito Cereno." The problem is the relation of its form as tableau, which relies on types or typological gestures for its construction of "meaning," to any genuinely subversive critique of nineteenth-century racial discourse of types and their destinies. Delano, Benito, and Babo are not three-dimensional characters in a narrative of indeterminacy, but rather two-dimensional figures in a tableau of doom with one survivor, Delano, who, like Ishmael perhaps, survives to tell the tale. In contrast to the Yankee Delano, Cereno, the Spaniard, is not only "blackened" temperamentally ("saturnine," "hypochondriac," "moody," "despotic"), but, moreover, physically marked as non-Anglo or nonwhite in accordance with the transmutation of the Black Legend into nineteenth-century racial discourse. Note the anti-Semitic-sounding combination of "a sort of Castilian Rothschild" (186) with the attribute of "small, yellow hands" (177) and the repeated insinuations that Benito is a moral *marrano*, a "Jew" merely passing as a Christian, a "trickster" (186), an imposter, "some low-born adventurer, masquerading as an oceanic grandee" (ibid.). Thus, the narrative plays over and over again, and in none too dispelling a fashion, with the notion that "[t]here was a difference between the idea of Don Benito's *darkly* preordaining Captain Delano's fate, and Captain Delano's *lightly* arranging Don Benito's" (193; my emphasis).

Africans, furthermore, are referred to as "raw," "unsophisticated" (167), "snakish" (233), and "Indian-like" (235) and are dehumanizingly compared to a veritable menagerie of animals—"shepherd's dog" (167), leopardesses, doves, bats (209), "cawing crows" (234), and wolves with lolling "red tongues" (237). Shortsighted simpleton or not, the Yankee "American," by contrast, is associated with only flattering descriptives—"good nature" (162), "benevolent," "charitable" (170, 196), "generous" (247, 248, 250), and "superior muscular strength" (258). Perhaps "Benito Cereno" is really a case of flattering the fool in which the fool is Amasa Delano with his belief in progress, his New England transcendentalist faith in nature (257), and his "planter's remark[s]" (220). Perhaps the reader is really meant to interpret him as equally deserving of the doom that befalls Benito and his servant, Babo. But, to the extent that, as Karcher and Nelson have pointed out, one is forced to view Babo as a type, "the black man"—and, I would add, not only "the black man" but "the Spaniard" as well—and, furthermore, the story closes with a tableau scene that effectively "seals" the African mutineer and the dejected, abject Spaniard in the doom predicted by nineteenth-century pseudoscientists for such types, the story leaves intact white and presumably Anglo-American manifest destiny even as it casts upon it "the aura of fatality." Benedict Anderson has observed that "nationalism always carries with it an aura of fatality."[64] In relation to "Benito Cereno," this observation also applies in reverse. "Benito Cereno"'s "fatality"—its inexorable Law of Doom—effects, despite its critique, national community not only as an American jeremiad of woe and warning, but also by the elimination of certain possibilities such as the success of Babo's revolt or the survival of the brother captain, the Spaniard, despite his Cain-like guilt. Instead, the last scene of the story violently embalms these figures:

> Some months after, dragged to the gibbet at the tail of a mule, the black met his voiceless end . . . For many days, the head, that hive of subtlety, fixed on a pole in the Plaza, met, unabashed, the gaze of the whites . . . three months after being dismissed by the court, Benito Cereno, borne on the bier, did, indeed, follow his leader. (258)

The scene is yet another *mise en abîme* of the story as a whole. It becomes clear that "to rush from darkness to light was the involuntary choice" (229). The light of the last scene reveals that death is the figurehead, the head figure, of Don Benito's domain and Babo's mutiny against it. Together, master and slave constitute a doubly "black" Black Legend fixed and preserved for the reader, who, like the American captain moving from innocence to experience, can walk through the gallery of pictures or tableaux in which the grotesque figures are so arrested that they might as well be made of wax; hence, "Cereno" with its several-edged connotations in Spanish of a man on guard, a man becalmed, and a dog the color of wax (*cereño*).

Let me stress that the story "Benito Cereno," however "incisive in its recognition of the conceptual, epistemological, and representational structures that support the racist economy,"[65] (and, I would add, imperialist economy), sentences to death both the "black" Babo whose head is described as a "hive of subtlety" and the Spanish "Benito Cereno" whose complexion and name suggest the ochre-yellow off-white color of wax. That gray or whatever murky color might be obtained from the mixture of black and yellow (the hive and the wax), an even more off-white amalgam than that encountered in Poe's stories, is not merely "antecedent" to the oppressive binarism of black versus white. Its determinism is projected into the future in the service of an Anglo-American white-supremacist manifest destiny intolerant of any complicity between black and Spaniard and focused on an image of Spanish rule as enabling not only complicity between, but the miscegenation of, master and slave, white and black. Such fears of a hybrid empire where power relations are not clear between blacks and whites on account of "familiarization" (in all senses of that word), blackmail, and so forth are expressed in passages such as the following:

> But if the white has dark secrets concerning Don Benito, could then Don
> Benito be any way in complicity with the blacks? But they were too stupid.
> Besides who ever heard of a white so far a renegade as to apostatize from his
> very species almost, by leaguing in against it with negroes? (201)

As the story unfolds, the reader is made cognizant of the fact that Don Benito was Babo's captive following the slave mutiny and thus not a free agent. This unfree status is precisely what likens him to Babo and, of course, makes Benito answerable to him instead of to the white Captain Delano. Hence, Benito's death is glossed by the words "[he] . . . did, indeed, follow his leader" (258).

Taking as exemplary the representations of Spain and Spaniards in *Wieland* (1798), "William Wilson" (1839), "The Pit and the Pendulum" (1843), even "The Facts in the Case of M. Valdemar" (1845), and certainly "Benito Cereno" (1855), at least two important developments can be traced. First of all, these texts manifest an increasingly explicit conjunction of metaphysical and physical taxonomies and thus the progressive racialization of crime culminating in the transformation of the shadow of the Black Legend into a stain. Second, they plot a three-dimensionalizing triangulation between the Anglo-dominated United States, the contested frontier zones (land and sea), and Spain or between the United States,

South America, and Spain—a triangulation in which Anglo-America aspired to be at the apex and not indebted to the two other points of geopolitical power. This triangulation sometimes expands into a tetrahedral constellation to include allusions to not only the Moorish, the Arabic, the Semitic, and the African, but also the Ottoman and even the Far Eastern. Hence, the reference in Melville's tale to Benito Cereno's "yellow hands" (177) may actually be interpreted as more than an anti-Semitic epithet for "the Castilian Rothschild" (186), but furthermore as another trace of the Far East or Asia along with the mention of "Lascars or Manilla men" (166), "Malay pirates" (191), and "Malacca cane" (211). In effect, a narrative about the fate of "the Spaniard" in "Benito Cereno" is mapped across the four continents—Europe, the Americas, Africa, and Asia. Spain in the imaginary is no longer confined to the United States and France as in *Wieland*, or England and Italy with a dash of the "Saracenic" in Poe's stories.

I argue that the move from the earlier bilateral (United States versus Old World) to later triangular or tetrahedral geographic and cultural configurations is highly significant. Ironically, as the actual economic and political clout of the vast Spanish Empire waned, its symbolic "domain" (to use that word well loved by Poe) was growing. In answer to the question "Where is Spain?" one might say that by the mid-nineteenth century "Spain" and "Spaniards" were not only in a state of dissemination around the globe (for such had been the case for two centuries already) but most especially within the Anglo American imaginary. "Spain" and "Spaniards" meant African, Asian, Middle Eastern, and "Indian" (Amerindian, West Indian, and even East Indian). "Spain" and "Spaniards" were north and south, east and west. Increasingly from mid-century onward, "Spain" and "Spaniards" signaled within this Anglo-American context hemispheric conflict, particularly over the lands, borderlands, and even seas of all of the Americas, South as much as North, and the presence of "Other Americans" (whether Native American or Spanish American or both) within that "New World." It is no accident that Benito Cereno and his boat are connected with Chile, with Buenos Aires, and with Lima. Nor is it any accident that the everywhere-ness of "Spain" and the everyone-ness of "the Spaniard" should have become a growing obsession within Anglo-American culture at the time (late 1840s–early 1850s) that the tide of Anglo expansion began to rise and shadow, with its own breaking wave, the borderlands—Texas, California, and so on—once claimed for the king of

Spain. Readers would do well to remember Melville's passages from *Moby Dick* implicitly equating Anglo-American empire with the whaling industry on which it so depended for oil to light its path and transforming Spain and its dominions, present or past relative to the composition of his novel, with fish for the catching or the taking:

> "Spain—a great whale stranded on the shores of Europe." Edmund Burke. (Somewhere.)[66]

> What was America in 1492 but a Loose-Fish, in which Columbus struck the Spanish standard by way of waifing it for his royal master and mistress? What was Poland to the Czar? What Greece to the Turk? What India to England? *What at last will Mexico be to the United States? All Loose-Fish.*[67]

In the process of land grabbing, or to extend the whaling metaphor, fish grabbing, the loose fish is transformed into the consumed or ingested fish. And once ingested, that fish becomes an inevitable part of its consumer, except in the miraculous case of Jonah and the whale. The question or the tremendous anxiety then arises as to the nature of the ingestor. If, to return to the particulars of the narrative obsessions of "Benito Cereno," Anglo-America consumes Africans as slaves, annexes parts of Mexico as U.S. territory, and eyes other former or continuing possessions of Spain, then what does Anglo-America become? It risks transculturating into something other than ethnocentric, geocentric notions of "itself" as white, Protestant, and New World.

In "Benito Cereno" the details signifying Asia or the Far East—particularly the Philippines ("Manilla" [*sic*]) and Southeast Asia ("Malay" and "Malacca")—in the descriptions of Benito's ship are illustrative of an awareness of a much more vast and *heterogeneous* Spanish Empire than that confined to the mainlands and islands of the New World. The triangular or tetrahedral structure of association—linking Spain and Spaniards with Africans, "Indians" (162, 200), and Asians—might be viewed as the expression of an almost admiring fascination with the variety of peoples within the territories and trading posts of the Spanish Empire. Hypothesizing an admiring fascination, the increasingly explicit racialization of Spaniards might be seen as an expression of celebratory awe over the historical "Orientalization" or Africanization or tropicalization or general miscegenated status of Spaniards and Spanish peoples despite pretensions to a mythic purity. However, the mutinous, anarchic state of affairs aboard Benito Cereno's ship, the *San Dominick*, is pictured as anything but desirable. Rather, this intimate congress between the sailors and the captain is shot through with intimations that things are out of their proper order, not so much because of the homoeroticism (although all of Melville's works are highly ambivalent in this regard), but because of the bewildering mixture among the ranks of the crew, racialized in this text. The story trades on the chaos resulting from and produced by a desegregation of hierarchicalized roles among what, according to imperial seafaring regulations, is supposed to be a highly scripted crew subject to a disciplined, disciplining combination of enforced communality and segregation.

I purposely use the word *desegregation* with reference to "Benito Cereno" because the inversion of naval authority, the mutiny on board, the improper congress between the captain and the sailors, master and slave, is figured in such racialized terms with the image of a spreading or contaminating shadow turned stain seeping throughout the text and punctuating its end. I claim that, rather than a celebration of the tropicalization of Spain and Spaniards, this mid-nineteenth-century narrative and most racializations of Spain and Spaniards at this time functioned as morality tales, however ambiguous and contradictory, about what they envisioned as the potentially horrific consequences of becoming an empire. They attest to anxieties about the impossibility of containing such a variety of people and still maintaining an alleged purity of race and command, in other words, "racial" and cultural dominance free of the political chaos and moral and physical degeneration attributed to miscegenation. A common Anglo criticism of Spanish imperial rule was that the Spaniards had mixed too much with "racially" inferior and pagan peoples, thus dooming their already suspect culture. Furthermore, the Spanish Empire is not the only empire about which "Benito Cereno" is concerned. As other critics have pointed out, its real concern is with the part played by slavery as a stain on the aspirations of Anglo-American manifest destiny. As suggested earlier, if Benito Cereno's ship is a tableau, a gallery of pictures, a cabinet of strange and unnerving wonders, it is just such a spectacle for the eyes of the "American" captain Amasa Delano, whose "dusky moors of ocean— cawing crows escaped from the hand of the fowler" (234) may or may not succeed in gouging out those very eyes. And, if those "dusky moors

of ocean"—note how "moors" may refer as much to Spain as to Africa—
do succeed in gouging out those Anglo-American eyes, then the Anglo-
American captain and his crew would be plunged into darkness, into
shadow not only as a racial stain but as the very multidimensional space
of culture. "Benito Cereno" articulates this layer of fear obliquely as this is
precisely what is not allowed to happen to Amasa Delano, though Benito
Cereno acknowledges that it has happened to himself in the last words
exchanged between the two captains:

> "You are saved," cried Captain Delano, more and more astonished and
> pained; "you are saved: what has cast such a shadow upon you?"
> 　"The negro." (257)

Just as Poe's "The Pit and the Pendulum" (1843) three-dimentionalizes the
Spanish Inquisition's initially two-dimensional-seeming picture of Time
with a crescent-shaped scythe-like pendulum, "Benito Cereno" (1855)
multidimensionalizes Anglo-American fears and fascinations with the
shadow of the Black Legend against Spain as racial stain and the trace
of historical doom cast by the still powerful but lowered sun, a black sun
if you will, of the hybridized Spanish Empire.

chapter 2

IMPERIAL VISIONS

Moor, Gypsy, and Indian

It may strike some readers as strange or perhaps too neat that the Black Legend against Spain should have resulted, representationally speaking, in the physical as well as moral "blackening" or the progressive darkening of Spaniards and those people deemed in some way "Spanish." But such was the case; it certainly bears itself out in the narratives from the end of the eighteenth century to the mid-nineteenth century examined thus far. However, I do not want to leave readers with the impression that every nineteenth-century invocation of the Black Legend involved this physical blackening or that the Black Legend was the one representational mode through which Spain, Spaniards, and "Spanishness" were depicted. In fact, chapter 1 is titled "The Shadow of the Black Legend" precisely to underscore that Brown's, Poe's, and Melville's representations of Spain are inflected by that legend but have a shape and substance of their own that contribute to an Anglo-American-made shadow of the Spaniard—furthermore, an Anglo-American identity dependent on that very fabricated shadow. With this metaphor I wish to recall to readers some essential features of the relationship between substance and shadow within the original paradigm of the Lacanian mirror image. In Lacan's mirror-stage scenario, the image in the mirror is dependent on a body that views the image. But the converse is also true. As Lacan theorizes throughout his work, the *imago*—the image in the mirror—calls forth a viewing body. The image exerts a shaping power over the viewing body and that is precisely why the viewer looks upon it—to have the illusion, now taken for real, of unified corporeal substance. In like manner, the late-eighteenth- to mid-nineteenth-century texts I have been analyzing reworked the Black Legend to conjure shadow figures of Spain, projecting thereby a virtual body politic to meet in rivalrous reflection the shaping force of these shadows.

As a representational mode, the Black Legend and its shadows were particular in their coordinates of reference in that the tropes of the "Black Legend" pointed to Spain and Spanish empire in the Americas. At the same time, however, not all representations of Spain fell or fall within this rubric. For instance, although it is clear that the determining shape lent by the infamous Black Legend against Spain was increasingly racialized in nineteenth-century U.S. visual and verbal artifacts, not all racializations could be attributed to the Black Legend. Negative racializations were usually inflected by the Black Legend, whether those racializations involved the whitening or darkening of the Spaniard. But the increasing and largely nineteenth-century concern with racializations per se called upon another representational mode with a much larger purview than the Black Legend—Orientalism, a mode used to represent the Mideast or the East versus the West (entire regions and multiple countries, including the Moorish and Ottoman empires, not just one country and its empire). In contrast to the Black Legend as a representational mode, Orientalism, as I will discuss later in this chapter, revolved around the fantasy of a colonized or subjugated and exoticized Other, not a hated and feared rival as with the Black Legend, though these distinctions were by no means hard and fast in all cases. Even in the cases I analyzed in the preceding chapter one can see strains of an Orientalist mode, just as one may see strains of the Black Legend in Orientalizations of Spain. Furthermore, Orientalizations of Spain were predicated on a contrast—on something non-Oriental that was either posited as not-Spanish or as Spain not Orientalized. In other words, in the nineteenth century, and increasingly as the century wore on, the Orientalizing version dominated as the major mode through which Spain, Spaniards, and "Spanishness" were made to signify. Because the Orientalizing one cast Spain in an ultimately inferior or subordinated position, however romanticized or alluring, it was more easily reconciled with the Black Legend than the non-Orientalizing one that whitened, Christianized, Westernized, Europeanized Spain, though this version was also available to be passed through the knot of the Black Legend.

With regard to Anglo-American self-constructions out of shadow play with Spain, readers may wonder about the relationship between the representational modes of the Black Legend and orientalism. If the Black Legend performed its office, why was another mode necessary? And what is the relationship between the more particular mode of the Black Legend concerned as it was with Spain and Spanish empire in the Americas and the much more generalized mode of Orientalism? The Orientalist mode was not as clearly pejorative as the Black Legend mode. In fact, as I shall demonstrate, in many cases it involved a seemingly admiring romanticization of Spain. Such a mode vis-à-vis the rival colonizer, imperial power Spain became popular in the United States in direct proportion to the United States' confidence in its own growing power. Equally important to recognize is that this mode was in a dialectical relationship with that confidence building. It was no mere reflection of it; it was supposed to produce confidence and not only confidence but a sense of entitlement over many peoples and places both internationally and domestically or internally. This sense of entitlement was, of course, intimately linked with aggression. It was aggressive.

This chapter analyzes the relationship between Anglo-Americans' admiring exoticization and self-righteous, bellicose aggressivity toward Spain and Spaniards in the "Old World" and those elements and peoples associated with Spanish empire in the Americas. And, it does so by taking the reader on a brief tour of the rhetorical dynamics of Anglo-American travelers' involvement in the Grand Tour of the Continent, which may or may not have included Spain (the exclusion of Spain is as telling as its inclusion); through a consideration of the Orientalizations of U.S. Hispanophiles' histories of Spain in relation to French and British Orientalizations of Spain; through an examination of some major commissioned paintings of Spain's role in the New World, paintings informed or inspired by the work of these Hispanophiles; through a simultaneous analysis of three major romances of Anglo-American manifest destiny evidently necessitating figures of Spain to propel their errands into the wilderness or "civilization"; and concluding with an in-depth analysis of one of the most famous nineteenth-century visual representations of Spain, one with symbolic resonance to this day, judging from the well-publicized restoration of the painting for its 1992 exhibition in National Gallery of Art (Washington, DC). Its exhibition was followed in the same year by a more immediately consumable version in the nation's capitol (down the block from the Shakespeare theater), a Spanish tapas restaurant bearing the name of the painting by John Singer Sargent: *El Jaleo*.

ORIENTING THE SPANIARD:
IMPERIALISM AS REPRESENTATIONAL MODE

In nineteenth-century Anglo-American discourse, "European" indexed France, Germany, Italy, and England, unless England was seen to be distinct from the "Continent." Nineteenth-century narratives of travel—from novels such as Nathaniel Hawthorne's *The Marble Fawn* (1860), Mark Twain's *Innocents Abroad* (1869), and Henry James's *The American* (1877), *The Europeans* (1878), and *The Portrait of a Lady* (1881) to texts of travel literature like Bayard Taylor's *Views a-Foot; or, Europe Seen with Knapsack and Staff* (1891)—map "European" as that which connoted the fine arts, refinement, education, civility, sophistication, a history that legitimated social institutions, and imperial power. Spain, though not entirely excluded from the categories of Europe or European, was, in narratives of the Anglo-American goes to Europe, frequently overlooked or avoided as a daunting, dangerous land on the other side of the Pyrenees. That "other side" both in and out of Europe is distinguished by climate, temperature, and even temperament as hot—hot-tempered, hot-blooded, bloody-minded.[1] The imputed discomfiting heat of Spain kept Spain off the Grand Tour itinerary for the Anglo-American upper classes.[2] Rather, hot, dark, enigmatic Spain was generally considered the starting point for a completely different sort of trip—a journey to North Africa and to the Near East.

Although Spain, along with Italy, was sometimes considered part of "southern Europe" (in juxtaposition to "northern Europe" which included England, France, Germany, Switzerland, etc.), Italy, with the exceptions of Sicily and Venice, was not treated as a bridge to Africa, the Near East, and that deemed as "Oriental."[3] The major destination of the European Grand Tour, Italy was reinscribed by centuries of tourist travel as the cradle of Western artistic achievement signifying both Roman Empire and glorious Renaissance. Old World peninsular Spain, on the other hand, conjured fantasies and anxieties about strange and volatile mixture, purging and contamination, attributed to and provoked by the traces and remnants of the Muslim Conquest, the Christian Reconquest, and the Inquisition.

New World Spain, the Spanish Americas, was, in Anglo-American imperial discourse, equally a site and sign of miscegenation and contaminating rather than regenerative hybridity. The figures of the Moor and the Gypsy, already signs of Old World hybridity, came to stand for what was represented as the further degeneration of the Spaniard in the New World through contact and intercourse with African peoples brought over as slaves and with Native Americans.[4] The discourse of Anglo-American imperialism in the period leading up to the Spanish-Cuban-American War (1898) was increasingly one of race articulated as a way of seeing. Imperial vision cataloged hierarchically and simultaneously reduced the peoples and histories of contact in the Iberian Peninsula and the Americas into a set of interrelated types—Moor, Gypsy, and Indian—that stood for migration, expulsion, racial and cultural intermixing, and ineradicable stain. Imperial vision was a representational mode or practice through which Spaniards, Moors, Africans, Jews, Gypsies, and Native Americans, the Old World and the New, colonizer and colonized, were transformed into tropes of doomed racial mixing: dark-skinned minstrels or dancers; dark-haired, dark-skinned, black-eyed maidens or women in "native dress"; and sometimes dark-skinned, often aggressive, male figures in full regalia, whether dressed in feathers and war paint, a pirate's outfit, a Moorish or Gypsy costume, a bullfighter's garb, or a beggar's rags.

Throughout the nineteenth century, Anglo-Americans had been consolidating their power—over Native Americans by genocide and Indian removal policies, over Mexicans in the Mexican-American War (1846–48), and over their rival imperialist in the New World, the Spaniards, in the Spanish-Cuban-American War (1898). Native Americans, free blacks, black slaves, and Spaniards posed a common threat to Anglo-American expansionism and empire building. In certain historical instances, this threat was a united one, as in the case of the Seminole (Muskogee and Miccosukee Creeks) and Yamasee tribes whom the Spaniards incited to attack Anglo-American colonists in the eighteenth and early nineteenth centuries. The Spanish empire in the Americas, the lands south of the Mississippi, especially the Spanish Floridas, represented not only territorial insecurity but a potentially threatening counterstate of Creeks and Seminoles who wanted their lands back, Spanish officials with neither the will nor the military power to restrain them, and runaway slaves from the U.S. territories whom the Spanish government allowed to live as free farmers.[5] However,

Anglo-American imperial representation of the Spaniard was not a mere matter of reaction to New World experience or historical contact in the Americas. Rather, Anglo-American imperial representation involved a complex two-way reorientation of the Spaniard, a mapping of New World mixing onto the Old World and Old World hybridity onto the new.

Into the latter part of the nineteenth century, Anglo-American imperial discourse replayed the early triangular drama of Spaniards and Native Americans against Anglo-American colonists, specters of black slave revolt and supposed anarchy in Spanish territories, Black Legend versions of the Spanish Conquest of the Americas and the decimation of native populations, as well as lurid versions of the Inquisition, the Reconquest, and the expulsion of Moors, Gypsies, and Jews from the Iberian Peninsula. This replay labored to displace and/or absolve Anglo-Americans' own bloody history in the Americas and to pose the Anglo-American empire as an antiempire, as anticonquest. These retellings of New and Old World Spanish history formed figures of the "white Spaniard," Moors, Gypsies, Jews, Africans, and Native Americans into tropes of the Moor, Gypsy, and Indian. Figures of colonizer and colonized, Old World and New were made into a united threat or prehistory of conquest through a racializing representational practice that purported to empirically and ethnographically identify and distinguish. Using the pseudoscience of physiognomy, theories of racial polygenesis, and moral allegories of race, Anglo-American imperial discourse constructed and mobilized a set of types—conquistador, "white Spaniard," Moor, Gypsy, and Indian—into tropes by which the United States was constituted as the rightful heir to the Americas.

Anglo-American imperialism, I argue, was a representational mode or practice by which Spain's ethnically mixed heritage and history at home with Moors, Gypsies, and Jews and in the Americas with Native Americans and Africans were made into physical proof and cause of the decline of the Spanish Empire. Over the course of the nineteenth century the Spaniard went from a figure of moral blackness and alien whiteness to a figure of dangerous, implosive "racial" mixture as a justification for further aggression and expansion on the part of the United States.

Rather than a celebration of ethnic and cultural fusion, Anglo-American imperial discourse took what Spanish empire had endeavored to expel (Moors, Gypsies, Jews) from the Iberian Peninsula and those whom the Spanish Empire in the Americas had worked to death (Native Americans and Africans) and put them under the skin of or transformed them into physical marks on the imagined body of the Spaniard. This representational practice projected Anglo-Americans' own fears and fantasies about miscegenation/hybridity as degeneration onto Spanish empire in the New World and the Old.

In this chapter, I focus on a number of allegorical works, novels, and paintings that retell history, U.S. and Spanish, construct racial types, and, in the process, transform typology into implied or overtly stated fate. Through readings of William Gilmore Simms's *The Yemassee* (1835), Nathaniel Hawthorne's *The Scarlet Letter* (1850), Oliver Wendell Holmes's *Elsie Venner* (1861), I will argue that type is transformed into fatal trope in order to articulate in visionary form the claimed manifest destiny of U.S. empire as racially and morally inevitable anticonquest. Fatality takes a seductively different form in works such as John Singer Sargent's painting *El Jaleo* (1882). Through a close analysis of this tableau of flamenco performance (*tablao*) as a synecdoche of Spanish culture, I consider the way in which admiring exoticization of type is semiotically linked to and may unwittingly reinforce typology as destiny.

IN AND OUT OF EUROPE: TWO VERSIONS OF SPAIN

Anglo-American texts and images from the colonial period to the nineteenth century represented the Spaniard as a figure of alien "whiteness" marked as different by moral blackness. The "white Spaniard" in pre-nineteenth-century Anglo-American discourse signified Europe and the Old World but with important differences: geographical isolation from the rest of Europe and a reputation for zealous, if not inquisitorial Catholicism. The alien "white Spaniard" took the form of noblemen ("Spanish grandees"); knights on the land or captains of galleons on the sea; Castilians; and, most popularly and resonantly, conquistadores and discoverers. This "white Spaniard" version persisted into the nineteenth century in iconic drawings and paintings of Spanish discovery and exploration of the New World, as well as in tableaux of burial and return home, the latter implying a narrative of the survival and even triumph of Anglo-American empire.[6] The white, European, Catholic/Christian version of Spain was generally composed by certain iconographic details:[7] white-skinned, neatly bearded men; the cross borne aloft like a flag; standards of the crown

(usually with the initials of Ferdinand and Isabella or with the castle and
the lion of Castile and Aragon) or of the church (a stylized cross); brightly
polished armor and coats of mail; lances, shields, and great two-handed
swords; plumed helmets or hats (the accessories of a grandee); some reference to the possession of land and/or sea—a boat, a military encampment
or procession, a globe; and sometimes figures of Native Americans gesturing in deference or cowering and fleeing in fear.

Numerous histories of Spanish empire and especially of the period of
discovery, exploration, and conquest were published in the first half of the
nineteenth century by Anglo-Americans. Washington Irving's *History of
the Life and Voyages of Christopher Columbus* (1828), Robert Montgomery
Bird's *Conquest of Mexico* (1834), John Fiske's *The Discovery of America*
(1840s), and William Hickling Prescott's *History of Ferdinand and Isabella*
(1838), *History of the Conquest of Mexico* (1843), *History of the Conquest of
Peru* (1847), *History of the Reign of Phillip II* (1849), and *The History of the
Reign of the Emperor* [Charles V] (1857) were all concerned with Spaniards
as discoverers, conquistadores, and colonizers. These imperial histories
served to reinforce the "white Spaniard" typology of Spain. Such texts provided U.S. readers with a usable past, that is, both a model and an antitype
for empire.[8] Legends of civilizing and glory-gaining accomplishments, as
well as sensational retellings of Spanish atrocities against the Native Americans, served a double narrative function in providing justification for
the expansionist ambitions of the United States. These double narratives
of magnificence and atrocity implicitly identified the nineteenth-century
United States with discovery, exploration, and triumph while disavowing
and displacing Anglo-Americans' own extermination of Native Americans
and expropriation of their lands back onto the early decades of Spanish
empire in the Americas.

Washington Irving's *History of the Life and Voyages of Christopher
Columbus* (1828) casts the "white Spaniard" in a rehearsal of the account of
Bartolomé de las Casas, who gave, in Irving's own words, "an indignant
picture of the capricious tyranny exercised over the Indians by worthless
Spaniards."[9] The "white Spaniard" plays a double role as the exalted and
vilified alter ego. Irving's history immortalizes "discovery" and condemns
the "white Spaniard," the conquistador, as a figure of tyranny and bar-
baric conquest from whom the text repeatedly distinguishes the Anglo-
Americanized self-reliant hero of the imagination, Columbus.

In novels, poems, short stories, and visual culture the alien "white Spaniard" was also figured as an agent of his own burial, as degenerate or degenerating whiteness consumed by the reprisal of that which he has abjected (Moors, Gypsies, Jews). The noble knight or hidalgo was the incarnation of physical and/or spiritual weakness, a white man who had forfeited control of his destiny through his addiction to leisure and luxury, inquisitorial Catholicism, or both as in inquisitiveness as acquisitiveness in the pursuit of others' property. This trope of alien whiteness decaying from within, of Spanish Empire as personal and historical doom, is a feature of Washington Irving's *Journals*, Ned Buntline's novel *The Last Days of Callao* (1847), Bret Harte's short stories (thirty thematizing the dying away of Spanish imperial influence in California), a paradigmatic example of which is "A Knight Errant of the Foothills" (1853), and Henry Wadsworth Longfellow's poem "The Theologian's Tale: Torquemada" from *Tales of a Wayside Inn* (1863). Longfellow's retelling of the Inquisition as a family drama in which an old knight accuses his own daughters of heresy and sacrifices them to the pyre is "a double picture, with its gloom and glow."[10] The black-white allegorical contrast of this "double picture" signifies the hidalgo's doubleness, his alien whiteness and moral blackness. The "double picture" takes on a narrative dimension in the two fires, first the auto-da-fé of the hidalgo's daughter, and then, that very evening, the immolation of the old knight by a raging fire that consumes his castle. The poem concludes with the triumphant pronouncement that "no trace remains on earth of his afflicted race."[11] The "gloom and glow" of the "double picture" accrues a historical prospect through the narrative of a doom for the Spaniard (and Spanish empire) which sets glory in potentially appropriable relief for the Anglo-American reader.

The daughters of hidalgos (figures of sympathy in Longfellow's tale of the Inquisition) were, in fiction and social history, objects of appropriable and redeemable alien whiteness. If, like Doña Inez, daughter of the wealthy landowner Don Augustin de Certavallos in James Fenimore Cooper's novel *The Prairie* (1827), she was an inheritor of vast chunks of land in the Southwest and West of North America, then she was treated as a "valuable" asset to the Anglo-American hero who, through his marriage to her, helped to fulfill the territorial goals of manifest destiny.

Some scholars such as Norman P. Tucker have treated nineteenth-century Anglo-American interest in Spain and Spaniards as wholly benign.

The imperial histories, novels, and short stories I have mentioned are generally taken merely as evidence of the sympathetic interest in Spain on the part of their producers. The works of the men of letters acclaimed as the first "Hispanophiles"—Henry Wadsworth Longfellow, Washington Irving, and William Hickling Prescott, as well as Alexander Everett (noted for the assistance given to Irving and Prescott and his *America, or a General Survey of the Political Situation of the Principal Powers of the Western Continent, with Conjectures on Their Future Prospects, by a Citizen of the United States*, 1827) and George Ticknor (also acclaimed for the aid given to Irving and Prescott and especially for his *History of Spanish Literature*, 1849)—are lauded as signs of the sympathy of their authors rather than read as complex works of imperial representation.[12] The general claim is that the Hispanophiles were taken with a "romantic concept of Spain."[13] However, even under or, rather, within the rubric of the "romantic concept of Spain," one can find these same scholars discussing the unavoidable, that is, the Hispanophiles' fascination with Spanish national unification and subsequent discovery, conquest, and colonization of the Americas; the golden age of Spanish "cultural achievement"; and/or with Andalusia and all that was deemed "Oriental" about Spain. Without question, the Hispanophiles fomented academic and imaginative interest in the Iberian Peninsula and the history and cultures of what became "Spain" and helped to construct a forum for intellectual exchange between Spain and the United States. Nevertheless, in addition to a dynamic of projection and wish fulfillment at work in the attraction of nineteenth-century U.S. historians and writers to the story of Spain's unification and rise to imperial power, I contend that there were tropological continuities between Anglo-Americans' admiring exoticization of Spanish types and their condemning and finally warmongering demonization of them as too hot-blooded, primitive, and racially tainted to govern any part of the Americas.

The version of Spain as a figure of alien "whiteness" has persisted into the twentieth century. However, in the nineteenth-century United States an Orientalist view of Spain and Spaniards was constructed by travel literature such as Alexander Slidell MacKenzie's *Year in Spain* (1829) and Bayard Taylor's *The Lands of the Saracens; or, Pictures of Palestine, Asia Minor, Sicily, and Spain* (1855); by collections of tales such as Washington Irving's *The Alhambra* (1832); by novels such as William Gilmore Simms's *The Yemassee: A Romance of Carolina* (1835; reprinted in 1853), Nathaniel

Hawthorne's *The Scarlet Letter* (1850), and Oliver Wendell Holmes's *Elsie Venner: A Romance of Destiny* (1861); as well as by paintings such as John Singer Sargent's *Court of Myrtles in the Alhambra* (1879), Frederick Arthur Bridgman's *In Spain, at the Time of the Moors* (n.d.), and Walter Gay's *Cigarette Girls, Spain* (1894). Through the imperial gaze of these works the Spaniard is likened to or becomes the Moor, the Gypsy, and/or the "Indian" in terms of empiricizing and fetishizing detail of physical appearance, behavior, gesture, dress, and other exotic and yet banal particularities of daily life. Spain is distinguished from "Europe" as the place of the volatile mixture of the Moorish, Gypsy, and Semitic by its haunting past incarnated or concretized in depictions of its inhabitants and of its Moorish and/or Arabian (versus Roman, Visigothic, or Iberian) antiquities. The Orientalization (including Orientalized Africanization) of Spain was also mapped onto the former Spanish territories of the U.S. Southwest. Charles Lummis, writing in the mid-1880s, articulated what he imagined as a dangerous mixture of Spanish and Native American cultures in the terms of the Orientalization of Spain: "It [the American Southwest] is a land of quaint, swart faces, of Oriental dress and unspelled speech . . . of polytheism and superstition, where the rattlesnake is a demigod . . . where Christians mangle and crucify themselves—the heart of Africa beating against the ribs of the Rockies."[14]

The imperial gaze, in Edward Said's model of Orientalism, is generally that of the colonizer on the colonized. U.S. imperialism vis-à-vis Spain involved a twist on that model. Spain was never a colony of the United States. It was, however, for many Anglo-Americans during the second half of the nineteenth century, an imperial power in decline or a failed imperial power. The image of Spain as a great imperial power in decline losing its grip on the Americas was a gratifying one. Such an image provided not simply a convenient foil, but a truly significant foil to the growing prosperity and power of the United States. Nations such as Mexico, France, and Great Britain were invoked to prove "America"'s status as an exceptional nation, as the nation destined to lead the world, but for historical reasons Spain was the prized booty of the ideology of manifest destiny. Anglo-American imperialists could identify with what was, on account of its New World possessions, the largest imperial power since the time of the Romans, as well as use Spain to define an Other that bolstered their sense of being civilized and finally "chosen" above all peoples.

In nineteenth-century Anglo-American imperial discourse, "Oriental" often went from marking the *not-European* to signifying that which is radically Other or anti-European.[15] Inasmuch as the Orient was considered not-European, it was "exotic"; inasmuch as it was seen as anti-Europe, it was imagined, experienced, and represented as dangerous. For many Anglo-Americans of the nineteenth century, the Moor, the Gypsy, and the Indian were represented as seductive or even hypnotizing and, therefore, potentially threatening. In the words of James Albert Harrison's travel narrative *Spain in Profile: A Summer among the Olives and Aloes* (1879), "In Cordova [Córdoba] you feel a strange geographical remoteness from the rest of Europe; at all events certain habitudes of mind are rather *violently upset* after a certain degree of intimacy with the Orientalism all around you."[16]

U.S. Orientalization of the Spaniard did not exist in isolation from the Orientalizing strategies of other imperial powers. The Orientalization of Spain was promoted most by the French. Shortly after the French invasion and defeat of Spain between the years 1804 and 1814, French writers, painters, and scholars turned their gaze on Spain, plundering it imaginatively for, above all, what was identified as its Moorish past. In his *Impressions de voyage de Paris à Cadix* (1847–48) Alexandre Dumas wrote of a misadventure en route from Toledo to Aranjuez. The inn at which he and his traveling companions were to have stayed the night is the scene of a fandango (a dance associated, in the text, with Moors and Gypsies but also called a "national dance"), which the hostess refuses to interrupt, sending the unhappy travelers back on the road. Only a few hours from Aranjuez—the royal country estate that Dumas writes "claims to be the Versailles of Madrid"—the author finds the Moorish, that which has been abjected by the city, the true "picturesque" in the form of the anticivilized or the savage:

> For travelers in search of the picturesque it really was exhilirating to discover at night in the midst of a desert, in a *venta* isolated and almost in ruins, this gay company of dancers in national dress. Madrid, charming but civilized, has banned the picturesque as all civilized capitals must, and there we sought it vainly, finding little more than stereotyped, inadequate performances on stages erected in the squares, whereas this revelry, surging up so spontaneously and unexpectedly before our eyes, seemed a harmonious whole.[17]

French texts and paintings of this period also often located the history of the Moors of Spain in specific architectural relics: the Alhambra and Generalife of Granada and the Mezquita (mosque) of Córdoba. These monuments were dramatized as places or landmarks of unbridled sensuality, unrequited love or jealous lovers, blood, and death. This representational practice oriented Spain ethnographically and geographically as part of Africa and Asia. The expulsion of the Moors and the Jews was made to come back and haunt; Africa and Asia were now seen as the constitutive and distinguishing elements of essential Spain. As Victor Hugo wrote in the preface to *Les Orientales* (1829), "Spain is half African, Africa is half Asian."[18]

Lurid retellings of Spanish history and fabulous re-scenarizations of the past made of the Alhambra, the Generalife, and the Mezquita enlivened dioramas of history and, by implication, present Spanish character. Paintings such as Henri-Alexandre-Georges Regnault's *Execution without Trial under the Moorish Kings of Granada* (1870) and works by the painter Edme-Alexis-Alfred Dehodencq (1822–82), who spent long periods of time in both Andalusia (southern Spain) and Morocco, where he painted scenes of violence supposed to be intrinsic to the "Oriental," were not celebrations of the ethnically mixed heritage of Spain. Instead, they represented another version of destruction from within. The Spaniard is not a figure of decaying whiteness, but rather a volatile "Oriental" mixture destined to violently implode or languorously putrefy. As Alfred de Vigny (1797–1863) declared: "[A] Spaniard is an Oriental, he is a Catholic Turk, his blood either languishes or boils, he is a slave to indolence, ardor, cruelty."[19]

A number of Anglo-Americans who wrote about Spain in the nineteenth century cited these French writers as authorities. For example, William Howe Downes, in his book *Spanish Ways and By-Ways* (1883), writes: "Spain is un-European. Gautier says it is a part of Africa, and should still belong to the Moors by right."[20] Even into the twentieth century, Anglo-American writers such as William Dean Howells in his *Familiar Spanish Travels* (1913) continued to reference Gautier's *Voyage en Espagne* with deference.[21] Many U.S. painters (among them, F. A. Bridgman, Walter Gay, and John Singer Sargent) went to Paris to study in French academies such as the École des Beaux-Arts or the Académie Julian and in the studios of various French artists such as Léon Bonnat, Jean-Léon Gerome, and Carolus-Duran, where they would have been directly exposed to the French Orientalizations of Spain.[22]

As France's colonial and imperial competitor, Britain also played a major role in the Orientalization of Spain. Spain was the object of British imperial desires as a potential satellite ally against the French and because of Gibraltar, part of the Iberian Peninsula that had been disputed British territory since 1704. British artist-travelers represented Spain in the form of landscape and genre scenes and architectural views that focused on Islamic architecture in the south of Spain.[23] Rather than depict the Roman antiquities in Spain, James Cavanah Murphy published *The Arabian Antiquities of Spain* (1815). David Wilkie, who traveled with Washington Irving in the 1820s, painted scenes of the Alhambra and David Roberts and John Frederick Lewis spent much of their time on their travels through Spain in the 1830s sketching the monuments of Spain's Islamic past. For the British, as for the French, the Alhambra and Generalife in Granada, the Giralda in Seville, and the Mezquita in Córdoba came to stand in, synecdochically, for Spain as a whole.[24]

Anglo-American imperial discourse appropriated from the Orientalizing strategies of the French and British, adding to the figures of the Moor and the Gypsy that of the Indian. For example, Downes's *Spanish Ways and By-Ways* (1883) represents Spain by poverty in the form of a beggar in Burgos with the "physiognomy of a North American Indian" and some Celtic features:

> We . . . wandered about the town [of Burgos] aimlessly, avoiding the beggars as best we could. One of this tribe, who was seated in a warm corner in front of a big, massive door, holding out his hand and muttering mechanical appeals, had a parchment skin of the rich tone of old mahogany, and the physiognomy of a North American Indian, modified by some very decided Irish characteristics . . . The beggars in Burgos are numerous but not aggressive; it is only in Granada that they wage open warfare upon strangers, pursue them, surround them, threaten them.[25]

Downes's text locates poverty that erupts into violence or what he calls "open warfare" in Granada. Like their French and British counterparts, Anglo-American writers and visual artists "mastered" Spain and its history by treating the south, specifically the region of Andalusia, as the "key" to the dark enigma of the country. In the writings and visual representations produced and consumed by these competing imperial powers, Andalusia (particularly the cities of Córdoba, Granada, and Seville) became the geographic and cultural locus not only of Spain's Islamic past but of Spanish essence, which they associated with voluptuousness, carnality, fanaticism, and brutality. As U.S. writer Washington Irving wrote:

> I think that I better understand the . . . Spaniard . . . the country, the habits, the very looks of the people, have something of the Arabian character. The general insecurity of the country is evinced in the universal use of weapons . . . the most petty journey is undertaken with the preparation of a war-like enterprise.[26]

No one made the Alhambra as famous or Spain as synonymous with the Alhambra for his contemporaries and for future generations as Washington Irving.[27] Many nineteenth-century Anglo-American travelers to Spain journeyed to Granada fully conscious that they were following Irving's footsteps. In 1855, twenty-three years after Irving published *The Alhambra* (1832), Bayard Taylor dedicated his book *The Lands of the Saracens* (1855), in which he describes the Alhambra in some detail, to Washington Irving.[28] In 1934, more than a century after the publication of Irving's *Alhambra*, Edith Wharton attested to the lasting influence of Irving's narrative, as well as Prescott's histories, in her autobiography *A Backward Glance*.

> I remember that the Spanish tour was still considered an arduous adventure, and to attempt it with a young child the merest folly. But my father had been reading Prescott and Washington Irving; the Alhambra was more of a novelty than the Colosseum.[29]

The Orientalized version of Spain produced and circulated by Anglo-American writers and visual artists was as doubled as the "white Spaniard" version. Along with bloody narratives and sensuous description came elegy. Laments for the vanished Moor, like those of Washington Irving from his *Alhambra,* mourn the passing of one empire to foretell the eventual doom of another:

> Never was the annihilation of a people more complete than that of the Morisco-Spaniards . . . The exiled remnant of their once powerful empire disappeared among the barbarians of Africa, and ceased to be a nation . . .

A few broken monuments are all that remain to bear witness to their power
and dominion, as solitary rocks, left far in the interior, bear testimony to the
extent of some vast inundation. Such is the Alhambra.

A Moslem pile in the midst of a Christian land; an Oriental palace amid
the Gothic edifices of the West; an elegant memento of a brave, intelligent,
and graceful people, who conquered, ruled, flourished, and passed away.[30]

Anglo-American Orientalizations of the Spaniard put back into the heart
of Spain what had been expelled in the Reconquest. The expulsion and
annihilation of the Moors was made to haunt the Spaniard just as the
Spanish Empire's treatment of the Native Americans was made into a
representational agent of their demise. Irving treats the Moors in this passage as James Fenimore Cooper treats the good Indians in his novels—as
laudable because they are doomed, vanquished, and vanishing. However,
Orientalizations of the Spaniard endeavor to dispel through displacement
rather than raise the ghosts of Anglo-Americans' own bloody history with
Native Americans. The praise given the "Morisco-Spaniards," like that
given throughout the nineteenth century to Native Americans in the
United States, was dependent on the certainty that they had been deprived
of their lands and their power. Elegy endeavored to keep it that way.

Although the "white Spaniard" conquistador representation preceded
the orientalization of Spain, in nineteenth-century imperial discourse
these two versions were often combined to form a united representational
strategy. The two versions were imbricated in texts such as Irving's *The
Alhambra* (1832) and visual images such as Emanuel Leutze's *Columbus
before the Queen* (1843) and *The Storming of the Teocalli Temple by Cortez
and His Troops* (1848) so that the "white Spaniard" is shadowed by some
trace or specter of what he has expelled.[31] Irving's *Alhambra* conjures a
vision of Columbus "the future discoverer" and the "Catholic sovereigns"
Ferdinand and Isabella giving thanks for their "victory" over the Moors,
which the text "returns to oblivion":

I picture to myself Columbus, the future discoverer of a world, taking his
modest stand in a remote corner, the humble and neglected spectator of the
pageant. I see in imagination the Catholic sovereigns prostrating themselves
before the altar, and pouring forth thanks for their victory; while the vaults
resound with sacred minstrelsy, and the deep-toned Te Deum.

The transient illusion is over—the pageant melts from the fancy—
monarch, priest, and warrior return to oblivion, with the poor Moslems
over whom they exulted. The hall of their triumph is waste and desolate.[32]

The victory of "Catholic sovereigns" quickly gives way to the ghost of
"the poor Moslem." The Spanish Empire of the Old and New World (signified by the neglected Columbus) becomes like the Islamic empire in the
Iberian Peninsula, that is, in Irving's text, a "transient illusion," a piece of
exotica that cannot last, like one of the dreams in Shakespeare's *Tempest*
or like Othello the Moor's short-lived career in the service of the Venetian state. Columbus, the figure of identification for Anglo-Americans, is
placed in the spectator position—in, and yet appropriable from, the fleeting mirage of Spanish empire.

Emanuel Leutze's painting *Columbus before the Queen* (1843) revisits this
history in the form of a slightly different set piece (Figure 1). The iconic

Figure 1. Emanuel Leutze, *Columbus before the Queen* (1843), oil on canvas,
38¾ × 51³⁄₁₆ inches. Brooklyn Museum of Art. Dick S. Ramsay Fund and
A. Augustus Healy Fund B.

scenario is that of Columbus, or Cristóbal Colón, being received and pardoned on December 12, 1500, by Isabella I of Castile "la Católica" and Ferdinand V of Aragon "el Católico" at the court they had moved to Granada after the expulsion of the Moors. Columbus, the celebrated "discoverer," served as governor and viceroy of Spanish settlement on the Caribbean island of Hispaniola (now Haiti and the Dominican Republic) from 1495 to 1500. It was these years of forced subjugation, and decimation of the Tainos under Columbus and his brothers that gave immediate rise to the Black Legend. However, it was Columbus's inability to control the Spaniards on the island that led to his being taken back to Spain, along with his brothers, in chains.[33] In Leutze's painting the Catholic monarchs Isabella and Ferdinand sit on their royal throne surrounded by court attendants distinguished by a detailed variety of skin tones and hair color. The scene is set within the multifoil arches and tiled walls of a Moorish-style edifice. The architecture serves as a reminder that the Spanish Empire was constituted not only by the expulsion of the Moors, but also by the reclamation of their territories and cultural symbols. Upon seizing Granada, the "Catholic sovereigns" are supposed to have marched into the city dressed in Moorish costume and, after their deaths, they were finally buried in the Gothic-style Capilla Real specially built opposite the Alhambra. However, like Irving's re-scenarization of the Alhambra, Leutze's painting of this particular tableau of history, which allowed the opportunity to set the Catholic monarchs within a Moorish-style edifice, also implies the reverse, that the fall and lasting influence of the Moorish empire has doomed the Spanish one.

Furthermore, although the scene is ostensibly of Columbus before the queen and Ferdinand removed his chains, the painting presents a liberated Columbus gesturing to his chains on the floor, as well as to a priest and a young boy holding gold and silks signifying the riches he had promised and which were at that time just beginning to be mined. The monarchs are depicted looking away in shame: Isabella with her head in her hand and Ferdinand gazing up into the distance. The two versions of Spain, the Orientalized Moorish version and the "white Spaniard" figure of alien whiteness and moral blackness, work together in this retelling of history to doubly shame, condemn, and doom the Spanish Empire. Columbus, the figure appropriated by the United States as the first "American," appears before the Spanish court as the agent of condemnation, like Christ before the Romans. He looks at the monarchs and points to his chains on the tiled floor. With this gesture Columbus condemns the Spanish monarchs in their Moorish castle as false Christians and cruel tyrants unable to govern without enslaving their subjects. The contrast between shamed monarchs and freed Columbus suggests that slavery has left its mark not on the New World (Columbus) but on the Old (Spain). The Orientaliza- tion of the Spaniard into a figure of enslavement also held out the prospect or vision of a displacement of Anglo-American empire's own dependence on slavery. Ironically, therefore, Anglo-America depended on Spain to de- flect from its own dependence on a slave system. The deflection func- tioned like a magic trick—distracting viewers from slavery here and now with gestures to over there or an elsewhere. William Gilmore Simms relies heavily on this trick in his romance *The Yemassee* (1835), as I will demon- strate, except that in his case he does not abjure slavery so much as defend a "righteous" Southern slave system. In Leutze's painting, the same ges- ture by which Columbus, as imagined Anglo-American hero, points to the New World riches denounces the Spanish Empire for its incapacity to appreciate what he has "discovered." The gesture also makes an implicit link between the chains and the wealth extracted from the New World by the Spanish. The implication is that the Spanish Empire is enslaved by greed and, furthermore, that the Spaniards' conquest has been unjustified because they have only stolen, not planted or produced. Leutze's tableau retells Spanish imperial history, New World and Old, through a juxta- position of the tropes of "white Spaniard" and Orientalized Spaniard in order to foretell the doom of the Spanish Empire from within and set the stage for the goods of the New World to pass to those who, by impli- cation, would appreciate them, know how to govern, and produce more riches with these goods. The implied Anglo-American imperial subject need only walk up the steps and take what is laid out for the grabbing.

Leutze also revisioned the history of the Spanish Empire in the Ameri- cas in *The Storming of the Teocalli Temple by Cortez and His Troops* (Figure 2). Although based in part on Prescott's *History of the Conquest of Mexico* (1843), the painting had a more immediate historical referent for inspira- tion than the conquest of the Aztec empire by Hernán Cortés in 1521: the U.S. conquest of two-fifths of Mexican territory in the Mexican-American War (1846–48). The war concluded with the signing of the Treaty of Guadalupe Hidalgo (February 2, 1848) in the year that the painting was produced. U.S. aggression against Mexico, the aggravating annexation of Texas in 1845, and efforts by President Polk to acquire California by deal making or military force culminated in the U.S. declaration of war against Mexico in 1846. Two years of armed conflict ensued through which the United States seized most of what is now known as the "Southwest."

Leutze's painting replays this immediate history through the previous violent conflict between Spaniards and Aztecs. The scene is a carefully chosen condensation and confrontation of historical moments and allegorical types. In the siege of Mexico City in 1847, the battle cry of U.S. soldiers had been "To the Halls of the Montezumas." The iconic symbol of the eventual occupation of Mexico City was the "storming of the

Figure 2. Emanuel Leutze, *The Storming of the Teocalli Temple by Cortez and His Troops* (1848), oil on canvas, 84.74 × 98.75 inches. Wadsworth Atheneum, Hartford. The Ella Gallup Sumner and Mary Catlin Sumner Collection Fund.

Castle of Chapultepec" by U.S. troops. This garrison on a hill was of no great military importance but had profound historical resonance for both the United States and Mexico. The hill had once been the site of an Aztec palace destroyed in the Spanish Conquest. In its place the Spanish viceroys had built a summer palace that, with Mexican independence, had been taken over by the Republic of Mexico as the site of the Mexican Military College. The Teocalli Temple was a sacred pyramid in the Aztec capital that became Mexico City. Leutze's painting condenses time and place, the "storming of the Teocalli Temple" by Hernán Cortés and his men and the "storming of the Castle of Chapultepec" by the United States.[34]

However, this allegorical condensation of time and place allows a central displacement and transformation. Symbolically, what U.S. soldiers battled and took over at Chapultepec is revisioned by Leutze's painting as the destructive confluence of what are represented as two equally savage "races." At the far right of the scene, an Aztec priest with a knife in his teeth lifts up a bloody, already sacrificed baby. Diagonally across the composition, on the upper level of the temple, a Spanish conquistador is in the process of hurling another Aztec baby over the edge to the stone floor below. At bottom left a Catholic priest attempts to give last rites to a dying Aztec warrior who turns away in refusal. Meanwhile, a Spanish opportunist behind this pair seizes the gold chains from around a dead Aztec warrior's neck. Across the composition at top right Aztec women and children are represented prostrate before the grotesquely rendered sacred carvings crowning the temple. Just below them another Aztec woman gestures in a hopeless appeal to the setting sun. The violent clash of Spaniards and Aztecs is made over by these formal crossovers and typological analogies into a unified tableau of false religion, barbarity, and greed.

While the painting makes clear by the Spanish flag being erected at the top of the temple that victory in this battle will go to the Spanish Empire, it is the "white Spaniard" figure who abjectly drapes the stairway leading up to the stage of this drama. His outstretched hand points to two figures, an Aztec boy and an adult Spanish fighter. Both are differently marked than the other Aztec and Spanish figures. The Spanish fighter is distinguished by the bandage wrapped like a Moorish turban around his head. The Aztec boy, the one figure in the entire composition looking directly at the viewer, is differentiated by his distinctly darkened face. I would suggest that, by these three central figures—the dead "white Spaniard," the Moorish Spaniard, and the dark-faced "Indian"—the moral allegory of the painting's violent synthesis of Spanish and native cultures is also made into a racial one. Not only are the Spanish and Aztec empires represented as foredoomed by their fabulously represented practices, but so too is newly independent Mexico as the descendant and inheritor of these two cultures. Furthermore, the figure of the fallen "white Spaniard" and the figures of Old and New World hybridity, the Moorish Spaniard and the Indian, compose together an allegory of fatality implying that the Spanish Empire and the offspring of its physical conquest of Native Americans are foredoomed as well by racial mixture.

The problem that faced the United States was the legitimation of conquest. Retelling the history of Spanish empire in the New World through a fabricated tableau of Spanish imperial history provided the opportunity to displace U.S. territorial ambitions and violent expansionist tactics, as well as Anglo-Americans' own fears and fantasies of miscegenation, back in time onto colonial encounter between Spaniards and Aztecs. The composition of the scene as a raised platform reached by stairs conveys the possibility of a further transformation. The suggested illusion for the viewer is that one may march up into the scene like the U.S. soldiers scaling the walls of Chapultepec. The fantasy conveyed by such an illusion is that conquest may become, in a vision of U.S. empire as anticonquest, a resolution of the overdetermined anarchy of this tableau of history.

ROMANCES OF ANGLO-AMERICAN IMPERIAL IDENTITY: SIMMS, HAWTHORNE, HOLMES

The mythic "white Spaniard" version of Spain did not die on the steps leading to the imagined antitype of empire in Leutze's *Storming of the Teocalli Temple*. The imbrication of the two versions of Spain as a united representational strategy became less pronounced, however, over the course of the nineteenth century. It was the Orientalized version of Spain that formed the constitutive contrast, both typological and narratival, in the formation of Anglo-American imperial identity. In what I am calling the romances of Anglo-American imperial identity, identity is constructed by retelling national and imperial history on the level of personal triangulations of desire and local territorial conflict. I take up three popular examples— William Gilmore Simms's *The Yemassee* (1835), Nathaniel Hawthorne's *The*

Scarlet Letter (1850), and Oliver Wendell Holmes's *Elsie Venner* (1861)— all by novelists who knew one another and were familiar with the work of writers such as Washington Irving more commonly associated with the "romance of Spain."[35] These allegorical fictions use the device of going back to some foundational moment in what is specifically marked as the "American" past in order to articulate a myth of origins by which Anglo-American empire is projected into the future as a foretold vision with the force of destiny.

Simms's *The Yemassee* (1835) weaves a tale about the war undertaken against the further encroachment of English settlement in South Carolina by the Yemassee and Creek nations (1715–17). Although historical accounts do not agree to what extent the Spanish governors in Florida assisted the Native Americans in this uprising against the English settlements, the plotting of Simms's novel implicates not only the Spanish governors of Florida but the king of Spain in the planning as well as the supplying of arms and mercenaries for the war. Simms's tale of Spanish empire and Indian nations taking revenge against the fledgling Southern English colonies is told through the frame of family drama and the marriage plot. Battle over the land of South Carolina is waged alongside internal agony between the chief of the Yemassee and his traitorous son Occonestoga (who ultimately pays with his life for dealing with the English). Interwoven with these battle fronts is the romantic conflict between the two Anglo heroes, Hugh Grayson and the governor palatine of South Carolina, Lord Craven (the pseudonymous Gabriel Harrison, who leads the English colonists in their defeat of the uprising), and the emissary of the Spanish Empire, an English buccaneer named Richard Chorley, who vie over the same Anglo woman, Bess Matthews.

Hawthorne's *The Scarlet Letter* (1850) retells the antinomian controversy (1636–38) among the New England Puritans of the Massachusetts Bay Colony as an adultery story of conflict between passion and law, the spirit and the letter. At the heart of the book is a troubled triangle of desire and revenge between two Anglo men, the minister Arthur Dimmesdale and the physician Roger Chillingworth, and the Anglo woman, Hester Prynne, who must wear the letter "A" on her breast. All are in some way marked not merely by the scarlet letter that implicates them all. Dimmesdale, Chillingworth, and Hester are figures of alien whiteness doomed by signs of blackness, which, in the case of Dimmesdale and Chillingworth, take the forms of Catholic ritual. Dimmesdale and Chillingworth are locked in what is represented as a sequestered, unholy association like that between a priest and his confessor that violates the sacred relationship between an individual and his god. This bond takes on the further characterization of the Spanish Inquisition at home with Chillingworth as the inquisitor leech who cannot exist without his victim-patient Dimmesdale.[36] Hester is semi-Orientalized, that is, represented as somewhat darkly Other in her features. Her name, Hester, resonates with that of the Old Testament heroine Esther. This suggestive Semitic characterization is reinforced by the descriptions of her "abundant" dark hair "with at once a shadow and a light" (192) and "deep black eyes" (61).

Spain figures in Hawthorne's text typologically and narratively as that which threatens the Massachusetts Bay Colony and prospectively Anglo-American empire spiritually and politically from within and from without as inquisitorial Catholicism or, more generally, heresy, as the Spanish Empire in the New and Old World, and as a utopian inversion of the laws of the New England experiment and, thus, potentially a counterexample and a leave-taking of that experiment. The antinomian controversy introduced the threat of political disorder, as well as potentially contagious doubt, which held out the possibility of undermining Puritan theocracy's claims to legitimacy. The Black Legend in Puritan discourse was used to type Catholicism (represented as pagan, anti-Christian, a blasphemous "solution" in the emphasis on works to the debate over spirit versus law) in the figure of the Spaniard as a visible devil, an inverted mirror image of the visible saint. Spanish empire, envisioned by Philip II as a single united Catholic realm, became the demonic obverse of the expansion of the Puritan city on a hill and that darkness against which the light and moral right of Puritan destiny might be rhetorically and politically formulated. The tropes of the Black Legend in Puritan discourse were also a primary means by which to shame, morally blacken, and alienate Puritan enemies within. Hawthorne's text draws heavily on this rhetoric of blackness, which internally defined Puritan theocracy, and combines these tropes of alien whiteness and moral blackness with the romanticism and racialization of the Orientalizing version of Spain in order to ambiguate his narration of the foundational past and the future of Anglo-American empire. The ship from the Spanish Main marks the presence of another America, another order within the Americas that offers Hester an escape.

Although the setting of the adultery story itself is the seventeenth-century colony, there are multiple temporalities to the novel. Like Simms's narrator, the narration of Hawthorne's text is situated in the present looking back at the past. This "present" narration irrupts at critical junctures into the historical drama. The book not only endeavors to encompass multiple times within its frame but also reverses the linear progress of time. The recent past including the other New England utopian experiment, that of the existentialists at Brook Farm, is evoked at the beginning of the book by the "Custom House" "introductory." The tale piece "Endicott and the Red Cross" printed after the conclusion goes further back in time than the adultery story, conjuring an allegorical tableau of the colony under its first governor.

Holmes's *Elsie Venner* (1861) is set closer in time to the temporal moment of its narration than either *The Scarlet Letter* or *The Yemassee*. Framed as the (omniscient) recollections of a professor of medicine, the novel takes up a medical case history rather than a war or a major community crisis.[37] However, childhood, heredity, and education in *Elsie Venner*, like the war between the Yemassee and the Anglo colonists in South Carolina and the antinomian controversy in the Massachusetts Bay Colony, are narrated as foundational pasts that govern the present and ultimately the future. The novel concerns itself principally with narrating an experience that tests the fitness of its protagonist, Bernard Langdon, who is presented as evidence of the existence and superiority of the "Brahmin caste of New England" (15). *Elsie Venner* takes its title from the name of the half-Spanish, half-Anglo protagonist, a young woman the mysterious circumstances of whose birth (her mother, it is finally revealed, was named Catalina and may have been bitten by a rattlesnake while she was pregnant) have corporeally marked Elsie and will doom not only her but any man with whom she might become physically entangled. Master Langdon or Mr. Bernard (as he is variously called) takes a leave from his medical studies in order to work for a year as a schoolteacher at a girls' finishing school, the Apollinean Institute, in the New England town of Rockland (the actual name of towns in Massachusetts, Connecticut, Rhode Island, and Maine) with its ominous Rattlesnake Ledge. At the Apollinean Institute he encounters Elsie, one of his students, who exerts the fascination of her "diamond eyes" upon him, enmeshing him in a dangerous triangle of jealousy with the contender for her interest, her cousin Dick Venner, also described as a "half-breed"—"the son of a South American trader and a lady of Buenos Ayres [*sic*] of Spanish descent" (137). Although Elsie provides the main obstacle to the potential remarriage of her father and to the progress of the hero Bernard Langdon, and it is her case that furnishes the subject of Langdon's eventual master's thesis, "Unresolved Nebulae in Vital Science" (424), it is the providential future of the racially and morally exemplary case of the "New England Brahmin" Bernard Langdon that is to be demonstrated by the narratival conflict with dark forces and by the constitutive contrast with figures of fatal mixture or hybridity.

The Yemassee, The Scarlet Letter, and *Elsie Venner* were all originally published with a subtitle classifying each work as a romance: Simms's novel as "a romance of Carolina," Hawthorne's novel as simply "a romance," and Holmes's novel as "a romance of destiny." The performative and seeming generic claims for the romance made by Simms in the introduction to *The Yemassee* and by Hawthorne in *The House of Seven Gables,* as well as in the "The Custom House" "introductory" to *The Scarlet Letter,* were used by post–World War II U.S. literary critics, most famously by Richard Chase, to argue that the romance is a distinctly "American" literary form.[38] However, it is not their forms that connect these romances to ideas of "Americanness." The romances of Simms, Hawthorne, and Holmes are neither formally identical nor are their forms essentially "American." Rather, I would argue, their "Americanness" or their "Anglo-Americanness" is not a quality but rather an effect of the representational practices of these novels, their rhetorical truth claims and disclaimers, and their construction and narratival mobilization of racial types, particularly "Spanish" types. Each of the novels' prefaces makes some kind of claim for the truthful nature of its material, whether historical, psychological, or medical. Furthermore, the romance of each tale is described as a quality of the novels' "real" referents rather than exclusively a function of their narrative fabrication. This is not merely a matter of creating room for license or getting the writer off the hook. The disclaimers of responsibility give the reader a sense of "independence." The illusion conveyed is that the readers of these romances are not led along by the tales or indoctrinated by ideology, but rather, are in the position to adjudicate for themselves the implications of the narratives and the destiny of their types.

In the preface to the second edition of *The Yemassee* (1854), Simms puts the responsibility on his material. The difference between the romance, which he claims as "American," and the English novel is, he writes, "one of material, even more than of fabrication."[39] This material, Simms contends, is that of "adventure" sought for "among the wild and wonderful" (xxx). Not only is the substance and the referent of the material claimed as "romance" but the "Americanness" of the Simms narrative is made over as found, not made:

> "The Yemassee" is proposed as an *American* romance. It is so styled as much of the material could have been furnished by no other country . . . The natural romance of our country has been my object and I have not dared beyond it. (Ibid.)

The phrase "so styled" points to the unavoidable, that the text constructs the nation in a particular, ideological way. However, the preface keeps this didactic function at bay by swerving immediately into the fiction that "our country" has already been so formed as simply to furnish what the text fabricates as the nation's "natural romance." The emphasis on "our country" also transforms into the national fiction the story's expansionist narrative and visionary ambitions.

Nation as empire is suggested in the form of a lament at the conclusion of the preface: "How much do we lose by our gains—how much do our acquisitions cost us!" (xxxi). The preface was added to the second edition, published after the Mexican-American War (1848). The massive territorial acquisitions made by the United States through the war raised the issue of slavery to an increasingly widespread pitch. The question was not only whether slavery would be extended to the new acquisitions, but whether not reestablishing slavery in the new territories would result in slave revolt in the Southern states. Simms's novel attempts to sentimentalize slavery in the Anglo colonies (against the negative example of the "real" slavery displaced onto the Spanish Americas) through the figure of Hector, the faithful black "servant" of the Anglo hero Gabriel Harrison. Hector's greatest fear is twofold: being made free, which he describes as abandonment, and being abducted and sold into slavery on the Spanish island of Cuba. Through the acceptance of the "superiority" of Gabriel Harrison on the part of the black slave Hector and the Anglo farmer's son, Hugh Grayson (who makes long speeches about how he will not abase himself by enslaving his will to any man),[40] the tale attempts to make the enslavement and forced labor of Africans into a gentle, uncoerced, and affectionate relation, and government into the right and necessary leadership by those whom, by nature rather than class, title, or force, are supposedly innately fit to rule. Forced enslavement and anarchy are transposed onto the other America represented by Spain and Spanish empire's representative, the lawless and brutal buccaneer pirate Chorley. The tale concludes with a vision of the black slaves fighting to uphold the Anglo colony against Native Americans and the encroachment of Spanish empire. The fiction, the text proclaims, was that

> [t]his was an ally upon which the Spaniards had largely counted. They had no idea of that gentler form of treatment which, with the Carolinians, won the affections of their serviles; and, knowing no other principle, in their own domestic government than that of fear, and assured the instability of any confidence built upon such a relationship between the ruler and the serf, they had miscalculated greatly when they addressed their bribes to the negroes, as well as to the Indians of Carolina. (378)

The concluding lament of the preface also suggests fears about racial mixture that the novel makes not only undesirable but narratively impossible. The lament does not so much dispel expansionist ambitions. Rather, it points to the terrors and desires around the expansion of the nation. During the Mexican-American War, Simms militantly championed the idea that only Anglo-Saxons or Anglo-Normans deserved to inherit the Americas. Shortly after the Mexican-American War, he declared: "Never Don or Savage . . . yet with the Saxon could endure!"[41] The anxiety that Simms's novel betrays and yet attempts to keep at bay is that U.S. empire would become something other than Anglo-American with the annexation of formerly Spanish territories such as northern Mexico, previously part of New Spain. Ultimately, Simms's *The Yemassee* takes up the Orientalist romance of Spain as an antitype against which to constitute the nation as Anglo-American empire, foreclosing any possibility of a romance with figures of Spain.

Despite its concluding lament, Simms's preface to *The Yemassee* is triumphal in tone. Its tone and its construction of romance as the modern answer to Greek and Roman imperial epic work to position Simms the writer as a kind of poet laureate or imperial epic seer. As the preface proclaims, "The modern Romance is the substitute which the people of the present day offer for the ancient epic" (xxix). In sharp tonal contrast, a lengthy, ambiguous, and ambivalent prefatory to *The Scarlet Letter,* "The Custom House," frames the adultery story of Hawthorne's novel. However contrary in tone, the negative apologetics of "The Custom House" nonetheless defends, as it constructs, a model of visionary expansion and empire for its writer as well as the nation. "The Custom House" is more than a *mise en abîme* of the book as a whole or an elaborate conceit. It is a defense accomplished through a self-castrating (beheading), quasi abdication of authority: the *Posthumous Papers of a Decapitated Surveyor* (52).

The book that has been written is set against the far better book about the present life of the customhouse that the narrator alleges that he has not penned (46). The truth claims of the book are represented as an obvious hoax: in the form of a relic (the scarlet letter) and the anointing ghost of Mr. Surveyor Pue. The narrator asserts that "the main facts" of the story about the origin of the embroidered scarlet letter "are authorized and authenticated by the document of Mr. Surveyor Pue" that the narrator protests are, along with the scarlet letter, in his possession and may be shown to those who desire a sight of them (42). At each turn, the narrator would seem to leave the question of belief and decision-making power to the reader by outrageous, comical claims to authority combined with abdications of the storyteller's authority over his own tale and its "facts."

"The Custom House" opens with the customary view of empire: the entry of people and goods from various parts of the globe into the borders of the nation regulated by government outposts and tolling stations like the customhouse in the port town of Salem, Massachusetts. The novel would seem to draw back from this prospect of the colonial trade with South America and Africa, the maritime commerce, and government regulation that have traditionally defined empire. The customhouse view is the book that the narrator professes he has not written. Instead, "The Custom House" constricts to the "neutral territory" of "our familiar room" (45) in which the narrator is still unable to write the romance that such a space should enable, and finally narrows to a desk defined only in terms of where it is not, that is, not in the customhouse. This narrated act of writing the text expands, however, in that this office is analogized to the heroic deeds of the General, the "stalwart soldier of the Niagara frontier"

(33) who fought in the Revolutionary War for independence, and to those who "go to dig gold in California" (48). The General, "on the very verge of a desperate and heroic enterprise," says, "I'll try, Sir!" (33). This scene is replayed when the narrator takes up his charge to write the tale of the scarlet letter with the declaration of "I will!" (43). Although the relation of the narrator to the General is articulated as one of difference, even opposition, in the very sentence that is to establish their distinctness the phrase "individuals unlike himself" is preceded by the qualifier "to be brought into habits of companionship," which suggests commonality (34). Likewise, though the narrator does not leave the enslavement of the customhouse and Uncle Sam's wages to prospect for gold in California, the narrator finds the relic of the scarlet letter with its traces of gold embroidery and agrees to the office of writing its tale, which promises, "[D]o this and the profit shall be all your own!" (43).

The independence that the preface makes a show of giving to the reader is a persistently invoked necessity for the text's creation as well as for the nation it prospects in another sense of that word, that it foresees. The text's authorization is structured upon what it is supposedly independent from: Uncle Sam's gold and bureaucracy. This gold, to which is attributed "a quality of enchantment like that of the Devil's wages" (48), is equated with enslavement as opposed to the ruggedness and independence of the Niagara and California frontiers, with their respective heroism and gold. Enslaving government and gold were often made into the distinguishing features of Spanish empire. "The Custom House" preface negatively contrasts the domain of Uncle Sam, the customhouse, with the restricted domain of the romance: imagination and sentiment. However, it is precisely imagination and sentiment that enable another kind of empire to transcend that of Uncle Sam and the customhouse. The text expands in and over time, covering past, present, and future. Although scenes of writing are constricted to that "neutral territory" of "our familiar room" and to the desk, the act of writing the tale about the scarlet letter takes the place of territorial expansion into far from neutral territory (e.g., battles against the British and French in the Revolutionary War and the War of 1812, expropriation of Native American lands, the annexation of California and the mass rush of Anglos to California with the Gold Rush of 1849). The empire of romance, the empire of the text that supersedes and yet depends on territorial conquest for its independence, enables

"The Custom House" preface to envision Anglo-American empire as an antiempire.

This visionary antiempire is one that expands while yet keeping its roots embedded in a local place, that retains its Puritan character even despite being a major commercial port in "contaminating" contact with all continents of the world. The naturalizing rhetoric of farming and plantation is used in "The Custom House" to limit who may be considered a "Salemite." In a complex, negatively toned, retrospective and perspectival gesture, the immigrant "from a foreign land" is displaced in favor of the "old settler" who from instinct "cling[s] to the spot where his successive generations have been imbedded" (22). The narrator's seeming negation of this "creeping," weed-like hold on a place expressed in the desire that his children "shall strike their roots into unaccustomed earth" (23) suggests, rather, a vision of the expansion of Salem to include other places by the transplantation of its future generations. This image of the narrator's progeny taking root like plants in unfamiliar, supposedly uninhabited soil transforms imperial conquest into a pastoral prospect of territorial expansion not as displacement and annihilation of other peoples but as freedom—the fiction of getting out of the purview of custom and the customhouse (22–23). However, with the concluding prospect of the town pump, this imperial, newfangled frontier is made over into the already accustomed and familiar and the narrator's office, his tale, into that which, from pump to English rosebush, will make this habitation of the soil flourish.

Turning to Holmes, the book the narrator of *Elsie Venner* does claim to have written but not published is an ethnology titled "Anglo-American Anthropology" (16). According to this undisclosed thesis on race, the "handsome face" of the novel's hero, Bernard Langdon, the exemplar of the "Brahmin caste of New England," puts him in "Section B of Class 1," or just under the first rank in a hierarchy of those designated as superior (ibid.). Langdon is the only character assessed by recourse to this study. The other Anglo figures and, most important, the figures of racial hybridity, the half-Anglo and half-Spanish cousins Dick and Elsie Venner, are deployed as evidence of an authority that underlies both the novel *Elsie Venner* and its dubious off-shoot, "Anglo-American Anthropology": "Through all the disguise of fiction a grave scientific doctrine may be detected lying beneath some of the delineations of character" (v).[42]

Although told from the perspective of a medical professor and based on a "scientific doctrine" that supplies the "machinery of his story," the novel is positioned by the preface not as a medical case study or a scientific proof but as a "romance" (v). Although the characterization and narrative deployment of racial types in the story endeavor to function as evidence of the "reality" of its racial typology, the operative fiction is that "the reader must judge for himself what is the value of various stories cited from old authors" (vi). Here the narrator Holmes speaks, like Hawthorne, as if he and his text have already passed into tradition and become a future part of the rhetorical machinery by which the nation as empire continues to constitute itself. As with *The Yemassee* and *The Scarlet Letter,* the preface to *Elsie Venner* performs as a disclaimer of authority and responsibility— "In calling this narrative a 'romance,' the Author wishes to make sure of being indulged in the common privileges of the poetic license" (v)— which adds precisely to the effect of seductive readerly independence. The narrator, furthermore, attempts to suspend the necessity for belief on the part of the reader:

> He [the author] has used this doctrine as part of the machinery of his story without pledging his absolute belief in it to the extent to which it is asserted or implied. It was adopted as a convenient medium of truth rather than as an accepted scientific conclusion. (Ibid.)

The story can work, this preface implies, whether one believes or not in this "grave scientific doctrine," that is, in theories of the existence of distinct races, a hierarchy of races, racial polygenesis, and hybridity as degeneration and/or fatality. The preface suggests that the rhetoric of science, medicine, physiognomy, and ethnology employed to fabricate the romance are a medium or formal conduit for "truth" rather than its basis. The preface makes an appeal to another kind of truth, that of common sense, experience, and sentiment:

> The Author must be permitted, however, to say here, in his personal character, and as responsible to the students of the human mind and body, that since this story has been in progress he has received the most startling confirmation of the possibility of the existence of a character like that which he had drawn as a purely imaginary conception in Elsie Venner. (vi)

Thus, it is crucial to the task of *Elsie Venner* that it be declared a "romance" in the sense of a tale of the imagination and that it also be plotted narratively as a romance in the sense of a love story of impossible and fatal liaisons versus providential ones. The preface of *Elsie Venner* makes a rhetorical move similar to that of *The Scarlet Letter* by suggesting that the realm or empire of the imagination may have more personal, experiential, commonsensical truth than that which can ultimately be proven by historical accuracy or science. In the case of Holmes's romance, this appeal to the imagination is put explicitly to the task of making pseudoscientific theories a truth of the heart. Racial stigmatization as sentimental truth becomes a moral.

In Holmes's later travel narrative *Our Hundred Days in Europe* (1887), "goodness" is associated with Anglo-Saxons as a "race." Although the word *race* does not occur explicitly in all the descriptions, it is clearly the operative category inasmuch as Holmes designates those Anglo-Saxons not simply by cultural characteristics, but by physical ones as well. Giving his first impressions of England and the English in *Our Hundred Days,* Holmes wrote:

> I trust that I am not finding everything *couleur de rose;* but I certainly do find the cheeks of children and young persons of such brilliant rosy hue as I do not remember that I have ever seen before. I am almost ready to think this and that child's face has been colored from a pink saucer. If the Saxon youth exposed for sale at Rome, in the days of Pope Gregory the Great, had complexions like these children, no wonder that the pontiff exclaimed, "Not *Angli,* but *angeli*!"[43]

The "Angli" (plural for Anglo) become, in this legend, *angeli* (Italian for angels), the highest order of beings in traditional Christian cosmogony. Holmes's novel *Elsie Venner* is a "romance of destiny" not for the Anglo-Saxon "race" but for what is constructed as its preordained successor, the "Anglo-American." The novel both assumes and fabricates an "Anglo-American" race defined not by place (e.g., born in the USA) but by genealogy, which is narratively and typologically structured to physically determine personal or individual fate and the nation's imperial future. Anglo-American empire is projected by this text, as with Simms and Hawthorne, as anticonquest, which in the case of *Elsie Venner* takes the

form of an ascendancy of intellect in which empire is not created by
territorial appropriation and battle. Rather, by the consumption of texts,
by education, study, and scholarship—in which the novel endeavors to
demonstrate that Anglos, particularly those of the "Brahmin caste of New
England," naturally excel—the world is "tamed." At the beginning of the
novel, the narrator/professor maintains that, although he is unable to
determine yet "positively" whether Bernard Langdon is one of this sort,

> [t]here are horse-tamers, born so, as we all know; there are women-tamers
> who bewitch the sex as the pied piper bedevilled the children of Hamelin;
> and there are world-tamers, who can make any community, even a Yankee
> one, get down and let them jump up on its back as easily as Mr. Rarey
> saddled Cruiser. (18–19)

The novel constricts the world to New England while expanding Anglo-
American domination everywhere within its encompassing narrative.
Through the machinery of the novel, the world becomes a "Yankee community." Ultimately, the characters of racial mixture and otherness are
either banished or die. Elsie expires from a kind of internal congenital
combustion, her cousin Dick is sent back to South America, and Elsie's
loving and faithful black governess Sophy is crushed by a giant boulder
from Rattlesnake Ledge, the last remnant of Native American possession
of Rockland. The novel completes the enclosing and circular logic of its
initial prediction with two Anglo couplings, the second marriage of Elsie's
father, this time to the Anglo schoolteacher Helen Darley, and the engagement of Bernard Langdon to Letitia Forrester, "daughter of the great
banking firm . . . Bilyuns Brothers and Forrester" (427). This story of
the Anglo-American empire of letters, of empire as anticonquest, independence, and survival, reproduces itself as the professor/narrator is succeeded by Bernard Langdon, whose "family pride would not let him be
dependent" (19; my emphasis) and who escapes from his fascination with
Elsie and his attempted ambush by Dick in order, finally, to take up his
narratively and typologically predestined position as a professor of medicine at an "ancient and distinguished institution"—a thinly disguised reference to Harvard (427).

Each of these novels deploys the "romance of Spain" in order to produce
by contrast Anglo-American-ness as type and trope, which is personal and

romantic on the level of the story as well as imperial and prophetic in its
forecasting logic. Although each of the novels is, in terms of location, a
New World story, Spanish empire in the Americas figures in these stories
in the form of characters with Black Legend Old World associations,
as well as most prominently Orientalized features of both New and Old
World, likened as these figures are to Moors, Gypsies, and/or Indians.
Rather than an imbrication of the two versions, Spain as a figure of alien
whiteness and moral blackness is washed up and washed out in the voyage
over the seas, degenerating into a pirate. It is the Orientalized version that
is used as the defining material for these romances of Anglo-American
imperial identity. The Spaniard is a figure of racial mixture, characterized
as closely associated with or like Native Americans and blacks, and oriented as much toward South America and the Caribbean as to peninsular
Spain, which in these tales is made fatally "romantic" by Moorish and
Gypsy features.

The friend of the Spanish governors of Florida and representative of
the Spanish crown, Chorley, in Simms's *The Yemassee,* is "the bucanier and
Spanish emissary, for in those times and in that region, the two characters were not always unlike" (282).[44] Although readers later learn that the
pirate-captain was born in England and even, in his young and delinquent
days, knew Anglo heroine Bess Matthews's father, the minister missionary,
Chorley is described as so like a Spaniard that he, essentially, through his
actions, becomes one. Explaining his business to the minister, Chorley
states, Carwin-like, "I drive a good business there [in Florida] with the
Spaniard. I'm rather one myself now, and carry his flag" (113). In turn,
Spanish empire becomes one of piracy, double-dealing, and violence. The
Anglo hero Gabriel Harrison declares aphoristically, "To be a pirate and a
Spaniard are not such distinct matters" (106).

Figures of the Native American or Indian are ennobled insofar as these
characteristics are appropriated to the Anglo characters and doomed as
treacherous, racially and politically inferior, and bloodthirsty in their association with figures of the Spaniard and Spanish empire. The Anglo hero
Gabriel Harrison arrogates to himself what is represented as the best combination of qualities from the English, the "American," and the Native
American, as exhibited in his dress combining the English cavalier (a
vest in the "purest white" showing "the taste of the wearer") with what is
deemed most natural to and appropriate to the "American forests," buskins

"like those worn by the Indians" (27). The Yemassee nation is represented as "something of a republic" (86) and thus like, but inferior to, the supposedly true republic of Anglo South Carolina. In contrast, the Spanish Empire symbolized by the "Spanish totem" on the "Belt of Wampum" by which the Yemassee and other nations made their war pact with the Spanish government of California against the Anglo colony is positioned "directly below the simpler ensign of the Yemassee" (62). The Spanish Empire is signified by "the high turrets, and the wide towers of its castellated dominion, frowning in gold" (ibid.). Spanish empire and the Yemassee nation are similar in that neither is afforded the transparency of the Anglos; both may be reduced to what is represented as a primitive signifying system, that of hieroglyphs. However, whereas Chorley sees in the "Spanish totem" "greatness and magnificence" and "gorgeous embodiments and vaster associations of human agency and power," the Yemassee chiefs become the vehicle by which the hieroglyph of Spanish empire signifies ridiculous, "dilating" pomp: "a lodge so vast and cheerless in its aspect, seemed rather an absurdity than anything else" (62–63). Spanish empire by its own sign system is read against itself as a tyranny ("castellated dominion") of fear and misery ("frowning" and "cheerless"). Anglo-American empire, by implication, becomes an antiempire, a "republic" of smiles and cheer.

Further damningly, Spanish empire in the figure of Chorley takes on all those negative stereotypes by which the Indian becomes, in the novel, more savage than noble. Chorley wields a hatchet (as a sign of his bellicose nature) and is well practiced in the arts of bribery and "Indian giving." This savage representative of the Spaniard is a buccaneer from the West Indies and is further oriented and Orientalized by his characterization as not only "Indian" but Turk. Chorley is introduced to the reader wearing "pantaloons, free, like the Turkish" (21). However, it is more than sartorial affinity that makes the savage, piratical Spaniard a Turk. The governor palatine of South Carolina, Lord Craven (aka Gabriel Harrison) interrupting a fight between Chorley and the Indian chief Sanutee demands to know Chorley's name and his origin. Chorley refuses and Harrison retorts, "For me you shall be Hercules or Nebuchadnezzar—you shall be Turk, or Ishmaelite, or the devil—*it matters not whence a man comes when it is easily seen whither he will go*" (29; my emphasis). In the end, history is foretold by typology while type is determined by forecasted conclusion. In this imperial fiction, though Chorley, and hence Spanish empire, may be arrogant and formidably strong with a history of conquest like the labors of Hercules and the Babylonian king's destruction of Jerusalem, they will, like the Turks, the Muslim descendants of Ishmael (son of Abraham and Hagar exiled into the desert), and devils, eventually be cast out, if not exterminated.

The narrative of *The Yemassee* bears out the narrative logic of this typology. All those men fighting under the Spanish crown perish. The only figures of Otherness who survive are the black slave Hector and the Native American woman Matiwan (wife of Sanutee and mother of Occonestoga), who both risk their lives (and, in the case of Matiwan, she betrays her nation) to save the governor palatine of South Carolina. This tale of war, death, and conquest depends on imagination and sentiment to transform this Anglo-American empire of force into one of affection. Hector, Matiwan, Hugh Grayson, and Bess Matthews all submit to the Anglo hero, Lord Craven, not through fear or force, but voluntarily out of what is represented as love. The defeat of the Native Americans becomes rather a regrettably necessary consequence of what is represented as their yet more lamentable fall to the seduction of the enslaving Spanish empire. This is played out in negotiations between Chorley and the Yemassee chiefs, and then again closer to "home" in Chorley's efforts to beguile Bess Matthews with his Moorish gold:

> Having said enough, as he thought, fairly and fully to dazzle the imagination of the girl—and, secure now of a favourable estimate of himself, he drew from his bosom a little casket, containing a rich gold chain of Moorish filigree work, arabesque wrought, and probably a spoil of Grenada, and pressed it on her acceptance. Her quick and modest, but firm rejection of the proffered gift, compelled the open expression of his astonishment. (110)

The chain is linked to the English-controlled island of Grenada in the West Indies, the "gold and jewels" of which Chorley speaks to Bess, attempting to charm her with tales about the "ease of their attainment" (ibid.). The arabesque pattern of what is termed its "Moorish filigree work" associatively connects Grenada to Granada and the site of the defeat of the Moors in southern Spain. The casket perhaps foreshadows their fate, as well as that of Spanish empire. Gold and specifically gold chains are what signify Chorley's corruption and captivation to Spanish empire:

He [Chorley] wore a blue jacket, studded thickly with buttons that . . .
formed so many pendent knobs of solid gold; and there was not a little
ostentation in the thick and repeated folds of the Spanish chain, made of
the same rich material, which encircled his neck. (21)

Spanish empire circulates in this text as Spanish gold that ensnares and
dooms those who put on its chains. In Chorley's rhetorical effort to court
Bess, Spanish empire becomes gold chains that lock and enslave, and
though "girls of Spain" are described as racially inferior to Bess of the
"whitest" neck, the text suggests that these chains stain those who wear
them:

The chain [of Moorish filigree work] is not unbecoming for the neck,
though that be indeed the whitest. Now, the girls of Spain, with skin nothing to be compared with yours, they wear such necklaces as thick as grape
vines . . . The chain is rich, and worth a deal of money. Let me lock it now
about your neck. You will look like a queen in it—a queen of all the Indies
could not look more so. (110)

Spanish empire as chains of gold blackens, morally and racially, those who
are captivated by it. Chorley, the Indianized, Orientalized, piratical Spaniard, becomes also the Moor, as in Shakespeare's *Othello,* which the novel
enlists. Although Chorley exhorts Bess, "Bessy did not, it is true, incline
the ear after the manner of Desdemona to her Blackamoor" (ibid.). With
the entrance of Gabriel Harrison upon this scene, the link of Spanish
empire, Spanish gold, tyranny, looting as opposed to planting, idolatry,
slavery, and blackness is solidified. Harrison demands of Chorley:

Have you no . . . highly wrought gem and ornament—in the shape of cross
and chain, which a sharp master of trade may have picked up, lying at watch
snugly among the little islands of the gulf? . . . I would buy such a jewel—
a rich chain, or the cross which the Spaniard worships. (123)

Chorley refuses and Harrison reveals that the black slave Hector is being
held captive on Chorley's ship so that he may be sold into what is represented as forced slavery displaced onto the Spanish-controlled island of
Cuba, rather than affection attributed, by contrast, to an Anglo-America.

The Yemassee narratively consolidates Anglo-American empire through victory and process of elimination set in motion and justified by the affections of the romance plot. This engineered vision of empire as a state of purity is effected by typological contrast with Spanish empire as hybridity and mixture. The representative of Spain, Chorley, though once English, has become Spanish and is thus at once Indian, Turk, and Moor. It is this mixture that ultimately dooms the Spaniard. The Spanish ship, Chorley's vessel, is a sign of dangerous mixture:

> Why, sir, she's neither one thing nor another in look, but a mixture of all. Now, when that's the case in the look of a vessel, it's a sign that the crew is a mixture, and that there is no one person regulating. (106)

Mixture signifies not only lack of leadership but anarchy, a state that is doomed from within. Thus, by this trope of Spanish empire as fatal hybridity, Anglo-American empire becomes not conquest but inevitability.

It has become *doxa* to argue that the letter of Hawthorne's *The Scarlet Letter* "has not done its office." This is partly because the narrator of *The Scarlet Letter* asserts that the letter has not done its office and critics have tended to bow to this assertion, like so many other assertions made by Hawthorne's ultimately coercive narrators. Furthermore, the letter has not done its office because it has more than one to do. The letter "A" prods the reader in a multipronged fashion. Numerous readers and scholars have remarked on the difficulty of assigning one fixed referent to the letter as in A = adultery or A = America. The "A" may correspond to both these concepts and many others in an apparently endless list in which the items often directly contradict one another or would seem to, as in the case, for example, of "angel" and "adulteress." Ironically, such contradictions and equivocations have led readers and critics to a consensus about *The Scarlet Letter* that they have not reached about *The Yemassee* and *Elsie Venner*. Or rather, *The Scarlet Letter* has become famous for one quality commonly attributed to it both as novel and "letter"—its ambiguity, its ability to signify both ways at once and actually create a magic circle from which it seems impossible to escape and which distinguishes its rhetoric from ambivalence that would merely seesaw back and forth between two possibilities.

Ambiguity has long been misunderstood as "anything goes" or as open-endedness. Of the many critics who have fastened on ambiguity as the hallmark of Hawthorne's *The Scarlet Letter,* Sacvan Bercovitch cautions against equating ambiguity with open-endedness, particularly in this novel:

> Hawthorne's meanings may be endless, but they are not open-ended. On the contrary, they are designed to create a specific set of anticipations, to shape our understanding of what follows in some definite way.[45]

Bercovitch explains that *The Scarlet Letter* combines ambiguity or what he terms interpretive process with purpose or telos, with a working toward a definite end or outcome: "Hawthorne's fusion of process and telos transmutes opposition into complementarity."[46] He harnesses this insight to an exploration of why Hester Prynne, the supposed rebel and nonconformist, returns to the site of her indictment as an adulteress when she had the opportunity to leave for good. I would like to follow Bercovitch's lead on the double office of ambiguity, but, for my purposes, to shift the emphasis and underscore its involvement in teleology as typology and typology as historical destiny. If ambiguity complements telos and vice versa, it does so as apologetics, a negative apologetics of empire in which the "A" performs the office of double sign, an AA, if you will, that homogenizes, whitewashes, and excludes. Despite the text's moments of embracing diversity or what is marked as Other within its purview, the tricky double A's effect, if not its a priori referent, is the construction of the future of the nation, U.S. empire, as Anglo-American.

From the opening chapter, "The Market Place," through "The New England Holiday," to the conclusion, alternatives to Puritan law, to the "settlement" of the Massachusetts Bay Colony, to the practices and ways of seeing of its theocracy are introduced, typologically doomed as savage, heathen, Papist, Indian, Spanish, and/or black, and then banished from the enclosure of the tale. Although Hester's return and voluntary reassumption of the scarlet letter give the illusion at the conclusion of the story that the New England colony is constituted by free will, there is, within the frame of the novel, no other choice figured as "real" or tenable. Although Hester had come from England and vanished with Pearl from the colony upon Dimmesdale's revelation and death, "real life" is equated with New England and the rest of the world recedes into a nothingness marked merely as "that unknown region where Pearl had found a home" (244). The only descriptions of another place beyond the borders of the

New England settlement come in the form of Hester's visions as she stands displayed on the scaffold in the marketplace: her "native village in Old England," "her paternal home; a decayed house of gray stone," and the architecture of a "Continental city, where a new life had awaited her" (65). The possibility of going there is foreclosed by their very descriptions. These places are not simply of the past ("native," "home," "had awaited") but are disappearing or "decaying." Furthermore, these visions are predicated as insubstantial and unreal "phantasmagoric forms" (ibid.). In the "Minister in a Maze" chapter, the Old World is introduced not as a place for a new life, but only as a place to hide. Habitable (as opposed to "wild") "America" is reduced to the "European" settlements of New England—no Spanish America is described in this text—and the Massachusetts Bay Colony as "America" would seem to extend across the globe, making it necessary to "conceal" in order to live:

> It had been determined between them that the Old World, with its crowds and cities, offered them a more eligible shelter and concealment than the wilds of New England, or all America, with its alternatives of an Indian wigwam or the few settlements of Europeans, scattered thinly along the seaboard. (202)

There are signs of rival Americas, as well as of a potential link to the Old World—Indians and the "Indian wilderness" and Orientalized pirates of the "Spanish Commerce" and the "Spanish Main." These potential other places are remotely signified by their figural representatives but remain "wild," lawless, undescribed, and implicitly unrealizable within the novel's domain. The ship from the Spanish Main is the one vehicle out of the Massachusetts Bay Colony and yet, within the frame of the novel, there would seem to be nowhere to go. The Spanish Main historically denoted either the mainland of the Spanish-controlled "America" adjacent to the Caribbean and between the Orinoco River and the Isthmus of Panama or to the Caribbean Sea. In *The Scarlet Letter*, the Spanish Main, and hence the Spanish Empire, figures not as landed empire, but is rather put out to sea:

> [I]t so happened that a ship lay in the harbor; one of those questionable cruisers, frequent at that day, which, without being absolutely outlaws of

the deep, yet roamed over its surface with a remarkable irresponsibility of character. This vessel had recently arrived from the Spanish Main, and within three days' time would sail for Bristol. (203)

Furthermore, this landless Spanish Empire is also lawless. Thus, even the vehicle from the Spanish Main that might lead out of "The Minster's Maze" and the world as New England colony altogether is "questionable" and characterized by "irresponsibility."

Although it is difficult to deny that *The Scarlet Letter* shrinks the world to the Massachusetts Bay Colony and expands the reach of Puritan theocracy even to the "Old World," in the wake of arguments by critics such as Werner Sollers and Sacvan Bercovitch it has become common to emphasize that the novel's imagined community is diverse, demanding assent, not homogenization. Thus, I would like to focus the problem of the "character" of the text's imperial vision on the chapters centering on Election Day, as these are the scenes that imagine New England as an assembled community and feature figures marked as Other among the convocation. In addition to Hester of the "antinomian" views, who "had in her nature a rich, voluptuous Oriental characteristic" (87) and whose letter created its own "magic circle" around her and Mistress Hibbins the witch, the congregation is envisioned to include "a party of Indians" and pirates of the "Spanish Commerce," "the crew of the vessel from the Spanish Main":

A party of Indians—in their savage finery of curiously embroidered deerskin robes, wampum belts, red and ochre, and feathers, and armed with the bow and arrow and stone-headed spear—stood apart with countenances of inflexible gravity, beyond what even the Puritan aspect could attain. Nor, wild as were these painted barbarians, were they the wildest feature of the scene. This distinction could more justly be claimed by some mariners—a part of the crew of the vessel from the Spanish Main—who had come ashore to see the humors of Election Day. They were rough-looking desperadoes with sun-blackened faces and an immensity of beard; their wide, short trousers were confined about the waist by belts, often clasped with a rough plate of gold, and sustaining always a long knife, and, in some instances, a sword. From beneath their broad-brimmed hats of palm-leaf gleamed eyes which, even in good nature and merriment, had a kind of animal ferocity. (218)

The Indians and the crew of the vessel recently arrived from the Spanish Main are associated with wildness and savagery in the form of animality. The Indians are clad in "savage finery" of "deer-skin robes" and "feathers"; the crew have eyes that gleam "with a kind of animal ferocity." Both the Indians and the crew carry weapons that even in the seventeenth century might have been considered "primitive" or backward. The Indians are armed "with the bow and arrow and stone-headed spear"; the crew, with long knives and the proverbial sword. Both the Indians and the crew from the vessel from the Spanish Main are represented as morally and physically blackened. The crew are typed as "desperadoes with sun-blackened faces"; the Indians have "snakelike black eyes" (230). Furthermore, both the Indians and the crew are made to embody the extremes of temperament or attitude. The Indians have "countenances of inflexible gravity" that rival those of the Puritans; the crew are "rough-looking desperadoes" who even in their merriment look ferocious.

The members of the crew are not assigned a nationality or a geographic point of origin besides that of the Spanish Main. Their physical and moral characterization draws on both versions of Spain, emphasizing, however, physical blackness as sign of lawlessness. They also possess, on their belts, the precious commodity that emblematized Spanish empire in the New World—gold, hence the phrase "Spanish gold." Furthermore, a little later on, they are represented as guilty of "depredations of the Spanish commerce," a phrase that suggests that all "Spanish commerce" is piracy (219).

Although the Indians and the crew are introduced together, they represent contrasting degrees of alterity and danger. The transition from the Indians to the figures of the Spanish Main is one of gradation or degradation: "Nor, wild as were these painted barbarians [the Indians], were they the wildest feature of the scene." The pirates are the "wildest feature." If "Indian" in *The Scarlet Letter* connotes those who are pagan, those who are idle or vagrant, those who are bellicose, those who may have taught Roger Chillingworth how to make poisons with herbs, and those who are by no means trustworthy, then the crew of the vessel recently arrived from the Spanish Main are displayed as more savage than the "Indian":

They transgressed, without fear or scruple, the rules of behavior that were binding on all others; smoking tobacco under the beadle's very nose,

although each whiff would have cost a townsman a shilling; and quaffing,
at their pleasure, draughts of wine or aquavitae from pocket flasks, which
they freely tendered to the gaping crowd around them. It remarkably characterized the incomplete morality of the age, rigid as we call it, that a license
was allowed the seafaring class, not merely for their freaks on shore, but for
far more desperate deeds on their proper element. The sailor of that day
would go near to be arraigned as a pirate in our own. There could be little
doubt, for instance, that this very ship's crew, though no unfavorable specimens of the nautical brotherhood, had been guilty, as we should phrase it,
of depredations of the Spanish commerce such as would have perilled all
their necks in a modern court of justice. (218–19)

The crew of the vessel recently arrived from the Spanish Main are the
ultimate antinomians. They are not governed by any laws—certainly not
by those of the Puritan community, nor even by the supposed "laws of
nature" to which the Indians seem to be bound in small ways. After all,
the Indians are represented as standing apart from the Puritans. They
seem to be sensible of some kind of unspoken law that they should not
mingle with the "civilized." The crew, on the other hand, transgress; if
the law is composed of boundaries, they cross them all because they are
constructed as without law. The crew, and by implication Spanish empire,
signify an ultimate form of lawlessness, an existence without foundation
outside the "pale" of the Puritan social order.

Those who have commerce with the crew or the captain of the ship
from the Spanish Main are threatened by a blackening by association.
Dimmesdale faces a number of temptations on his return home from the
forest where he planned his escape with Hester. Luring him to transgress
is "one of the ship's crew from the Spanish Main," described as a "tarry
blackguard." Again, moral blackness or criminality (being a "blackguard")
is made into an outward, physical covering ("tarry-ness"). Dimmesdale
"longed, at least, to shake hands with this tarry blackguard" (207–8); however, the danger is that this moral and physical tar might rub off and stick.
Dimmesdale, of course, refrains. Yet, what is interesting is that the mere
presence of this pirate represents a "crisis" (220).

Chillingworth, who makes his first appearance in the community
dressed in part like an "Indian" and accompanied by one, is also shown to
know the captain of the ship from the Spanish Main. The captain tells

Hester that Chillingworth will travel with her and Dimmesdale and that, therefore, "our only danger will be from drug or pill; more by token, as there is a lot of apothecary's stuff aboard, which I traded for with a Spanish vessel" (ibid.). Chillingworth and the "stuff" from a "Spanish vessel" are figured as the only dangers. In the captain's next message to Hester, Chillingworth becomes a "black-a-visaged hump-shouldered old doctor" (229). Although "the generation next to the early emigrants, wore the blackest shade of Puritanism, and so darkened the national visage with it, that all the subsequent years have not sufficed to clear it up" (218), to become *black* in this text is to have commerce with things Spanish or to become like them by leaving the enclosure of the law. Those who submit in either mind or body to the Puritan theocracy are drained of their signs of "Otherness." Hester, who near the beginning of her penance (long before the letter has accomplished even part of its office) is described as having "in her nature a rich, voluptuous Oriental characteristic" (87), becomes by the conclusion one with a face of "marble quietude" (213). Dimmesdale goes from being called a priest to being reverentially invoked as minister once he has prophesied the great destiny of U.S. empire and submits to the law of the letter. As Dimmesdale makes his way to the scaffold, he is marked as "pale" (234). Mounting the scaffold and revealing his chest, he demonstrates that to submit to the letter is not to "blacken your fate" (235) as the "black-a-visaged" Chillingworth warns. The letter, the "portent," the tale has, "done its office" (241). All signs of wildness, antinomianism, blackness are banished from the body politic after the revelation and Dimmesdale's prophecy. That imperial vision is articulated as "a high and glorious destiny for the newly gathered people of the Lord" (232) and takes the form of plantation—"the New England they were planting in the wilderness"—as opposed to the gold associated with Spanish empire as illegitimate piracy. A large pumpkin had sprung up in the governor's garden directly beneath the window "as if to warn the Governor that this great lump of vegetable gold was as rich an ornament as the New England earth would offer him" (107). This vision of New England and U.S. empire as a garden with alchemical vegetable gold (the "true" gold) that is made, not stolen, is in strategic contrast with the gold metal that distinguishes the crew from the Spanish Main with their "rough plates of gold" and the captain who is set apart by the "gold lace on his hat, which was also encircled by a gold chain" (219). This motif of different kinds of gold appropriates the goods of Spanish empire to that of the United States, while converting its value into a fiction of anticonquest, empire as planting and sowing or, in the case of Hester's embroidery, sewing.

A strange, Orientalist triad of signs runs from Simms through Hawthorne to Holmes, that of Spanish gold, snakes or coils, and blood. In Simms's novel the Anglo heroine Bess Matthews who almost ended up ensnared by Chorley's chain of Moorish filigree and Spanish gold is saved from the "fatal power of fascination" (155) of a rattlesnake. The Yemassee chief Occonestoga, who killed the snake, tells Harrison not to worry as "[t]he blood is good in her heart" (160). In *The Scarlet Letter,* Hester's daughter Pearl runs into the group of mariners, "the swarthy-cheeked wild men of the ocean, as the Indians were of the land" (229). The captain of the ship is enchanted with Pearl and tries to kiss her. Unable to catch her, he instead

> took from his hat the gold chain that was twisted about it, and threw it to the child. Pearl immediately twined it around her neck and waist with such happy skill that, once seen there, it became a part of her, and it was difficult to imagine her without it. (Ibid.)

Pearl is thus the one character to actually exchange with the representatives of Spanish empire. Putting on the gold chain, the sign of Spanish commerce, she not only becomes like them but the description also suggests that the wildness and lawlessness associated with the crew from the Spanish Main were already part of her. Pearl is a figure of alterity as the offspring of adultery, but even more because of her unknown and questionable paternity. Throughout the text there is speculation that she is a hybrid child produced by a union between Hester and the "Black Man." Although the "Black Man" represents the devil in the text, moral blackness becomes physical blackness for those who do not, in the end, submit to the letter. Furthermore, anxieties about mixture or miscegenation if not with Africans, then with the Indians, Catholics, and Spanish pirates who represent heathen lawlessness and a moral blackening that becomes a physical, racial stigmatization, center on Pearl. Chillingworth named her as his heir, thus transforming Pearl into "the richest heiress of her day in the New World" (243). The text concludes with the suggestion that because of this change in economic status, had she stayed, she "might have mingled her wild blood with the lineage of the devoutest Puritan among them all" (ibid.). However, after twining the gold chain around her body and appearing on the scaffold, Pearl disappears from the enclosure of the tale never to return. Her "wild blood" does not "mingle" with that of the body politic. The effect of the tale is, thus, not only "Anglo-Americanness" but a fiction of purity in the discourse of blood.

In Holmes's novel, the character of mixed Anglo and Spanish ancestry, Elsie Venner, is the rattlesnake, and her blood is represented as tainted. Elsie's body and those of the other principal characters are minutely represented. Physical description plays an especially important role in this romance as it is the body that is the product of biological heritage and that determines not only individual fate within the narrative but, moreover, the destiny of the body politic, the social order as a whole. Accounts of the features of the main characters are more than introductory descriptive passages used for the purposes of initial characterization. The narrator's representation is only one of the many views, especially of the bodies of Elsie and Dick Venner. The various discussions about the meaning of the appearances of these two young "half-breeds" is the main action of the narrative. The primary social activity of the "romance" is the different attempts to determine the fate of Dick and, especially, Elsie from analysis of their appearance. The novel uses the interpretations and impassioned reactions and discussions of a cast of Anglo characters—the narrator doctor, a judge, another medical doctor, the hero Bernard Langdon, the Reverend Doctor Honeywood descended from a long line of Puritans, the schoolteacher Helen Darley, the Reverend Chauncy Fairweather of a "liberal" Protestant church—as well as those of Elsie's faithful black nurse, "Old Sophy," in order to reconstruct through emotional drama the pseudosciences of phrenology and ethnology as home and heart(h) truths born out of the personal experiences of the characters. These characters, particularly the professionals, dispute between themselves in dialectical arguments setting science against religion, Puritan theology against "liberal" Protestantism, original sin against grace, and heredity against salvation. Each debate is a congenial one ending in a synthesis of views that enlists Puritan theology in order to biologize sin.

The primary anxiety of the novel centers on the supposedly higher form of whiteness, Anglo-Americanness and the "Brahmin caste of New England," it constructs. The "white satiny skin" (37) of its Anglo-American,

New England Brahmin caste hero Bernard Langdon is produced as imperiled, as promising much but requiring protection. The two characters of Spanish descent, Elsie and Dick Venner, narratively and typologically represent Anglo-Americanness contaminated by Spanish empire of Old World and New. As Spanish empire that has insinuated itself into the New England enclave of Rockland, Elsie and Dick represent internal hazards to the hero and to the U.S. body politic. Dick arrives in Rockland from South America seeking to marry Elsie, but is also described as already there:

> This boy [Dick] had passed several of his early years at the Dudley mansion, the playmate of Elsie, being her cousin, two or three years older than herself, the son of Captain Richard Venner, a South American trader, who, as he changed his residence often, was glad to leave the boy in his brother's charge. The Captain's wife, this boy's mother, was a lady of Buenos Ayres, of Spanish descent, and had died while the child was in his cradle. These two motherless children were as strange a pair as one roof could well cover. Both handsome, wild, impetuous, unmanageable, they played and fought together like two young leopards, beautiful, but dangerous, their lawless instincts showing through all their graceful movements. The boy was little else than a young Gaucho when he first came to Rockland; for he had learned to ride almost as soon as to walk . . . An ancestry of wild riders naturally enough bequeaths also those other tendencies which we see in the Tartars, the Cossacks, and our own Indian Centaurs. (137–38)

Like the figures of Spain in the romances by Simms and Hawthorne, Dick and Elsie represent lawlessness. However, Holmes's novel takes the Orientalizing version of Spain, especially the association of Spain with the "Indians" of East and West, and transforms this trope of danger firmly and explicitly into biological heritage (passed on from mother to children). The mythologized past becomes medical and psychological case history making the undesirable characteristics—impetuousness, lawlessness, reckless horsemanship—of legend into irreversible congenital defects. This transformation marks a shift in nineteenth-century U.S. imperial discourse. This change is seen most clearly in the contrast between the line about "wild riders . . . the Tartars, the Cossacks, and our own Indian Centaurs" from Holmes's *Elsie Venner* and a passage from Washington Irving's

Astoria (1836) in which Irving describes the supposed effect the Spaniards had on certain Native American nations with whom they came in contact:

> The Spaniards changed the whole character and habits of the Indians when they brought the horse among them. In Chili, Tucuman, and other parts, it has converted them, we are told, into Tartar-like tribes.[47]

The difference between the passage from Irving's book written in the 1830s and Holmes's book published in 1861 is the emphasis, in the latter, on biological essence as causality. Through the trope of providing the reader with a scientific, rational explanation for Dick's wild riding, Holmes used the words "ancestry [that] bequeaths . . . tendencies"—that is, in contemporary language, genetic inheritance—to construct a supposedly "essential" similarity between Spaniards and Indians, that is, their inextricability from horses. Significantly, Holmes referred to the mythological half-man half-horse, the "Centaur" (described as a wild beast by Homer and traditionally associated with brutal, drunken, and lecherous behavior), to cloak his pseudoscientific, racist theories in a myth of origins that works to dehistoricize and, consequently, to naturalize them. Unlike Holmes's explanation, that of Irving rests, at least in part, on a notion of historical change—the Spaniards introduced horses to the Native Americans and they thus formed new habits. Although both texts serve to produce Spanish empire in the New World and Native American nations as an allied threat, the difference in structure and language between them marks a historical shift in consciousness.

Dick, who like Elsie has a mixed heritage (part Spanish, part New England), is represented as a person torn by "a double consciousness":

> On his New England side he was cunning and calculating, always cautious, measuring his distance before he risked his stroke . . . But he was liable to intercurrent fits of jealousy and rage, such as the light-hued races are hardly capable of conceiving—blinding paroxysms of passion, which for the time overmastered him. (315)

The explanation offered for the jealousy, rage, and uncontrolled passion is Dick's "Spanish descent"—his Spanish "blood," which elsewhere is referred to as his "Southern blood":

His Southern blood was getting impatient. There was enough of the New-Englander about him to make him calculate his chances before he struck; but his plans were liable to be defeated at any moment by a passionate impulse such as the dark-hued races of Southern Europe and their descendants are liable to. (299)

This Punch-and-Judy show animation of the fiction of two distinct strains of blood, Spanish and New England, at war with one another in Dick's consciousness is made to color his body. Dick is described as that "olive-complexioned young man" (258) and by the judge as having a face "indictable at common law" (161). Furthermore, although Dick's mother is described as a "blue blood," the implication is that so-called Spanish blood is never pure:

> [H]is father, who, though he had allied himself with the daughter of an alien race, had yet chosen one with the real azure blood in her veins, as proud as if she had Castile and Aragon for her dower, and the Cid for her grandpa. (180–81)

Through the figures of Dick's mother, the "lady from Buenos Ayres," and Dick himself the text's own racism and Anglo culture's own prejudices, caste system, disgusts, and antipathies find a convenient site of displacement in those of Spain and Spanish America. It is Dick Venner, the "olive-complexioned young man," who frankly declares that he prefers his cousin to the women he encounters in Latin America because of her "race":

> He was tired of worshipping or tyrannizing over the bistred or umbered beauties of mingled blood among whom he had been living. Even that piquant exhibition which the Rio de Mendoza presents to the amateur of breathing sculpture failed to interest him. He was thinking of a far-off village on the other side of the equator, and of the wild girl with whom he used to play and quarrel, a creature of a different race from these degenerate mongrels. (141)

Figures of Spain are the mouthpieces of the text's discrimination and hierarchization among those of "Spanish descent." Everyone in this romance loves "whiteness," and especially that which is represented as somehow whiter than they are. Dick of the "olive complexion" desires Elsie, Elsie thinks she loves Bernard Langdon (although she supposedly lacks the capacity to love), Langdon catches the "angel" and daughter of the banking firm Bilyuns Brothers and Forrester, Letitia Forrester. Elsie, though "white," is so dangerous that no one loves her but the black nurse Old Sophy. However much all the characters in this circular romance of race may love "whiteness," only the figures of true "whiteness" that form the "Brahmin caste of New England"—Bernard Langdon, the "Puritan" minister Honeywood (Letitia's grandfather), and the doctor narrator—have what is represented as the superior acuity to discern degrees of whiteness, in this case, Elsie the white-ringed serpent from the true Anglo-Americans. By contrast with the figures of Spanish empire—Dick and especially Elsie Venner—and the racial threat to the body politic they are made to represent, Anglo-Americanness is made to seem besieged and, therefore, U.S. racial prejudice is transformed by narrative magic from racism into a necessary tool of personal, national, and imperial self-defense.

Ultimately, Dick is not represented as "white," nor, despite his racism, is he able to distinguish supposedly pure whiteness, the real "Anglo-American," from that which is fatally tainted. Furthermore, Dick's olive-skinned body is not the site of the identificatory crisis that Elsie's body represents. Although Dick, the "Spanish bandit" (145) from South America who arrives with a "belt heavy with gold and with a few Brazilian diamonds sewed in it" (141), represents Spanish empire in the New World, Dick is not as much of a threat to the Anglo-American male hero. Although he does attempt to kill Langdon out of jealousy (because he fears a match between Elsie and Langdon), the danger he represents is direct combat at which Langdon, and by implication U.S. empire, is demonstrated to be a more technologically advanced and emotionally and intellectually controlled opponent. Dick's primary characteristic is his wild riding, while Elsie is represented as a rider as well. Empire is articulated in the novel through the metaphor of riding:

> It makes men imperious to sit a horse: no man governs his fellows as well as from this living throne. And so, from Marcus Aurelius in Roman bronze . . . the saddle has always been the true seat of empire. (137–38)

Dick uses his South American lariat or *bola* and skill in the "Spanish saddle" to lasso Langdon, but Langdon uses the revolver—described as "more modern and familiar" than the "Spanish dagger" (195)—to unseat Dick by shooting his mount. The "Spanish bandit" and gaucho is finally shipped back to South America. Through this allegorical scene Langdon is shown to be more than a "horse tamer," unlike Dick and Spanish empire in the New World. Rather, the implication is that Langdon, and, thus, Anglo-American empire, may be the "world tamer" predicted by the narrator doctor.

Dick and the Spanish empire in the New World he represents are, moreover, less of a menace than Elsie. He represents political threat as proprietary and territorial conflict that, as in the scene of Dick's unseating, would seem to be easily and straightforwardly accomplished. Elsie, on the other hand, who is described as the "wilder of the two" (138), represents the romantic insinuation of Spanish empire. Her father, Dudley Venner, is supposed to have suffered from a bout of "doubled consciousness" (244) during his romance with Elsie's mother Catalina, that is, until her early death. Elsie is both the physical product and the portent of what is constructed as racial contamination. As a woman (at least on the outside), she, unlike Dick, might be able to bear a child by Langdon. Thus, Elsie is potentially capable of what is, according to the novel's logic, the gravest danger: the possibility of fatally altering the hero's lineage and, by implication, the nation's imperial future. However, as in the case of her father, romance with Spain has potentially destructive consequences (e.g., "doubled consciousness") for the lover as well as the offspring. The greatest threat to Langdon's "destiny" and that of the nation is the romantic danger of Spanish empire in the form of female figures of alien whiteness such as Elsie Venner. The daughter of one of the "first" families in Rockland, a rich and beautiful woman upon whose cultivation nothing had been spared, this female figure of contaminated Anglo-Americanness is the most dangerous element most subversive to the "health" of the body politic envisioned by the novel because she would seem to be perfect marriage material. An obvious play on her last name, "Venner" is venery and it is the opportunity for venery, illicit or licit, that she holds out for the Anglo hero like a poisoned apple.

The novel in a sense works as a course in visual discrimination. As it builds a hierarchy of races, of classes, of religions, it also preserves the future for an Anglo-American elect. However, there still remains the problem of those who might pass in appearance and/or familial association as

Anglo-American. The novel's characters all study Elsie, but it is, of course, Langdon who can see the dark vein spoiling the text's artifact of Anglo-Americanness, white marble:

> Here was a magnificent organization, superb in vigorous womanhood, with a beauty such as never comes but after generations of culture; yet through all this rich nature there ran some alien current of influence sinuous and dark, as when a clouded streak seams the white marble of a perfect statue. (350)

Elsie has a double problem. She is half Spanish and, owing to some mysterious accident—an "ante-natal impression" (383)—while she was still in her mother's womb, she is effectively a woman on the exterior and a rattlesnake at heart. Elsie's strangely transfixing diamond eyes, the circle of pale pigmentation around her neck hidden always by a gold chain, the long braided coil of her dark hair, the bracelet with enameled scales and the other one like Cleopatra's asp turned to gold, her lithe movements, lisping speech, and wild, lawless, and poisonous habits signified by the white powder kept in a secret hiding place and the two small white scars she left in Dick's arm all serve to characterize her as a snake-woman. As serpent- or rattlesnake-like, Elsie becomes associated with the last vestige of the "Indians" in Rockland. She disappears for days to join the rattlesnakes that infest the Mountain of Rockland and its feared Rattlesnake Ledge. These rattlesnakes are analogized to the "Indians" as the rattlesnakes had historically "next to the Indians [been] the reigning nightmare of the inhabitants." The "screeching Indian Divell" had, the story begins, been easier to "drive away" because they could not crawl into the crevices of the rocks (47). The rattlesnakes, however, have remained and, like Elsie, have insinuated themselves. Furthermore, her intimate association with the rattlesnakes, her ability to handle them without harm to herself, makes Elsie like the Gypsy woman who brings Bernard Langdon some specimens for him to study in order to determine whether rattlesnakes (and Elsie) really can exert a special fascination with their diamond eyes. The "dark, gipsy-looking woman" who delivers them tells him, "Lord bless you . . . rattlers never touches our folks" (186). The idea is that certain "primitive" peoples can handle snakes with impunity because they are like snakes at heart.

Elsie's snaky peculiarities further link her to Spain. The first discussion of the death of Elsie's mother and the suspicion that she may have been bitten by a rattlesnake while she was pregnant come not much before the revelation of the mother's tombstone and her name, "Catalina." Although there is little doubt by the conclusion of the novel that Elsie is neither quite right nor, in the novel's terms, quite "white," it is made a romantic mystery whether her "congenital defect" comes from Catalina and from Spain or Spanish empire in the New World, from Rattlesnake Ledge and the snakes and Indians associated with that last vestige of "wilderness," or from some mixture of these elements. Elsie is characterized as impervious to all outside influences, except for those associated in some way with Spain. The one governess she does not terrify away or try to poison is a "young Spanish woman" who taught her the Spanish language and Spanish dances, the fandango and the sarabande (134, 165). Elsie's father caters to all of her eccentric demands so that she may dress herself in snake bracelets, diamonds like her rattlesnake eyes, and "precious old laces, too, almost worth their weight in diamonds,—laces which had been snatched from altars in ancient Spanish cathedrals during the wars" (178).

Whether it is the snake in her that responds to things associated with Spain or the Spanish in her that is serpent-like, the danger and fatality of the rattlesnake is so entwined with the Spanishness constructed by the tale that the trope of the danger of coils of Spanish gold becomes in and on the body of Elsie Venner a rattlesnake-like white ring around her throat and a "congenital obliquity" in her blood that ultimately consumes her. Elsie, and by implication the Spanish Empire she represents, is oriental, snakelike, "American" Indian, and East Indian, Gypsy, and Moorish. Elsie's dancing, more than her riding, turns her into a figure of Spain as snake-like, Moorish, and Indian of the East and the West:

Elsie was alone in the room, dancing one of those wild Moorish fandangos, such as a *matador* hot from the *Plaza de Toros* of Seville or Madrid might love to lie and gaze at.[48] She was a figure to look upon in silence. The dancing frenzy must have seized upon her while she was dressing; for she was in her bodice, bare-armed, her hair floating unbound far below the waist of her barred or banded skirt. She had caught up her castanets, and rattled them as she danced with a kind of passionate fierceness, her lithe body undulating with flexuous grace, her diamond eyes glittering, her round arms wreathing and unwinding, alive and vibrant to the tips of the slender fingers. Some passion seemed to exhaust itself in this dancing paroxysm; for all at once she reeled from the middle of the floor, and flung herself, as it were in a careless coil, upon a great tiger's-skin which was spread out in one corner of the apartment. (135–36)

Elsie's castanets are her rattler. She is both snake and charmer. The "wild" Moorish dances, the fandango and the sarabande, make her alive and dangerous in her allure, like the bull to the matador, and the tiger to the hunter. Furthermore, her dancing is a sign of fanaticism and "mania" suggesting lack of free will:

> The sound of the castanets seemed to make her alive all over. Dick knew well enough what the exhibition would be, and was almost afraid of her at these moments; for it was like the dancing mania of Eastern devotees, more than the ordinary light amusement of joyous youth—a convulsion of the body and mind, rather than a series of voluntary modulated motions.
>
> Elsie rattled out the triple measure of a saraband[49] . . . The chain of mosaics she had on at that moment displaced itself at every step. (316)

Elsie the Indianized, Orientalized, Moorish, and Gypsy snake-woman figure of Spain is both sign of doomed empire (Spanish, Moorish, the Native Americans of the New World) and the potential agent of its downfall. In the narrator doctor's reply to Langdon's questions as to whether human beings might be capable of the "power of fascination" found in certain animals and whether there may be "predispositions, inherited or ingrafted, but at any rate constitutional, which shall take out certain apparently voluntary determinations from the control of the will" (197), the narrator doctor responds that answers to such questions may only be found in that "middle region between science and poetry" (198). That is precisely the domain that Holmes's novel stakes out for itself. The subject in question is, of course, Elsie, and to explicate her potential the narrator doctor recounts a legend of a snake-woman from the Indies sent to destroy Alexander's empire:

> Mizaldus tells us, in his *Memorabilia,* the story of the girl fed on poisons, who was sent by the King of the Indies to Alexander the Great. ". . . Aristotle saw her eyes sparkling and snapping like those of serpents . . . and sure

enough the young lady proved to be a very unsafe person to her friends. (198–99)

Unlike the girl from the Indies fed on poisons, Elsie is congenitally marked by her destiny for those who can see it. Langdon believes that "she had brought her ruling tendency into the world with her" and that the origin of her "alien impulses" "reaches far back into the past" (352). Elsie is represented as both incapable of exercising free will, that is, she is a slave to her innate passions, and, turning the phrase around, might also make others slaves to her "ruling tendency."

The novel rehearses the competing discourses of religion, science, medicine, ethnology, phrenology, romantic legend, and law in order to forge a cumulative synthesis about the origin and future that this figure of fatal Spanish empire and tainted Anglo-Americanness represents. The novel biologizes sin and moralizes physiognomy, creating "pure" Anglo-Americans (Bernard Langdon and his fiancée Letitia Forrester) as the types of angels and grace, while the tainted Anglo-American Elsie—the Moorish, Gypsy, Indian figure of Spanish empire as fatal attraction—becomes at once the racial type of the criminal, the insane, the devil, and the damned. Puritan election is Darwinized in *Elsie Venner* and the conclusion would suggest that those who are congenitally damned cannot be healed, educated, or saved by grace, works, or reason. Elsie consumes herself, allowing the consolidated Anglo-American community to demonstrate its sensitivity in mourning the death that gives them evident release and relief.

The most disturbing aspect of this "romance of destiny" is its sentimentalization of a theory of criminality and sin as a congenital defect in certain peoples—especially "Indians" and those of "Spanish descent"—which must, according to the novel, however regrettably, be "extirpated." Then, according to the narrator doctor's letter, the agents of this extirpation should sit down and contemplate "them" charitably (203–5). This pattern of expulsion, extermination, and/or expropriation and then romantic elegy puts the fate of Native Americans in the United States and the "destiny" of those of Spanish descent in the Southwest, Cuba, and Puerto Rico in the naturalizing rhetoric of biology and the self-saving terms of charity and feeling. Holmes's *Elsie Venner* was published in 1861, between the Mexican-American War (1846–48) and the Spanish-Cuban-American War (1898). It was so popular that it was published and republished as a

book and serialized in the *Atlantic Monthly,* to which Holmes became a
leading contributor. He was well-known among his contemporaries as
an advocate of scientific rationalism and, specifically, for his views on
heredity and abnormal psychology.[50] The term "manifest destiny" had
been coined and widely circulated in 1845, sixteen years prior to the publication of *Elsie Venner.* The fulfillment of manifest destiny at the expense
of certain so-called "races"—Native Americans and those of "Spanish
descent"—whose presence in or near the continental United States was
seen as a threat to the security and to the material and moral progress of
the nation as empire was an idea that was increasingly finding expression
and justification among scientists, theologians, and writers. One cannot
say with certainty what Holmes's views on the Spanish-Cuban-American
War (1898) might have been as he died four years before "the splendid
little war" (to borrow John Hay's phrase) was instigated. The typing of
those of "Spanish descent" as at once inherently doomed and dangerous
in Holmes's *Elsie Venner* was available both to those who saw the war as a
necessary means to expel the tainted and threatening Spanish Empire from
the New World and to those who, like Charles Francis Adams, opposed
this imperial venture out of fear of miscegenation that would occur with
the contact of intervention and who believed that those who were not
properly "Anglo-Saxon" would eventually consume themselves.[51]

Regardless of what might be conjectured about the personal views of
Simms, Hawthorne, or Holmes, each of these novels has a visionary
dimension. As Lauren Berlant has pointed out so incisively with reference
to *The Scarlet Letter,* the narration of the "The Custom House" preface is
not just in the past tense but is also in the future perfect. The preface's
address endeavors to project its inscribed author Hawthorne as one who
will "have already altered the future form of the nation by the production
of literary texts."[52] Although Hawthorne's book is, of the novels I discuss, the most complexly arranged in terms of temporal structure, each
of these novels retells the past but places the site of its reading, and thus
its effects, in the future. As I have endeavored to demonstrate, these
romances produce an effect of Anglo-Americanness as a personal identity
as well as a political and social destiny for the nation as empire. The vision
of U.S. empire they project is one of antiempire. Although such a vision
relies, no less than actual territorial conquest, on the demonization and
elimination of Others from its frame of desire, each of these romances uses

imagination and sentiment to make U.S. empire as Anglo-American seem not only inevitable but emotionally gripping or, one might say, persuasively conscripting.

SARGENT'S *EL JALEO: TABLAO* OF SPANISHNESS

Before I turn, in the next chapter, to the consolidation of Anglo-American imperial identity around the Spanish-Cuban-American War (1898), I would like to return one last time to the question of the romance of Spain exhibited by the Hispanophiles—those U.S. citizens who traveled to and spent a considerable amount of time in Spain; who studied Spanish history, culture, art, and society; and/or who produced work representing Spain that is generally understood as evidence of a kind of love affair with Spain. As I have discussed, the romances of Anglo-American imperial identity by Simms, Hawthorne, and Holmes take up the exotic, Orientalized types that feature in the romance of Spain but narratively preclude or punish any romance *with* Spain. In this section, I focus not on a historical novel, but rather on one of the many paintings produced in the nineteenth century by U.S. painters of what were to represent "real" Spanish types based on being there and being in some way sympathetically involved in the heat and passion attributed to Spain. I pose the question of whether there was any semiotic relationship between the admiring exoticization of "Spanish" types in U.S. cultural production and the condemning and finally warmongering U.S. demonization of the Spaniard in that invented war by which the United States claimed to "liberate" Cuba and appropriated Puerto Rico.

I bring this question to bear on one of the most ambitiously scaled and complexly elaborated paintings of a scene located in Spain produced by a U.S. artist in the nineteenth century: John Singer Sargent's *El Jaleo* (Figure 3). Sargent (1856–1925) completed this tableau of a flamenco performance or *tablao* in 1882. Done on the scale of a history painting, the work was his largest Salon piece (94⅘ × 140⅘ inches or roughly 8 feet × 11.5 feet). Although the painting was first displayed before the public in Paris, that same year, 1882, the painting was exhibited in London, then New York, and finally in Boston, where it was on view at the Williams and Everett gallery after it was purchased by Thomas Jefferson Coolidge, a Boston businessman, heir to the Coolidge fortune, and descendant of

Thomas Jefferson. Sargent's tableau of flamenco as typically Spanish was a major critical sensation at the time. Painting "Spanish" subjects seems to have been quite advantageous for his career. However, Sargent was also evidently deeply fascinated with the paintings of Goya and Velázquez he studied, the music and dances of the Gypsies in Spain that he made some effort to learn, and the work of contemporary Spanish artists, particularly the painters of the Catalan modernist circle whose work he introduced to collectors in the United States.[53] Through a close analysis of *El Jaleo* I will argue that the representational practices even of this painting so heavily invested in Spain as a locus of passion—and of desires disavowed at home—rehearse and confirm, however unwittingly, many of the tropes through which the United States was envisioned as a predestined Anglo-American empire.

At the time of its initial reception, critics of *El Jaleo* were divided over whether the work realistically depicts a scene from life in Spain or whether it is, on the contrary, sensationalistic, displeasingly impressionistic, and unrefined.[54] Some critics found nothing to offend their sensibilities, while

Figure 3. John Singer Sargent, *El Jaleo* (1882), oil on canvas, 237 × 352 cm (94⅘ × 140⅘ inches). Isabella Stewart Gardner Museum, Boston.

others were particularly disturbed by the "'repulsive' face of the dancer, and the 'disagreeable suggestiveness' of her movement" (Fairbrother, *John Singer Sargent and America*, 57). None of the critics disputed, however, what they all took to be the typicality of its subject matter. I would suggest that the critical controversy over its handling points to the complex coding of the picture. The painting combines a realist and an allegorical idiom with the visual articulation of homoeroticism in the ambivalent forms of surrogacy (the flamenco dancer and singer) and displacement (Spain). I will argue that the layered doubling of idioms, realist and allegorical, works to encode its historical, literary, and erotic tropes about Spain in the visual language of the real, thus transforming legend about hot, dark, queer, passionate, and fatal Spain into essence.

The impassioned and cathectic center of the composition would seem to be the figure of the masculinely rendered female flamenco dancer, on which the U.S. critics (as well as the French and British) focused their attentions. The *New York Times* review of October 13, 1882, remarked on the "enthusiasm and abandon in the pose of the dancer" and maintained that "there is nothing debasing nor suggestive of the unseemly" (56). The very stress on the inoffensiveness of the figure of the dancer suggests that other critics were leveling charges of indecency or obscenity. Indeed, the review of November 7, 1882, in the U.S. art journal *The Art Amateur* described the dancer's face as "repulsive" and insisted that the figure's movements were disagreeably "suggestive" (57). A number of U.S. critics were dismayed by Sargent's drawing of *El Jaleo*, which they considered "loud, almost coarse, slipshod in execution, fearfully and wilfully wrong" (ibid.). These same critics frequently pointed to the dancer—to the supposedly awkward if not impossible angle of her forearm, the ungraceful, backward slant of her body, and the heaviness of her features.

The figure of the dancer was indeed controversial and the controversy over execution (i.e., "drawing") was freighted in moral terms suggesting that it was the ambiguity of the figure of the dancer—the "impressionistic" and ambiguous handling of the visual signs of gender and sexuality—that engaged and disturbed critics. Linking the technique of the painting to its coded qualities, Sargent's close friend Henry James remarked about *El Jaleo* that "it looks like life, but it looks also, to my view, rather like a perversion of life, and has the quality of an enormous 'note' or memorandum, rather than of a representation."[55] James's comment is itself ambivalently loaded. The painting's seductively queer perversity becomes in this sentence "a perversion of life." Nonetheless, James's quip points to the double idiom and double-talk of this ostensibly "realist" work, to the allegory and the "perversity" encoded within a framework of details that may also be taken as ethnographic observations of actual performance. Furthermore, calling the painting an "enormous 'note' or memorandum, rather than . . . a representation" brings out, if not its queer desire, its textuality rendered within a pretense of musicality, the painting as a highly composed but seemingly casually "written" note under the flamenco notes and the noise or *jaleo*.

The figure of the dancer is at once correct and fantastic, ambiguously gendered and eroticized to suggest a perversely masculine woman and yet ghosted by other possibilities. The bright white paint of the dancer's costume takes the eye to the skirt's ever so slightly raised hem and the revealed shoe. This emphasis on the dancer's large and heavy black shoe is a gesture that critics have interpreted as pointing to the zapateo: the boot and heel tapping as well as the stomping rhythms of flamenco dance. Traditionally, it was the zapateo or zapateado that characterized male dancers' performances. Although flamenco dance was open to individual interpretation, generally male dancers were expected to express themselves more through toe and heel beats (clicking and stomping) than were female dancers, who were expected to emphasize hand, arm, and body movements. The figure of the dancer has both: there are the brightly punctuated heel and toe of the dancer's large black shoe and the twisting, massive, and athletic arms.

This strong and muscular rendering of the figure of the dancer, as well as the profile of the face, suggest comparison with one of a number of portraits of young boys that Sargent produced in Italy. The dancer's facial features and coloring and the articulation of the arms and hands are very similar to those of the figure of a young Italian man leaning against a white wall and covered only partially by a dark toga-like garment in Sargent's *Young Man in Reverie* (1878). Sargent was also already playing with gender ambiguity in the sketches he made of flamenco dance subjects while in Spain. Three years before the completion of *El Jaleo*, he made a pen-and-ink sketch titled *Spanish Male Dancer before Nine Seated Figures* (1879) (Figure 4). Of the various sketches Sargent produced while in Spain this is the only one that compositionally prefigures, with its nine figures watching a lone dancer perform, *El Jaleo*'s eight figures plus one conspicuously

empty chair behind the dancer. In the place eventually occupied by the
gigantic female dancer suggesting a travesty is a "male" dancer whose hips
and protruding buttocks are strikingly curvaceous to the point of caricature. If it were not for the title, one might construe the figure to be a
woman dressed as a man. In any case, it is that archly curved back leading to the heavily outlined and jutting distention of the *culo* (or buttocks)
that arrests the eye and turns this sketch often claimed as the direct nota-
tion of experience into what one is tempted to call a camp performance
of a performance. Ethnographic representation here becomes more akin
to a wink and a twist of the hips than to documentation. Likewise, in *El
Jaleo,* for which this was one of many early preliminary sketches, the bodily gestures of the dancer are exaggerated and in their illegibility border on
the obscene in the sense of off-scene or not seen. Furthermore, the obscu-
rity surrounding the dancer suggests that something is occulted and yet
withheld, that things are not quite as they might seem.

Figure 4. John Singer Sargent, *Spanish Male Dancer before Nine Seated Figures*
(1879), drawing, brown ink and brown wash on off-white paper, 13.3 × 20.7 cm.
Courtesy of Fogg Art Museum, Harvard University Art Museums. Gift of Mrs.
Francis Ormond. Photograph by David Mathews; copyright 2003 President and
Fellows of Harvard College.

The sketch was not exhibited publicly during Sargent's lifetime. As for *El Jaleo*, although none of Sargent's contemporaries went so far as to state that they considered the dancer to be the impersonation of a woman or that the figure appeared to them to be a man in a dress, their critiques circle around the topic. Sargent may well have been engaging in and evoking for his viewers the Orientalist fantasy of Spain as a country where so-called Eastern excesses and exoticism were figured in a hypermasculinization of the men (e.g., bloodthirsty bellicosity) and a hyperfeminization of the women (e.g., fatal sensuality), as well as in precisely the opposite, the supposed effeminacy of the men and the presumed masculine aggressiveness of the women. In such Orientalist representation, as Edward Said writes, "The Orient [and one might include anything deemed 'Oriental'] becomes a living tableau of queerness."[56]

The charge of suggestiveness and indecency made by some critics may have been specifically provoked by the gesture of the dancer's long, outstretched arm and hand. The fingers are curled and extended in such a way as to resemble horns or a gesture known as *los cuernos*. Although not exactly equivalent to "giving someone the finger," the *cuernos* is generally understood as a gross insult. The two pointing fingers, most commonly a sign of sexual betrayal, particularly of a man outwitted by an adulterous woman, are sometimes literalized in their significance as the two penises in an unfaithful woman's sex life. The gesture is emphasized further by repetition, first in the raised hand of the figure of a woman in a vermilion shawl (extreme left) and then again in the shadow on the wall. As with almost every other detail of the composition, the gesture, though exaggerated and physically impossible, has a surface justification. It might also be interpreted simply as playing the *pitos* or snaps that add to the rhythm of flamenco.[57] Nonetheless, there is still something at once titillating and obscene about the illegibility and repetition of the gestures as well as the expressions of complicity and the compositional lines of connection that unite the two seated women at the far left with the dancer in a circuit of energy, desire, or even blood pact suggested by the drips of red paint (de)forming the fringe of their costumes.

Out of the shadow of the dancer may be discerned the illuminated torso of the figure who forms the actual center of the composition. This male figure with head thrown back to expose his bare throat, mouth wide open and eyes closed, is, I would suggest, the erotic center of the painting.

If the dancer is the surrogate figure of homoeroticism, this male singer is both queer desire's expressive sign and its obscure object. The gesture of the head conveys a sense of transport or abandon and could, to that extent, also function as a sign of that Romantic obsessive construction, the "Spanish Gypsy spirit," or of the art of *cante jondo* as something more or less than human, like the howling of a wolf. However, the figure is portrayed not as predator, but more as prey. The sense of vulnerability is accentuated by the bareness of his neck, revealing his neck muscles and Adam's apple. The wide-open mouth, echoing the well-like mouth of the second guitar on the wall, suggests that he is open, ready to be or already pierced by the agent of his ecstatic transport or by the viewer's gaze. The ambivalence of the facial gesture and posture of the singer—enraptured abandon of deep pain, profound pleasure, and/or gut-wrenching grief— might also connote an eroticism charged by a sense of danger and the lure of the very fatality allegorically encoded into the seeming actuality of the performance. Although fatalism may describe the lyrics and even the style of flamenco deep song, fatality takes on the added charge of sexual danger. When Isabella Stewart Gardner, who inherited the work from Coolidge, proposed hanging the painting in the "Spanish Cloister" of her "house museum" Fenway Court with its Hispano-Moresque window and colored tiles, Sargent wrote: "It might be like a mummy at the feast unless I give her a new gauze gown all spangles and pull the sword out of her heart."[58] Although Sargent is most probably discussing some refurbishment of the canvas, this witticism steeps the painting itself (her) in the Orientalizing tropes of Egyptian mummies and the erotics of pain and death. For many U.S. travelers and expatriates of the nineteenth century, countries viewed as "Oriental," including Spain, were often the fantasy sites both to engage in and represent sexual practices disavowed and disallowed back home. Through a displacement of location to Spain, the surrogacy of the mas- culinized female dancer, and the layering of figure with shadow and aban- don and openness with lurking concealment, the painting does become at once a simply flamenco *tablao* and a tableau of queerness and fatality as typically Spanish.

Returning to James's metaphor of the "note," I would like to take a close look at the writing on the wall. Double entendre is quite literally written across the backdrop of the scene.[59] Over the empty chair two guitars are painted on the wall. The left guitar, far less distinctly drawn, is like the spectral echo of the other, just as these strange guitars are the ghostly doubles of those being played. In their chiasmic, doubling relation to the two guitars that the male musicians are playing, the implied notes or sound and movement of *El Jaleo* hang in tonal contrast with the silent suspension and stillness of these guitars on the wall. These signs of suspended silence also function to convey, even unconsciously, the sense that something is being deliberately withheld, not articulated aloud. Writers have remarked on the importance of ritual pauses and silences in flamenco; however, beyond the obvious realist referent of artistically arranged stillness and silence, these silently suspended guitars also call attention to the wall as a text of notes in the other sense, that of writing. The exclamation *olé* plays doubly across the wall at the far right. Painted faintly in red just above the figure of the woman clapping, this call of the bullring is balanced on the far left by another deep red stain, the indistinct hieroglyph of a bull. The head and horns are more solid and better defined than the rest of the body, which is sketchily outlined with quick brushstrokes of reddish orange paint. The slightly lowered angle of the head suggests that the bull is charging toward the faintly outlined shape of a *banderillero* in action. To the right of this hieroglyph of the bullfight and below the more substantially rendered guitar is the red "print" of a human hand. More than other marks, with the exception of writing, handprints imply human agency. Apart from connoting energy, vitality, and passion, the red stain of the handprint also suggests violence, anger, and blood. If the wall is an "enormous note," it is one signed with a blood-red handprint like the trace of some terrible fight or violent crime. Beneath this stain is the curiously unoccupied chair, empty except for an orange.

None of these details—the guitars on the wall, the painted notes "olé, olé," the hieroglyph of bull and *banderillero,* the bloody handprint, the empty chair, and the orange—are conventions of flamenco performance, but may rather here serve as allegorical signifiers of the thematics and psychosexual and metaphysical states invoked by the darkest of flamenco song styles.[60] *Cante jondo,* or "deep song" in Andalusian Spanish, has often been used to emblematize the flamenco vocal style associated with the Gypsies in Spain. The most moving and tragic of flamenco song styles, *cante jondo* tells impassioned tales of death, loss, and ill-fated love. Whether the empty chair marks absence or loss as an ill-fated love or a violent death, the orange, the bloody handprint, and the writing on the wall lead allegorically to Andalusia and to stories of fatal passion, revenge, and eroticized death.

The spot of orange may be, quite literally, a piece of local color, an allusion to the nineteenth-century descriptive cliché of Andalusia as a land of oranges and the conventional travel narrative use of Andalusia as the key to Spanish temperament and character. The orange, the hieroglyph of the bullfight, the bloodstained handprint, and the exclamation "olé, olé" also direct one to Andalusia, and specifically Seville, by a different path, the story of the Spanish Gypsy femme fatale Carmen from that initially controversial and later internationally celebrated opera by Bizet (first performed in 1875) and the novella by Prosper Mérimée (first published in 1845) on which it was based. As is often remarked, Sargent painted this tableau of a flamenco performance during the height of the notoriety and popularity of the opera and renewed interest in the novella in Europe and the United States.[61] It is not that Bizet's opera or Mérimée's novella must be understood as direct sources for Sargent's painting, but rather that these odd details of the orange, the empty chair, the bloody handprint, and the writing on the wall exceed the logical bounds of the realist frame and call for, as well as invoke, other shadow texts and narratives that helped to make Andalusia, the tobacco factory and Spanish Gypsy quarter in Seville, the Gypsies as a romanticized group, bullfighting, guitar music, and bold, seductive dance movements typical of Spain as an imagined whole. The basic plot of Mérimée's story of Carmen was retained by Bizet. The story begins at the tobacco factory in Seville where Carmen works and culminates outside the bullring in this capital of Andalusia. Carmen enchants a young officer, Don José, stabs (according to Mérimée) or disfigures (according to Bizet) a fellow tobacco factory worker, but eludes incarceration because Don José sacrifices his honor and rank by arranging her escape. Don José joins Carmen's band of smuggling bandits in the "Egyptian business" (Bizet) and is reduced to a seller of oranges (Mérimée) and becomes what Carmen disavows (but is eventually shown to be) in the Bizet opera: "I don't belong to this country [Spain] of crooks, of peddlers of rotten oranges."[62]

Ultimately, the foreshadowed rival to Don José for Carmen's overdeterminedly intense but fleeting passions appears in the figure of a toreador. In the Bizet opera, the toreador enters the Gypsy dance scene of Don José's release from prison and reunion with Carmen. Bullfighting, fatally triangulated passions, scenes of betrayal and eroticized death, and the song and dance of the Gypsies are made culturally synonymous and nationally characteristic ritual psychodramas. Don José fatally stabs Carmen when he realizes that he can never possess this "devil," "witch," and "wolf" just as his toreador rival sacrifices the bull. Although the Bizet opera makes Carmen the totem animal, there is also the shadow narrative of the toreador's erotic death dance with the bull.

Throughout Mérimée's tale and as a minor note in the Bizet opera, Carmen, the Gypsies, and Andalusia are also associated specifically with oranges. When Mérimée's narrator first meets Carmen and goes to her lodging, there is "a pile of oranges in one of the rooms."[63] Carmen consumes oranges as she devours men in both the novella and the opera. In the Mérimée novella, the orange as sign of Carmen's sexual appetite takes on a further allegorical load. When Carmen wishes to manipulate or enchant men, she offers them one or more oranges, which they do not refuse. The oranges sold and consumed outside the bullring before Carmen's fatal stabbing in the Bizet opera, are, in the Mérimée novella, Eve's apple in another guise, and what follows the acceptance or consumption of these oranges is trouble, a fall of sorts that, in the Bizet and Mérimée tales, falls most heavily on the Spanish Gypsy woman Carmen. Whereas the sword is in Carmen's heart at the conclusion of these shadow narratives, if there is any sword through "her," the painting's heart, it goes through the pierced center point of the figure of the male singer. However, despite this queer twist, El Jaleo allegorically encodes the blood sports of bullfighting and ill-fated love triangles behind the foregrounded realist codes of a flamenco song and dance performance. The work puts flamenco performance into the realm of history painting not merely by its scale, but, moreover, through the writing on the wall and other allegorical signs that turn bloody conflict, fatality, and danger into the fundamental drama of Spanish history. Spanish history becomes a foreshadowed story of corruption and decay.

This sense of foreshadowing leads back to the most obvious aspect of the painting, its tonal contrasts, deep, dense shadows, and dark underlayer both formally and allegorically. The figures along the wall are articulated out of darkness, that is, by the shadows that frame them. Looming over the painted company is an expansive area of dark sepia, gray, and black covering a large portion of the canvas. This gigantesque shadow takes its alibi from the assumed footlights invited by the realist conventions of the work. No footlights are figured in the painting and the shape of this large shadow is far less distinct than any of the other shadows presumed to be cast by these imagined footlights. Again, there is the surface logic of the performance scenario. The indistinctness might signify movement. However, in its monumentality the shadow also points out of the frame to the Spanish paintings Sargent had studied and with which critics were, in the case of Sargent's other submission to the Salon of 1882, *Lady with a Rose,* so eager to associate him. Although it was to Velázquez that critics connected *Lady with a Rose,* I would suggest that the dominating shadow of *El Jaleo* recasts the most well known shadow in Spanish painting, Francisco Goya's *The Colossus* (1808–12).

The significance of the shadowy giant in the sky, towering above a valley with his back to a fleeing multitude of people, and with his left arm and fist raised as if in some kind of challenge against an invisible enemy, has long haunted studies on Goya. There is little doubt, given the dates of the painting's composition, the crowds in flight, and the artist's own dismay at the horror of the French invasion of Spain and the ensuing Peninsular War, that the painting is a response to those war years. Nonetheless, whether the giant signifies the French invasion or conversely the Spanish resistance, whether the giant is an irrational demon out to wreak havoc on Spain or a kind of avenging angel working on behalf of the invaded country, whether it suggests the resistant spirit of the Spanish people looming large in the face of invasion or an irrational destructive and self-destructive force bent on revenge at all costs has vexed attempted interpretations.[64] The inscrutability of Goya's *Colossus* ghosts the similarly defiantly enigmatic shadow dominating the background of *El Jaleo.* One might take the shadow as a tribute to the dancer and to flamenco as romantic embodiments of the resistant spirit of the persecuted Gypsies and the stigmatized and marginalized underclasses who were flamenco's practitioners. The shadow might also be a sinister sign, an intimation that something irrational or threatening has been released through the song and dance, as in a séance. Furthermore, the portion of the wall to the right of the large shadow of the dancer is marked by the shadow of the hands of a man clapping and the shadows of the hands, arms, and heads of the two female dancers who are seated. The shapes of the shadows and their undulated pattern on the wall suggest flames, as if they were part of some dark fire burning in that corner of the painting.[65] This sense of conflagration is reinforced by the dripping red ostensibly of the fringed costumes. One may see this as the fire and smoke of passion, a romance that threatens the viewer; however, this may just as easily be a scene of self-consuming flame. But the red and orange paint are the only relief in what is primarily a black, gray, and sepia palette.

What hits the eye most immediately is the voluminous white skirt, the most pronounced element on this otherwise overwhelmingly dark canvas. Sargent often used black and white contrast to emphasize skin tone in his portraits. The chalky whites of the skirt have the effect of making the skin tones of the figures look not only dark, but like mixtures or mid-tones between the black blacks and white whites. The tonal and allegorical darkness of the work signifies more than an ethnographic comment on the lamenting resignation of many *cante jondo* lyrics. I would suggest that the Manichaean aspect of the sharp tonal contrast is used to mark these figures of Spanishness as a racially and morally hybrid mix of white and black. However admiring a connoisseur Sargent may have been of flamenco music, Gypsy performers, the paintings of Goya and Velázquez, and the work of Catalan modernists, the romance with Spain visually articulated by *El Jaleo* is nonetheless implicated in the very representational practices by which Spain and Spanish empire were typed as Moor, Indian, or, in this case, Gypsy, and thus implicitly fated as corrupted and decaying, like the "rotten oranges" of the Bizet libretto. Crucially, *El Jaleo* does not in itself set this typology of Spain as Gypsy against an image of Anglo-Americanness. However, the painting is rife with signs like those by which Anglo-American imperial discourse projected U.S. fears and fantasies about hybridity as degeneration onto Spain and agonistically produced the fiction of the United States as Anglo, white, pure, and predestined to become rightful heir to the Americas. Romances with Spain like *El Jaleo* could be as available to imperial vision as the romances of Spain in the narratives of Anglo-American imperial destiny.

chapter 3

CONSOLIDATING ANGLO-AMERICAN IMPERIAL IDENTITY AROUND THE SPANISH-AMERICAN WAR

THE ORIENTALIZED ALTER EGO

In 1898, in response to the conflict in the Caribbean between the United States and Spain over Cuba in particular, the Berlin paper *Kladderadatsch* published a remarkable cartoon (Figure 5). The cartoon figured the United States as Uncle Sam and Spain as an armor-clad Quixotic knight challenging each other, nose to nose and foot to foot. Uncle Sam and the Spaniard are each stepping on Cuba with a forward lunging foot while Uncle Sam's other foot is poised on Florida and the Spaniard's on Spain. The caption reads, "This encounter does not seem, at present, exactly a happy one for poor Cuba." The cartoon is remarkable for the way in which it "sized up" not only the positions of the various parties involved in what has been designated the Spanish-American War, but, moreover, the way in which Spain functioned as both historical and symbolic contestant in the formation of Anglo-American national identity with imperial ambitions.[1] The cartoon shows Spain as none other than an imperial alter ego. Despite U.S. rhetoric about the liberation of Cuba (and Puerto Rico), Spain is figured as Uncle Sam's primary object of attention in a tango-like contest—a love–hate dance—between two colonizers for dominance. Even the popular nineteenth-century U.S. term for the war, the "Spanish-American War," rather than the more historically accurate "Spanish-Cuban-American War," underscores the extent to which Anglo-American imperial identity was forged in distinct counterpoint to images of Spain and Spaniards.

Figure 5. Anonymous, *This encounter does not seem, at present, exactly a happy one for poor Cuba* (1898), cartoon. From Berlin, *Kladderadatsch* (1898). Reprinted from *Cartoons of the War of 1898 with Spain from Leading Foreign and American Papers* (Chicago: Belford, Middlebrook, & Co., 1898), 35r. Courtesy of the President and Fellows of Harvard College.

As with John Singer Sargent's *El Jaleo,* a potential temptation arises to read U.S. wartime images like the one presented by the Berlin *Kladderadatsch* as homoerotic and, on account of being homoerotic, as subversive statements about equivalence or sameness between the United States and Spain that "dissolved" war between two countries into a dance of desire. Such a move assumes that homoeroticism is inherently passive, nation and/or empire deconstructing, which, despite stereotypes, is not necessarily so. In the case of the Berlin *Kladderadatsch,* one might interpret the image of the tangoing Uncle Sam and Spaniard as an ironic, even campy, comment on the war—a comment not necessarily performing the function of inciting it or of feeding into the imperial designs of either the United States or Spain. But homoerotic images or, following Eve Kosofsky Sedgwick's thesis in *Between Men,* even repressed homoerotic—or rather, *homosocial*—images were by no means necessarily outside an economy of war and imperial aggression, as Lori Merish argues persuasively in "Not 'Just a Cigar': Commodity Culture and the Construction of Imperial Manhood."[2] Through her analysis of U.S. cigar imagery as an "index of the racial and sexual unconscious of American imperial masculinity in the late nineteenth century" she demonstrates how, with regard to Cuba in the Spanish-Cuban-American War,

> the cigar embodies Anglo American men's desire for Cuban "manliness" and, simultaneously, repudiation of that desire, a repudiation that takes the form of an insistence on white supremacy over blacks and U.S. imperial dominance over "unruly" and excessively independent "mongrel Creoles."
> (277)

According to Merish, the homoerotics of the cigar exchanged between men hardly qualifies as pacifist or antiwar. In fact, in the case of the U.S. war cartoons that Merish analyzes, it marks both desire and the channeling of that desire into socially sanctioned aggression—war and imperial capitalist expansion.

Moreover, that representational homoeroticism—just like what I call "imperial erotics" more generally (whether homo-, hetero-, or migratory in its object)—is implicated sooner or later in "racial stratification" or hierarchicalization (303). Such stratification is not evident in the image of the tangoing Uncle Sam and Spain from the Berlin *Kladderadatsch,* but it was in Anglo-American Orientalizations of Spain, as I argued in the preceding chapter on mid- to later nineteenth-century Anglo-American representations. In this chapter I contend that Orientalizations that had been a way of turning the colonizer into the colonized on a "soft-core level" in the mid-nineteenth century took on "hard-core" manifestations around the time of the Spanish-American War (1898). The phrases "soft-core" and "hard-core" are usually employed to characterize erotic and pornographic material, respectively. I use them deliberately to signal the close relationship between desire and aggression in Anglo-American representations of Spain, a relationship that around the war collapsed concepts of "desire" and "aggression," making them virtually indistinguishable, because, for one thing, they were never ever simply about representing the Other (Spain). They were also about representing the Self (Anglo-American identity), a point that Merish develops not in relation to the United States and Spain, but certainly in relation to the United States and Cuba, particularly Afro-Cuban insurgents against foreign domination, whether Spanish or Anglo.

With regard to Spain, representations of Spain and Spaniards at the end of the nineteenth century in the United States were not merely a symptom or a consequence of being at war with a foreign power. These representations and the general concentration on "Spain" or "Spaniards" were at the center of the development of U.S. national identity as an Anglo-American imperial power. The closer the United States came to becoming Spain, as William Graham Sumner complained had happened less than a year after the war, the more the representations symptomatized an attempt to stratify Spain and Spaniards *beneath* and *away from* Anglo-Americans. The images generated far exceeded even a complex homoerotic economy of half-expressed, half-repressed desire. The collapsing of desire and aggression in the late 1890s meant that many of the images hardly looked or seemed "desirous" in any way. Rather, they revolved around *repulsion,* the turning of philia into phobia and phobia defined as the phantasmic representational space in which mechanisms of identification and desire are not allowed to coexist. Thus, one impulse is experienced independently from the other, a mental state that tends to invert desire into its mirror opposite—aversion—with only a trace of its former aim. This is what often happened with the Oriental version of Spain in and around 1898.

During the Spanish-American War, for instance, the *Syracuse Herald* published a satiric cartoon about Spain captioned "Entertaining a delusion" and showing two figures sitting across from each other at a small tavern table (Figure 6). The scene is reminiscent of a passage from Cervantes's *Don Quijote*. With a drink poured from a bottle labeled "diplomacy," the figure on the right is toasting a ghostly medieval knight on the left. In contrast to the premise of *Don Quijote*, the figure on the right, who has conjured up the phantasmic knight in armor with a white facing peeking out from beneath the visor, is not the deluded Man of La Mancha but an "Africanized" matador whose headgear, resembling a cross between a bullfighter's hat and a turban, is topped by three human skulls. The

Figure 6. *Entertaining a delusion* (1898), cartoon. From *Syracuse Herald* (1898). Reprinted from *Cartoons of the War of 1898 with Spain from Leading Foreign and American Papers* (Chicago: Belford, Middlebrook, & Co., 1898), 10r. Courtesy of the President and Fellows of Harvard College.

ghostly knight is a representative not merely of heroic medieval chivalry, but of "European aid," as indicated by the words written on the cartographic plume emanating from the top of the helmet. Effectively, this cartoon stages the two versions of Spain—the white European one and the Orientalist one—and has these two versions sitting down at the table with each other. However, the cartoon equates with the delusional the notion that Spain is "European" or in congenial alliance with European "civilization" and power. The cartoon implies that the European version of Spain is not real. What is posited as real is a character who, with three human skulls aboard his turban-like headgear, a protruding nose (both hooked and rounded), and thick lips sandwiching a gibbous tongue, suggests, in a grotesque racialization, the Semitic African or "Blackamoor." "Moor" is the conceptual category that historically has been deployed to denote the mingling of the "Semitic" with the "African." The "Africanization" of the Spaniard in this cartoon points not only southward, but also eastward. "African" subsists within an Orientalizing paradigm that was central to ethnographic discourse about Spain and Spaniards in the United States and even in Spain itself from the mid-nineteenth century onwards. In the cartoon, however, this ethnographic discourse and its apparatus of exoticization are condensed into a shorthand grotesque demonization of Africa, of the Middle East, and particularly of Spain.

Furthermore, the map of the cartoon's implications cuts westward as well as south and eastward. The three human skulls atop "Spain"'s turban-like hat put into play the trope of the cannibal, fundamental since the fifteenth century to colonialist discourse about Africa, "the East," and the Americas, especially the Caribbean. In other words, the triangulation implicit in the figuration of Spain as a "Semitic African cannibal" underscores the extent to which a westward or "Americas" reference point is at stake in this cartoon and other wartime material. Not only were Cubans, African Americans, and Filipinos considered "Negroid," as Amy Kaplan has argued persuasively in her essay "Black and Blue on San Juan Hill," so too, I maintain, were Spaniards and "Spain" itself.[3] Moreover, Spaniards, like Cubans and Filipinos, were considered "Negroid" according to an Orientalizing paradigm. Earlier in the century and later, some time after the Spanish-American War, Anglo-Americans tended to make distinctions between Spaniards from Spain or Spanish Creoles in the Americas and other Spanish-speaking peoples, but less so during the Spanish-American

War. Although there are many reasons to dispute the commonly used name for the war of 1898, the irony is that Cubans, Puerto Ricans, Filipinos, and Spaniards were all being judged as subcivilized—given to various kinds of "cannibalism" and other distasteful behaviors unless under the guiding or chastising hand of U.S. intervention. According to Anglo-American imperial ideology regarding the Americas, "Semitic African cannibals" and people imagined to have been tainted by such a biological and cultural legacy were unfit to govern without being tutored in or overseen by the supposedly democratic and civilizing ways of the Anglo. Of course, the desire to govern or tutor people figured as repulsive cannibals and also, as I shall demonstrate later on, as rapists is inherently contradictory. If the Other or the "enemy" is rendered too disgusting or repulsive, another desire is being expressed under the cover of reform or correction—and that is elimination, which, though facilitating the incorporation of formerly Spanish territories into the sphere of Anglo-American empire, translated into a highly ambivalent and often openly hostile incorporation of the people in question, whether Cubans, Puerto Ricans, Filipinos, or Spaniards.

With regard to the Spanish-American War, as with so many other wars and campaigns of aggression, much of the scholarship on wartime representation has focused on men and the construction of masculinity. Merish's work on the war, for instance, focuses not only on men, but on specifically homoerotic/homosocial desire between men, the simultaneous indexing and deflection of that desire into aggression and the circulation yet containment of it within commodities—in more concrete terms, the way in which the phallic cigar is not just a cigar and yet must per force remain a cigar. That desire should manifest itself and be legible in terms of an investment in specific objects and yet also be subject to rechanneling from people to things to shore up against the threat of castration or lack is a fundamental principle of psychoanalysis and one that Merish traces convincingly in her analysis of male homosocial desire in relation to national identity and imperial expansion. Such an analysis, however, marginalizes the role of women in the consolidation of Anglo-American imperial identity in and around the Spanish-American War and elides questions of class, an irony when one considers that the rest of the book *Sentimental Materialism* is dedicated to precisely these questions, but not in terms of the Spanish-American conflict. The very last section of the

chapter on the Cuban cigar makes mention of the New Woman in relation to the phallic object of cultural contestation—the Cuban or, as
becomes apparent, the not-so-Cuban cigar. The section appears somewhat as an afterthought, as does the discussion of the sexual, gender,
and racial identifications in white lesbian appropriations of the cigar traceable, according to Merish, in "The Bloomer Club Cigar" advertisement
(302). This discussion is very brief and ends with the point that though
these appropriations destabilized the national and imperial sex-gender
system, they also did the work of empire, both domestically and abroad,
by subordinating black women (depicted serving white women) to white
women.

Concluding a brief discussion of women's investment in the phallic,
torpedo-like Cuban cigar of the Spanish-American war period with cigar-
wielding, cigar-smoking lesbians—Merish reiterates nineteenth-century
sexologist Richard von Krafft-Ebing's and Havelock Ellis's interest in a
supposed "cultural identification between lesbians and cigars" (ibid.)—
reinforces the cultural trope that war and transnational transaction are the
province of masculinity, either of men or of lesbians figured not in terms
of femininity or some other representational constellation but, explicitly,
in terms of culturally constructed masculinity (masculine women). This
conscription of lesbians into the province of masculinity is problematic,
as Monique Wittig pointed out a long time ago, for, if lesbians are not
women or (patriarchically) "proper" women, neither are they men or necessarily masculine. Furthermore, collapsing the New Woman into lesbians
who have been collapsed into masculinity does not elucidate more generally women's investment (or lack thereof) in the war. Finally, figuring desire
in terms of desired objects, whether people or commodities or people as
commodities, ignores manifestations of desire as libidinal energy or psychic investment that seems to have little to do with what one might think
of as being in the realm of *eros* and the pleasure principle. What of desire
as *thanatos,* particularly of the Other or the not-me, as the repulsion and
elimination of persons or objects? Although Merish's chapter on the
Cuban cigar deals with the imbrication of eros and the death drive in
her discussion of lynching—that is, with the simultaneity of white male
desire for black men's reputed phallic potency and yet also their "need" to
murder the bearers of that imagined potency so as to both appropriate and
contain it—lynching is still treated within a critical framework of desired,

not repulsed, objects. In fact, *Sentimental Materialism* assumes and even sporadically celebrates an economy of desired objects.

The underlying emphases of this chapter are somewhat different. I explore desire and women's relations to the Spanish-American War not so much in terms of possession or lack as in terms of negotiations with their own publicly and patriarchically recognized roles as social harmonizers and peacekeepers, a highly mediated kind of desire appearing as the absence of desire or as passivity rather than as active libido. I also explore desire beyond this seeming absence or quiescence—that is, in terms of active abjection and repulsion. It is a mistake, I contend, to trace desire only in terms of desired objects. Equally important is to figure it in terms of its abjected and repulsed objects. Spain and Spaniards became such an "object" in and through hard-core Orientalizations. It/they became, in a word, the quintessence of the not-me, the negative objects through which Anglo-American imperial identity established its "me," its self-definition, and, moreover, conscripted those who were not upper-middle-class Anglo-American men, those not centrally located within its power structure, to its cause.

This chapter explores four interrelated issues: (1) how women were recruited and contributed to the consolidation of Anglo-American imperial identity, often symbolized as a heroic white Columbia; (2) how, despite various kinds of exceptions, a racially encoded vision of manifest destiny served to consolidate a consensus overruling class differences in the cultural production around the Spanish-American War; (3) how the tying together of Orientalist representations of Spain and Spaniards (like a turban) over and around the Black Legend of Spain (the inherited rope) produced a kind of Turk's-head knot that served to create a symbolic teleology foredooming the end of the rope for Spain as an imperial power; and (4) how the racial typecasting of Spaniards figured the "repulsiveness" of Spain at the same time that it justified Spain's repulsion/expulsion from the Americas. My examination of constructions of Spain and Spaniards around and during the Spanish-American War seeks to demonstrate that these representations were not the sole province of "eminent men of letters." Thus, I explore these issues across a range of materials—from the travel novel of Mary Nixon, an upper-middle-class woman, and William James's immensely popular *Varieties of Religious Experience,* to cartoons, songs, and war memorabilia. As I am interested in demonstrating the formation and extension of an Anglo-American consensus, not simply in making an inventory of "responses," I concentrate on how Spain and Spaniards figured in published works, not unpublished ephemera, around and during the war. These works constructed access for "Americans" with a little pocket money and leisure time to a sense of status that came from imaginary acquisition of elite education and travel through, for example, travel literature; to a sense of racial superiority that came from encouraged identification with the model of moral, cultural, and biological fitness in, for example, cartoons; and, finally, to a sense of participation or belonging via seductive conscription through, for example, songs and medals. Songs, medals, and speeches all contributed to a cultural recruitment of individuals into a personal and national manifest destiny against not only the last of the Spanish Empire, but, moreover, against what was viewed as the unruly abjection of Spaniards as a "race."

THE IRONIST, THE ANARCHIST, AND THE "AMERICAN GIRL": WOMEN AND THE WAR WITH SPAIN

Anglo-American representations of Spain and Spaniards published or otherwise publicly disseminated in the seventeenth, eighteenth, and nineteenth centuries were mostly written or produced by men, not women, of the upper-middle and upper classes. Men such as Washington Irving, Henry Wadsworth Longfellow, George Ticknor, George Bancroft, John Hay, William Hickling Prescott, Nathaniel Hawthorne, William Gilmore Simms, Oliver Wendell Holmes, Frederick Arthur Bridgman, Walter Gay, William Dannat, and John Singer Sargent came from comparatively privileged backgrounds and, furthermore, formed a network of direct and circulating influences with respect to the "study" and representation of Spain and Spaniards. As Stanley T. Williams argued throughout his two-volume *The Spanish Background of American Literature,* there never before existed in the United States such a group of eminent men of letters devoting their combined efforts to Spanish subjects. The scarcity of representations by women may be attributed to several factors. In general, men had much greater access to the means of production, canonization, and subsequent preservation of representations, whether textual or visual. Furthermore, the historical structuring of the public and private spheres, especially in the nineteenth century, discouraged women from publicly concerning themselves with topics related to history, trade, foreign policy, border disputes, land acquisition, and war. The topic of Spain and/or Spaniards involved a historical subtext, if indeed it was not overtly about border disputes, land acquisition, war, and the like.

This is not to say that women did not write history books and, in particular, books of Spanish history. Elizabeth Wormeley Latimer was the author of more than half a dozen popular histories, among them *Spain in the Nineteenth Century*, first published in 1897 and again in 1898.[4] It is significant, however, that she felt it necessary to contain and belittle her venture into a field of endeavor that was considered the rightful domain of men:

> I again disclaim, as I have done in several previous prefatory Notes, any right to be classed as an "historian," and deprecate being judged by the high standards properly applied to those who look beneath the surface of events, and elucidate the causes of history. (iii)

Nevertheless, Latimer's history of Spain in the nineteenth century is more than four hundred pages long. The last chapter, about Cuba and some preliminaries to the Spanish-American War, concerns itself with a sweeping panorama of topics: (1) a brief history of Spain's colonization of and colonial policies in Cuba; (2) bitter struggles during the nineteenth century between what she terms "Peninsular Spaniards" (those born in Spain) and "Creoles" (those of Spanish descent born in Cuba) over political representation and the racial caste system and among the Creoles over the question of slavery; (3) a scheme proposed in 1836 by a few people from the Spanish administration to sell Cuba to France and another proposed in 1850 by President Polk to buy the island from Spain in order to annex it to the United States; (4) trade disagreements (the "Black Warrior" affair) between Spain and the United States, which provided a convenient occasion for the United States to draft the Ostend Manifesto (1854) declaring that the possession of Cuba by "a foreign country" was a menace to the United States; (5) the growth of revolutionary movements among insurgent Creoles, fugitive slaves, and a great many Afro-Cubans against Spanish rule in Cuba beginning in 1868 with the Ten Years' War and renewed in 1895; and (6) speculation about whether Cuba "could sustain herself as a republic?—with her race hatreds; her domestic broils; her mongrel population" (414–15). Latimer's text ultimately differentiates between Spaniards and Spanish history and Cubans and Cuban history. Although it attributes political instability to Spain as much as to Cuba—"one continued tangle of revolutions" (9)—a distinction is made on the basis of a trope, the trope of "race":

> Why have Spanish-American republics been for years the opprobrium of liberty, but because of the nature of the people who inhabit them?—the dilution of the blood of the proud and boastful Spaniards with that of the servile races. Spanish-Americans have crude ideas of freedom, and apparently no capacity for self-government. (414)

In the final analysis, the argument of Latimer's book seems to be that if self-government is difficult for Spain, it is impossible for Cuba—"no capacity for self-government"—owing to miscegenation between "Creoles," "mulattoes," and "blacks." One might have wished that this woman historian would have had more independence of thought than to rehearse the status quo arguments of many Anglo-American male historians and politicians as well as of the Jesuit father whose blaming statement about "half-castes" and social discord she quotes at the end of her history of Spain and her chapter on Cuba (422).

The explosion of representations of Spain and Spaniards shortly before, during, and after the Spanish-American War did not provide many exceptions to the public/private division I mentioned earlier. Other women, of course, did cross the gender/representation boundaries, occasionally in a disguised fashion, often indirectly, and sometimes boldly. Mary F. Nixon's travelogue novel *With a Pessimist in Spain* published in 1897, a year before the war, is an example of the encoded approach. The book narrates her travels through Spain, starting at Gibraltar and terminating in Catalonia, with a female friend identified as "the Pessimist" who, she writes, "looked irresistible on her donkey."[5] The Pessimist has several important functions that allow Nixon to create a nonthreatening position from which the narrator can comment on the impending conflict between the United States and Spain. The Pessimist serves as the narrator's travel companion, chaperone, romantic friend, and constant partner in dialogue. The relationship between the narrator and the Pessimist is patterned after the one between Sancho Panza and Don Quijote in Miguel de Cervantes's *Don Quijote*.

Instead of the realist and the idealist, they represent the ironist and the pessimist. Their relationship is quite literally a dialogic one. While the Pessimist voices negative attitudes toward travel, and especially travel in Spain, the ironist often echoes the stereotypes about Spain and Spaniards in order to overturn them or to turn them back on the implied Anglo-American reader. Many of the negative attitudes toward Spain expressed by the Pessimist correspond to specific prejudices Anglo-Americans inherited from the British in the seventeenth century as part of the Black Legend against Spain and which in the nineteenth century, and particularly in the late 1890s, fueled and merged with the more virulent aspects of the Orientalist version of Spain. At one point, the Pessimist declares, "When I write a history, it will be that of a less bloody country than Spain." The first-person narrator replies, "All history is bloody. One gets used to it in time" (274). The remark and the retort are significant because they represent a debate between two women about writing history, culturally designated as the province of the male historian, and specifically about writing the history of Spain. The question of whether an invocation of the figure of the cruel and bloody-minded Spaniard is justified or whether cruelty and bloodthirstiness are endemic to the history of all countries (the United States included) is explored in light of the impending war between Spain, the Spanish colonies, and the United States. One of the exchanges between the Pessimist and the narrator contains an allusion to the Spanish-Cuban-American situation:

> "There's something that ought to make your patriotic breast beat with joy. Look! Among those superb statues of Daphne, Apollo, and Lucretia, is one of America."
>
> "I'm having too nice a time to be patriotic," said the Pessimist.
>
> "What! the Pessimist enjoying herself! *Mirabile dictu!* Hurrah for La Granja!" I exclaimed wildly.
>
> "Be quiet, the guard is looking at you, and you'll be arrested for a Cuban sympathizer," said my friend sternly. (235)

The reference to the impending conflict between the United States and Spain over Cuba in the Pessimist's mention of "a Cuban sympathizer" occurs within a setting and in the context of other remarks that question what is "Spanish" about Spain. The setting for the dialogue is La Granja de San Ildefonso, a pleasure palace with extensive gardens near the town of Segovia. Commissioned by Philip V and modeled after Versailles, it betokens an emulation of the French prevalent among the Spanish nobility of the Enlightenment. The discussion of the generally anti-Spanish Pessimist's enjoyment of her Spanish travels begins with the narrator's exclamation over a statue of America among the pantheon of mythical figures that compose one of the fountains in the gardens. The framework for the reference to Spain's continuing designs on Cuba, an imperialist enterprise serving nationalist interests, is Spanish "captivation" with and by foreign models of imperial grandeur: the *afrancesamiento* (Frenchification) of the Spanish upper class; the historical subjugation of Spain to French policies both under the Bourbons in the eighteenth century and with the French invasion in 1808 and Napoleonic rule from 1808 to 1814; and the Spanish tribute to the mythic/heroic idea of America.

With a Pessimist in Spain functions as a critique of stereotypical notions about the "Spanishness" of Spain. The heavy reliance on irony, however, produces two possible readings, a chauvinistic one and a sympathetic one. They are not mutually exclusive but, rather, are held in tension by the dialogic structure. The chauvinistic reading, on the one hand, is encouraged by a more sophisticated version of vulgar stereotypes about Spain voiced in the exchange between the Pessimist and the ironist. The ironic mode employed may have reinforced Anglo-Americans' sense of distance and security from the object of their tourist and imperial gaze. The ironic use of extreme versions of the stereotypes would have allowed the readers to congratulate themselves on their comparatively refined judgment. The sympathetic reading, on the other hand, is abetted by the dialogic form in which bias and belligerence against Spain are vented and displaced, or at least juxtaposed, with an enjoyment of and an appreciative stance toward Spanish culture. At one point the narrator exclaims:

> Of all things in Spain, I think the manners of the people strike one as most remarkable . . . In Andalucia they are gay; in Aragon, grave; in Castile, deferential; but everywhere, prince or pauper, noble or peasant or beggar, each and all are courteous and thoughtful of the comfort of others. (207)

If this remark is another twist on the topos of the noble savage, it is startling to the extent that it equates Spaniards with social refinement at the very moment in U.S. history when reporters and politicians often made "Spaniard" synonymous with "tyrannical barbarian" in order to prime the public for war.

With a Pessimist in Spain argues that social harmony is preferable to war. The message is a pacifist one, but also a socially conservative, if not an elitist, reactionary one. The narrator contrasts the Spaniards' "calm self-respect" and "courtesy" with the social discontent of "an American chambermaid" who "spent her time in alternate fits of trying to show herself as good as you, and sulking because she felt she was not" (ibid.). Extrapolating from this passage and returning to the reference to "the Cuban sympathizers," I conclude that Nixon praises the Spaniards' "manners" at the expense of the Cuban revolution and the struggle for social and economic justice in U.S. society. At the end of the nineteenth century, pacifism was not necessarily coextensive with social radicalism as it was frequently inflected by class as well as racial prejudice. It is possible to argue for a disturbing correlation between Nixon's association of Spain with Old World gentility and France and her ability to identify herself with its inhabitants rather than with the rebellious Cuban sympathizers of unspecified origin.

Emma Goldman, perhaps because of her triply marginalized status as a radical Russian-Jewish immigrant woman, boldly crossed the gender/representation lines. Critical of the ideology of manifest destiny expressed at every turn by the Rough Riders and the jingoistic journalism that preyed upon people's sympathies for the Cuban and Puerto Rican insurgents, Goldman refused to be silenced by calls to the patriotic "duty" presumed appropriate for women. That duty was twofold: upholding the "American" soldiers' cause and showing motherly and protective sentiments toward the insurgents supposedly "orphaned" by the Spaniards' undemocratic tyranny. With this analysis I do not wish to minimize the suffering of thousands of Cubans who died rebelling against the Spaniards or from mistreatment, starvation, and unsanitary conditions in the concentration camps that were created under the order of the Spanish captain-general Valeriano Weyler y Nicolau to control and punish the Cuban rebels. My point is to indicate the ways in which anti-imperialists, pacifists, and others who opposed the United States' "splendid little war" were silenced, particularly if they were women. A decade after the Spanish-American War, when the war was still a popular topic, Goldman wrote unsparingly about the hypocrisy of the "American" position toward Cuba and of "American" representations of Spaniards as barbarous and cruel:

> How our hearts burned with indignation against the atrocious Spaniards! . . . when the smoke was over, the dead buried, and the cost of the war came back to the people in an increase in the price of commodities and rent—that is, when we sobered up from our patriotic spree—it suddenly dawned on us that the cause of the Spanish-American War was the consideration of the price of sugar; or, to be more explicit, that the lives, blood, and money of the American people were used to protect the interests of American capitalists, which were threatened by the Spanish government . . . When Cuba was firmly in the clutches of the United States, the very soldiers sent to liberate Cuba were ordered to shoot Cuban workingmen during the great cigarmakers' strike which took place shortly after the war.[6]

Goldman sought to expose the hypocrisy of the rhetoric of newspapers and politicians and to expose the underside of U.S. involvement in Cuba. What appeared to many Anglo-Americans as well as U.S. citizens (such as the African American and Native American soldiers) from other ethnic groups recruited for the cause to be a patriotic investment in the fulfillment of the United States' new role as liberator of the oppressed in the Southern and Eastern Hemispheres, was, according to Goldman's Marxist analysis, an alienation of the workers, the employees, both Cuban and "American," from the products of their labor. In short, she suggested that big business had manipulated the "American people" with effigial images of Spaniards and sentimental appeals to patriotism. Goldman's analysis was "popular" to the extent that it told the unofficial story and was persuasive to and provided a rallying point for a large number of early twentieth-century leftists. She was eventually deported from the United States for her essays, speeches, and other political actions.

For the most part, however, the recorded and preserved popular constructions of the Spanish-American War and its history were written and designed by men. Men enlisted and fought as soldiers; men painted and sculpted work after work celebrating and monumentalizing U.S. victories in Havana and San Juan; men rushed to the battle lines to take pictures and glean stories for newspaper columns; men formed and joined in large numbers both the Rough Riders and the Anti-Imperialist League. One man's reference to the war became the name ingrained in the minds of people at the time and, later, in history books: that "splendid little war."[7] Unlike the American Civil War, the Spanish-American War proper (the part of the war fought against Spain over Cuba and Puerto Rico, not the subsequent seven-year Philippine-American War) was too brief, a mere three months, to give a significant number of women time to overcome the restrictions on their authority to speak out about the war, except as supporters of the troops at train stations and wharves. Such was not the case when the United States became involved in the protracted and extremely bloody annexation of the Philippines and Guam, a situation that provoked the vocal opposition of women reformers such as Jane Addams.[8]

Women figured most often as allegorical representations of U.S. imperial ambitions in the form of an ideal type—the "American" Girl imagined exclusively as Anglo-American. Martha Banta has observed that "many variations on the American Girl functioned actively at the turn of the century to represent a variety of ideals, but once the Girl became the symbol for the nation as a political entity, she was assigned as a strong image harboring explicitly imperialistic connotations."[9] Banta, in the "Poster Lives" chapter of her book *Imaging American Women: Idea and Ideals in Cultural History* (1987), reprints two versions of the American Girl often found in newspapers, magazines, and other printed material referencing the Spanish-American War. I would describe these as the genteel passive vessel of patriotism (Figure 7) and the emancipated New Woman fighter. The genteel passive vessel of patriotism on the cover of the music sheet titled *The American Girl Battleship March* is, as Banta points out, "a fine example of the merger of wartime sentiment and the feminine touch." To complete the logic of Banta's remark, I argue that the image of Miss Maude Mears, the woman who devised the idea of a fund-raising campaign for a warship called *The American Girl Battleship* to complement the *American Boy Battleship*, afforded women a model and channel of participation in the Spanish-American War that would not compromise their status and that promised, in fact, the opposite: genteel, bourgeois respectability. Such an image represented the deployment of the "domestic woman" for the war effort and an ideological consensus about the new, belligerent role of the United States in world affairs. Similarly, the image of the New Woman that appeared in the cartoon captioned *The "Newest" Woman* (Figure 8) from the *St. Louis Globe-Democrat* (1898) signaled the appropriation of the

Figure 7. *The American Girl Battleship March* (1898), cover of a music sheet. From
W. H. Krell, *The American Girl Battleship March* (Chicago: The S. Brainard's Sons
Co., 1898). Courtesy of the Lilly Library, Indiana University.

Figure 8. Hedrick, *The "Newest" Woman* (1898), cartoon. From *St. Louis Globe-Democrat* (1898). Reprinted from *Cartoons of the War of 1898 with Spain from Leading Foreign and American Papers* (Chicago: Belford, Middlebrook, & Co., 1898), 42r. Courtesy of the President and Fellows of Harvard College.

rhetoric of the suffragettes as well as the stance and attire of those who espoused exercise and radical dress reform (e.g., bloomers) for U.S. imperialist interests.

The rhetoric of sisterhood was also rearticulated to espouse a sentimentally inflected U.S. imperialist agenda. In a memorial address delivered on February 27, 1902, in Washington, DC, John Hay declared emphatically, "Our sister republics to the south of us are convinced that we desire only their peace and prosperity."[10] Earlier, in 1898, Anglo-American painter, art instructor, and critic Kenyon Cox had done a nude study titled *Columbia and Cuba* (Figure 9) for a magazine cover. Banta interprets this image of the tall, strong Columbia as protecting Cuba, "a lovely but frail and naked maiden in distress."[11] Besides connoting the stronger/ weaker sister relationship, the drawing plays on an older/younger sister or mother/daughter relationship. It suggests a scenario in which the older sister/ mother (Columbia) has just finished disciplining the younger sister/ daughter (Cuba) and is standing proudly while Cuba clings contritely to Columbia, who wields a big stick, paddle, or bat. Banta proposes that images of Columbia like this one needed no support from male representatives of "American" power because such militantly masculinized images incorporated them already. However, Columbia's muscular, mannish arm leading down to the hand that grips the phallic stick may also be interpreted as leading back to these male representatives.[12] The club is a clear reminder of the long arm of Uncle Sam and the "big stick policy" articulated by Theodore Roosevelt. The gazes of the figures lead out and triangulate as well. Both the Columbia and Cuba of Cox's study gaze out at the viewer. One might imagine that this viewer could be a "new woman" herself, a suffragette for whom such an image of female power, however imperialistic, might still have had particular emancipatory appeal. And not only might it have had an emancipatory appeal, but a subversive one as well if one thinks of it in relation to Lori Merish's analysis of the lesbian erotics supposedly embedded in "The Bloomer Club Cigar" advertisement. It is not hard to see a naked Cuba clinging so intimately to an equally naked Columbia who appears to approve of the skin-to-skin contact as a highly gynoerotic image. I am not so sure that I would call it a "lesbian" one, though. If it was supposed to be referencing a special degree of intimacy between two women, the "lesbian-ness" or lesbian subversiveness of it is contained by a patriarchal framing gaze directed toward the figures

Figure 9. Kenyon Cox, *Columbia and Cuba* (c. 1898), pencil drawing nude study for magazine cover. Courtesy of the Library of Congress, Prints and Photographs Division (LC-USZ62-68463).

who are staring not at each other but at some invisible third presence. The point to which the figures' looks are directed might just as easily be a position of superior authority, Uncle Sam's controlling gaze. Columbia's posture is remindful of that of a soldier standing at attention before this gaze that, in the cartoon, is not embodied by a corresponding cartoon character, but rather transparently conscripts the viewer. Columbia is not so much a masculine woman as male authority in the drag of a female body disciplined by the gaze of yet another male authority above "her."

A cartoon that appeared in the *St. Louis Globe-Democrat* during the war makes graphically explicit what in the Cox study manifests itself merely as the implied gaze of Uncle Sam on such scenes of "sisterhood," gynoerotic or otherwise (Figure 10). In the cartoon, Columbia, figured as tall and fair and with one arm around the U.S. flag, hails with a long trumpet Cuba, "Porto Rico," and the Philippines, represented as shorter and darker than Columbia and gratefully outstretching their arms to their "liberator." Broken manacles and chains lie on the ground beside them. In the center background of this scene, a self-satisfied Uncle Sam sits in a chair puffing contentedly on his pipe and leering at the three dark beauties, his new possessions. Outfitted respectively with trumpet and pipe and both facing their new charges, Columbia and Uncle Sam reinforce rather than countermand each other. Banta also reproduces this image in the same chapter ("Poster Lives") in which she discusses *The American Girl Battleship, The "Newest" Woman,* and Cox's study *Columbia and Cuba.* In her analysis, she precedes Cox's *Columbia and Cuba* with the cartoon in question, proposing a progression from cartoon to study. Reversing the ordering logic of analysis to supersede the study with the evidently much more popular cartoon—not only published but anthologized and republished during 1898—I wish to reemphasize the degree to which the spectrum of women's publicly recognized roles or positions and the discourses shaping these roles had been co-opted for the imperialist cause.

Part of the co-optation involved the simultaneous creation of a female figure of Spain, not the dangerously seductive dark-skinned belle, but a rickety old woman—the typical hag barely standing, in contrast to the robust but graceful Columbia, the ideal type of Anglo-American woman. The figuration of women in U.S. wartime posters and cartoons was designed to channel Anglo-American women into patriarchally and patriotically controlled mother-and-sisterhood. Spain, on the other hand, is associated with social uselessness—a mother country and mother empire very much past her prime, as in a cartoon from the *Syracuse Herald* captioned *Spanish markmanship* (Figure 11) of a wretched old woman stationed on the shore, punting stones at Uncle Sam's phallically armored hat, which floats in the water, a cross between a battleship and a submarine. Aside from the implication of the United States' technological superiority over Spain, the cartoon strongly suggests that Spain, unlike the potent floating hat, symbol of the U.S. ship of state, is barren, *her* apron holding nothing but stones.

Figure 10. Russell, untitled (1898), cartoon. From *St. Louis Globe-Democrat* (1898). Reprinted from *Cartoons of the War of 1898 with Spain from Leading Foreign and American Papers* (Chicago: Belford, Middlebrook, & Co., 1898), 81v. Courtesy of the President and Fellows of Harvard College.

CLASS AND CONSENSUS:
THE STICKING POWER OF MANIFEST DESTINY

I propose that written and visual representations of Spain and Spaniards be thought of in terms of a dialectic between classes (class as defined by an interplay between the factors of property, money, education, occupation, and geographic location), as well as in terms of a hierarchy in which "middlemen"—journalists, illustrators for magazines, cartoonists for journals and papers, public speakers such as politicians—were able to meld the sentiments and aspirations of the larger population with the interests

Figure 11. *Spanish marksmanship* (1898), cartoon. From *Syracuse Herald* (1898). Reprinted from *Cartoons of the War of 1898 with Spain from Leading Foreign and American Papers* (Chicago: Belford, Middlebrook, & Co., 1898), 18r. Courtesy of the President and Fellows of Harvard College.

of the upper-middle Anglo-American class (landowners, industrialists, big businessmen, expansionists, and so forth). I should clarify here that in this chapter I distinguish a cultural elite from the middle class and the working class. This cultural elite was composed of individuals privileged by a combination of an extensive or classical education, wealth, travel abroad, property ownership, family name, and social and institutional connections to other individuals with some or all of the same privileges. I do not posit the cultural elite as the originators of ideas about Spain and Spaniards, the middle and working classes as receivers, or the members of the working class as furthest from the "origins" of those representations. I favor a model that takes into account the dialectic between all parts, categories, strata of society and culture, and which, at the same time, acknowledges a hierarchy of control over the production and dissemination of written and visual representations. However, this model recognizes that the access that middle and working classes may have had to the means of textual and visual production and dissemination may have been partially or largely erased by the canonization process.

Throughout the nineteenth century, and especially in the second half, ideas about Spain and Spaniards were part of both the "political unconscious" and the consciousness of the nation. The Spanish-American War was instrumental in catalyzing onto paper ideas, notions, and images in large quantities. During the 1890s, and especially in 1898, the subject of Spain and Spaniards was extended to a greater number of genres. Instead of being represented only in novels, learned poems, histories, and paintings, Spain and Spaniards figured in magazine stories, newspaper articles, songs and newspaper verse, cartoons, political speeches, photographs, drawings, and paintings reproduced in magazines and journals, battle memoirs, letters to newspapers, and on commemorative medals. Many of these genres were more accessible to general audiences in terms of both circulation and signification than were complicated novels and history tomes that required concentration and leisure to read or paintings often only privately exhibited. Furthermore, a wider range of people besides Anglo-American men of the cultural elite were involved in the production of works with Spain and Spaniards as subject matter. Ordinary journalists (some of them virtually unknown because their stories were printed anonymously), photographers, soldiers (both Anglo-American and African American), and civilians with other occupations (e.g., who sent verse to the newspapers) were creating representations. Also generating representations were Anglo-American men of privilege and power, such as Teddy Roosevelt, Henry Cabot Lodge, John Hay, and William Randolph Hearst. Then there were Anglo-American writers and journalists who were not born into privilege, nor acquired it during their careers, but were well known, such as Stephen Crane and Ambrose Bierce. There were also writers, such as Frank Norris, who were indeed from the upper-middle class and who were also quite well known at the time magazines such as *McClure's* hired them to report on the U.S. campaigns during the war.[13]

A direct relationship between class privilege and racist, warmongering expansionism cannot be established. Although a pattern between Anglo-American privilege, power, and imperialism may be discerned, people from all classes were creating, especially after the entry of the United States into war, pro-war and anti-Spanish representations. Furthermore, partial defection from the interests of one's class was a possibility. William James, for example, born into a prominent New York family that eventually moved to Newport, Rhode Island, and then on to Boston, was both a founder and a member of the Anti-Imperialist League. James evinced an admiration, similar to that of the Hispanophiles, for the energy, tenacity, and heroically "indomitable spirit" of legendary Spaniards—in James's case, "the Spanish mystics" Saint Teresa of Ávila, Saint Ignatius of Loyola, and Saint John of the Cross.[14] Although James did not engage in racial stereotyping with respect to "Spaniards" or "Spanish-speaking people" (unlike his contemporary and self-proclaimed "anti-imperialist" Charles Francis Adams), he did not entirely abandon the enterprise of racial typing promoted in his day as a respectable form of "knowledge," particularly by people such as the Harvard-based naturalist Louis Agassiz, whom James served as an assistant while studying medicine. In James's *Address on the Medical Registration Bill* (1898) clauses such as "[e]very nation has the Jews it deserves" and "[l]et us cultivate the robust Anglo-Saxon spirit" make their appearance.[15] In his private correspondence, phrases may be found such as "[t]he German character" and "the Anglo-Saxon race."[16] On the whole, however, his writings remained quite free of the apparatus of racial classification that pervaded the rhetoric of Louis Agassiz, Oliver Wendell Holmes, and other close acquaintances with a public profile. Although William James's writings in no way amount to a critique of racial typing, they do reveal a concern with the end that I have claimed that discourse was serving: justified imperialism. The Spanish-American War became a focal point for his increasing absorption with the problem of jingoism. According to his son Henry, several years before his death in 1910 he had begun to collect material for "a study which he sometimes spoke of as a 'Psychology of Jingoism,' sometimes as a 'Varieties of Military Experience.'"[17] He never completed the study, but it was part of his extended campaign as a public philosopher against U.S. imperial ambitions that expressed themselves so clearly in the Spanish-American War. James opposed this war on the grounds that appropriation of Cuba, Puerto Rico, and the Philippines was a hysterical, hypocritical, and savage course of action not worthy of the United States: "We had supposed ourselves (with all our crudity and barbarity in certain ways) a better nation morally than the rest . . . Dreams! Human Nature is everywhere the same; and at the least temptation all the old military passions arise."[18] He preached pacifism in the name of tolerance and civility. While there is a fine line between his position and that of other U.S. anti-imperialists of his class who espoused their isolationist doctrine because they wanted to preserve the future of "the republic" from what were considered the lazy, dirty, or unruly inhabitants of another country,[19] William James's writings suggest a person guiltier of Anglophilia and hope about "American" exceptionalism than of Hispanophobia or other forms of racially motivated "anti-imperialist" isolationism.[20]

Partial defection from the dominant class's interests, however, is sometimes one of the markers of privilege. A counterpoint to the case of William James is that of Stephen Crane. Although Stephen Crane's family settled in the North American colonies in the mid-seventeenth century, he was not born into privilege. He rebelled from what social standing his family possessed, identified with the urban poor, and lived the life of an artist pauper. His insolvency and his desire to be as close to harrowing "realities" as possible persuaded him to take a job at Joseph Pulitzer's *New York World* to cover the Spanish-American War. Although he was not a warmonger, he earned his living off of wars, both in his fiction and in his journalism. Although his articles were not jingoistic, he worked for one of the "leading propaganda organs," a journal "in the business of whipping up war-passion and increasing [its] circulation."[21] In general, his journalistic output on the Spanish-American War was not sensationalistic. The descriptions of the war that he wrote from Cuba and Puerto Rico often

betray a deep weariness with the whole business of war. With some exceptions, they do not encourage the reader to romanticize any aspect of it—
either the purported heroism and selflessness of the U.S. troops or the purported villany of the enemy, the Spaniards and the pro-Spanish Cubans,
who were shown to be less demonic and less despicable than many Anglo-
Americans assumed. Crane's ability to convey the suffering, physical and
psychological, of those involved in the war had a leveling effect—all were
equal in the face of mutilation and death. The following paragraph from
a dispatch written in July 1898, printed in the *World* on July 8 and titled
"Spanish Deserters among the Refugees at El Caney," is a prime example
of this leveling:

> [A]s the truce advanced, it changed the number and the character of these
> refugees. More men flocked in, young men and strong men. Certainly
> among them were deserters. There was the air of the true Spaniard about
> them. They had cast aside their distinguishing uniforms, to be sure, but
> they could not so easily disguise the ways and bearing of the soldier. Un-
> doubtedly they were renegades. But then—what matter? . . .
>
> One saw in this great, gaunt assemblage the true horror of war. The sick,
> the lame, the halt and the blind were there. Women and men, tottering
> upon the verge of death, plodding doggedly onward. (184)

The first paragraph in the passage maintains distinctions between people—
between the renegade Spaniards and the rest of the crowd. The second
paragraph, however, erases distinctions between ethnicities, cultures, gen-
ders, and injuries. Everyone is "tottering upon the verge of death." This
passage could easily have come from *The Red Badge of Courage* (published
in book form in 1895). Appearing in Pulitzer's *World,* it was an unusual
piece of writing because it was quite impartial with respect to the "enemy"
and did not construct a picture of U.S. national heroism to divert attention away from and justify the atrocities of war. As Crane wrote in a dispatch published on October 6, 1898, "after all—and after all—and again
after all, it is human agony and human agony is not pleasant" (220).
Nevertheless, despite these leveling moments, there are descriptions of
the Spaniards and Cubans as hot-tempered, impulsive, lazy, dishonest,
and childish that would have appealed to the prejudices of the readership of the *World* and the *New York Journal,* as well as to the prejudices

of readers in general, Anglo and otherwise. These descriptions were probably to be expected from a man who a few years earlier, reporting on the Greco-Turkish War, had written, "The Greeks I can see and understand, but the Turks seem unreal. They are shadows on the plain—vague figures in black" (43). Later, Crane wrote, "Turks, Turks, Turks; but then that is a mere name used to describe these creatures who were really hobgoblins and endowed with hobgoblin motives" (71). Moreover, in a dispatch printed in the *London Westminster Gazette* a day or two after the preceding dispatch, he had referred to a Turk as "the Oriental," a designation further erasing the distinctiveness of the individual "Turk" and positing the usual Orientalist trope of difference from "Western" peoples (81). Despite his distance from privilege, his identification with the poor and the downtrodden, and his ability to convey the suffering of all parties in a situation, Crane had his contradictions. His position as a reporter for the "yellow press" made him a useful "middleman" indeed—serving the interests of Anglo-American big business and expansionism by selling his name to those papers, unable to make any critique of manifest destiny that wasn't already co-opted by the context in which it was appearing, and perhaps all the while believing that he was merely being a faithful reporter, writing what he saw.

An example of a middleman who inhabited a world of privilege but who determinedly constructed himself as a man of the people, who was a well-known expensive artist but who promoted an image of himself as a frontiersman contending with "Indians," Spaniards, and the elements to eke out a living, was Frederic Remington. Not surprisingly, William Randolph Hearst enlisted him to cover the Spanish-American War with the well-known order, "You furnish the pictures and I'll furnish the war."[22] The illustrations of Spanish atrocities Remington sent back to Hearst's *Journal* were published and, according to Lawrence I. Berkove, used to "build a popular revulsion against Spanish rule that only needed a spark to kindle it into a demand for war."[23] In general, Remington was the quintessential melder of the sentiments of the larger population with the interests of the Anglo-American upper-middle class—the newspaper impresarios such as Hearst seeking to expand the circulation of their papers, capitalists minding the price of sugar, and captains of industry hoping to deflect public attention from the labor unrest that had been gaining momentum throughout the 1880s and 1890s.

These decades were marked by large fortunes in the hands of a few thousand millionaires and by labor unrest, as well as by the increasing negotiating power of labor unions. The Spanish-American War served as a major "diversion" from issues of class conflict in U.S. society. The war per se was one more manifestation of the old trick of finding an enemy outside the country to prevent class warfare within. A racially encoded imperial vision of manifest destiny functioned as sticky saltwater taffy that kept the different classes of society more or less bonded together in a common cause despite dissensus. I use the metaphor of saltwater taffy to describe the workings of the ideology of manifest destiny as I suggest that many Anglo-Americans experienced this ideology as natural, sweet, innocent, and flattering.[24] Manifest destiny could be consumed not as a construct, but as a reality; not a bitter oppression, but a desirable goal; not a lie or cover-up, but a combination of nostalgia, hope, and idealism about themselves.

A romantic, racial nationalism had been developing throughout the nineteenth century as a belief system not necessarily tied to class interests, but easily mobilized to serve them. A middleman such as Frederic Remington, who had published stories and illustrations in *Harper's Weekly, Harper's Monthly, Century, Cosmopolitan, Colliers, McClure's,* and *Scribner's* and who wrote descriptions such as the following—

Cuba is not a new-born country, peopled by wood-cutting, bear-fighting, agricultural folks who must be fresh and virtuous in order to exist. It is an old country, time worn, decayed, and debauched by thieving officials and fire and sword. The people are negroes or breeds, and they were sired by Spaniards who have never had social virtues since they were overrun by the Moors[25]—

in which he associated "negroes," "breeds," "Spaniards," and "Moors" with vice was the consummate candyman and fixer for his like-minded contemporaries. The idea that Remington was selling and that his audiences were eager to buy can be summed up in this line from his story "They Bore a Hand": "Indians, greasers, Spaniards—it was all the same."[26] According to this perspective, if Anglo-Americans eliminated Native Americans, Mexicans, and Spaniards, they were merely fulfilling the "prophecy" Remington had made in 1889 in his story "Horses of the Plains":

He has borne the Moor, the Spanish conqueror, the red Indian, the mountain-man, and the vaquero through all the glories of their careers; but they will soon be gone, with all their heritage of gallant deeds.[27]

Remington's vision, which he translated into innumerable paintings, illustrations, and stories and which was shared by many of his contemporaries, was that of the brave, physically and morally "fit" Anglo-American winning the West and the tropical frontier of Cuba and Puerto Rico from "the Moor," the "red Indian," and the "Spanish conqueror" who, despite their "heritage of gallant deeds," could not compare biologically or morally to the advanced and advancing Anglo. On May 27, 1909, Remington was elected an honorary member of the New York branch of the Roosevelt Rough Riders Association, according to a letter written two days later to Remington by Colton Reed, Secretary of the Association.[28]

MAKING A TURK'S-HEAD END OF SPAIN

Adjectives such as *bloody, atrocious, decayed, cruel,* and so forth, which appear in the works of Anglo-Americans arguing for or against the validity of their application to Spaniards at the end of the nineteenth century, merit attention because they crop up repeatedly in written representations. They also feature prominently in both the Orientalized version of Spain and in the negative side of the "white," more or less European, Catholic/Christian conquistador version of Spain witnessed in the Black Legend that equated Spain with intolerance, cruelty, and tyranny or misrule. In the 1880s and 1890s, and specifically with the advent of the Spanish-American War, the Orientalist version of Spain and vestiges of the Black Legend frequently appeared together, the demonizing tropes of the latter passing into and through the representational loop of Orientalism. This particular roping together or conjunction of versions served Anglo-Americans' need to find an adequate justification for taking over Spanish colonies and killing Spaniards as well as other Spanish-speaking peoples (namely, Cubans and Puerto Ricans). The Orientalist version in conjunction with the Black Legend reflected and perpetuated the renewed conviction that Spaniards were biologically and culturally "unfit" to rule any part of the Americas. The conjunction of the two versions to make a mutually reinforcing argument for "the expulsion of the Spaniard, and the final termination of Spanish rule in America" is patently evident in Andrew S. Draper's manifesto *The Rescue of Cuba: An Episode in the Growth of Free Government* (1899).[29] In Draper's first chapter, "Historic Misgovernment by Spain," he claims:

> [C]orruption seems to prevail among Spaniards more widely and persistently than in any other European nation; it is the trait that has most undermined the Spanish character, and has been more effective than any other in retarding Spanish progress, while other European nations have grown more honest and humane with the progress of civilization. Corruption and cruelty have held backward a nation of splendid possibilities, and have led Spain to commit acts almost as unwise and atrocious as those of Turkey.[30]

Draper's characterization of Spaniards as prone to "corruption" and "cruelty" echoes the familiar motifs of the Black Legend. His comparison of Spain with Turkey is a clear indication that the Orientalist version is operating metanarratively, as is the Black Legend:

> Four centuries ago all nations were shockingly cruel compared with the present standards, but the Spaniards at that time exceeded all other peoples in mercilessness; and while other nations have grown humane and gentle with the advance of better civilization, the Spaniards have lagged behind, and have continued to hold sentiments so savage as often to impel them to war against helpless prisoners, women, and children with the same ferocity with which they fight against soldiers in arms . . .
>
> It is not pleasant to tell this story, but it is part of the world's history, it bears upon the course of the United States concerning Spaniards, and it has at last settled the fate of Spain.[31]

That the Black Legend is invoked to justify U.S. aggression in the Caribbean and continuing U.S. intervention in "Spanish" America is apparent in the phrases "four centuries ago" (harking back to the beginnings of Spanish colonization of the Americas), "exceeded all other peoples in mercilessness," and "the course of the United States concerning Spaniards."

The comparison to Turkey, however, should not be overlooked. Without an understanding of the existence of an Orientalist version of Spain this comparison would seem to be quite arbitrary, when in fact it is anything but random. Comparisons between Spain and Turkey were especially common in the last years of the nineteenth century on the part of those who took an interest in both the Greco-Turkish War and in the Spanish-American War and who drew parallels between Turkey and Spain as "Oriental" countries. In December 1897, as the Greco-Turkish War was being fought, Charles Francis Adams, then President of the Massachusetts Historical Society and self-proclaimed "anti-imperialist," quoted Cotton Mather's 185-year-old remarks about the Turks as he, Adams, referred to "the approaching fall of the Ottoman Empire" and "Spanish rule in America."[32] Adams deployed Mather's remarks to make an elaborate comparison between the "Ottoman Empire" and "the Spanish domination in America" with respect to the Cuban challenge to Spanish control that had been building for several decades prior to 1897 and that was renewed in 1895 when a war for independence broke out:[33]

> What is now taking place in Cuba is historical. It is the dying out of a dominion the influence of which will be seen and felt for centuries in the life of two continents; just as what is taking place in Turkey is the last fierce flickering up of Asiatic rule in Europe, on the very spot where twenty-four centuries ago Asiatic rule in Europe was thought to have been averted forever. The two, Ottoman rule in Europe and Spanish rule in America, now stand at the bar of history . . . I have been unable to see what either has contributed to the accumulated possessions of the human race, or why both should not be classed among the many instances of the arrested civilization of a race, developing by degrees an irresistible tendency to retrogression.[34]

Charles Francis Adams's address to the Massachusetts Historical Society is indicative of the fact that the fusion of the Black Legend with the Orientalist version of Spain was not merely the province of Anglo-American imperialists per se. After all, Adams was one of the Anti-Imperialists. As such, the address furthermore betokens the extent to which notions of Anglo-American manifest destiny buttressed by this story about Spain and "Spanish" peoples exceeded doctrinal differences between "imperialists" and "anti-imperialists." In the mouth of an "anti-imperialist," for instance, manifest destiny reached its imperialistic apogee—it attained the incontestable status of providentially ordained natural law. The comparison between "Ottoman rule in Europe" and "Spanish rule in America" played a pivotal role in the elevation of the Anglo-American construct "American manifest destiny" into a "natural" law. Adams's comparison both rested on and advanced what by the late nineteenth century had become an organicist model of the naturally occurring westward progression of empire. The comparison of Spain with Turkey was dictated by a view of history according to this model that effectively turned history into teleology. Rather than speaking of the sixteenth-century rivalry between Spain and the Ottoman Empire, mentioning Spain's victory against the Ottoman Empire in the battle of Lepanto, or referring to particulars about the impending conflict between Spain and the United States in 1898, Adams's address conflates the Ottoman and the Spanish empires to make way for the new victor—the United States and Anglo, not Hispanic, "American" rule in the Western Hemisphere.

Draper and Adams were by no means unique in their formulations of a blend between the Black Legend and the Orientalist version of Spain. A similar combination of elements can be found in Bernard Moses' address "The Recent War with Spain from an Historical Point of View" delivered at a meeting of the Teachers' Association of Northern California, and published in 1899. Moses asserted that "Spain failed . . . because she was proud," "because, she was greedy of wealth," "because of her moral weakness," and "because she was intolerant, and in her intolerance made religious belief the test of good citizenship."[35] The vestiges of the Black Legend are easy to discern in these statements, as is the Orientalist version in the following lines:

> Spain, in her culture and in her experience, stands nearer the Orient than any other European nation. If, therefore, national decay and death are on the trail of the civilized nations, we might reasonably expect them to appear first in Spain. If for Spain there is no revival, if she must be wasted as the nations of western Asia have been wasted, then in the process of the centuries other nations may be expected to share in the same fate. (13–14)

Implied in these lines is the theory that Spain, inasmuch as it was associated with the "Orient," was a "natural" prey of "national decay" and "death." Moses was ultimately concerned with the rise and fall of empires, and although he never explicitly stated that "Oriental" nations were actually *doomed* to fail, his address more than hinted at such an idea. He clearly subscribed to the westward progress of civilization and his vision of "westward progress" was a specifically racialized one. He located the highest achievements of civilization with Anglo-Saxons and Teutons, with the English, Anglo-Americans, and Germans, praising those of "English stock" above all others for their "progressive form of civilization," their "traditions of freedom and toleration," of "practical independence without revolution," and of "efficiency in furnishing a method for governing communities" (12–23). He closed his essay by placing the fulfillment of American manifest destiny firmly in the hands of *Anglo*-Americans:

> [T]here is no reason to doubt that, under a like stimulus, the American branch of *the English people* may have at least an equally beneficent influence; and that along the lines of political supremacy it will carry the ideas born of our broader experience and our freer life, to establish, wherever the Americans dominate, the basis of a better social existence. (22–23; my emphasis)

For Moses the contrast between Spaniards and Anglo-Americans was not simply a matter of tyranny versus democracy. This point elucidates the import of Draper's words—"the expulsion of the Spaniard and the final termination of Spanish rule in America"—and of the almost identical phrase in chapter 1 of Henry Cabot Lodge's book *The War with Spain* (1899), "the final expulsion of Spain from the Americas."[36] The similarity between the phrase "the expulsion of the Spaniard" and the phrase "the expulsion of the Moors and the Jews in 1492" found in popular nineteenth-century history books such as William Hickling Prescott's *History of the Reign of Ferdinand and Isabella the Catholic* (1837), Samuel Astley Dunham's *History of Spain and Portugal* (1854), John S. C. Abbott's *The Romance of Spanish History* (1869), James Albert Harrison's *Spain* (1882), Henry Edward Watts's *The Christian Recovery of Spain* (1894), and Elizabeth Wormeley Latimer's *Spain in the Nineteenth Century* (1897) is not a mere coincidence, but rather was determined by the logic of the Orientalist version of Spain shared by many Anglo-Americans.[37] It should be noted that in many of these history books the phrases "the expulsion of the Moors" and "the expulsion of the Jews" are employed with degrees of condemnation or of embarrassment over the policies of the Catholic kings of Spain. On the other hand, most of these histories, though they seem to empathize with the Muslims, conclude by celebrating the "Christian" Reconquest. By the 1890s, it is clear that the phrase "the expulsion of the Moors" was both a stock expression and a familiar trope in U.S. and British books of history and travel, so familiar that Latimer wrote in 1897, "There are many excellent books, both of history and travel, which tell us about Spain in the days of her glory,—about Ferdinand and Isabella, *the expulsion of the Moors*."[38] In the late 1890s, the implication of the equation of Spaniards with Moors was that Spain was racially and morally degenerate. Within the framework of Anglo-American imperial ideology, the mark of distinction or election as opposed to the stigma placed on Spaniards and those of Spanish descent was born of another kind of *sangre pura* (pure blood)—not that of *el cristiano viejo* (the old Christian), but of "English" blood. The fraternity between Uncle Sam and John Bull (the personification of "the English people"), a popular theme in many wartime posters and cartoons, was thought to be more than political or even cultural. Whether implicit or explicitly stated, the basis of the alliance was presumed to be a racial one as well.

The Orientalist version of Spain in combination with the Black Legend was not confined to the writings and speeches of educators, historians, and politicians, to the journalism of well-known literary figures, or to the illustrations of well-known artists. It could be found in poems and songs contributed to many newspapers around the country by unknowns, in war cartoons printed in journals published quarterly and in papers published daily, among war memorabilia such as commemorative medals, and in letters written to newspapers by American soldiers serving in the war. In these representations Spaniards are portrayed as Turks, Moors, "dusky" bullfighters, dancers, guitarists, and skulking Indians.

The similarity between portrayals of Spaniards in newspaper verse published in 1898 and the addresses, essays, and books of the 1890s by men of letters attests to a representational continuity. It supports the theory that a phrase such as "the Spanish Turk" in Earl Marble's poem "Gineral Fitzhugh Lee" published in a newspaper in 1898 and the reference to "the 'unspeakable Turk,' the treacherous, barbarous Spaniard" made by N. C. Bruce, an African American who volunteered to fight in the Spanish-American War, were suggestive to Americans (Anglo and otherwise) not simply because the Greco-Turkish War had taken place shortly before the Spanish-American War, but because the Orientalist representation of

Spaniards had been so thoroughly disseminated during the nineteenth century.[39] Furthermore, all these "texts" belonged to the nation's public discourse about itself, about its purposes or "destiny."

TYPECASTING AND THE REPULSION OF THE SPANIARD

Among cartoons of the Spanish-American War, those of "Bart" (Charles Lewis Bartholomew) were some of the most popular. Twice as many of Bart's cartoons as of any other cartoonist were selected for the collection *Cartoons of the War of 1898 with Spain from Leading Foreign and American Papers* issued by the publishing house Belford, Middlebrook in 1898.[40] Bart's war cartoons appearing in the *Minneapolis Journal* present Spaniards as composites of types that, especially in the second half of the nineteenth century, embodied for Anglo-Americans what they deemed "Oriental"— dusky little bullfighters, guitar-playing minstrels, pirates with pantaloons, scimitars, turban-like headgear, and so on. Other cartoonists produced images in publications such as *Harper's Weekly,* the *Philadelphia Inquirer,* the *Philadelphia Press,* and the *Syracuse Herald* that caricatured Spain as an inept matador, a rapacious pirate on his last legs, a renegade "Moor," or a Semitic African cannibal with delusions of imperial grandeur. Bart's cartoons, however, were especially popular. First of all, they are particularly effective in packing together the many types and motifs from the Orientalist version of Spain and Spaniards to create a composite racialized physical type serving as an emblem of Spain. Second, despite the composite nature of the cartoon representations, highly theatrical scenes featuring facial expressions and dramatic actions make their messages abundantly clear. The Spaniard is presented as physically repulsive—big-nosed, bug-eyed, hairy, dark, racially tainted. In contrast, the Anglo-American viewer can feel superior and self-righteously certain that Spain and Spaniards, lampooned and punished, are receiving their just deserts. Cartoons by Bart such as *This Will Settle It* (Figure 12) depict a piratical Spaniard with a huge hooked nose and a broken dagger being run over by a U.S. biker steaming with anger and using his two-wheel technology to leave the "barbarian" in the dust. *If This Is Intervention Let U.S. Intervene* (Figure 13) shows Uncle Sam holding a large basket of provisions for "starving Cuba" and aiming his revolver at the head of a small, monstrous Spaniard cravenly clutching a scimitar-like dagger. Finally, *No Room for Him on This*

Figure 12. Bart (Charles Lewis Bartholomew), *This Will Settle It: The American Wheelman Will Join in the War on Spain—Poor Spain!* (1898), cartoon. From *Minneapolis Journal* (March 4, 1898). Reprinted from *Cartoons of the Spanish-American War by Bart with Dates of Important Events from "The Minneapolis Journal"* (Minneapolis: Journal Printing Company, January 1899), 6r. Courtesy of the President and Fellows of Harvard College.

Figure 13. Bart (Charles Lewis Bartholomew), *If This Is Intervention Let U.S. Intervene. Uncle Sam to Spain—I Propose to Feed Starving Cuba—with Your Consent if You Please, without It if You Don't!* (1898), cartoon. From *Minneapolis Journal* (March 22, 1898). Reprinted from *Cartoons of the Spanish-American War by Bart with Dates of Important Events from "The Minneapolis Journal"* (Minneapolis: Journal Printing Company, January 1899), 11r. Courtesy of the President and Fellows of Harvard College.

Side (Figure 14) offers up the image of a Spaniard in composite oriental-izing costume—bullfighter's hat labeled "Spain," turban-like bandanna, shawl or serape, curved sword dropping out of his hand—being ignomin-iously booted by Uncle Sam out of the "Western Hemisphere" back toward Spain. For the most part, Bart's cartoons packed the many types and motifs from the Orientalist version of Spain into one ultimatum summed up in this poem from the *Cleveland Plain Dealer* in 1898:

> *Don't You Hear Your Uncle Sam'l?*
>
> Land of garlic and tortillas,
> Land of xebecs and mantillas,
> Land of mules and smuggled bitters,
> Land of raisins and of fritters,
> Land of Pedro and of Sancho,
> Land of Weyler and of Blanco,
> Land of bull fights and pesetas,
> Land of dusky senoritas [*sic*],
> Land of manners stiff and haughty,
> Land of Isabella naughty,
> Land of Boabdil and Hamil,
> Don't you hear your Uncle Sam'l?
>   "Git!"[41]

Such ultimatums functioned to typecast Spain and Spaniards as culturally and historically backward (of the past) and racially unfit, while simultane-ously conferring upon the United States and Anglo-Americans in partic-ular a mission and a manifest destiny that was not so much the fulfillment, as the extension of the Monroe Doctrine to encompass the globe. With the caption *No Room for Him on This Side* and the icon of a banner read-ing "Western Hemisphere," the cartoon plays out an offensive version of the Monroe Doctrine that in 1823 had been formulated as a more defen-sive measure to protect the United States and the newly independent re-publics in Latin America from interference by a European power.

With reference to Spain, the poem also carries a trace of the Black Leg-end in the verses "land of manners stiff and haughty, / Land of Isabella naughty" alluding to Spaniards' alleged pride and deceitfulness, but most of it references the tropes of the Orientalist version—brigandage ("xebecs,"

Figure 14. Bart (Charles Lewis Bartholomew), *No Room for Him on This Side* (1898), cartoon. From *Minneapolis Journal* (April 5, 1898). Reprinted from *Cartoons of the Spanish-American War by Bart with Dates of Important Events from "The Minneapolis Journal"* (Minneapolis: Journal Printing Company, January 1899), 15v. Courtesy of the President and Fellows of Harvard College.

a word with a Turkish etymology referring to ships used by corsairs or pirates, and "smuggled bitters"), "mantillas" (a word conjuring up images of veiled women), "bull fights," "dusky senoritas [sic]," and defeated Moorish leaders ("Boabdil and Hamil"). The abject effeminization of the figure of the Spaniard in the cartoon transvestism; broken, dropped, and inverted swords; and "poetic" vanquishment work along the logic of rape, a rape no doubt devised to avenge the Spaniard's supposed rape of Cuba.

The broken, dropped, and inverted swords that render the abject effeminization of the figure of the Spaniard are echoed in one of the repeating details that unites the various representations of Spaniards in the cartoons: the large, pendulous, hooked nose. This bent nasal orifice appears as an attribute of "the Spaniard" in all the cartoons I have cited, thus effectively hanging "Spaniard" on a hooklike nose. Uncle Sam and the U.S. Scorcher also bear prominent noses, but these are not represented with the same highly distorted proportions, magnification in size, and twisted shape. Martha Banta contends that in the late nineteenth century, nativist "Americans," partly in reaction to the waves of immigrants from Europe, Eastern Europe in particular, became preoccupied with defining the ideal "American" type. They identified this ideal with "whiteness" and "regularity of features": "the straight, slender nose, the full yet controlled line of the lips, and the high 'pure' brow made familiar from endless plaster casts of Greek statuary."[42] Banta quotes from *The Bazar Book of Decorum* of 1870 to prove her point:

> It is common for foreigners to praise our people for their good looks, and the American face is certainly remarkable for its regularity. It seldom presents those extraordinary deviations from the classical ideal so frequently observed in foreigners . . . As people of all nations come hither, we have, of course, every kind of face. There are, accordingly, all varieties of disproportion and degrees of ugliness to be occasionally seen. These, such as the . . . nasal appendages fleshly and pendent, like abortive elephants' trunks. . . .[43]

In Bart's cartoons, Spaniards are given the features associated with "foreigners" and frequently, though not exclusively, those associated with Semitic foreigners. About the representations of Jews in the 1890s, Banta writes that Jews were rendered in a ludicrous fashion, given noses "whose enormity signal[ed] their difference from 'Americans.'"[44] Although no overt comparison between Jews and Spaniards can be found in the cartoons, it seems that there was an implicit association being made, one that was supposed to stigmatize the Spaniard—racially as "Oriental" and morally as non-Christian. Protestants often considered the Catholicism of most Spaniards to be a type of anti-Christianity, a formulation that rested on, among other things, an association of Catholicism with its converts (forced or otherwise), Jews and Muslims. Hence, the reference, popular in the nineteenth century, to Spaniards as Catholic Turks.

The curved sword, dagger, or knife that visually underscores the hooked nose in material relating to the Spanish-American War also works to link together many of the tropes of the Orientalist version of Spaniards. It also represents the combination of the Orientalist version with the negative side of the white conquistador version presented by the Black Legend. The sword, dagger, or knife is an accessory as inevitable for the Spaniard as bloodthirsty, vengeful Turk and/or Moor, bullfighter, pirate, and tyrannical conqueror/ruler as a knife is for Injun Joe, "the half-breed" who disguises himself as "a deaf and dumb *Spaniard*" (my emphasis) in Mark Twain's novel *The Adventures of Tom Sawyer* (1876). It is not surprising that the sword, dagger, or knife is featured in cartoons, illustrations, and poems; it functioned as an easily comprehended sign associating Spaniards with violence, barbarism, death, and, to the extent that the sword works as a phallic symbol, with rape. The following stanza from a newspaper poem titled "The Passing of the Don" by E. L. Bowker expresses the full import for pro-war Anglo-Americans of the sword, dagger, or knife in connection with Spaniards:

> As a person drowning makes one final clutch for life,
>   And knows that all is fruitless, yet still he struggles on;
> So Spain, a dying nation, *grips Cuba with uplifted knife,*
>   But, thank God! America has stepped between to end the bloody strife.[45]

The image of Spain as a "dying nation grip[ping] Cuba with uplifted knife" is reminiscent of the image, central to "American" captivity narratives, of the Anglo-American woman on the point of being ravished by the demonic Indian. "America" is figured in the poem as the heroic rescuer thwarting Spain's violent captivation of Cuba.

Both writers and visual artists capitalized on three versions of the threatening image of Spaniards bearing their swords: (1) the sensationalistic image of a dagger plunged into the heart of some victim, as in Howard Chandler Christy's painting *An Awful Tragedy of the Spanish War* (Figure 15); (2) the self-indulgently elegiac image of the Spaniard taking a last stand with his sword unsheathed, as in Christy's *Heroic but Fruitless Defense by the Spaniards of the Last Fort in Front of Caney* (Figure 16); and (3) the ridiculous images of a Spaniard losing his grip on his sword and being kicked in the buttocks and of a Spaniard terrified by the realization that his dagger or sword is useless in the face of Uncle Sam's U.S.-made revolver or rifle. The last two images were probably very gratifying to those U.S. citizens who could identify with the figure of Uncle Sam proving himself endowed with virile strength despite his hoary locks and Ichabod Crane body.

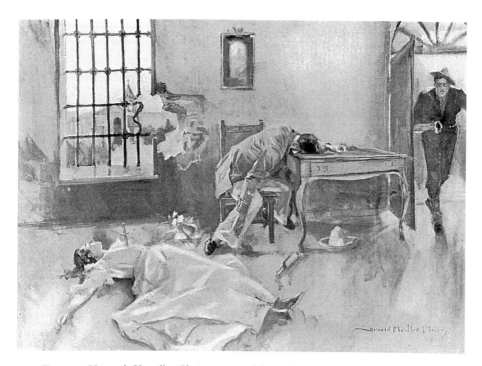

Figure 15. Howard Chandler Christy, *An Awful Tragedy of the Spanish War* (1898), painting. From *Leslie's Weekly* 87, no. 2249 (October 20, 1898): 313. Courtesy of the President and Fellows of Harvard College.

Even more pleasurable, perhaps, was the image accompanied by the inscription "YANKO SPANKO/1898 WAR" on one side of a commemorative medal dating from the end of the war (Figure 17), the other side of which reads "DEWEY,/REMEMBER/THE/MAINE/HE DID."[46] The image is of a big, tall Uncle Sam sitting on a bench, spanking a puny Spaniard who is lying facedown across his knees in bullfighter-like costume with no accompanying sword or dagger. Such an image represented the ultimate defeat and humiliation of the Spaniards. The "vengeful" Turk or Moor, the daunting conquistador/governor, and the "bad Indian" of the captivity narratives about the Cuban situation published daily in the Hearst and Pulitzer papers had been reduced to a bawling bullfighter/matador without a sword, lying helpless under Anglo-America's hand uplifted in a paternal, imperial gesture of reprimand. "Maternal" counterparts to this image of paternal reprimand also existed, as can be appreciated in Charles Dana

Figure 16. Howard Chandler Christy, *Heroic but Fruitless Defense by the Spaniards of the Last Fort in Front of Caney* (1898), pen and wash drawing. From *Leslie's Weekly* 87, no. 2251 (November 3, 1898): 346–47. Courtesy of the President and Fellows of Harvard College.

Gibson's illustration *Come, Let Us Forgive and Forget* printed in *Life* on August 11, 1898 (Figure 18).[47] Gibson's image shows "America," or rather, Columbia, embodied by a monumental, white-skinned woman with a "classically" proportioned face and a star-spangled, Phrygian cap on her head, offering the olive branch of peace to a sulking, dark-skinned, hook-nosed, little Spanish bullfighter who is a third her size and is bound up in his own cape.[48] The scene on the commemorative medal and Gibson's illustration encapsulate the extent to which Anglo-Americans had equated their victory against the Spaniards with righteous judgment and imperial destiny through the supposed fulfillment of what they considered to be their ultimately exclusive *Anglo-Saxon* revolutionary heritage of "freedom," "liberty," "equality," and "virtue."

Tremendous ironies inhere in this vision of *Anglo-American* manifest destiny and the hard-core Orientalist version of Spain lending it a definitional center. This seemingly independent Anglo-American imperial identity was internally dependent for its identity on the very figure of Spain it was attempting to eject or repulse from its psychic and claimed territorial domain; that is, Spain—the image of its decline—was the supporting object around which this Anglo-American imperial identity consolidated itself like a circle of linked buttresses. This hollow edifice of identity was

Figure 17. Commemorative medal from the Spanish-American War (1898), white metal. Obverse: YANKO SPANKO / 1898 WAR. Reverse: DEWEY,/REMEMBER/THE/MAINE/HE DID. The Mariners' Museum, Newport News, Virginia.

fabricated with the aid of the sticky taffy of the ideology of manifest destiny sealing up gender and class fissures. The Turk's-head knotted rope of history as teleology foredoomed Spain and Spaniards at the same time that, like the rope on a pulley wheel, it was employed to raise up an Anglo-American imperial identity and empire. The greatest and most ominous irony is that the construction of modern "American" nationalism, built up on a grand scale—as Anglo-American imperialism—depended on a racially stigmatizing system that resembled the one applied by Spain to define itself against its "Others" in its own campaign of national unification and self-aggrandizement.

Figure 18. Charles Dana Gibson, *Come, Let Us Forgive and Forget* (1898), drawing. From *Life* 32, no. 818 (August 11, 1898): 110–11. Courtesy of the President and Fellows of Harvard College.

chapter 4

SACRED BULLS OF
MODERNISM

TOTEMIC GROUND

During the nineteenth century, Anglo-Americans had been especially interested in typing and explaining the inhabitants of Spain in terms of "race" and "racial origins"—attributing the presumed distinctiveness of Spaniards from "Europeans" to their "Oriental" heritage, to the traces of Moorish, Gypsy, and Jewish "blood." As I have argued in chapters 2 and 3, Anglo-Americans' interest in Spaniards as Moors, Gypsies, Jews, and "Indians" was heavily determined by the dynamics of a racially encoded vision of manifest destiny. The defeat of Spain in the Spanish-Cuban-American War (1898) and the acquisition of most of its remaining colonies marked the debut of the United States as a world power. Spain was no longer a fearful rival or an undesirable obstacle to Anglo-American imperialism. In the years immediately after the war, sundry essays and books were published discussing the causes of Spain's decline and contrasting the country's retrogression with "America"'s advancement. The prevailing U.S. sentiment toward Spain was pity, a mixture of disdain and clemency. The conqueror had been conquered and, having been vanquished, would eventually be imagined as a kind of colony, a place where the United States might extend and cultivate an idealized vision of democracy and enterprise. As Jeremiah Zimmerman's *Spain and Her People* (1902) proclaims: "Many of them [Spaniards] wish that we had taken Spain also, for the Spaniards are a badly governed people, and they have no hope in their government"; and "American enterprise, thrift and industry would make much of Spain, fair as a garden of the Lord, for the mountainous regions and barren places that defy cultivation are no excuse for the neglect of the districts that are capable of the highest productiveness."[1]

This chapter is concerned with what expatriate U.S. modernists writing and publishing between the early 1920s and the late 1950s had to say about Spain and the extent to which, less imperialistically and in a more eulogizing manner, but perhaps in a no less proprietary way, they figured Spain not as a well-charted colony, but as a last frontier, a land to be discovered. Unlike the writers of the nineteenth century obsessed with racial origins and the physiognomic aspects of race, twentieth-century writers such as John Dos Passos, Waldo Frank, Gertrude Stein, and Ernest Hemingway shifted away from a specifically racial typing of the inhabitants of Spain in favor of figuring them in relation to their country as land. Dos Passos in *Rosinante to the Road Again* (1922); Frank in *Virgin Spain; Scenes from the Spiritual Drama of a Great People* (1926; revised in 1942); Stein in *The Autobiography of Alice B. Toklas* (1933) and *Picasso: The Complete Writings* (1934); Hemingway in *The Sun Also Rises* (1926), *Death in the Afternoon* (1932), the script for *The Spanish Earth* (1937), and *For Whom the Bell Tolls* (1940), and even Richard Wright in *Pagan Spain* (1957) were primarily interested in Spain as land. Their writings engage with the idea of the Spanish land as a transforming force determining national character, temper, soul, or spirit; as raw material waiting to be transformed (redistributed, fertilized, and tilled); and, most significantly, as a medium that would help them to vitalize their work. Spaniards usually figure as peasants, artisans, villagers, laborers, bullfighters, dancers, and guerrilla soldiers—representatives of a primal, authentic relationship to the land, if not actual embodiments of both its creative and its destructive forces.

This kind of fascination with the land, the soul of the nation, and regeneration was not an exclusively U.S. phenomenon. Gripped by the idea of the primacy of the Spanish land in relation to Spanish identity were British, American, and also Spanish writers, especially those promoting the cause of anarchist, agrarian collectives, but also less radical writers such as Ángel Ganivet (*Idearium español,* 1897) and Miguel de Unamuno (*En torno al casticismo,* 1902).[2] Preoccupied with the issue of national regeneration a few years prior to Spain's defeat in the Spanish-Cuban-American War (1898) and in the face of the presumed identity-eroding consequences of "Europeanizing" industrialism, these writers subscribed to what Donald Shaw has called a "nationalist mystique."[3] Other Spanish writers of the first two decades of the twentieth century who extolled the purportedly quintessentially "Spanish" part of the Spanish land—that is, Castile— and the rural laborer as part of the dream of spiritual reorientation and national regeneration were Antonio Machado (*Campos de Castilla,* 1912) and José Martínez Ruiz ("Epiloga en Castilla," *Lecturas españolas,* 1912), alias Azorín, also members of the so-called "Generación del '98." These various writers differed with one another over how the land had shaped "the Spanish soul," but, nevertheless, they were concerned with very similar questions. Dos Passos, Waldo Frank, and Hemingway were familiar with the writings of Unamuno when they wrote their works on Spain. Dos Passos himself was especially interested in the writings of the Generation of '98, as was Hemingway, whom Dos Passos purportedly introduced to much of the literature. According to Ángel Capellan, Hemingway read closely from the work of Unamuno, Ganivet, Antonio Machado, Pío Baroja, José Ortega y Gasset, and Salvador de Madariaga.[4] In fact, one of Hemingway's Spanish friends and himself a novelist, José Luis Castillo-Puche, has documented that Hemingway not only read Baroja's work but visited him on his deathbed in 1956. Castillo-Puche's book contains a photograph of Hemingway dedicating a copy of *The Sun Also Rises* to the Basque novelist.[5]

The parallels between the Spanish and U.S. writers' concerns and the influence of the Spanish writers on certain of the U.S. ones are undeniable. Both the Spanish and the American writers were interested, one way or another, in the idea of the rebirth of Spain. The Spanish civil war (1936–39) itself triggered, so to speak, the hopes of liberals and radicals in the United States that Spain would become the symbol of the triumph of liberal democracy against fascism and all that was seen as retrogressive. However, I do not make U.S. writers' involvement in the civil war per se the focus of my examination. That subject has been well documented and thoroughly discussed by Allen Guttmann, John Muste, and others.[6] Rather than concentrate solely on the civil war, I cut to the core of what I contend was the lure of Spain for U.S. writers between 1920 and the late 1950s, many of whom were not directly involved in the war, spent time in Spain either before or after the war, or demonstrated interests in Spain that extended beyond it. The U.S. writers had their own agendas.

The trend I am analyzing had as much to do with reactions to industrialism, mass production, mass technologization, and ontological alienation (symptoms of capitalism) as it did with the issues of class, distribution of wealth, and land ownership in the conflict between "los republicanos y los nacionales." Although the interest in Spain as country/land and in Spaniards as peasants, villagers, workers, and so forth came to a head during the war years, it was not simply produced by or confined to the war experience.

Spain represented for many U.S. writers and thinkers of the first half of the twentieth century the transposition of certain ideals held to be particularly "American"—such as "democracy"—into a largely agrarian setting, a place with ties to the land, ties that, it was felt, had been lost in the United States through industrialization, mechanization, increasing urbanization, physical and psychological dislocation, and discontinuity. As Dos Passos writes in *Rosinante to the Road Again* (1922):

> In this day when we Americans are plundering the earth far and near for flowers and seeds and ferments of literature in the hope, perhaps vain, of fallowing our thin soil with manure rich and diverse and promiscuous so that the somewhat sickly plants of our own culture may burst sappy and green through the steel and cement and inhibitions of our lives, we should not forget the northwest corner of the Mediterranean.[7]

Spain also represented the place where what was missing from life in the United States—ritual, passion, a sense of the sacred—could be acquired, actively or osmotically. Spain, or the idea of Spain—to borrow the distinction implicit in Wallace Stevens's well-known poem "The Idea of Order at Key West" (1936)—was one of the chief elements in a "modern" myth of the soil, a myth propagated against modernity's own entropic forces. "Spain" was at the center of the response of U.S. writers and artists to modernity, particularly those who imagined themselves as modernists responding aesthetically (formally and ideologically) to the "crisis" of modernity and who felt the need to fashion themselves and their art practice at a seeming remove from mainstream U.S. culture or, more to the point, Anglo-American U.S. culture. Why did Spain figure so centrally in modernists' contradictory quests to be moderns, but to contain modernity by making sense of its cultural entropy; remove themselves, either imaginatively or literally or both, from the Anglo-dominated United States while simultaneously always addressing their country of birth not as the geographically plotted and bounded United States, but as the mythic "America"? A brief version of the answer is surely contained in these two stanzas from Wallace Stevens's poem "The Idea of Order at Key West." In these stanzas the poet addresses the explorer "Ramon Fernandez" with the by now well-known epithet "pale Ramon." The address or apostrophe consists of a question, a "tell me, if you know" how, why, and to what ends the night, the sea, and distant lands ("emblazoned zones and fiery poles") are mastered, ordered. The mastery and order or, more precisely, desires for them ("the maker's rage to order") apply to geophysical space as much as to words on the page.[8] These stanzas suggest that for U.S. modernists Spain or traces of Spain ("Ramon Fernandez . . . pale Ramon") figured so centrally because of the historical and symbolic association of Spain with the "discovery" and the conquest and colonization of the greater part of the Americas or the "New World." Spain doubled both as symbol for and destination (if only metaphoric) of the poet-writer-discoverer-and-creator of new worlds. Hence, the question leveled at Ramon Fernandez about "mastering," "positioning," "fixing," "arranging," "deepening," "enchanting" and the references to "[t]he maker's rage to order words of the sea" and "words . . . of ourselves and of our origins." These modernists, aspiring to "make it new" in a world already old and mapped and increasingly mediated by the machine, wanted to begin afresh. They were drawn to Spain and Spaniards to retrace the dream of the invention and discovery of America. This inquiry after "ourselves and our origins" translated for the modernists into a simultaneously nostalgic or retrospective and future-oriented or prospective voyage toward a world in the making, a "last frontier" to be appropriated in their own image. Allusions to Spaniards in Hart Crane's book of poems *The Bridge* (1930) (Luis de San Angel, Juan Pérez, Fernando De Soto) and in Archibald MacLeish's epic poem *Conquistador* (1932) (Alvarado, Cortés, Bernal Díaz, Francisco López de Gómara, Jerónimo de Aguilar, etc.) occur, as in Stevens's poem "The Idea of Order at Key West," in the context of apostrophe. The allusions compose an address to the vanished Spaniard whose remains, however insubstantial, conjure up the dream of a New World and that promise of the return of newness, not to the Spaniards, losers of empire, but to the U.S. modernist writers:

And the west is gone now: the west is the ocean sky . . .
O day that brings the earth back bring again[9]

While U.S. modernists who did not expatriate were attracted to an identification with Spaniards as seafarers, explorers on the high seas—"Here
waves climb into dusk on gleaming mail . . . slowly the sun's red caravel
drops light" (Hart Crane) and "We could not lie in our towns for the
sound of the sea . . . We looked to the west" (MacLeish)[10]—U.S. expatriate modernists enshrined images of Spain as land even when they denaturalized, as with Stein, the trope of the Spanish "earth." To expatriate
modernists, Spain meant "land," partly perhaps to compensate for their
own uprootedness. Spaniards as "primitives" were supposed to have an implicit connection to it, even if that connection was expressed opposition-
ally in the form of a deliberate architectural discontinuity between "nature"
and "man," as one sees in Gertrude Stein's representations of Spain. U.S.
expatriate modernists clinched the centrality of the role of Spain in a modern myth of the land down to the very soil.

"Sacred Bulls of Modernism," the title of this chapter, refers not merely
to the fact that the expatriate modernists who went to Spain wrote about
bulls and bullfights, though most did, and that they did is in itself meaningful. Their interest in bullfighting proceeded from their wish to see
Spain as a primitive country with a strong bond to the land. Bulls have
long been regarded as quintessentially "grounded." Modernist writers'
interest in bullfighting also had the effect of reinforcing for their readers
the linkage between Spain and primitive cultures, not necessarily negatively, but certainly with all the attendant cultural baggage of the anthropological investigation of one country by another. The title "Sacred Bulls
of Modernism," however, is primarily intended to flag the fundamental
claim of this chapter—that Spain and Spaniards played a totemic role in
rituals of U.S. expatriate modernist self-fashioning and mythmaking about
their own discovery-creation of a last frontier, a proving ground of experience and artistry. The bull is, after all, a totem animal. Innumerable books
have been written on the symbolic value placed upon bulls as signifiers of
potency, sexual, psychical, and political, and of a formidable, if not deadly,
but necessary confrontation on the labyrinthian path to self-knowledge
and self-possession. The symbolic antecedent of the bull writ large is generally considered to be the Minotaur. Theories abound about the origin

and function of totems, and specifically of the bull as totem. As I mentioned in my Introduction, in *Totem and Taboo* (1913), Freud suggests that the totem originated subsequent to the murder by the brothers of the primal or ancestral father. The totem animal functioned as a substitute for the father. When sacrificed for the commemorative totem meal, it was a means of appeasing him for the outrage inflicted on him and assuaging the guilt of the parricidal brothers. Furthermore, according to Freud, the incorporation through ingestion of parts of the father's surrogate in the totem meal is indicative of the brothers' desire to become like the father, to accrue his qualities and thus take his place. And, Freud writes, the celebratory sacrifice of the totem animal expresses satisfaction at the earlier father-surrogate having been abandoned in favor of the superior concept of God, or a transcendental ideal.[11] As Freud himself declares, totemism, and particularly totemic sacrifice, has to do with "the relation of the son to the father" and with the need to both celebrate and atone for the murder of the father by the sons.[12] Although hypothetically any animal can qualify as a totem, Freud's essay pays more attention to human fear of and fascination with, love and hate toward, animals that impose in their rival, generally larger-than-human scale—bears, lions, horses, and bulls. Regarding the bull, Freud mentions the "religion of Mithras": "We may perhaps infer from the sculptures of Mithras slaying a bull that he represented a son who was alone in sacrificing his father and thus redeemed his brothers from their burden of complicity in the deed."[13] In all cases, Freud stresses the mechanisms of identification with the totem and the emotional ambivalence toward it. Totemism involves a complex set of emotions and desires: rivalry, hostility, parricide, identification, guilt, longing, and idealization. The totemic representation of Spain and Spaniards is not quite the same as that under the sign of *imago* and or alter ego, though continuities exist and any given representation may evince several functions simultaneously. Totemic representation implies a different set of historical relations in which that which has been totemized is something that belongs to the past (even to an atavistic past) and recuperated for some beneficial use in the present.

I call attention to Freud's theory of totemism and its relation to the title "Sacred Bulls of Modernism" to frame this chapter's concentration on three expatriate modernist writers: Gertrude Stein, Ernest Hemingway, and Richard Wright. But, I reference Freud not to run Stein, Hemingway, and Wright as individuals through the psychoanalytic mill. I shall resist that temptation; these figures only too easily attract this kind of approach— and have, in literary biographies of them. Such an analysis would reduce their interest in Spain to case studies of individual pathologies. Instead, I read these works as symptomatic of a larger cultural agonism with Spain as totemic ground. All three writers actually went to Spain and "mapped," wrote with pictures and drew with words, the contours of the land. For both Stein and Hemingway, their respective journeys, "cartographic" each in its own way, were the product of a desire to "discover" a last frontier, a "last wonderful country" (to quote a remark that Hemingway and John Huston shared in the late 1950s) supposedly unspoiled by indus- trialism (technology and mass production) where they could prove them- selves pioneers of an ultimately individualistic, not socialist-collectivist, vision of personal, artistic, cultural, and, one might venture to assert, inter-national regeneration. They did so by claiming for themselves and their work an original or authentic relationship to the earth through their insiders' understanding of the Spanish people's relation to their land and, furthermore, by suggesting in the course of their descriptions that their writings had incorporated and were embodying the spirit, the *Geist,* pre- sumably arising from the Spanish soil and its people. As polar antithesis, Richard Wright's *Pagan Spain* purported to document the degradation of human life and the impoverishment of self-determination in Spain, and it drew explicit similitudes between a "primitive" landscape and a "pagan" people.

I find Freud's theory of totemism and the metaphor of the "sacred bull" useful in explaining the general historical and cultural pattern of U.S. responses to Spain between the 1920s and the 1950s, if not from the turn of the century onwards. Much scholarship in "American" literature and culture, taking its cue from British and U.S. literature itself, has explored the idea of Britain as parent and the United States as son or daughter. The "American" Revolution and its aftermath have been discussed within this paradigm. The metaphors of mother country and colonial dependents achieving "independence" is so familiar, so much a part of the myth of "America," that it is no longer viewed as metaphor or as descriptive of only one historical relation—that of what became the United States with Eng- land. What I have been advancing is the argument that Spain occupied a similar position to England, if not more significantly complicated by the fact that it functioned historically and symbolically as both tyrannical father or "Old World" parent country and fraternal rival for the Americas. Recall, for instance, Melville's long tale "Benito Cereno" (1855) or the alter-ego depictions of "the Spaniard" in cartoons from the Spanish-Cuban-American War (1898).

Having made the comparison of Spain to father and brother figures, the comparison is complicated by the fact that nations are spoken of in the feminine and thought of as much as the "motherland" as they are the fatherland or *la patria*. The feminine gendering of the word *patria* should be noted as a sign of a certain amount of gender ambiguity in the concept of country. An association of Spain with a mother is strikingly evident in Walt Whitman's poem "Spain, 1873–74" in which he suggests that "out of that old entire European debris" Columbia may glimpse her own face, as though she where birthed by mother Spain. A search for mother Spain on the Internet, for instance, yields a far greater number of links than "father Spain," and this in itself is significant. However, when a country is figured as tyrannical, it is usually masculinized representationally. Perhaps within patriarchal logic the idea of a tyrannical motherland is far too threatening, even more so than the nation as a tyrannical fatherland. The fact that wars were and still are largely fought by men over their "possessions" has the effect of masculinizing and phallicizing the mother country, though not in a particularly subversive way, as I demonstrated in the preceding chapter. If figured as a mother, a country is a phallic one upholding patriarchal law, not setting herself up as rival.

In the "family drama" of war, the resounding defeat of Spain in the Spanish-American War was generally representationally analogized to the murder of a male authority figure, both a primal father and one of the brothers from the rivalrous band of brothers contending for possession of the Americas. Once Spain, the tyrant-father and rival-brother, had been vanquished and, as the cartoons loved to show, kicked back across the Atlantic, historical and cultural "space" opened up for other emotions besides hostility, especially with the passage of time. Stein's and Hemingway's treatment of Spain, their sacred bull, emblematizes the longing, identificatory curve of the totemic spiral of emotions circling from idealization around to hostility and back. In Wright's *Pagan Spain* (1957), Spain as sacred bull becomes the abjected scapegoat upon which a hostile narrator heaps the sins of both "Western" and "non-Western" history.

The cultural authority granted to it by other modernists is sacrificed in a Gothic portrayal of the country as a wasteland and its inhabitants as irredeemably pagan. The fact that Franco was in power at the time that Wright wrote *Pagan Spain* and that Wright composed his book as, among other things, an anthropological reconnaissance trip through Spain under the dictator/father figure Franco may have contributed to the appeal for Wright of the Black Legend and its image of Spain as paternal tyrant. Significantly, Spanish women fare relatively well in *Pagan Spain;* Spanish men do not. They are, for the most part, depicted as petty tyrants.

Despite the seemingly wide disparities between Stein and Hemingway, on the one hand, and Wright, on the other, the narrators of all the works I discuss in the following three sections react as if they had found long-lost kin in Spain and Spaniards. An avenue of speculation beyond the scope of this chapter is the role that going to Spain on Stein's recommendation may have played in displacing or complementing the search for or creation of father figures with the search for or creation of strong maternal figures in Hemingway's and Wright's texts about Spain. Both Hemingway and Wright were, at one point or another during their time in France, close to Stein, who influenced their writing and introduced them to many people helpful to their careers. The association of this country with strong women features conspicuously in both *For Whom the Bell Tolls* (1940) and *Pagan Spain* (1957). In fact, Stein herself seems to have represented Spain largely in terms of Saint Teresa, who figures as a kind of pioneering foremother, a woman with a mystical design or mission. Furthermore, as discussed later, Stein represented Spain, among other ways, in terms of women, specifically *women,* wearing black. While the three writers' texts are manifestations of different aspects of the totemic relationship, Stein, Hemingway, and Wright all appropriated Spain as their sacred bull by using it (some might say abusing it) as the tough hide and ground of their self-constitution, in the posture of something like bullfighters—a parallel that Hemingway was at no pains to occult.

To put this last point aphoristically, Stein, Hemingway, and Wright seized Spain like a bull by the horns to test, strengthen, and confirm through contact with this totem and through ritual initiation their standing as "great" modernist writers, pioneers, discoverers who survived to tell the tale. In other words, they seized the bull by the horns to turn themselves into sacred bulls of modernism. Given the relationship between totemism and tradition, it is ironic that, although Spain was the proclaimed site of U.S. expatriate modernists' confirmation as writers and shapers of modern literature, this focus of intense interest and literary activity has been ignored in scholarly and curricular accounts of "American" literary history. Such omission of figures of Spain in U.S. literary and cultural history is, in large part, an effect of the workings of Anglo-American imperial ideology, the vicissitudes of which I have been tracing. The relative valuation in U.S. universities of France and Britain over Spain has been given added weight by the association of Spain, despite its history of resistance, with fascism. Under the first two decades of Franco's regime, during which so many Spanish intellectuals went into exile and foreign scholars either avoided the country or thought of it as an intellectual and cultural desert, the Black Legend was renewed as a political descriptor and Spain was dubbed by foreigners the "Cinderella [ash girl] of Europe"—yet another turn of the family drama of gender and class, this time featuring Spain not as fatherland or motherland nor as fraternal rival but as an orphan in a household not her own.

For U.S. modernist writers, Spain, nonetheless, became a figurative and also a very literal "ground" of experience ("Solid Spain! The earth is clotted, corrugation, furrow," as Waldo Frank exclaimed) upon which to constitute their art practices and their own identities as expatriate "Americans" or "Americans" abroad. Whether they joined the Lincoln Brigade to shed their blood on Spanish soil with the hopes of helping "New World democracy" triumph over "Old World totalitarianism/fascism"; whether they became the first "American" aficionados of a ritualized contest between man and nature in bullfighting; or whether they suddenly appreciated the "rhythm of the visible world, the relationship between the external and the internal," to quote Gertrude Stein, what links them is the fact that Spain became for them a new frontier where they could prove themselves variously as pioneers, making it "new," beginning again, or, in Wright's case, surviving a desolate wasteland, the sinister side of a new frontier. In general, this project took the form of an individualistic idealism finding a vision of *communitas* on the open, unpaved road running across "desolate abandoned dun-colored spaces" (Dos Passos and also Waldo Frank); of the "modern" revivified and made ultranew, avant-garde, through contact with the "primitive" (Stein); and (with Hemingway) of the reenactment of American frontier values such as rugged individualism, courageous deeds, ritualized battles with nature (through bullfighting, hunting, and fishing) and with the "natives" (in the Spanish civil war); the camaraderie of male companions (bonding with guerrilla soldiers); and an authentic relationship with the soil (ingesting, like a peasant, the fruits of the earth, being baptized in bulls' blood, getting covered with Spanish sand and dust, baking, like clay, in the Spanish sun).

Figures of Spain and Spaniards were central to Stein's and Hemingway's hopes for the discovery/creation of a "New World" in the "Old World" and Richard Wright's attempt to attain a postcolonial status by indicting the "Other" colonizer of the Americas, Spain and Spaniards. After the U.S. victory over Spain in the Spanish-Cuban-American War (1898) until the advent of Franco's regime (1940), the appeal of the Black Legend as the "truth" about Spain receded considerably. This trend reversed itself in the first two decades of Franco's dictatorship. Wright's *Pagan Spain,* published in 1957, is a prime example of the revival of the Black Legend. Meanwhile, however, the country that in the seventeenth and eighteenth centuries had been considered by Anglo-American colonists to be the "home" of the Papist infidel, the tyrannical monarch, and the location of a degenerate and oppressive feudal system became for a number of U.S. expatriate writers and writer-travelers abroad a liminal space of personal and artistic transformation during the 1920s and 1930s and even the early 1940s. The taboo had turned into the totem. Much the same may be said of territory in or off North America claimed at one point by the Spanish crown—Cuba and "New Spain" (or Mexico) for Archibald MacLeish; Florida and Havana, Cuba, in Wallace Stevens's poetry; Baja California, associated with the early-sixteenth-century Spanish explorers in John Steinbeck's *Log from the Sea of Cortez* (1941); and San Francisco in Eudora Welty's short story "Music from Spain" (1949). The land(s) of Spain and the figure of the Spaniard, including the conquistador and immigrant, became for these Americans what the earth was for Antaeus, the giant who wrestled with Hercules and whose strength derived from his physical connection with his "mother Earth." Such a relation partakes of a classic aspect of totemism in which, as part of an initiation ritual on the way to establishing a certain degree of status, the participants incorporate some aspect of their elders or of that deemed to have residual special power. The respective ventures of Dos Passos, Frank, Stein, and Hemingway partook of a visionary colonialism. Despite their leftist and liberal agendas, these writers used Spain as raw material for their retrospective radicalism without staying and becoming permanently involved with the country and the people about whom they wrote. In a sense, they took the goods and ran—went to Spain, mined it for its possibilities, and left its continuing problems for its inhabitants to handle. Ezra Pound observed caustically that "Spain is an emotional luxury to a gang of sap-headed dilettantes." It is a hyperbole with a measure of truth in it. Aesthetic engagement without sustained political participation was a luxury that the U.S. expatriate and writer-traveler could afford. The irony is that such harsh criticism came from a fascist sympathizer. Evidently, Pound had not stopped to consider the similarities between their retrospective radicalism and fascist visions of the regeneration of the national spirit or consciousness through a return not only to the essence of blood, but to that of the soil as well. Although Richard Wright's *Pagan Spain* was written a good deal later than the works by Stein and Hemingway I examine, its inclusion in the discussion is important because Wright's book transvalued the celebratory optimism of that visionary colonialism into a kind of despairing critique that nevertheless remained in the shadow of an imperial ideology. Wright viewed Spain as an antiprogress nightmare, a blood-soaked land of "brown hills, red lands, russet-gray vineyards, dun-colored olive groves" and "gruesome mountain tops," a land "far . . . fallen to the rear of her sister European nations."[14] Wright's text, as I will demonstrate, is implicated in the very discourses of race and metaphysical judgment with which Anglo-American imperial ideology framed people of "color" and other "whites" who were not Anglo-Teutonic or Protestant.

I explore the valences of Spain as frontier and Spaniard as frontier inhabitant, including representations of the peasant as noble savage ("good Indian" and cicerone) and as a locus of ignorance, superstition, treachery, and violence (the "bad" Indian of the captivity narratives). In the course of my discussion, I examine how the variables of gender, ethnicity, creed or ethos, political affiliation, and the issue of "home" influenced their representations. A designation such as "Anglo-American" can only be understood in relation to other identity positions. I consider how Stein's and Wright's representations of Spain and Spaniards problematize the representations found in the dominant Anglo-American culture. Nonetheless, I elucidate the ways in which all three of these writers' portrayals fall between Anglo-American conventions about Spain. Although Stein, Hemingway, and Wright were modernists, they did not always avoid conventions or write in opposition to the dominant culture.

GERTRUDE STEIN'S SPANISH LANDSCAPES: A DIFFERENT "GEOGRAPHICAL HISTORY" FOR MODERNISM

The centrality of "Spain" to both a formulation of modernist discourse and its representation has hitherto been ignored in studies of Gertrude Stein's work. Literary scholars have continually plotted U.S. modernism on a map connecting the United States to Britain and France. Specifically, U.S. modernism has been represented with reference to urban sites and the much-vaunted triangulation between New York, Paris, and London. These cities have been treated as standing in for, in a synecdochical relation to, their respective nations. Paris, in particular, has been foregrounded as "another country" for expatriate U.S. modernists. Some of Stein's work, such as *Paris France* (1940), in which she writes, "Paris was where the twentieth century was," or her quips "writers have to have two countries, the one where they belong and the one in which they live really" and "America is my country and Paris is my home town," would seem to reinforce this map of relations.[15] However, Stein's *Autobiography of Alice B. Toklas* (1933) and her portrait of Picasso published in 1938 alter this familiar geography of modernism to give a foundational "place" to Spain in her inscription of herself as both a champion and a pioneer of the avant-garde. I focus on the 1938 "Picasso" and bring in the *Autobiography,* published five years earlier, to elucidate particular issues concerning Stein's use of Spain to remap modernism and her identity as a modernist. Unlike the *Autobiography,* the title of which signals a disjuncture between the ostensible subject matter and its "agenda," the 1938 "Picasso" has been read in two ways: as a legendizing portrait of Picasso, and as a manifesto of Stein's involvement with analytic Cubism and what she saw as its most important feature—its defamiliarization of the habit of knowing what one looked at into successive moments of seeing rendered simultaneously. Literary critics have underplayed, if not entirely overlooked, the fact that not only is the artist Pablo Picasso and an avant-garde practice the subject of the piece, so is the location of this practice. The location is designated as being not merely with a Spaniard (i.e., Picasso, the Spaniard in France), but with "Spain." As Stein writes, "Cubism is part of the daily life in Spain."[16] Ironically, though literary critics have underplayed or generally overlooked Stein's Spanish remapping of modernism, her fellow writers did not, as is evidenced not only by Hemingway and Richard Wright, who went to Spain quite literally following her advice, but also by those who fled from the East Coast and the Midwest in the other direction—to Southern California, one of the most Spanish and Mexican parts of the United States. For example, 1930s writer Nathanael West in one of his four novels, *The Day of the Locust* (1939), created a character named Mrs. Jennings, a cultured madam of a Los Angeles sex workers' house, whose favorite topic of conversation is "discussing Gertrude Stein and Juan Gris [the famous Spanish Cubist painter whose work, with its emphasis on constructed rhythms and abstract components, radicalized the Cubist movement's development]."[17]

Spain in the 1938 "Picasso," like France in *Paris France,* is depicted within a recognizably regionalistic rubric. By "regionalistic" I mean that the text's syllogisms about Spain are phrased in terms commonly employed to define or circumscribe a particular area of a nation—the lay of the land, habits of mind or daily life (hence the statement about Cubism being part of the daily life in Spain), descriptions of cultural expressions with attention to local architecture, and the like. Of course, all these terms come into play in descriptions of national characteristics as well, the chief differences being that the regionalistic model is interested in stating its generalities in terms of particularisms, its "wholes" in terms of "parts." This is exactly what Stein does in her explanations of the difference between France and Spain. If, for her, France is a "city" in relation to the "soil," Spain is a series of "villages" in relation to their "landscapes." The regionalistic rubric is operative to the extent that the country Spain is scaled down to villages and landscapes. Although the concepts of "region" and "regionalism" have been theorized in numerous ways, since the mid-nineteenth century they often have been formulated in reaction to industrial capitalism with its mass production, technologization, and machinic urbanization. Writers of the first half of the twentieth century, and particularly U.S. writers such as John Dos Passos, Ernest Hemingway, and Waldo Frank who, like Stein herself, went to Spain, were drawn to the project of envisioning a country in a regionalistic way even if they never actually employed the term "region" but only wrote as if within a vague but powerful paradigm. In such cases, this paradigm involved a fascination with the indigenous and the folklike—for example, a primary interest in a country

as "land," as raw material waiting to be transformed and also as a transforming force, and, with respect to Spain, Spanish peasants, villagers,
manual laborers, bullfighters, and/or guerrilla fighters inasmuch as these
were understood to be close to the "land," if not embodiments of its
vital forces. It is significant, for example, that in the *Autobiography* Stein
describes Picasso as a bullfighter.[18] It is also significant that, although the
1907–14 chapter of the *Autobiography* indicates that on their several trips
to Spain Stein and Toklas visited or sojourned in main cities such as
Barcelona, Madrid, Toledo, Granada, and Palma de Mallorca, as well as
in large towns such as Cuenca and Ávila, in the 1938 "Picasso" Stein refers
to Spain not in terms of its cities and towns, but in terms of villages and
landscapes and the relation between the two. The effect, I argue, is to
activate a set of expectations—habits of mind on the reader's part—about
a supposed organic relation between figure and ground that is a central
tenet of regionalistic rubrics despite variations in focus.

Spain, however, is treated within a recognizably regionalistic rubric
with some significant disorientations. In both the 1938 "Picasso" and the
Autobiography, the relation between figure and ground, between village
and the landscape, is denaturalized. Descriptions do not accord with the
trope, widespread from the 1920s to the 1940s, of "the Spanish earth"
serving as the tangible, raw material for an organic relation between it, the
human body, and human works of art, including architecture. A sign of
Stein's deliberate denaturalization of the popular trope of "the Spanish
earth" (here I allude to the title of the 1937 documentary film for which
Hemingway wrote the screenplay in collaboration with Joris Ivens, John
Dos Passos, Archibald MacLeish, and Lillian Hellman) is her repeated use
of the word *landscape* rather than *earth. Landscape* denotes, among other
things, the visual re-presentation of nature as in a painting or drawing. In
the *Autobiography* and the 1938 "Picasso," the relation between the Spanish villages and their landscapes is portrayed in terms of human art and
ritual—as an opposition between nature and man acknowledged and cul-
tivated by Spaniards, as Cubism (the "natural" expression of that opposition), as the art of camouflage in modern warfare with its lines, colors, and
flatness being not merely analogous to, but imitative of, Picasso's Cubism.
To quote Stein on the relation between the Spanish villages and their
landscapes, "the architecture of other countries always follows the line of
the landscape . . . but Spanish architecture cuts across the landscape . . .

The work of man is not in harmony with the landscape, it opposes it and it is just that that is the basis of cubism and that is what Spanish cubism is" ("Picasso," 53). These Spanish villages and their landscapes, in their stark "elementality," are pictured as challenging nineteenth-century French and British positivist notions of organic unity and historical continuity and progress. Stein's association of Spain with the "elemental" would seem to evoke a long tradition of French, British, and Anglo-American representations of Spain and Spaniards as "primitive" or backward. However, her texts transvalue notions of the primitive into the "elemental" *as* the fundamentally modern. Rather than equating "elemental" with closeness to nature, with organic continuity, with the preindustrial past, she associates it with art, with the culturally constructed, with the full force of modernity with all of its promise and destructiveness. For Stein, the "elemental" signified a quintessentially modernist mode of cultural revitalization—the active search for and practice of that strange quality ascribed to Picasso's Spanish Cubist work in the final lines of her 1938 portrait—"of an earth that one has never seen and of things destroyed as they have never been destroyed" (ibid., 91). To clarify, she never uses the words *primitive* or *elemental* in the 1938 "Picasso," but both words appear in the *Autobiography*—and in the same paragraph on Picasso, Spanish Cubism, and her aesthetic preferences:

> In these early days when he created cubism the effect of the african art was purely upon his vision and his forms, but his imagination remained purely Spanish. The Spanish quality of ritual and abstraction had been indeed stimulated by his painting the portrait of Gertrude Stein. She had a definite impulse then and always toward elemental abstraction. She was not at any time interested in african sculpture . . . She says that as an american she likes primitive things to be more savage. (*Autobiography,* 64)

"Elemental" is here associated with abstraction and is counterposed somewhat against "primitive," although "primitive" is valorized to the extent that it is "savage," which does not mean "backward" or "barbarian" but uncultivated, raw, original, anticonventional, disencumbered from tradition and history. Of "african sculpture" she writes, "it is very ancient, very narrow, very sophisticated," implying that it has too long a tradition for her "taste."

Examining Stein's use of "primitive," "elemental," and "savage" may seem a divergence away from the issue of the creation of a "different 'geographical history' for modernism" and how her disorienting regionalistic rubric fits into the making of that history. However, the transvaluation of the "primitive" into the elemental *as* the modern occurs within the context of two startling "geographical" transformations: (1) the transformation of Spain into a region of villages and landscapes that exist not in relation to history (unlike the cities in the *Autobiography*, the villages remain unnamed), but in relation to art and philosophy; and (2) the intersection of Spain with "America" on the basis of a supposedly modern understanding of the elemental discontinuity and disagreement between things:

> Spaniards know that there is no agreement, neither the landscape with the houses, neither the round with the cube, neither the great number with the small number, it was natural that a Spaniard should express this in the painting of the twentieth century, the century where nothing is in agreement . . . America and Spain have this thing in common, that is why Spain discovered America and America Spain, in fact it is for this reason that both of them have found their moment in the twentieth century. ("Picasso," 54, 57)

This passage on Spanish Cubism enacts a variation of modernism by locating the cutting edge of modernist art practice not in Paris, London, or New York, but in Spain and along a no-man's-line of similitudes between "Spain" and "America" composing a composite frontier region of the mind.

Taking these two geographical transformations to be definitional examples of Stein's transvaluation of the primitive into the elemental as modern, it becomes clear that "primitive" for her has nothing to do with backwardness, crudity, or regression along a horizontal time line or within a chronology. Instead, "primitive" is associated with its root *primus*, meaning not merely "prior," but also "first," "original," and "fundamental." It is understood to have everything to do with existing in vertical time and space, like those villages against their landscapes functioning as horologes or sundials telling the time—hence, "Spain discovered America and America Spain . . . both of them have found their moment in the twentieth century." That time as space is modernism.

These two geographical transformations—of Spain into a region of villages and landscapes and of "Spain" and "America" into a composite frontier region of the mind—also exemplify the relation between Stein's disorienting regionalistic rubric and abstraction. Like other terms discussed, "abstraction" has numerous significations. It can mean an abstract or general idea; something visionary or unrealistic; the act of considering something as a general quality or characteristic apart from concrete instances; the act of taking away or separating; the state of being lost in thought; or a nonrepresentational work of art. In the 1938 "Picasso" all of these meanings are at work, but three in particular apply to Stein's disorienting regionalistic rubric. First of all, the reduction of Spain to villages and their landscapes and the reduction of "America" to skyscrapers ("Picasso," 44) is an act of considering something as a general quality or characteristic apart from concrete instances. Villages and skyscrapers are relatively concrete instances, but unnamed and unplaced and devoid of distinguishing features they are not. At most, they are abstracted particulars. However, these abstracted particulars are allowed to assume the status of general qualities about their respective countries. They hint at region (province, metropolis), but stand for much more—for Spain, for "America." Second, lifting these villages and skyscrapers out of the settings habitually reserved for them—the country, the city—into the realm of art and philosophy is an act of subtraction or separation of the figure from the ground. Third, the synthesis of these villages and skyscrapers and of Spain and "America" under the aegis of discovery is Stein's deliberate creation of something visionary or unrealistic. This visionary synthesis represents her break not only with nineteenth-century notions of progress, but also with nineteenth-century realism. Stein writes: "[R]eality for them [Spaniards and Americans] is not real and that is why there are skyscrapers and American literature and Spanish painting and literature" (ibid.). In the 1938 "Picasso" and the *Autobiography,* the choice between the real and the visionary is the no contest between the known and the new. Privileging the act of discovery, Stein chooses the latter. Although there are no references to the history of Spain, except the phrase "Spain discovered America," the conjunction Spain-America for her composite frontier region of the mind is anything but random. Within Euro-American culture, the embeddedness of these territories in a narrative of "New World discovery" is unparalleled. However quixotic Stein's project of creating "another country" out of the synthesis of two abstractly regionalized ones (Spain and "America"), she has on her side the pull of history turned legend—the legend of the Spanish discovery of the Americas, a legend she reciprocates *in her discovery of Spain.*

In *The Geographical History of America* published in 1936, Stein writes: "Geography does not look like it does in relation to the human mind."[19] The *Autobiography,* and especially the 1938 "Picasso," draw Spain in accordance with a design that undercuts regional and national boundaries as we habitually think of them. In these works Stein creates a different geography for modernism, like that "earth that one has never seen" which she mentions in connection with Picasso's Cubism. Instead of France, Britain, and the United States, it is "America" and Spain, "a big [and] a little country" (*Geographical History,* 85). Like "pictures [commencing] to want to leave their frames and [creating] the necessity for cubism" ("Picasso," 38), these two geographical entities—Spain and "America"—are freed, in Stein's work, from their conventional borders and made to meet, forming one earth as if seen from a plane: "the mingling lines . . . coming and going" (ibid., 88) and "one piece of it . . . not separated from any other one" (*Geographical History,* 85).

The boldness of this new geography may be appreciated in light of her position as an expatriated woman writer daring to play with cultural authority, history, geography, and ethnography. A U.S. citizen living in France, Stein originally wrote the 1938 "Picasso" in French. It was published by the Librairie Floury in Paris. Later, she and Alice B. Toklas translated the essay from French into English. Although written and published in French, it was hardly flattering to France. It contained statements such as, "in the twentieth century it [painting] was done in France but by Spaniards" (21), "France for Spaniards is rather a seduction than an influence" (48), and "[a]fter all Spain is Spain and it is not France and the twentieth century in France needed a Spaniard to express its life" (51). Effectively, the piece audaciously rescinded in favor of Spain the allegiance paid to France by so many of Stein's U.S. predecessors and contemporaries. This was a daring move to make as a U.S. expatriate writing in French and in France, where both a French audience and a U.S. audience would have assumed that France deserved the credit, especially in matters of art and literature. It should be noted once again that Stein was tremendously influential in getting other writers interested in Spain. Whenever one mentions U.S. modernists and Spain, the figure most commonly recalled is Ernest Hemingway, but actually it was Stein who encouraged Hemingway to go to Spain in the first place as she had stayed there on numerous occasions more than a decade before he ever set foot on the other side of the Pyrenees.

Stein's endeavor to create a different geographical history for modernism and more or less confer upon herself the role of discoverer and pioneer of the avant-garde was intrepid not only because she was arrogating to herself, a woman, so much cultural authority, but also because she extended the terrain of "America" to include that of its former imperial rival, Spain, in the form of a claim to shared understanding. In "Picasso" she writes, "I was alone at this time in understanding him [Picasso], perhaps because I was expressing the same thing in literature, perhaps because I was an American and, as I say, Spaniards and Americans have a kind of understanding of things which is the same" (42). Although such assertions served the task of self-promotion, Stein was one of the first U.S. writers to take a substantive interest in the artistic and philosophical production of a country that, on the whole, in the late nineteenth and persistingly into the twentieth century, had been viewed as backwards, a historical and cultural failure, by Anglo-Americans in the wake of the defeat of Spain in the Spanish-Cuban-American War of 1898. It is true that Stein wrote this "Picasso" piece in the late 1930s and that Spain, with the outbreak of its civil war in 1936, was already the object of much international attention and interest. The *Autobiography,* however, was published three years before the war. In it, she articulates a debt to her experiences in Spain for a transformation in her "style" or the orientation of her writing: "[I]t was there [in Granada] and at that time that Gertrude Stein's style gradually changed. She says hitherto she had been interested only in the insides of people, their character and what went on inside them, it was during that summer that she first felt a desire to express the rhythm of the visible world . . . She always was, she always is, tormented by the problem of the external and the internal . . . These were the days in which she wrote Susie Asado and Preciocilla and Gypsies in Spain. She experimented with everything in trying to describe" (119).

Although, for the most part, Stein did not describe places and type inhabitants as many other writers did who subscribed to the scientific legitimacy of ethnography and who attributed the presumed enigmatic distinctiveness of Spaniards from "Europeans" to their "Oriental" heritage, certain passages in Stein's work would indicate that conceptually she was not as critical of the ethnographic clichés about Spain as "torment" over the "problem of the external and the internal" might indicate. As "discoverer of Spain," she nonetheless played the "American" frontier pioneer defining Spanish natives in relation to their land. The following sentences might be interpreted as a reminder of an earlier Stein given to "scientific" categorizing and typing that Wendy Steiner wrote about in her book *Exact Resemblance to Exact Resemblance* (1978): "Spain is the only country in Europe whose landscape is not European . . . therefore it is natural that although Spaniards are Europeans even so they are not Europeans" ("Picasso," 71) or "Spain . . . is not at all southern, it is oriental, women there wear black more often than colors, the earth is dry and gold in color, the sky is blue almost black . . . and the air is very light, so that every one and everything is black" (ibid., 30). At first glance, these sentences read as if they belonged to a regionalistic paradigm resting on the argument about the determining force of environment—on one-to-one "natural" correspondences between physical geography and "race," customs, belief systems, and the like. Sentences, however, were Stein's passion. She constructed them very thoughtfully. Within these sentences, which are syllogisms, one can detect a flying back and forth between assertions and negations of well-worn theses about Spain that assume a "natural" continuity between the land and the people. With regard to the statement "Spain . . . is oriental, women there wear black," she later contradicts the "oriental" part and the earlier "European" part with "Spaniards and Americans are not like Europeans, they are not like Orientals, they have something in common, that is they do not need religion or mysticism not to believe in reality as all the world knows it" (ibid., 44). By such contradictions, Stein's work shows conventional regionalistic and nationalistic rubrics to be tautological constructions in which a people's identity and, in this last example, especially that of the women, is defined in relation to a land assigned identifiable characteristics because of them. Of these habits of mind she sought to free herself so that her work—like the women in black against the earth dry and gold in color—would stand out starkly and resist the misreadings of those who would attempt to relegate her writing to mediumistic automatism, pretty nonsense, or "local color." Her boldest move as a woman was to turn history, geography, and ethnography into language games and philosophy. Spain and Spaniards, by all her accounts, gave her the courage.

HEMINGWAY IN THE DIRT: SPANISH EARTH AND THE INGESTION OF AUTHENTICITY

Unlike Stein, Hemingway and Spain have been discussed together for years, both anecdotally and from the standpoint of serious literary analysis. So famous was and is the association of Hemingway with Spain that an entire U.S. tourist industry thrives to this day revolving around those places in Spain he visited (Pamplona, San Sebastian, Bilbao, Madrid, Valencia, Seville, Córdoba, Granada, Málaga), those hotels he mentioned in his works (the Montoya, la Florida, the Montana, the Palace), those cafés, bars, and restaurants he frequented (Café Iruña, Café Suizo, Bar Milano, Chicote, Botín), and those events (bullfights, ferias, the fiesta of San Fermín, the Spanish civil war) in which he took part—if only vicariously—and monumentalized in his writing.[20] As for literary analysis of his work in relation to Spain, numerous books and articles examine within a more general investigation of his work the function of Spain as site and symbol for the elaboration of his code of discipline, courage ("grace under pressure"), killing, and dying well.[21] More specifically in reference to Spain or Spanish culture, there have been explorations of the influence of Pío Baroja on Hemingway's existentialism, explorations inspired, no doubt, by the repetition of the word *nada* ("nothing") in the story "A Clean Well-Lighted Place."[22]

Other areas of interest for scholars have been Hemingway's coverage of the Spanish civil war as a reporter for the North American Newspaper Alliance, his championing of the Spanish Republican cause (many have opined, for personal advantage), and his close, though eventually embittered personal and ideological relations with John Dos Passos and Martha Gellhorn. Dos Passos first went to Spain in 1916 and began familiarizing himself with its cultures and writing about the country before Hemingway embarked on his long literary campaign to claim Spain for himself. Martha Gellhorn also covered the civil war in Spain and took a much keener interest in the intricacies of politics than did Hemingway, to whom she was unhappily married from 1940 to 1945. In *For Whom the Bell Tolls* (1940), on account of his disillusionment with the role the Communists

played in sabotaging a united leftist front against fascism, Hemingway reiterated the strains of the Black Legend and condemned all of the Republic's leaders in a passage conveying the stream-of-consciousness of the
novel's Anglo-American hero Robert Jordan:

> Muck them to hell together, Largo, Prieto, Asensio, Miaja, Rojo, all of
> them . . . Muck the whole treachery-ridden country. Muck their egotism
> and their selfishness and their selfishness and their egotism and their con-
> ceit and their treachery . . . *They always muck you instead, from Cortez and
> Menendez de Avila down to Miaja.* Look at what Miaja did to Kebler . . .
> Muck all the insane, egotistical, treacherous swine that have always gov-
> erned Spain and ruled her armies.[23]

The story goes on to show Jordan's anger subsiding and his repentance
for having thought such things: "If that were true what are you here for?
It's not true and you know it. Look at all the good ones" (370). *For Whom
the Bell Tolls* never names those "good ones." Discriminating political
analysis never made its way into a book advertised as one of the best war
novels of all time. As for the Hemingway–Dos Passos friendship, it
foundered on Hemingway's jealousy of the literary success of his friend's
trilogy *U.S.A.* and, more important, on the 1937 execution by Stalinist
Communists in Spain of José Robles, then colonel in the Spanish Republican army and Dos Passos's translator, who was accused of being a fascist
spy. The somewhat more politically sophisticated Dos Passos suspected
that his translator had been the victim of an internal purge and broke with
the Communist Party, whereas Hemingway preferred to toe the party line,
although later in *For Whom the Bell Tolls* he denounced all the Republic's
leaders.

Aside from the tourist industry and the industry of scholarly articles
and books, the association of Hemingway with Spain gave rise to and continues to inspire a number of fiction and travel-book writers following
hard on the heels of Hemingway's itineraries and modes of consuming
Spain. Take, for example, Francis Davis's war novel *My Shadow in the
Sun* (1940), Barnaby Conrad's *Matador* (1952), *La fiesta brava: The Art of
the Bull Ring* (1953), *The Death of Manolete* (1958), and *Name Dropping:
Tales from My Barbary Coast Saloon* (1994), Hemingway's duplication of
himself in *The Dangerous Summer* (1960), Norman Mailer's *The Bullfight:*

A Photographic Narrative with Text (1967), and James Michener's *Iberia* (1968) and *Miracle in Seville* (1995).

Such perpetual identification of Hemingway with Spain and Spain with Hemingway is precisely what Hemingway hoped to achieve for himself in regard to the "last wonderful country." The mythic identification, however, has had the effect of blinding scholars to its very making—to the textual performances through which Hemingway forged such an identification and the ideological valences of his evocations of Spain or, more specifically, "the Spanish earth" to legitimate his expatriate modernist art practice. *The Sun Also Rises* (1926) and *For Whom the Bell Tolls* (1940) are the novels where the making of the mythic identification of Hemingway with Spain, via the author surrogate Jake Barnes and hero alibi Robert Jordan, takes place. In these two novels the myth is in different stages of its making—*The Sun Also Rises* representing the first stage and *For Whom the Bell Tolls,* the second. It is not a question of the chronological precedence of one over the other, but of how the relationship between narrator and country is presented, including the degree of "insider" knowledge and status. *The Sun Also Rises* is all about choosing one's "last wonderful country." *For Whom the Bell Tolls* is about "being there," the choice already having been made. *The Sun Also Rises* opens with a conversation in Paris between Robert Cohn, billed as the Jewish-American antihero, and the Anglo-American hero Jake Barnes over which country to visit from their expatriate perch, Paris. *For Whom the Bell Tolls* begins with the Anglo-American hero Robert Jordan lying flat on his belly "on the brown, pine-needled floor of the [Spanish] forest" (1). Prior to the commencement of the narrative, he has joined an antifascist guerrilla unit and is studying the lay of the land accompanied by "a short and solid old man" in a "peasant's smock" (ibid.).

To return to the opening conversation between Cohn and Barnes, Cohn asks Jake whether he would like to go to South America. Jake replies that he has never wanted to go, that he can see all the South Americans he wants to in Paris, and that he goes to Spain in the summertime. The narrator's running commentary to the reader about the conversation equates Cohn's desire to go to South America with silly romantic book knowledge and his own interest in Spain with the appreciation of bull-fighters who, according to Jake, know how to live: "Nobody ever lives their life all the way up except bull-fighters."[24] Thus, in this debate about a "last wonderful country," the text associates South America (and Cohn, the "Jew") with mere book knowledge and escapism whereas Spain is made synonymous with living, with reality, and the implied philosophy and aesthetics of realism. Stanley T. Williams has observed that "Spanish realism mattered to some American men of letters just as the realism of Velásquez mattered to Whistler."[25] Much could be written on the topic of the connection for U.S. writers of Spain and Spanish art, both literary and visual, with realism. However, what matters in Hemingway's text is not so much that Spanish literature and visual art signify realism, but that being in Spain is to give one access to "the real," while other forms of expatriation are made to lead only to the escapist or the fake. Such distinctions are, of course, the common tropes of "realism" itself as a representational mode.

While South America is consigned the realm of romance and escapism, Spain is made to occupy the proving ground of really living and living truly. *The Sun Also Rises* has the Jewish American expatriate's dream of going to South America signify the degeneration of expatriation into a hopelessly self-deceiving exile: "Listen, Robert, going to another country doesn't make any difference. I've tried all that. You can't get away from yourself by moving from one place to another" (11). Cohn is cast as the Wandering Jew with a bad case of wanderlust: "I [Jake] felt sorry for him. He had it badly" (10). In contrast, Jake's summertime voyages to Spain from the neighboring country of France are coded, not as escapism, but as confrontation, as a rite of passage. In the last chapter of *The Sun Also Rises,* Jake, entering Spain for the second time, tells his audience:

> I hated to leave France. Life was so simple in France. I felt I was a fool to be going back into Spain. In Spain you could not tell about anything. I felt like a fool to be going back into it, but I stood in line with my passport, opened my bags for the customs, bought a ticket, went through a gate, climbed onto the train, and after forty minutes and eight tunnels I was at San Sebastian. (233–34)

Made abundantly clear is that going to Spain is not easy, not a tourist dream, a romantic escapade, but rather a contest with oneself. It requires courage. Jake's initial crossover into Spain is also structured like a test. In all cases, this test has to do with experiencing the earth, ingesting the products of its soil. First comes the mountainous journey to the city of Pamplona after crossing "the Spanish frontier" (92):

> [A]nd then it was really Spain. There were long brown mountains and a few pines and far-off forests of beech-trees on some of the mountainsides . . . We climbed up and up . . . and we saw a whole new range of mountains off to the south, all brown and baked-looking and furrowed in strange shapes. (93)

Then comes the lunch at the Hotel Montoya: "The first meal in Spain was always a shock . . . You have to drink plenty of wine to get it all down" (94). Later on, having survived the first meal, Jake demonstrates that he knows how to handle a *bota* when he drinks with a Basque peasant out of a "big leather wine-bag" (103–5). Ultimately, the Fiesta of San Fermín, lasting eight days and nights (July 6–14), functions as an extended rite of passage for the hero Jake. During this time he runs with the bulls, braves the bullfights no matter how bloody or tragic, rubs shoulders with the *riau-riau* dancers, drinks bottles and bottles of red wine, downs cups and cups of Spanish coffee, sips *anis del toro* (150), vermouth, and cognac, and, most important, proves himself to be what he portrays as the Spanish equivalent of a visible saint, an aficionado with *afición:*[26]

> Afición means passion. An aficionado is one who is passionate about the bull-fights . . . These men were aficionados . . . Somehow it was taken for granted that an American could not have afición. He might simulate it or confuse it with excitement, but he could not really have it. When they saw that I had afición . . . it was a sort of oral spiritual examination . . . there was this same embarrassed putting of the hand on the shoulder, or a "Buen hombre." (131–32)

Buen hombre literally translated means "good man." Jake may not be able to have Lady Brett Ashley, his "English" (149) heartthrob, but he does win the respect of Montoya's men. The Spanish aficionados accept the "American" (16) expatriate into their tribe, paying tribute to him with a manly pat on the back. Although Jake will leave Spain to return to France, his choice of the "last wonderful country" has resulted in a sense of belonging. His "wound" (30–31) notwithstanding, he shows he knows how to live life to the fullest even when it is painful. More to the point, the Spanish aficionados recognize that he knows, conferring upon him the distinction of being a good man, a man with passionate know-how for a difficult thing. *The Sun Also Rises* treats life, bullfighting, and Spain as those difficult things. Spain is represented as the country of "obscure reason[s]"—dangerous, not "safe" (232) and "clear" (233) like France. But Spain is Jake's country of choice and in the story Spain reciprocates and chooses him through Montoya's men, unlike Cohn, whom it hits in the face in the person of Pedro Romero (202). Thus, *The Sun Also Rises* completes the first stage of the myth—the mutual election of the Hemingway hero and "his" country, Jake and Spain.

Ultimately, what ties Jake to Spain is physical intercourse, not with Lady Brett and not even in the congratulatory pats of Montoya's men, but with the dirt of the earth itself:

> The car was powdered with dust. I rubbed the rod-case through the dirt. It seemed the last thing that connected me with Spain and the fiesta. (232)

The Spanish earth—Spain and the fiesta—are the medium by which Jake, the first-person narrator (author surrogate in Hemingway's texts), wards off the accusation in Bill's joking remark during their fishing expedition in Burguete:

> You've lost touch with the soil. You get precious. Fake European standards have ruined you. You drink yourself to death. You become obsessed by sex. You spend all your time talking, not working. You are an expatriate, see? (115)

Jake may be sexually impotent, but he shows that, unlike his rival Cohn who dreams in vain of South America and cannot write his second book (37), he has not lost touch with the soil and, by implication, has not lost his creative capacities. The brief, chopped-up message he telegraphs to Brett at the book's conclusion indicating that they will meet up once more in the heart of Spain—"LADY ASHLEY HOTEL MONTANA MADRID / ARRIVING SUD EXPRESS TOMORROW LOVE / JAKE"—is meant to confirm his ability to write a real and true line.

If *The Sun Also Rises* reenacts the act of choosing a "last wonderful country," it exorcises other possibilities—South America—and, in exorcising them, conjures them up. The irony of the opening conversation between Jake and Cohn is that for Hemingway himself Spain was one country out of several he used as material for his expatriate modernist art practice. Besides France and Spain, he wrote romanticized adventure stories (only not in the purple prose attributed to Cohn) set in Italy, Africa, and Cuba. Hemingway himself went to these places and, of these three, became rather proprietary about Cuba. A few miles outside of Havana in the poverty-stricken village of San Francisco de Paula he bought himself a huge one-story Spanish colonial house and grounds called "Finca Vigía" (Lookout Farm), a piece of property explored as a symbol of Anglo-American imperialist fantasies in Cuban director Tomás Gutiérrez Alea's 1968 film *Memorias del subdesarrollo (Memories of Underdevelopment)*. The Hemingway who published *The Sun Also Rises* in 1926 cannot be held accountable to the Hemingway who in 1939, at the conclusion of the Spanish civil war, purchased Finca Vigía. The parallels, however, between Cohn's dreams of going to South America and Hemingway's later financial and literary investments in Cuba strongly provoke the question of why the idea of going to South America in *The Sun Also Rises* must be punished with such vehemence in the figure of Robert Cohn. *The Sun Also Rises* explicitly associates South America with romance, escapism, and self-deceiving exile, but it refuses any mention of the obvious: the long history of colonialism and neocolonialism. Jake's privileging of Spain over South America may be to doubly banish any association with that history, cast as he is as an aficionado of bullfights rather than as a participant in a colonialist fantasy and choosing a "last wonderful country" presumably never colonized and thus not discovered. Jake, therefore, and by extension Hemingway, can be its original discoverer. The scapegoat Robert Cohn is deployed so Jake can have a guilt-free experience of discovery. With this remark I would like to turn briefly to a passage from *A Moveable Feast* (1964) before discussing *For Whom the Bell Tolls* (1940), the second stage of the myth of identification between Hemingway and Spain.

In the first chapter of *A Moveable Feast*, published after his death, a certain passage functions as a revelation of his literary and cultural production as a modernist expatriate writer:

> I . . . finally came out on the lee side of the Boulevard St. Michel and worked on down it past the Cluny and the boulevard St. Germain until I came to a good café that I knew on the Place St. Michel . . . I . . . ordered

a *café au lait*. The waiter brought it and I took out a notebook from the pocket of the coat and a pencil and started to write. I was writing about up in Michigan and since it was a wild, cold, blowing day it was that sort of day in the story . . . [I]n one place you could write about it better than in another. That was called transplanting yourself, I thought, and it could be as necessary with people as with other sorts of growing things. But in the story the boys were drinking and this made me thirsty and I ordered a rum St. James. This tasted wonderful on the cold day and I kept on writing, feeling very well and feeling the good Martinique rum warm me all through my body and my spirit.[27]

The passage describes how the narrator enters a Paris café, orders in French, and commences to write in English a story about his boyhood in Michigan, where the weather is identical to the weather in Paris at the moment of composition. The justification given for not merely a familiar modernist trope of simultaneity, but, in this case, a coincidence of phenomena, is the necessity for and possibility of transplantation, uprooting oneself from one plot of ground and, it is implied, striking roots into another: "[I]n one place you could write about it better than in another. That was called *transplanting yourself* [my emphasis] . . . it could be as necessary with people as with other sorts of growing things." The succeeding sentences suggest that this transplantation entails a kind of arterial connection of roots and circulatory exchange between disparate geographical locations and between textual and physical bodies: "[I]n the story the boys were drinking and this made me thirsty and I ordered a rum St James . . . feeling the good Martinique rum warm me all through my body and my spirit." Rather than as a deliberately antinaturalistic Stein-like synthesis, literary production is presented in terms of an assumed continuity between body, nature, and art.

The geographical specifics of the connection between writer, text, and territory—the triangulation between Paris (France), Michigan (the United States), and Martinique (the French Caribbean)—betray the colonialist aspect of this organicist model. This model posits an organic relation between figure and ground, between the text and the elements, designed to compensate, it would seem, for modernist expatriate displacement. The flow of commodities, sensations, and textual production forms a triangle between the European metropolis, the North American heartland, and "the torrid zone," which implies another triangle—what is historically known as the triangular trade of rum, sugar, coffee, and slaves between Europe, Africa, and the Americas. This passage from *A Moveable Feast* offers no critique of its apparent investment in such a scenario. Rather, it partakes in a historically loaded triangular flow of commodities and so on, naturalizing it with references to the primary bodily sensations of taste and temperature: "tasted wonderful," "cold day," and "rum warm me." The socioeconomic history of exploitation becomes personal in a strange depoliticizing twist of the "personal as political" in which the narrator literally ingests the commodities that built the colonial empires and global capitalism—coffee and rum, *distilled from the earth* (the coffee plant and the sugar cane), first by slave and later by exploited labor.[28]

In the absence of critique, the question arises as to what is at stake. What desires lie at the core of this colonialist organicist model of modernist art practice, which rearranges, while maintaining, all of the basic components of the colonial process with its transplantation, appropriation, distillation, consumption, integration ("all through my body and my spirit"), and literary production signaling successful transplantation? Roland Barthes, in his essays "Wine and Milk" and "Steak and Chips," has argued persuasively that certain foods and beverages pertain to a cultural ritual of alchemical transmutation through physical incorporation designed to result in a procreative vitalism: "Wine . . . is a totem-drink, corresponding to the milk of the Dutch cow."[29] Granted that in this passage from *A Moveable Feast* the vitality imparting substances are coffee, milk, and rum, they too, like the red wine and various kinds of meat consumed in the tales about Spain, function as "mediumistic substances" that lead the expatriate man of letters "towards the original strength of nature."[30] They are not mere aliments, but tokens for something else—for the myth of an authentic relationship to the soil. To answer the question posed earlier, the desire for an authentic relationship to the soil lies at the heart of the colonialist organicist model of modernist art practice in this and all of Hemingway's texts, particularly those having to do with Spain, and especially in *For Whom the Bell Tolls* (1940).

In *Being and Time* (1927), Martin Heidegger defines "authenticity" as the condition of those who reflect on the identity they acquired at birth so as to critically assess the values and goals of that identity and "choose" their own identity. Heidegger also maintains that the practicalities of life

demanding immediate action make some degree of "inauthenticity" unavoidable. Had Hemingway read *Being and Time,* published a year after
The Sun Also Rises, he would probably have slated Robert Cohn's desire
to go to South America as a sign of "inauthenticity" (damnation) and his
hero's choice of Spain as a mark of "authenticity" (salvation). The passage including the line "Fake European standards have ruined you" quite
nearly duplicates Heidegger's distinction. As I suggested earlier, if *The Sun
Also Rises* is all about choosing the "last wonderful country," *For Whom the
Bell Tolls* is about being there, being in it. But, as for Heidegger, "being
there" passively is never enough. The problem of inauthenticity remains,
like the ever-present possibility of damnation. *For Whom the Bell Tolls,* for
all its seeming certainties, beginning with the John Donne quotation—
"no man is an Iland . . . every man is . . . a part of the maine"—is a text
that endeavors to resolve and is suffused with the anxiety about being
there inauthentically.

In a short story about the Spanish civil war titled "Under the Ridge"
and published a year before *For Whom the Bell Tolls,* this anxiety is clearly
voiced, once again in the form of an accusation. "The Extremaduran," a
character referred to after his province (Extremadura) goads the narrator-
author surrogate with the following words:

> We can give ourselves no illusions about foreigners. If you are a foreigner,
> I am sorry. But for myself now, I can make no exceptions. You have eaten
> bread and drunk wine with us. Now I think you should go.[31]

For Whom the Bell Tolls attempts to transubstantiate the act of eating
from colonialist consumption into the very act of communion with the
country and its inhabitants that the Extremaduran denies the narrator
in "Under the Ridge." Ironically, *For Whom the Bell Tolls* endeavors to
achieve this meaningful communion by turning everything and everyone
Spanish into comestible produce of the earth to be consumed by Robert
Jordan, the protagonist from whose point of view the story is told and
who thinks to himself, "You're a bridge-blower now. Not a thinker. Man,
I'm hungry . . . I hope Pablo eats well" (17). In *The Sun Also Rises,* Jake
consumes food and beverages presented as typically Spanish. Spaniards,
however, are not described as or closely associated with food in the earlier
novel. *For Whom the Bell Tolls* actually conflates people with food. Maria,

the young Spanish woman with whom Jordan falls in love, is portrayed in terms of cereal and animals hunted for their pelts and meat: "Her hair was the golden brown of a grain field . . . little longer than the fur on a beaver pelt" (22). The first time Maria and Jordan encounter each other, she is cooking rabbit—"with onions and green peppers and there were chick peas in the red wine sauce . . . [t]he rabbit meat flaked off the bones, and the sauce was delicious" (22–23). Jordan's pet name for Maria becomes "Rabbit." Nor is Maria the only Spanish person represented in terms of food. Some of the other guerrilla fighters are portrayed as cold cuts: "Robert Jordan looked carefully at the other three men at the table. One had a large flat face, flat and brown as a Serrano ham" (51). Not only are Spaniards rendered as food; they are specifically pictured as produce of the earth—not figures in a landscape in Steinian fashion, but vegetable growths from the soil. Jordan thinks, "Look at her [Pilar] walking along with those two kids [Joaquín and Maria]. You could not get three better-looking products of Spain than those. She is like a mountain and the boy and the girl are like young trees" (136).

The text also conflates topographical locations with food. For instance, according to the story, Jordan and his fellow guerrilla fighters spend much of their time sheltered in a cave in the Sierra de Guadarrama northwest of Madrid. That cave and all its contents are "ediblized," pun intended on "Oedipalized." The cave could be said to represent a return to the mother's womb as site of gustatory gratification:

> the warm air of the cave, heavy . . . with the odor of cooked rice and meat, saffron, pimentos, and oil, the tarry, wine-spilled smell of the big skin hung beside the door, hung by the neck and the four legs extended, wine drawn from a plug fitted in one leg, wine that spilled a little onto the earth of the floor, settling the dust smell. (59)

Jordan's comment that the hideout of the guerrilla fighters is "la cueva de los huevos perdidos" (the cave of the lost eggs) (199) reinforces the associations of the cave as a womb of food and the Spaniards as comestibles. Furthermore, evident in this womb-cave is the transubstantiating role of the distilled produce of the earth (wine from grapes). The wine dripping out of the pigskin onto the earthen floor of the cave, settling the dust smell, might as well be blood, the very lifeblood that Jordan, the Anglo-American communicant in Spain, imbibes so greedily and continuously. The admiring description of another character in the novel, Andrés, confirms that the logic of totemic sacrifice is in operation:

> In the dust and the heat, the shouting, the bull and man and wine smell, he [Andrés] had been in the first of the crowd that threw themselves onto the bull . . . They called him the bulldog of Villaconejos and joked about him eating cattle raw. (365)

What is at stake, so to speak, in the description of the pigskin filled with wine in the womb-cave and of Andrés throwing himself like a hungry lion on the bull is the imagined vitalism to be gotten from an authentic relation to the soil and those earth animals, the pig and the bull. That the desire for such a relation to the "Spanish earth" reaches cannibalistic proportions in *For Whom the Bell Tolls* is apparent in all the imagery rendering people into food. The metaphoric cannibalistic consumption of human beings expresses the same objective—to incorporate the qualities of a people regarded in the text as the embodiments of earthy, primitive procreative forces lacking or inaccessible in the expatriate's own culture.

Speaking of lack, *For Whom the Bell Tolls* does not content itself with ingestion to resolve anxieties about being in Spain inauthentically. Ingestion of the vegetable, animal, and human produce of the earth partly assuages anxieties about being there, but in itself it is not enough if readers are to think Jordan, and by extension Hemingway, a heroic man of action and not simply a man with a big and somewhat unsettling appetite, trying to incorporate all of Spain into himself. Thus, the text offers further solutions. Jordan is scripted as a writer-discoverer-ethnographer of Spain, presented as a frontier. It turns out that Jordan the bridge-blower was once upon a time an instructor in Spanish at the University of Montana (335) and that he wrote a book on Spain: "He had put in it what he had *discovered* about Spain in ten years of traveling in it, on foot, in third-class carriages, by bus, on horse and mule-back and in trucks" (248; my emphasis). This solution is imperfect, however. Other people before him have written books on Spain: "There had been such good books written by [George] Borrow and [Richard] Ford and the rest that he had been able to add very little" (ibid.). No U.S. writers are mentioned in the passage, only British ones. In other words, Hemingway simultaneously denies and asserts Jordan's originality in writing about Spain because Jordan is not British, but "American," as he emphasizes to his Spanish colleagues to keep them from calling him *Inglés* ("English"): "Not *Inglés*. American" (67). His nationality and that of his creator are certainly detectable enough in the presentation of Spain as frontier, a presentation that matter-of-factly, with no traces of ironic distance, rehearses an entire battery of nineteenth-century Anglo-American stereotypes about Spaniards. Gypsies are compared to "Indians in America," Indians and Gypsies are compared to Moors, and in the novel a Gypsy sings, "My nose is flat. My face is black. . . . Thank God I am Negro" (60).

To return to the question of the imperfection and incompleteness of Robert Jordan as writer-discoverer, writing and book knowledge are never enough according to the Hemingway code. It is imperative that readers see Jordan discovering Spain firsthand—with his body and all his senses—and not only discovering it, but incorporating himself into it. He must leave his mark not merely on the pages of a book and not merely on frontier territory, where others may have tread, but on virgin land or the closest to it he can find. This virgin land is provided in the form of Maria, who has been raped by fascists but has "never kissed any man" before Jordan. For him she is a virgin. As he tells her, "[N]o one has done anything to thee. Thee, they cannot touch. No one has touched thee, little rabbit" (71). Thus, besides exploring the wild mountainous country of the high sierra, he discovers Maria, whose body is rendered in terms of land— "her breasts like two small hills that rise out of a long plain where there is a well, and the far country beyond the hills was the valley of her throat where her lips were" (341). "Making love" to Maria gives him the opportunity to fill in the other side of the equation designed to equate him with the Spanish earth and vice versa, such that his consumption of it is his communion with it, a communion guaranteeing "being there" authentically. If turning everyone and everything Spanish into comestible produce of the earth allows Jordan to incorporate the Spanish earth into himself, having sex with Maria, who symbolizes that earth, is a way of incorporating himself into the land, infusing it with the very vitalism he has appropriated from it:

> [F]or her everything was red, orange, gold-red from the sun on the closed
> eyes, and it all was that color, all of it, the filling, the possessing, the having,

all of that color, all in a blindness of that color. For him it was a dark passage which led to nowhere, then to nowhere, then again to nowhere, always
and forever to nowhere, heavy on the elbows in the earth. (159)

The description of Jordan's and Maria's sexual encounter suggests that
Jordan is Maria's sun and she his roots or journey down them into the
earth. In a predictably gendered fashion—he as the sun, she as the earth—
they both become natural forces that together resemble the cyclical trans-
fer of energy in photosynthesis. Furthermore, not only does Jordan have
the chance to incorporate himself into the Spanish land through the body
of Maria, the novel implies in a comment made by "the Gypsy" to Jordan
that he may have impregnated Maria or, to follow the extended metaphor,
deposited his seed in the ground, an act that corresponds to that of God
making Adam in his own image from the clay of the earth. The Gypsy
exclaims, "You were supposed to kill one [a man], not make one!" (79). In
sum, sex with the willing Maria is the vehicle for the almost alchemical
transmutation of what otherwise might look too much like "inauthentic"
colonial consumption and conquest into a type of anticonquest—mutual
incorporation that, beyond Jordan's control, just happens to promise
self-perpetuation.

  For Whom the Bell Tolls leaves no stone—or perhaps, as Jordan jokes,
"stein"[32]—unturned in its quest to complete the mythic identification of
Jordan with Spain, to establish once and for all an authentic relation with
the soil that would rub off on its author and stick like the dust on the
rod-case in *The Sun Also Rises*. To bring the second stage of the myth to
a close—to make "being there" irrevocably authentic—and to put the
finishing touch on the mythic identification of Hemingway with Spain
and Spain with Hemingway, *For Whom the Bell Tolls* sacrifices its hero.
Mutual incorporation of the Spanish earth's products (Maria is described
as such) is still not enough to allay lingering anxieties about inauthenticity, particularly Jordan's (also Hemingway's) concerns about being a foreigner in Spain trying to be an insider: "[H]e never felt like a foreigner
most of the time; *only when they turned on you*" (135; my emphasis). This
last phrase calls forth the well-worn "type" of the treacherous Spaniard
to whose treachery Jordan's loyalty can stand in sharp contrast. The relation of loyalty to authenticity is a complex one, but may it suffice to say
that at the novel's end loyalty that demands ultimate self-sacrifice is what

conduces to the bridging of the gorge, so to speak, between native and potentially inauthentic expatriate or colonizing foreigner. Anselmo, the Spanish peasant by Jordan's side at the opening of the novel, is killed dynamiting the bridge to stop the fascist advance and Jordan is mortally wounded by enemy fire shortly thereafter. As in all Hemingway texts, death is the great leveler. Spaniard and "American" alike must die, or almost. Jordan is kept alive a little while longer so that through his consciousness—in a tactfully indirect manner—may be relayed the significance of his death in the still unfinished business of establishing an incontrovertibly "authentic" relation to the Spanish earth. Fighting impending loss of consciousness, Jordan thinks, "[H]e was completely integrated now" and he takes "a good long look at everything": "he touched the palm of his hand against the pine needles where he lay and touched the bark of the pine trunk that he lay behind . . . He could feel his heart beating against the pine needle floor of the forest" (471). Hemingway not only sacrifices his hero; he sacrifices him to the very earth of Spain. With this final gesture he effects the transvaluation of expatriate modernist visionary colonialism into dying for "one"'s country, dying for Spain, sealing for good the mythic identification of himself with Spain.

The "logical" extension of this death on the forest floor of Spain is full body ingestion by or incorporation into the earth, an incorporation surpassing in scope and permanence what Jordan was able to achieve with Maria. As for Hemingway, he worked out the fate of his alibi and surrogate to consummate a mystical union not so much between Jordan and Maria as between himself and Spain. Books such as *Hemingway's Spain* by Barnaby Conrad and Loomis Dean simply continue the equation, the implication of which is that to consume Spain you must consume Hemingway and vice versa. In some ways, Hemingway's association with the Spanish earth worked too well and he wound up "in the dirt." A few critics of his work—particularly of his first-person narrators—began to refer to him as a peasant with a bovine mentality. For instance, Wyndham Lewis wrote a review dubbing Hemingway's narrator (and barely disguising his real target, the writer himself) "the dumb ox," a Steinian and Picasso-like bull turned "cow": "[H]e Steins up and down the world, with the big lustreless ruminatory orbs of a Picasso doll-woman."[33] Hemingway's penchant for portraying Spain as earthy, primitive, and dangerous resulted in a myth that stuck to him almost too well. Not only was Spain primitivized; in the process so was Hemingway, whom writers Nancy Cunard and Frederic Prokosch both thought of as a feral man, a carnivore.[34] Whether cow or cannibal, prey or predator, a sign posted around Madrid's Plaza Mayor declaring "Hemingway did not eat here" might be read as a postcolonial retort to Hemingway's ingestion of authenticity.

RICHARD WRIGHT'S *PAGAN SPAIN:* THE DISPLACEMENT OF ALIENATION OR MODERNIST GOTHIC

Richard Wright's *Pagan Spain* (1957) is a late and comparatively little read work by the well-known African American expatriate, author of, among many other works, the acclaimed and by now canonized collection of stories *Uncle Tom's Children* (1938) and the novel *Native Son* (1940). According to Michel Fabre, Wright, haunted by Stein's advice given to him shortly before her death in 1946 that he should go to Spain, made his first visit in August 1954 and several other return visits thereafter. He kept a journal, took copious notes about life in Spain under Franco, and in 1956 began serious work on the manuscript that was published, following extensive editorial cuts, as *Pagan Spain*. Unlike Hemingway's novels, it was a commercial failure, although on the whole critics were not particularly hostile.[35] I shall return to the subject of this book's commercial failure later.

Since *Pagan Spain*'s publication, critics and scholars have taken it at face value—that is, as a nonfictional blend of journalism and anthropology—despite its experimental juxtaposition of first-person narrative, eyewitness reporting, commentary, anecdotes, vignettes, and dramatic dialogue. My claim is that Wright's formal experiment is held together by something that critics and scholars have overlooked in their haste to elide his representations of Spain with the "real," with "realistic" description—only slightly distorted by Freudian analysis and an obsession with phallic symbols—of Spain under Franco. Commencing with the chapter "Life after Death," ending with "The World of Pagan Power," and portraying Spain as a Western country lacking Western secular humanism and thus not Western (228–29) but distinctly "Spanish"—meaning unenlightened, superstitious, primitive, pagan, animalistic, brutal, uncivilized, and populated by visible ghosts, tortured Christs and bulls, and weeping virgins (243, 281)—that something is none other than the Gothic frontier mode complicated by and adapted to Wright's position as what Mary Louise Pratt has termed a hyphenated subject of empire.[36] I supplement and modify her rubric by maintaining that Wright's text is not the product of an internally critical European colonialist mentality (although one can detect echoes of Conrad's *Heart of Darkness*) so much as the inscription of an attempt by a subject of Anglo-American U.S. imperial ideology to attain a postcolonial status by turning the tables (26) on the "Other" colonizer of the Americas, Spain and Spaniards.

Pagan Spain is an example of a reversal of Western frontier Gothic east back across the Atlantic and a transposition of Southern Gothic onto a country not south of "the North" (such as Yoknapatawpha County) or of the U.S. border (such as Mexico or the Caribbean), but south and southwest across the Pyrenees relative to France as north. By "Western and Southern frontier Gothic" I mean the general form that arose in the adaptation and deployment of British Gothic modes to the frontiers and borderlands of the Americas, where Anglo culture ran violently up against "Other" Americans and scripted them as cannibals and savages. Regarding European versus American Gothic, Leslie Fiedler has argued that European Gothic is socially radical inasmuch as it supposedly often questions the righteousness of aristocratic rule and ancien régimes, whereas American Gothic, rather than subverting existing social orders, is implicated in showing their maintenance, or at the very least establishment. Fiedler's distinction seems too sharply drawn to me, but compelling is his argument about the socially conservative nature of American Gothic. I would extend that conservatism or, more appropriately, socially reactionary thrust in particular to what I am calling a combination of Southern Gothicism and Western Gothicism in Wright's case. Wright's reliance on these Gothic modes is complex because, on the one hand, it would seem to follow some of the characteristics that Fiedler associates with European Gothicism—questioning or undermining the status quo of politically and socially repressive order in *Pagan Spain,* that is, Franco's regime. On the other hand, it advances a critique of this regime in terms that perfectly correlate with the socially and culturally stigmatizing aspects of American Gothic according to Fiedler's model.

By Southern Gothicism I refer to the long tradition of literary and cultural representations from, of, and about the U.S. South exploring the equation of the South with "horror"—with incest, degeneracy, madness, race hatred, religious intolerance, and slavery. Wright's book represents

Spain as a repelling and fascinating enigma south across the border from a more or less civilized north, namely, France. Once across the border, Wright's "landscapes" of Spain, governed by Gothic tropes of darkness, desolation, and eeriness—"the look of the world darkened" (94), "dark and jagged mountains" (7), "a pall of heat and dust," "landscape of bald mountains" (67), "kingdoms of desolation, vast continents of perpendicular columns" (68), "surrealistically shaped mounds of red laterite" (136), "blood-red sun" (137), and "black Andalusian mountains" (188)—correlate with landscape descriptions emerging out of the long tradition of Western Gothicism. Just as Spain is treated as both "south" and "westward" (though not as part of "Western culture"), its inhabitants, Spaniards, are depicted as if they were in fact "Columbus's Indians [the native Americans upon whom the East was mapped] . . . the lost heathen" (26), as well as like ignorant white "Ku Kluxers" uncomprehendingly enacting primitive rituals of racial purity (284). Such reversals of identifications—of the denizens of Spain, once an imperial power, with the very people whom they conquered and with "primitive" white folks of the U.S. South—are examples of an avenging countercolonial discourse. Wright's daughter, Julia, observes that he, Wright, was "often fascinated in Spain by situations that echo or counterpoint his own experience of oppression in America."[37] Unquestionably, Wright represented Spain under Franco in such a way as to exorcise the persecuting demons of his U.S./Southern past. The problem with his attempt to turn the tables on history as well as on historically constructed discursive categories of "civilized" and "barbarian" is that the text does not extricate itself from the very discourses of race and metaphysical judgment it professes to abjure in the name of Western humanism.

In a sentence such as "Spain had been ready with one Will, one Race, one God, and one Aim . . . [a]nd . . . had remained stuck right at that point" (287) one can see a sincere attempt to describe Spanish Falangism, to explain it, as other writers have done, with German Nazism, as more than a political program, as an all-encompassing kind of "paganism," a totalizing reaction formation to the anxieties of modernity. Faith Berry points out: "[T]he manuscript took courage to write and to publish . . . Richard Wright was one of the few American authors who openly criticized the Franco regime during the climate of American cold war anticommunism in the 1950s" (xxv). However, if Gothic may be said to be the quintessential mode for the allegorization of "race" as Joan Dayan has suggested, Wright's reliance on this mode in this modernist piece of "nonfiction" about Spain is unfortunate.[38] The Gothic mode belongs largely to Anglo-Germanic cultural traditions. Despite the generalizations and a certain ahistorical nominalism of Claudio Véliz's book *The New World of the Gothic Fox: Culture and Economy in English and Spanish America,* Véliz's argument that Gothic is the mode of Northern Anglo-Protestant countries in contrast to the Baroque of southern European and Latin American Catholic countries is sound enough. More to the point, Gothic, with its obsessive fixation on identity and origins and its ultimately dualistic metaphysics of good and evil, black and white, has been and continues to be a representational tool of Anglo-American imperial ideology that insists on its own Anglo or Anglicized civilization in contrast to the alleged backwardness of non-Anglos, nonwhites, non-Protestants, and non-Westerners.

Moments stand out in *Pagan Spain* that read as endeavors to transvalue racialized metaphysical assumptions in the claim that "The Pyrenees . . . mark the termination of Europe and the beginning of Africa" (4). Wright discusses the Black Virgin of Montserrat with an "American" (of "Spanish" parents) named "Pardo" meaning, among other things, "mulatto" (69–73) and remarks on the fact that every time Spaniards exclaim "¡Olé!" they are uttering a Moorish word meaning "For God's sake!" (103). He admiringly describes the "swarthy, black-haired boys" (14) and "black-eyed teenage girls" (107) and declares that he felt as if he knew all of his life some fellow travelers he meets on a train from Madrid to Granada (189). He empathizes with the "aesthetic moods" of the Moors who built and arranged the gardens of the Alhambra (191), makes friends and establishes a deep rapport with several women flamenco singers in Granada (200–205), and plays at being a (black) bull with his new flamenco friends (203–5). He is fascinated by the scrawny children of Seville "clapping their hands in complicated rhythms" that remind him of the children's games he has seen "in the African jungle" (212), converses with a man who sells Spanish girls into what the slaver asserts is "not white slavery . . . [but] [o]live-skinned slavery" (217), and visits a nightclub in Seville named "the Congo" (218). The net effect would seem to be to underscore the similarities between Spain and Africa in a mischievously subversive, if not celebratory, manner. Such a "tropicalization" of Spain would seem to defy the historical preoccupation with *sangre pura,* with the fantasy of lineage untainted by Moorish (or, for that matter, Jewish) blood. It would also seem to fly in the face of the fearful or anthropophagic exoticization of Spain on the part of Anglo-American and non-Hispanic European travelers who swore by the phrase "Africa begins at the Pyrenees!" Moments such as the ones cited escape the judgmental Gothic mode. They attest to a profoundly utopian desire to go through alienation in order to recognize oneself, to be further expatriated so as to return "home." These moments remind the reader that *Pagan Spain* is the creation of an African American, not an Anglo-American or even a Jewish American, confronting and reworking the very legacy with which others have branded Spain and which Spaniards have alternately denied or championed as their mark of distinction from "Europe" or the rest of "Europe." In a word, these moments are evidence of a postcolonial sensibility slipping through the talons of imperial Gothic.

The problem is that, despite these postcolonial instances, the Gothic of Anglo-American imperial ideology maintains a vise-like hold on the majority of the text. To return to Mary Louise Pratt's thesis, Wright's work is a manifestation of hyphenated imperial subjecthood, which I see playing itself out as a deep ambivalence to the "African" in African American, an ambivalence at least as deep as the desire to expatriate from Anglo-America in order to fashion one's ground. The following passage about Wright's visit to Azpeitia, the birthplace of Saint Ignatius of Loyola, founder of the Society of Jesus (the Jesuits), is an unequivocal example of an ambivalence that does not teeter in the balance, but weighs quite definitely against the equation of either "Africa" or "Spain" with reason, with civilization—properties, supposedly, of "Western" culture from which *Pagan Spain* never excludes the United States, despite its history of slavery, its Klan, and its ongoing "race" wars:

> In the dimness I examined glass cases in which were locked fragments of clothing once worn by Loyola, yellowed letters written by him, a sword which he had once used, gilded boxes, etc.; and *I could not help but remember the fetish huts that I had seen in West Africa, huts containing the hallowed objects of ancestors.* (234; my emphasis)

If Spain evokes "Africa," the association is hardly always liberatory—quite the contrary. If, for example, adjectives such as *black, dark,* and *obscure* signify "African," as arguably they do in the previously cited postcolonial instances, they are consummately unstable signifiers. Dozens of examples may be found in which, true to the Gothic mode, they imply or simply denote irrationality, violence, paganism, barbarousness, and evil. In fact, given the context of the overall narrative—about "pagan" Spain—no use of any of these words in the text is entirely free of these significations, and certainly not their use in the closing chapters:

> There was undoubtedly a brand of demonism here [in the Society of Jesus], for these young men had become hopelessly entangled in the turbulent and *obscure* complexes of their own personalities. (235; my emphasis)

> Or did he [a young "Spanish Jewish businessman"] feel that I, a Negro, had no right to invade that *dark domain of his heart?* (267; my emphasis)

> The Inquisition . . . had whipped the Spaniards into a semblance of out-ward conformity, yet keeping intact all *the muddy residue of an irrational paganism* at the bottom of the Spanish heart. (287; my emphasis)

"Obscure," "dark," and "muddy" consign Spain and Spaniards to a realm of darkness and in these passages, one may note, literally to *a heart of darkness.*

As is apparent in the middle quotation, the text is not unselfcon-scious—"I, a Negro, had no right to invade that dark domain of his heart?" Ironic reversals and a keen awareness of the potentially exploi-tative nature of his journalistic enterprise—"go to poor countries to look at the natives" (239)—are discursively foregrounded. That a relation exists between the author's identity as a "black" person and his interest in the "dark domain" of his subject is made explicit in the use of the term "Negro," meaning "black" in both Spanish and English. If Spain occa-sioned utopian moments of connection and understanding—like black gospel singers "they [his flamenco women friends] sang and baptized me in their sorrow . . . words would have profaned what they communicated to me of their hurt and dejection" (202)—its history and culture drew Wright to it as part of, or at least as similar to, Africa, and the suffering of its people, to the suffering of African Americans and other oppressed minorities in the South and the United States as a whole. For example, about Protestants living in Spain under Franco, he writes:

What drew my attention to the emotional plight of the Protestants in Spain was the undeniable and uncanny psychological affinities that they held in common with American Negroes, Jews, and other oppressed minorities. (162)

He goes on to use the metaphor of "white Negroes" to describe these Protestants, "the assumption being that Negroes are Negroes because they are treated as Negroes" (ibid.). Nevertheless, the examination of Spain as similar to Africa and to the American South and its treatment as an opportunity to create successive canvases of black on white reminiscent of Robert Motherwell's series of paintings *Elegies to the Spanish Republic* (circa 1940–45) result in the separation of "blackness" into different kinds and levels, bearing out the very distinction made in the section on the Black Virgin of Montserrat:[39]

We know that the black color of the statue does not come from paint. Neither is this blackness racially representative. It is highly likely that the statue turned black from the smoke of incense that pagans burnt before it. (72)

Pagan Spain suggests that the blackness of Spain is ultimately not material artifice (paint) or biology ("race") but a sign and symptom of its philosophical and religious condition, of its paganism—black because it has been burned in the fires lit to pagan gods. The book presents Spain as a self-consuming land of fetish objects and bloody sacrifices. It avails itself of the Gothic mode to shift from the discourse of race—the physical aspect of persons—to that of metaphysical judgment. Thus, the text is imbricated in metaphysical judgment that closely parallels old Anglo-Protestant conventions dating back to the sixteenth century about Catholic countries (particularly Spain, the archrival of England), as well as non-Christian countries in general. More disturbingly, in *Pagan Spain* the metaphysical judgments are still invoked in the language of color, specifically "blackness," and are affixed on people in a particular place. The placing of traits raised out of historical contingency—in the end *Pagan Spain* makes claims not only about Spain under Franco but about Spain antedating 1492 (287)—echoes environmental determinism arguments popular in the first half of the twentieth century and that substituted for biological or phylogenetic definitions of race. Hence, *Pagan Spain* identifies not Catholicism in general but Spanish Catholicism in particular with "one of the fatalities of the world" (274).

The paradigm of the conjunction of place and timeless traits—"I sighed, realizing that, in Spain, all things were Spanish" (114)—is pushed beyond the frameworks of "region" or "ethnicity." The text defines both the Catalan barber who defends the cause of Catalan autonomy (93–95) and "the young Spanish Jewish businessman" as essentially Spanish. And, like a twist on Herman Melville's Gothic tableau tale "Benito Cereno" (1855), "Spanish" is made synonymous with a destiny "darker" than that of the African:

> The African, though thrashing about in the *void*, was free to create a future, but the pagan traditions of Spain had sustained no such mortal wound . . . This was a fact that made me feel that the naked African in the bush would make greater progress during the next fifty years than the proud, tradition-bound Spaniard! (229; my emphasis)

Ultimately, the "Spanish" Catalan barber is described as "the emperor of a bleak empire . . . he had made a monument of his *black defeat*" (95; my emphasis) and the "Spanish" Jew is compared to a "knife blade" swerving through the traffic in his "shining Jaguar" tearing down "*the night street* at a terrifying speed" and "seething with shame and burning with fury" (269; my emphasis). This latter set of images is nothing short of apocalyptic. In such passages, anthropological interests in constructions of regional identity and ethnicity give way to judgment lying in the register of biblical injunction.

By its final chapters, *Pagan Spain* has made of Spain not only a borderland between "the Western" and the "non-Western"—"it looked and seemed Western, but it did not act or feel Western" (228)—or, for that matter, between "the two Spains . . . the official Spain and the human Spain" (74), but also a hinterland of "rotting piles" (192) of architecture and a "bloody Sargasso of the irrational" (230); in other words, a wasteland and a backwater. It is worth pausing on the reference to the Sargasso Sea. The Sargasso is an unusually still sea, part of the north Atlantic Ocean between the West Indies and the Azores. It is the center of a swirl of confluent ocean currents and is known for the abundance of brown seaweed on its surface. In Wright's text it functions as a metaphor for irrationality and cultural brackishness or lack of progress. Although the text makes no mention of this fact, the Sargasso Sea is the geographical and historical site of the confluence of empires—British, French, and Spanish—fighting over ownership of the Caribbean and exploiting, if not decimating, the natives and African slaves in the process. This scenario of colonial/imperial struggle for domination of the Caribbean (and the Americas in general) is transmutingly displaced onto Europe and the struggle of the totalitarian powers to assume control of it. The text claims that "Germany and Italy had only recently been rescued from a bloody Sargasso of the irrational," but Spaniards "were as chaff before the totalitarian whirlwind" (ibid.). Of the imperial powers since the sixteenth century, the only one *Pagan Spain* puts on trial is Spain. It leaves off the hook France, Britain, and the United States, the latter being by the late 1950s most certainly an empire with specifically racist and ideologically intolerant domestic and foreign agendas. Similarly, putting aside the question of the difference between totalitarianism and Franco's Spanish Catholic Falangist Party, the only country portrayed as succumbing to a continuing totalitarianism is Spain. Thus, *Pagan Spain* projects its fear of empire and totalitarianism onto Spain—Gothically scapegoating it as the villain and badlands of history. Spain becomes the sign of self-imposed damnation in the modern world, damnation that *Pagan Spain* paints in colors befitting the book of Jude: "They [those who have 'taken the way of Cain'] . . . are wandering stars *for whom blackest darkness has been reserved forever*" (Jude 13; my emphasis).

To conclude, *Pagan Spain* reserves the "darkest blackness" for Spain—focusing not on biology, not on topography, though these are factors, but on its ontological status as the repository of "the primitive" understood as irrational paganism. Like many a British or Anglo-American text, *Pagan Spain* is, among other things, a projection of fear of the Other within or near the Self, of the supposedly "non-Western" within "the Western," of the Catholic beside the Protestant, of Spain in America for numerous Anglos and the Anglicized (Wright included). In *Pagan Spain* fear of Spain replays some of the main tropes of the Black Legend against Spain that equated the country with tyranny, cruelty, paganism, and backwardness. Although written by an African American, the text functions for the most part as an expatriation of Anglo-American Gothic, a tool of Anglo-American

imperial ideology, and precludes the emergence of its writer's hyphenated
subjectivity from beneath the long shadow cast by that very ideology.

The "primitive" that Wright found in Spain was not in the end the
primitive that Gertrude Stein, his friend and mentor in France, spoke of
to him when she said:

> Spain is primitive, but lovely. And the people! There are no people such
> as the Spanish anywhere. I've spent days in Spain that I'll never forget. See
> those bullfights, see that wonderful landscape. (*Pagan Spain,* 4)

For her, Spain's "primitiveness" was something she wished to emulate in
her writing, formally and philosophically, just as for Hemingway it was
something he wished to ingest for authenticity and ultimately potency's
sake. For Wright, Spain's "primitiveness" was something utterly resistant
to modernity and which took him a five hundred-page manuscript, the
unedited length of what became a greatly shortened book, to exorcise.
Granted, other modernists such as Stein and Hemingway wrote their major
works on Spain before the Franco era, whereas Wright wrote his work a
good decade and a half into the regime. But, besides attesting to the sour-
ing of the American modernist interest in Spain as "the last wonderful
country," to quote Hemingway, *Pagan Spain,* the artifact, corroborates
the theory that the flip side of dreams of cultural regeneration through
contact with a borderland imagined as primitive, virgin, or untamed by
one's own culture is a nightmare of regression—of being "sucked into a
maw" (230) of whatever is deemed alien to one's sense of self. On the one
hand, it is entirely possible to see within Wright's judgment of Spain a
hope that someday it too would become what in his writings are treated
as commensurate with one another: "modern," "Western," and "democratic," as in the widely advertised concept of modern Western democracy.
On the other hand, the "fear" of Spain in *Pagan Spain* may be viewed as
a displacement of the writer's anxieties as a hyphenated subject of empire
burdened to prove his own contested identity as a "modern" in every sense
of that word, which was carefully distinguished from the "primitive" other
that more "racially" unmarked thinkers and writers could afford to play
with and/or internalize.

Readers may wonder why, if *Pagan Spain* was as inscribed in the mode
of Anglo-American imperial Gothic as I claim, the book was a commercial

failure. Presumably it should have delighted its Anglo-American readership, especially those who had never gone to Spain, who were predisposed
to view a Catholic country under Franco as religiously and politically suspect, who might have been morbidly fascinated by the bloody descriptions of bullfights, Holy Week floats, and flagellants, and who would have
been titillated by the Freudian analysis of the repression and release of
sexual energies traceable in the religious rituals, statues, and monasteries.
About the book's commercial failure, Michel Fabre offers two explanations: (1) "perhaps, Spain was not in fashion" and (2) "the American public probably did not think that a black man without religion had the right
to dissect and judge the decadence of a white Christian nation, particularly one that was considered 'friendly' by the U.S. government."[40] The
first explanation is unconvincing. Although it is true that during the first
decade and a half of the Franco regime many leftist and liberal U.S. writers refrained from writing about Spain to signal their post–Spanish civil
war disillusionment (Spain was, to them, a lost cause with no romance in
it) and their disagreement with the domestic and foreign policies of that
regime, the topic of Spain was not dead. Allen Guttman points out in *The
Wound in the Heart* that several thousand books about Spain—histories,
biographies, memoirs, polemics, and novels—were written and consumed
in the United States between the years 1940 and 1960. Granted, these works
mostly concerned the Spanish civil war, not life under Franco. Although
Wright's work purported to be about "the reality of life under Franco" (1),
to borrow his words, the title *Pagan Spain* hardly announced sympathy for
the regime. Moreover, it provided no indication that it was about Spain
under Franco. The book mentions Franco by name no more than three
times and, as I have argued, is essentializing rather than historicizing.
Ironically quoted passages from the Falangist catechism aside, criticism of
the regime was lost in a generalized analysis of Spanish history, culture,
and psychology. Its generalized analysis, however, was not the reason for
its commercial failure, as generalized analyses of Spain had historically been
more palatable to the public than detailed sociohistorical or socioeconomic
treatises and were a familiar feature of travel literature. The interest in
Spain that smoldered on after the washout of pro-Republican hopes was
popular. Although many intellectuals kept their distance from Spain for
philosophical and pragmatic reasons (including difficulties obtaining visas
to do research), all through the 1950s U.S. films were being built around

figures of Spain, made about Spain, and even produced in Spain. Consider, for instance, *Don Juan* (1950), filmed in Spain, *The Bullfighter and the Lady* (1951), *Sombrero* (1953), *Lola Montés* (1955), *The Conqueror* (1956), and three films starring Ava Gardner—*The Barefoot Contessa* (1954), *The Sun Also Rises* (1957), and *The Naked Maja* (1959). Crowning the 1950s, Poe's short story "The Pit and the Pendulum" put in an appearance once again in 1961 as a film.

Regarding Fabre's second explanation for the commercial failure of *Pagan Spain*—that "the American public probably did not think that a black man without religion had the right to dissect and judge the decadence of a white Christian nation"—the evidence would point to the contrary. *Native Son* sold well precisely because it did advance such a critique, in this case of the United States. Furthermore, the U.S. public in general—especially the white, Anglo, Protestant public whose sympathies the book courts—were not adverse to consuming Spain through the premise of "paganism." To reinforce his second explanation, Fabre mentions the dismay of the Catholic press and of certain Protestant daily papers at Wright's criticism of a "white Christian nation, particularly one that was considered 'friendly' by the U.S. government." The influence of the Catholic press (and this press was not unanimously pro-Franco) and certain Protestant dailies should not be overestimated. U.S. fascist sympathizers were pro-Franco, as were a number of U.S. Catholics and a smaller number of right-wing Protestants who regarded the general as a defender of the Christian state against anarchy, Communism, and immorality. Only a small minority of the U.S. public, however, would have been offended by *Pagan Spain*. Fabre himself admits that the *New York Times Book Review* and the *Saturday Review* praised the book.

I would argue that the real problem was not subject matter or content, but genre and form, that is, the book's experimental juxtaposition of first-person narrative, eyewitness reporting, commentary, anecdotes, vignettes, and dramatic dialogue, all held together by what I have identified as a frontier Gothic mode. If the book had been an eyewitness account or a novel, it would have done better commercially. *Pagan Spain* was a belated modernist experiment released in the late 1950s, when even the literary world was coping with pressures to conform and standardize to the tastes of a mass audience and having to compete with television as the preferred medium of entertainment.[41] If Wright had novelized his experiences in

Spain and experimented within that historically legitimized form for experimentation and *Pagan Spain* had been advertised as a novel, it might have had a better chance for commercial success. As for its failure, it was not because the novel stood outside the reach of the representational strategies of Anglo-American imperial ideology.

Neither Stein's nor Hemingway's nor Wright's texts on Spain were beyond the reaches of Anglo-American imperial ideology. Each treated Spain as a frontier, a proving ground for experience and artistic practice. Each mined it for its possibilities and tragedies. For all the rhetoric of understanding, sympathy, and absorption, each writer came, "discovered," and departed. In differing ways and degrees, each was caught up in a visionary colonialism. Stein's writings on Spain, and especially the move to make of Spain and America a composite frontier region of the mind through the abstraction and equation of particulars, while offering an implosion of the environmental determinism of regionalistic ethnography, may also be read as the manifestation of a somewhat questionable incorporatist tendency. Unlike the Hemingway maneuver, Stein's incorporations take place through a kind of philosophically nominalist liquidation of matter rather than through its hypermaterialization in organicist metaphors. The question is who is benefited by such a liquidation of the resistance between concrete particulars. For her readers in France, Britain, and the United States, Stein's writings may well have put "Spain" on the map of international modernism and even pointed up "America"'s dependence on Spain for its categorical existence. Yet she chose only two persons to personify America and Spain, "Spain and America in their persons" (*Autobiography*, 16), herself and Picasso, both expatriates whom she empties of biographical particulars—including ethnic (though not national) backgrounds—and extols as geniuses. On the one hand, Stein's merger of America and Spain, a big and a little country, flew in the face of Anglo-American imperial ideology with its insistence on the independence and superiority of an "America" precisely not predicated on the Old World or "Spanish" America of the New World. On the other hand, one wonders whether the rhetoric of genius and discovery plays a compensatory role, making up for or conventionalizing an otherwise ideologically subversive remapping of the world. I do not want to minimize the amazing sentences that she did write and that must have stunned, surprised, and perhaps even angered complacent Anglo-Americans and those who constructed themselves according to Anglo-centric assurances of their Occidentality, their Westernness: "Oriental people, the people of America and the people of Spain have never, really never forgotten that it is not necessary to use letters in order to be able to write" ("Picasso," 73). Nevertheless, if Stein had brought out her Jewish heritage and not muted or dismissed traces of Africa in connection with Spain, her texts might have really expatriated beyond the borders of a potentially conformist "neutrality."

Hemingway can be more centrally located within the parameters of Anglo-American imperial ideology. Although his works sometimes read like textbooks on cultural appreciation of Spain and Spaniards, except when these works invoke the figure of the treacherous Spaniard, the real heros of his two famous "Spanish" novels—*The Sun Also Rises* (1926) and *For Whom the Bell Tolls* (1940)—are Anglo-Americans, Jake Barnes and Robert Jordan, and their antiheroes are a Jewish American, Robert Cohn, and a Spanish drunkard whose bed "smelt stale and sweat-dried and sickly-sweet the way an Indian's bed does" (360). As if to compensate for their expatriated status, Jacob and Jordan are scripted according to what Sacvan Bercovitch has identified as a Puritan typologization of "the American self."[42] In other words, they are modeled on biblical heroes drawn from the Old Testament. In the event readers might miss the biblical typology, blatant hints are provided in the *The Sun Also Rises* ("You've a hell of a biblical name, Jake" [22]) and in *For Whom the Bell Tolls* ("Roll, Jordan, Roll!" and "As Jordan goes so go the bloody Israelites. The bridge, I mean" [438]). Despite Hemingway's professed hatred of Puritanism and rejection of his Protestant upbringing, he seems to have chosen a classic Anglo-American Puritan Protestant identity-affirming solution for displacement.

The Sun Also Rises riffs off of the Genesis story of Esau and Jacob in its construction of the Robert Cohn–Jake Barnes rivalry, with Jake being the favored son, the chosen one who eats his bowl of "stew" (110) *and* appreciates his birthright. Deliberately or not, *The Sun Also Rises* equates Spain, "the last wonderful country," with that birthright to confirm the election of its Anglo-American Jacob-hero over its Jewish American Esau-anti hero Robert Cohn. The implications are disturbing. That the Esau and Jacob story had acquired self-serving racializing overtones in Anglo-American culture by the late nineteenth century is abundantly clear in Oliver Wendell Holmes's use of the motif in *Elsie Venner* (1861).

To the extent that Spain as "birthright" justifies and sanctifies the Anglo-American expatriate, a question ensues as to the ultimate nature of that birthright. Is it Spain as "Spain" that is desired or Spain as the longed-for and vanished "American" frontier? In *The Sun Also Rises*, Bill, a friend of Jake's, exclaims about the Basque country around Burguete near the Irati River: "This is country" (117). Is it just a coincidence that when Jake returns to rendezvous with Lady Brett in Madrid he checks into the "Hotel Montana"? The name, twice stated in the text, evokes the Far Western North American territory so designated by the Spanish explorers. Moreover, the very capital of Spain, Madrid, is described as a kind of outpost town in the wilderness, not quite the proverbial city on a hill: "I saw Madrid come up over the plain, a compact white sky-line on the top of a little cliff away off across the sun-hardened country" (239).

The allusions to the river Jordan and the Israelites in *For Whom the Bell Tolls* are direct encouragements to view Robert Jordan's mission to blow up the bridge for the cause of the Spanish Republic in light of Moses' mission to lead his people out of slavery in Egypt to the land of Canaan westward across the Jordan River. Like Moses, who is never allowed to cross the Jordan into the promised land and dies on Mount Nebo, where he is presumably "gathered to [his] people" (Deuteronomy 32:50), Robert Jordan is mortally wounded trying to escape the fascist attack after fulfilling his mission. He cannot travel on with Maria and the other surviving members of the guerrilla unit to the safety of the Gredos mountains southwest of the Sierra de Guadarrama. At the novel's end he is lying on the mountainside awaiting an opportunity to commit one more heroic deed, the killing of an oncoming fascist officer: "He was waiting until the officer reached the sunlit place where the first trees of the pine forest joined the green slope of the meadow" (471). At the hour of Jordan's death, he is not so much gathered to his people as to the Spanish earth. "His" people have left for Gredos and the grandfather he talks to in his head as he waits for the fascist cavalry to arrive is figured as absent—"*Who are you talking to?* Nobody, he said. Grandfather, I guess. No. Nobody" (469). The parallels between the Moses and Robert Jordan stories, however, point up a similarity more significant than any of the differences—their chosen-ness, their exceptionalism. As in *The Sun Also Rises, For Whom the Bell Tolls* reserves a place of distinction for an Anglo-American. Although not exactly arguments for Anglo-American exceptionalism, their overt imposition of biblical references on heroes in both cases singled out as "American" and no other kind of American but Anglo works, perhaps despite conscious intentions, as a recommendation with one important difference. Hemingway's "Spanish" novels change the topology of the familiar Puritan Protestant *Anglo-American* narrative of election. For Hemingway, it was not New England, not the United States, not even "America," but Spain as "the last wonderful country," the frontier or what "America" used to be. Spain is Jordan's Canaan, even if its promise for a guerrilla fighter for the Republic was, by the time Hemingway published *For Whom the Bell Tolls*, a thing of the past. In sum, the relation of Hemingway's exceptionalist stories of Anglo-American heroes in Spain to Anglo-American imperial ideology is one in which visionary colonialism is always both "colonialist" in its insistence on justified insider status and "visionary" in its utopian appreciation for the country it so desires to appropriate.

On the topic of cultural appreciation of Spain, Wright's *Pagan Spain*, despite its failure to extricate itself from the representational modes of Anglo-American imperial ideology, for all its self-divided shadowboxing with the black bull of Spain, actually resists the visionary colonialism at work in Stein's and Hemingway's texts. It may seem contradictory to point out how a text falls within the reaches of Anglo-American imperial ideology and yet is not characterized by the "incorporative" colonialist tendencies of Stein's and Hemingway's pieces. Such, however, is the case, and although one might cite Wright's seeming revulsion for Spain and things Spanish to resolve the tension, "revulsion" does not adequately describe his complex responses. As already mentioned, these responses are characterized by a certain unforgettable postcolonial sensibility instanced and summarized in these words of Wright's from *Pagan Spain:*

> The fate of Spain had hurt me, had haunted me; I had never been able to stifle a hunger to understand what had happened there and why. Yet I had no wish to resuscitate mocking recollections while roaming a land whose free men had been shut in concentration camps, or exiled, or slain. An uneasy question kept floating in my mind. How did one live after the death of the hope for freedom? (4)

However overstated his case against Franco's Spain—"concentration camps," for instance—or misguided his judgments of Spain, Wright certainly did not gloss over the curtailment of civil rights in a dictatorship. Stereotypical depictions notwithstanding, he seems to have been genuinely affected by the sufferings of the people he met and interviewed during his various note-gathering trips. That he was quite literally "haunted" by Spain is evident in the more than five hundred-page manuscript he churned out and the edited version that became *Pagan Spain*. Moreover, there are several moments in *Pagan Spain* of refreshing uncertainty or disorientation quite uncharacteristic of the Stein's and Hemingway's celebratory "manifesto" approach to their frontier country. For example, Wright declares, "Frankly, I had not been prepared for what I encountered" (227) and "The next Spanish intellectual I met roused so many conflicts, resistances, and confused emotions in me that I can only lay the matter and its negative outcome, for whatever it is worth, before the reader" (251).

Of the three writers' works, Wright's was the least assimilable to the tourist industry. It was least assimilable not so much because it was critical of the Franco regime, but because of its gloomy picture of social conditions in Spain and, as suggested earlier, because its experimental form thwarted readers' expectations for a novel or less "disorienting" travel account. Ironically, *Pagan Spain*'s imbrication in the Gothic of Anglo-American imperial ideology coupled with its formal experimentality generally kept it off the reading list of the neocolonialist phenomenon of tourism all about inexpensive "fun in the sun." By the mid-1950s, the Franco regime had grown mild compared to what it had been in the 1940s. If Richard Wright, formerly a member of the Communist Party in the United States, found it possible to travel and interview people in Spain in the mid-1950s, the average tourist had little to fear. The tourist industry to Spain that commenced in the mid- to late 1950s was in full swing by the mid-1960s. By then Spain was one of the world's most popular vacation destinations and U.S. citizens did their share of traveling to it, a phenomenon that continued through the 1970s and into the mid-1980s, as long as the dollar was high and the major destinations (Madrid, Barcelona, the Costa del Sol, etc.) were less expensive than other destinations in wealthier countries such as France and even Italy. U.S. representations of Spain and Spaniards in the 1960s and 1970s ran the gamut of tropes and types discussed. Interest still existed in warlords, conquistadores, knights, and other "heroic" figures more or less part of the trope of the idealized Castilian, *castizo,* or "white" Spaniard, as indicated by U.S.

films such as *El Cid* (1961), *The Castilian* (1963), and *Man of la Mancha* (1972). Other films such as *A Witch without a Broom* (1966), *Bandolero!* (1968), and *The Undefeated* (1969), the last based on Hemingway's 1927 short story by the same title, attest to a continuing fascination with Spaniards as "primitives" or lowlife characters, the closer to the earth the better, and with Spain as the site of the frontier-like confrontation between "man" and "nature" and between feuding peoples. Richard Slotkin's thesis in *Regeneration through Violence* (1973) about the dual function of the frontier—as a place of danger and death as well as revitalization—works well to summarize the function of Spain in such films. However, while these works tend to offer figures and images of the "Spanish earth" remindful of those prevalent in the works of expatriate modernists, there is not the same investment in personal, artistic, and cultural regeneration through interaction with the land and the people. This was the era of films such as *Sol Madrid* (1968) and books such as James Michener's *Iberia* (1968). The modernists' rites of passage had become an excursion into picturesqueness, difference, and exoticism. Spain as the modernists' "sacred bull" was now an image on a postcard from Córdoba or Seville, or more like the billboard-size cardboard bull on the highway wordlessly advertising Pedro Domecq sherry and brandy cellars.[43] The point was to *savor* its picturesqueness, to *view* its difference, its exoticism, from a car or train window, to take a snapshot or buy a postcard of it, to see it through a passing tourist's, not a more committed insider's, eyes—to enjoy its hotels, restaurants, beaches, bullfights, flamenco *tablas,* and colorful fiestas. At issue was not originality or authenticity so much as the animation of kitsch, living out the travel-poster image. U.S. travelers of the 1960s and 1970s in search of authenticity, exotic inspiration, or a spiritual harrowing were going further east and south—to India, Africa, and Central America. Spain was still an "elsewhere," but every passing year witnessed an increasing resemblance not to mythic images of the American frontier, but to the suburban homogenization of the United States.

(POST)MODERN DENATURALIZATIONS OF NATIONALITY

STAGING COMPARISON: "AMERICAN"/"SPANISH," MODERNIST/POSTMODERN, TEXT/IMAGE

In the works of many writers included in the traditional canon of "American" literature as well in the works of many U.S. painters and photographers, representations of Spain and its inhabitants involve an attempt to define "Spanish" blood, temper, or nature.[1] Such an attempt has had and continues to have the effect of reinforcing the notion of an essential "American" identity that is posited, either overtly or implicitly and without ironic distance, in contradistinction to the one figured as "Spanish." Rarer are the texts or visual works that critique the endeavor to define Spain and Spaniards in terms of racial heritage, temperament, geography, and environment; that treat the category "Spanish" as fluid, malleable, a continual construction on the part of foreigners and also citizens of Spain and, furthermore, that question the category of "nationality" per se so as to suspend the classification "American" as an equally constructed signifier. Texts and visual works such as these produced by residents within the territorial boundaries of the United States should be studied to interrogate and open up the traditional canon of "American" literature, which rests on, among other things, a tautology about its "Americanness."

Similarly, works by people who identify themselves as Spaniards that question notions of "Spanishness" or self-consciously invoke the tropes of "Spanishness" to destabilize, fragment, or deconstruct them should be included in the discussion. An examination of selected works by "Spanish" artists questioning "Spanishness" is an appropriate complement to an exploration of works by "American" writers such as Jenny Ballou and Kathy Acker because it elucidates the ways in which the "Other," despite expectations, does not rehearse the preassigned national characteristics. An attention to issues of self-representation in the film *La línea del cielo* or *Skyline* by Spanish director Fernando Colomo and in the work of two photographers from La Coruña, Galicia, Xurxo Lobato and Manuel Sendón, balances out a discussion of how works by U.S. artists such as Ballou and Acker, as well as nineteenth-century writers and painters who preceded them, do or do not question the existence of an essential, stable "Spanish" identity and to what effects, if not ends.

To break up the dichotomy produced by the categories "American" versus "Spanish," I also focus, in this chapter, on two novels by Barcelona-born Felipe Alfau, who identifies as an "Americaniard," to use his term for Spaniards transplanted to the United States. I consider Alfau's *Locos: A Comedy of Gestures* (1936), a novel written in short stories, and the novel *Chromos* (1948; 1990) in relation to Ballou's novel *Spanish Prelude* (1937) and Acker's novel *Don Quixote* (1986), respectively. Jenny Ballou was a member of the Ballous, Anglo-Normans who emigrated to the "American" colonies from England and gained prominence in New England as ministers, philosophers, educators, botanists, and publishers of, among other things, travel literature. Though Anglo-Normans (and before 1066, Normans), the Ballous became part of the Anglo-American establishment, just as they had been part of the British establishment. Nothing in Jenny Ballou's work indicates another ethnicity or socioeconomic background. Nevertheless, her novel *Spanish Prelude* puts up a significant degree of resistance, within the limits of its aesthetics, to the dominant culture or the ethos and discourse of Anglo-American ethnocentric, imperial ideology. Kathy Acker, who died in 1997, was Jewish American. As the author of *In Memoriam to Identity,* she does not claim this identity as the "ground" from which she writes. Rather than affirm a particular ethnicity or call a specific geographical location "home," she concentrated on constructing "geographies of enunciation," to borrow Karen Brennan's phrase.[2] Alfau, who was born in Barcelona, grew up in Catalonia and the Basque country for the first fourteen years of his life, emigrated with his parents to the United States in 1916, and eventually began to write highly ironic works in English.

Examination of textual and visual works produced by variously "located" artists is a tactic employed to question the assumed natural basis for grouping artists or artifacts together under a national rubric. This tactic aims to reposition "nationality" and the notion of a "national" literature or visual field, as well as periodicity itself (modernism/postmodernism, old/new), as constructs and, therefore, as theoretical problems inescapably linked, in this case, to the historical and imaginative relations between Spain and the United States, relations both inherited from the nineteenth century by modernists and inherited from modernism by postmodernism. By historical and imaginative relations I mean, in the case of the U.S. writers, the legacy that Jenny Ballou, writing in the late 1930s, and Kathy Acker, writing in the mid-1980s, inherited: the consolidation of Anglo-American imperial identity around the Orientalization and literal as well as figurative abjection of Spain and Spaniards during the nineteenth century (culminating in the Spanish-American War of 1898) and of the "missionary" or visionary colonialist stances sometimes found among U.S. citizens who volunteered to fight in the Spanish civil war and those expatriate modernists who treated Spain as one of their principal "grounds of being." To counter this legacy, Acker's novel, for example, alludes to the liberal Spanish Republic of 1931 within the context of references to the export abroad of hypercapitalism by U.S.-managed multinational corporations. The novel suggests that the "redeemer-nation" image of "America" as the great liberator, the torchbearer of civil rights, freedom, and democracy, is, in view of its actual exports, exceptionalism as hypocritical propaganda.

With respect to the texts and/or visual works of Spaniards and/or "Americaniards," the historical and figurative relations are shaped by the following interconnected issues: (1) U.S., particularly Anglo-American, assumptions about the racial, cultural, and moral inferiority of Spaniards; (2) the exigencies of transformation and assimilation on immigrants from Spain to the United States; (3) the pressures of Americanization on "Spanish" nationals within Spain's borders during the Cold War and current New World Order political and economic scenarios; (4) the commodification and commercialization of Spain by the tourist industries of both the United States and Spain; and (5) the desire evident in the last three decades among many Spaniards to emulate the "American way of life." The first two issues inform Alfau's novels *Locos* and *Chromos*. The last three issues are relevant to the work of Colomo, Lobato, and Sendón.

Although much has been written about the discontinuities between modernism and postmodernism, postmodernism, in many of its aspects, is not a new phenomenon. This chapter concentrates on the strategies that these particular postmodernist and noncanonical modernist works have in common: appropriation and reappropriation (including quotation and imposture), ironic distantiation, parody, incongruity, and disorientation. Elucidating the strategies themselves involves a consideration of their relative merits and limitations in terms of the denaturalization of "nationality," the critique of essential "Spanish" or "American" identities. Furthermore, attention to both textual and visual works is crucial in a discussion of the representation of nationality. Since the Renaissance, textual and visual images have been employed together to create a kind of emblem of the ideal nation, subject, or citizen, as well as a descriptive picture of the state of a nation and its subjects. In the past century, the relation between word/text and visual image has literalized in more media than ever before the potential correspondence between the two which, in Western culture, was elaborated by Horace (in *Ars Poetica*) and by other classical writers and which from the sixteenth century onward became the focus of much aesthetic speculation in treatises on the humanistic theory of painting. To achieve the effect of incongruity and disorientation, postmodernism and works with a postmodernist sensibility create, among other things, a disjuncture or a contradiction within the potential or assumed relation between words and visual images implied in the term "image," which denotes both a description of something in speech or writing and a physical representation "photographed, painted, sculpted, or otherwise produced."[3] In Alfau's *Locos* and Ballou's *Spanish Prelude*, the visual image conjured up through verbal description in the course of the "sketching" or modeling of characters generally does not "explain" their words, actions, or ideas. Both novels play with and frustrate the reliance on type characters, in this case "Spanish types" gleaned from Anglo-American and "Spanish" fiction, and the genre of caricature popular in the nineteenth century. In general, they use type ironically rather than straightforwardly, a technique that does not entirely displace the stereotypes, but that does destabilize them. Moreover, the verbal description evoking the image contains cues that distance the reader from the image as a transparent glimpse into the essential identity of a character. Additionally, the image transmutes in a way that recuperates mixed metaphor as a deconstructive tool. In Fernando

Colomo's *Skyline* (1983), what is said and what is seen often do not go together. For instance, although the film is titled *Skyline* and is set in New York, the typical panoramic view of Manhattan is absent. In fact, no clear vistas of New York are offered. Lobato and Sendón employ the titles of the photographs to create expectations that are not gratified by the photographs themselves. The disruption of the function of these photographs as mirrors of a stable nationality, as icons for the nation, is initiated in this disjuncture, a disjuncture that is furthered by the interplay of signs within the photographs themselves. Finally, in Kathy Acker's *Don Quixote* and Alfau's *Chromos,* verbal description—with the exception in Alfau's book of the representation of the *chromos* (old-style calendar pictures) and the narration of the frame tales told by the character named Garcia—chiefly countermines the formulation of conventionally imaginable visual images, producing instead "impossible" and certainly improbable heteroclites (to borrow Foucault's term) or pastiches. When a visual image of a person is offered, it generally metamorphoses into something other than it was; it is chameleonic, as are the "Americaniards," the transplanted Spaniards, in Alfau's novel. Both these novels deliver a subversive blow to Western culture's mimetic codes that construct the effect and expectation of a stable correspondence between word and image and between the work of art and its supposed real referent. A common complaint about these two works is that they produce an uncomfortable epistemological vertigo and confusion. I contend that this effect is created by their substitution of a constantly shifting performance for the type of verbal description that offers iconic stasis or familiar grounds according to readers' expectations.

BROKEN FIGURINES, CONCAVE MIRRORS, AND IRONIC RICOCHET: FELIPE ALFAU'S *LOCOS* (1936) AND JENNY BALLOU'S *SPANISH PRELUDE* (1937)

I examine Alfau's *Locos* and Ballou's *Spanish Prelude* to explore both the potential and the limitations of irony as a technique for denaturalizing nationality, specifically the notion of an essential "Spanishness." Despite the difference in their "origins," both Alfau and Ballou shared a common background in literature from Spain. Alfau wrote fiction influenced by that of Spanish writers Miguel de Unamuno and Ramón María del Valle-Inclán, as well as generally by the works of *el vanguardismo,* a movement in the first quarter of the twentieth century characterized not only by its literary experimentality but also by its heated polemics over how to disassociate "Spanish" culture from "blood and sand" both within Spain and beyond its borders.[4] Ballou, an American-born writer who went to live in Spain during the last years of Primo de Rivera's dictatorship (the late 1920s), was surprisingly well informed about the debates concerning "Spanish identity" in the writings of José Ortega y Gasset, Unamuno, Valle-Inclán, and Pío Baroja.[5] However, notwithstanding Alfau's and Ballou's shared background in debates among Spaniards about "Spanish identity," their primary audience were English-speaking U.S. residents. In their allusions to or explanations of these debates, they mediated Anglo-American stereotypes and expectations about Spain and Spaniards.

At first glance, both *Locos* and *Spanish Prelude* appear to endorse a number of stereotypes that reinforce the notion of an essential "Spanish identity," equating Spain and "Spanishness" with ignorance, illiteracy, close-mindedness, conservatism and reactionaryism, mysticism, fanaticism, monomania, fatalism, superstition, secrecy, deception, prostitution, mendacity, laziness, impracticality, obsession with death, madness, terror, and punishment. The contents of both novels might qualify them for a place beside countless other books that participate in the "Black Legend"-izing and Orientalization of Spain, that argue for the existence of a collective "Spanish soul" and tally it with pride, cruelty, sensuality, and irrationality. I maintain, however, that these two texts "ironize" the stereotypes they present by creating visual images through verbal description that then, through subsequent verbal descriptions, are broken, redrawn, or deconstructed, or that already contain cues distancing the reader from the image as a transparent glimpse into the essential identity of the "Spanish" characters and settings. These characters and settings are offered initially as potential signs of "Spanishness" and Spain's fate, but then are complicated, partially erased, or taken away altogether.

In Alfau's *Locos* this ironic handling of the iconography of the stereotype often takes place within an almost ethnographic presentation of common "types" of "Spanish" society extracted from everyday parlance and literature from Spain—*fulano de tal* (Mr. So-and-So with social ambitions), *el chulo* (the pimp), nuns, beggars, maids, priests, policemen, and so on. One of the most striking examples concludes the story/chapter titled "Identity."[6] Fulano (Mr. So-and-So), perpetually frustrated in his desire to be somebody important, decides that his only option is to commit suicide by jumping into the Tajo River, which runs alongside the city of Toledo. Just before he jumps, Fulano takes one last look at the city. The passage reads:

> And once more he saw Toledo covering its hill like a petrified forest of centuries. It was absurd. With all useful justification of its existence gone, the city sat there like a dead emperor upon his wrecked throne, yet greater in his downfall than in his glory. There lay the corpse of a city draped upon a forgotten hill, history written in every deep furrow of its broken countenance, its limbs hanging down the banks to be buried under the waters of a relentless river.[7]

A passage that initially promises a monumentalizing image of a city beginning with the dramatic words "And once more he saw Toledo covering its hill" is a verbal description furnishing a series of images that implode the potential icon into a performance of decay. The city becomes a "petrified forest" that changes into a "dead emperor upon his wrecked throne" that converts into a "corpse . . . draped upon a forgotten hill" that transmutes into the "deep furrow[s]" of a "broken countenance" that transform into "limbs" that are ultimately buried in water. What was presented as more or less solid and imaginable—Toledo upon its hill (an allusion perhaps to the well-known image of the city in the famous El Greco painting)—turns increasingly into malleable, crumpled, and crumbling matter (a "corpse" that is "draped" like fabric and plowed earth connoted by the word "furrow") and finally deliquesces into water. In Alfau's stories, water, like *niebla* or mist in Unamuno's *nivola* or little novel *Niebla* (1914), signifies dissolution and "nothingness." The image of Toledo, frequently used in Anglo-American literature (as in, for example, Poe's story "The Pit and the Pendulum") to reference the Spanish Inquisition and, as Alfau's narrator tells, "the dreadful historical nightmares" of Spain, metamorphoses beyond recognition and is, at the last, buried beneath a relentless river—that of time or oblivion. The passage functions as a kind of practical joke on the reader in search of an icon of eternal Spain, whether infernal or majestic.

In another passage from the same chapter/story, "Identity," verbal description initially conjures up an image of an object, a figurine, that is the very literalization of the definition of an image as a physical representation.

In the subsequent verbal description the original image of the figurine is changed, broken, with the accidental dropping of the figurine itself. This action suggests an attempt to frustrate the reader's expectations that ensuing verbal description will support and elaborate the image as originally constituted. The breaking of the figurine intimates that the relation between verbal description and "object," between signifier and signified, is "fantastic," that is, a product of the reader's fantasy. The narrator describes the figurine in question as "represent[ing] a herculean warrior with drooping mustache and a ferocious expression . . . The color of the face was not yellow but a darker color, more like bronze" (8–9). The narrator and the junk dealer argue about whether the figurine is Chinese or Indian. The junk dealer keeps insisting, "[T]his is a real Chinese mandarin warrior, I don't know which, and it is a real bargain." The very next moment, he accidentally drops the figure on a marble tabletop where it smashes into a "thousand pieces." The narrator comments, "I fancied I saw a furious look in the little porcelain head now detached from the body" (9). The breaking of the figurine suspends the whole endeavor to assign it an identity and value by achieving a consensus about its origins. The suggested rupture between verbal description and object, signifier and signified, is the formal means to dismember any stable relation between figurine and origin, identity and value—that stable relation which is necessary for the fiction of nationality to be read as other than a fiction/fantasy.

A complete reading of the book makes it possible to interpret the figurine, that is, the signified in the chapter/story "Identity," as itself a signifier of the signified in the chapter/story "Chinelato," that is, the character Señor Olozaga, otherwise known as Juan Chinelato. This character is described in the following manner:

> [H]is hair was still black, both on his head and in his drooping mustache. There was a strong suggestion of the Oriental in him which contrasted excessively with his European attire. He might have been taken for a Chinaman had it not been for his deep olive complexion. I mean olive in the literal sense, not the olive color with which we Spaniards are described, but the real color of the olive which marked this man as the type of the Malay. (102)

In the verbal description of the figurine, the same phrase "drooping mustache" is used. Furthermore, Juan Chinelato, like the figurine, is presented as a warrior whose origins and identity are a puzzle. His body is treated as a series of clues pointing to "the Oriental"; his clothes, to the "European."[8] The reader is told that he lives in the suburbs of Madrid, that "of course, he was not Spanish and undoubtedly the blood of all races was mixed in his veins," and that he is a "Spanish citizen" and has a "Spanish" passport (101, 103, 104). If he does have "the blood of all races . . . mixed in his veins," then he might indeed be "Spanish," for, despite centuries of conflict over *sangre pura,* there was and is no such thing. The text, however, deliberately sidesteps any mention of this possibility, leaving the reader to fill in missing information, an action that implicates the reader in an interpretation of what is meant by "Spanish"—race, citizenship, geography, and so on. In the context of the chapter/story "Chinelato," the smashing of the enigmatic little figurine, an event that suspends discussion about its origins, may be read as an "object lesson" aimed at the venture to define the Other for the purposes of commodification.

Ballou's *Spanish Prelude* (1937) draws character sketches that are redrawn in unexpected ways or contradicted and foiled by the performance of the character. For example, Doctor Monteagudo is initially portrayed as dressing in black, sometimes in "the blackest of black," intensely pale, obsessed with guns and hunting, and given to "bracing monologues" during which he exposes "the whites of his eyes blindly" and spins metaphysical theories like a crazed Don Quijote.[9] Furthermore, he is socially and politically conservative. An expectation is created that he is living in the past and is like a sixteenth-century sable-suited caballero—morbid, monomaniacal, and cruel, as the Black Legend would have it. At times he is heartless. His interests and gestures, however, often contradict or redraw the visual image initially provided of him. Further description redraws this apparently retrograde character from stereotype to renowned ear specialist, passionate scientific investigator, and one who cheerfully shakes hands without "any air of fatality" (21).

Successive brief descriptions of a character called "Saturnina" partially erase and redraw the image of gloom and darkness conjured up by her name, which translates as "Saturnine." Presumably fatalistic, superstitious, and ill-tempered by nature, as her name suggests, the first time she appears "on the scene" within the illusion of autonomous agency granted to her by the narrator, she is "boisterously preparing a little feast . . . her face red from frying and reciting" (lines from José Zorrilla's play *Don Juan Tenorio*

[1844]). The demonstration of her joviality in the context of performance functions as an ironic commentary on the supposed essentiality of her saturnine temperament. Moreover, Saturnina, potentially designated as a member of the country "folk" to embody the national temperament—the supposed fatalism and superstition of the "Spanish soul"—is shown learning to take on the mannerisms of a city person, in this case of a *Madrileña*. The text intimates that identity, national identity included, is a matter of mimicry, learned behavior, not a question of innate qualities.

In the quick "sketch" of the character referred to as "the caretaker," verbal description, rather than presenting and then redrawing a visual image, already contains cues that distance the reader from the image as a transparent glimpse into the character's essential identity and a view of him as evidence of the purportedly fundamental medievalism of Spain. The caretaker is sketched thus: "'Well!' he cried, in his natural voice, looking like a picture of some clown of the Dark Ages in a frame. 'I didn't frighten you, did I?'" (31). The unexpected juxtaposition of the word *natural* and the phrase "looking like a picture . . . in a frame" closes off the text as text from the phantasm of virtual space beyond it. Framing, rather than providing the boundaries of type and identity, prevents the effect of text as transparent window. Instead, the reader is left with a recession of representation: text as frame, picture of a clown of the Dark Ages in a frame, character resembling picture of a clown of the Dark Ages in a frame. Furthermore, the construction of "natural voice" presumably against "unnatural voice" in the context of the gesture "I didn't frighten you, did I?" sets up both voices and his resemblance to a medieval figure as parts of a performance over which the character has control. The caretaker directs his question to, among others, the narrator as character who he knows is a foreigner. Therefore, an impression is created that he is putting on a performance of what he suspects she associates with his national identity.

The use of irony to denaturalize nationality in Ballou's *Spanish Prelude* extends beyond the ironic handling of stereotypes and involves a reliance on the metaphor of the distorting mirror for the related acts of spying on "Spanish" society and extracting "characters" for a novel. Repeatedly, the narrator drops hints that she is a part of the scene she is describing, that objective distance is, therefore, impossible, and that her sojourn in Spain is a long journey through a hall of concave mirrors where the scrutiny of others identities is actually an unflattering judgment of her own. About the character Carmen, she observes, "She did not indeed look like the same person. She was wearing a flowered dress. I had a weird feeling I was looking at myself as she sat in the deep chair opposite me, smiling" (166). Carmen, one of the narrator's closest friends in Spain, becomes her alter ego. This identification of the Anglo-American narrator/character with a "Spanish" character belies the notion of essential differences based on "nationality" and suggests that whatever the narrator sees may be a projection of her own self-image. That a character named "Carmen," of all names, should be the narrator's alter ego-cum-*imago* suggests a deep familiarity on Ballou's part with the history of stereotypes about Spain and a knack for turning them around in relation to herself in a twinkling of a phrase or sentence.

A similar passage constitutes part of the description of the New Year's Eve masquerade ball in Madrid that the narrator attends: "I put on my mask in the vestibule of the Club and ran up the stairway. Looking at myself in the long mirror of the bright entrance, I saw Alberto, the future count, holding a bouquet of flowers. I turned around" (200). Traditionally, deceit has been one of the many moral flaws attributed in Anglo-American literature to Spaniards. In this scene, the Anglo-American narrator sees Don Alberto, the "future count" and arch-self-deceiver, an ardent supporter of the revolutionary Republic who is always glancing "at the society pages before turning to the news" (42), when she looks in the mirror to check her disguise, the bridal costume of a "Spanish" peasant. The double sighting—of herself in peasant disguise and of Don Alberto holding a bouquet of flowers for one of the socialites—points up the extent to which both she and he are, on the eve of the revolution, potential accomplices in the trivialization of the working class's struggle for social justice. Regardless of nationality, the two of them represent the liberal bourgeoisie's self-deception.

Irony as a strategy to denaturalize nationality has its limitations in both Alfau's *Locos* and Ballou's *Spanish Prelude*. For irony to work, readers must be willing to read the double significances, not just the surface layer. Subtle disjunctions between verbal description, the visual image evoked, subsequent description, and the like are easily overlooked or ignored. The reader has to be on the alert for an ironic statement to be read as an inversion of what it is ostensibly implying. In Alfau's *Locos*, for example, the image of Toledo as a dead emperor, a draped corpse, and limbs hanging down into a relentless river might simply serve to reinforce associations of the city and of Spain with death, decay, and degeneration. Likewise, the conversation between the characters about the origins of the "Chinese" figurine and the breaking of this figurine with a face like Chinelato's could easily be interpreted as rendering acceptable, or perhaps merely amusing, the racial typing, commodification, and ignominious treatment of those deemed "Oriental." Set in Spain (Toledo and Madrid, to be precise) and equipped with a cast of questionable characters (thieves, murderers, pimps, confidence artists, and so forth) with "Spanish" names, the novel, I argue, courts U.S. interest in Spain as an exotic country full of colorful types.

Many of the descriptions in Ballou's book pose a similar problem. A doctor who always dresses in black and who, in his obsession with hunting, even shoots at dying birds; a superstitious servant whose name connotes gloom; a caretaker who is associated with the Dark Ages; and a handful of "vanguardist" intellectuals who are supposedly ten years behind the times and about whom the narrator comments, "nowhere is the lost generation more lost than in Madrid" (94) are, to a significant extent, the very embodiments of stereotypes of Spaniards as cruel, fatalistic, medieval, and backward. A cursory reading of the book might miss the irony embedded in these portrayals.

Furthermore, not every ironic handling of an icon or type necessarily involves ideological change. In Ballou's novel, the character Margarita Vaquero is described as the owner of a boardinghouse who, influenced by foreign glamour magazines, decides to become thin. The narrator says, "It is true that with her modern figure her boardinghouse took on a brighter air, became known at the foreign embassies as a pension to be recommended . . . But in essence her life remained the same; she was not compensated for the daily martyrdom she underwent since she had reduced. *For having taken, according to her nature, the most violent treatment, she had ruined her stomach, and vomited, like Santa Teresa, every day*" (62; my emphasis). The passage literally overturns one of the most famous icons of Saint Teresa, the seventeenth-century statue by Bernini (Cornaro Chapel, church of Santa Maria della Vittoria) of the weakened saint: instead of leaning back in ecstasy, in Ballou's text she bends over, vomiting. However, the phrase "according to her nature," coupled with the comparison of Margarita's behavior to that of Saint Teresa, a famous "Spanish" mystic and a national symbol, prompts a reading of that phrase as an essentializing reference to her "Spanishness" that associates it with violence. Perhaps this vignette concerning Margarita's self-destructive efforts to attain and preserve a "modern figure" is merely caricaturing the self-hatred of those Spaniards who internalized the belief that Spain did not qualify culturally as a part of Europe. It is equally possible to interpret Margarita as an emblem of the "Spanish" body politic that is self-destructive because of its "nature." The use of the phrase "according to her nature" and the recapitulation of the historical and cultural associations of Woman with hysteria, narcissism, and abjection overload one side of the meanings, arresting ironic play. Irony fails to find its target (the stereotype), ricochets back as mimesis (a presumed imitation of things as they are), and kills the character, the image in the concave mirror, without implicating the narrator or reader.

Alfau's *Locos* never confronts the social repercussions of ironic ricochet, the potential failure or inability of irony to unfix the stereotypes, the danger that irony might in fact conserve and reinforce them. Perhaps this apparent lack of concern about the conservatism of irony as a technique can be explained by pointing out the extent to which *Locos* is organized around the idea that literature is self-referential and need not be accountable to historical persecutions of people because of their identities. After all, the absurdity of literalization is one of the main themes of the novel. *Locos* refuses to figure social relevance or consequences as anything but unfortunate literal-mindedness. The last story in *Locos,* "Romance of the Dogs," is about an old Spaniard named Garcia. He is a bohemian poet, hypersensitive to the advent of spring, and suffers a "whole degeneration of the system" when spring arrives like an invading army of light (199–200). To read this story as an antibohemian, almost fascist celebration of order and regeneration through an embrace of "life," "nature," and "an infinite force of creation" (198–200), rather than as a performance of romantic sensibility even more ironic than Poe's "Fall of the House of Usher," seems unfair, and yet the possibility remains.

In Ballou's *Spanish Prelude,* however, an anxiety about the ease with which irony may be co-opted by dehumanizing and, more specifically, reactionary forces surfaces repeatedly. I say dehumanizing and reactionary forces because a passage such as the following that underscores the limits of irony and related modes of parody and caricature cites two "liberal" thinkers—Henrik Ibsen (1828–1906), the Norwegian dramatist, in his capacity as a social philosopher concerned with the relation between representation and human rights, and Ralph Waldo Emerson (1803–82), New England transcendentalist philosopher who, despite his mixed record as a social activist and the contradictions of his own rhetoric that implicate as much as they may acquit him of an investment in racializing typologies and typology as teleological history, wrote numerous antislavery tracts that attempted to elaborate a theory of whole personhood as opposed to mere property:

> Before I returned to the mountains, I had learned to see people as subhuman caricatures. I saw in Madrid, as Ibsen had finally seen in cities, "only paunches, heads, and hands," but no men or women; only, as Emerson said, "mere sketches" of men and women. (301)

She seems to fear that the irony of the sketches she made in Madrid will fail to destabilize the dehumanizing stereotypes and the dangerously abstracting icons. Thus, when her pen rolls off a balcony at the Escorial and falls "at the feet of the promenading people, leaving a trickle of life fluid after it" (303–4), instead of bemoaning its loss, she describes that moment as more "beautiful" than anything she had ever "read" or "written" (303). At that moment, she experiences a humble self-transcendence as a writer, a transcendence that does not involve a final revelation about Spain or anything else, but rather a glimpse of a fluidity of representation surpassing that which she could achieve through irony: "[L]ifting my head, I watched my thoughts change their shape, moving, disappearing with the clouds over the mountain wall" (304).

VISTAS THROUGH FOG: "CLICHÉS" IN FERNANDO COLOMO'S *LA LÍNEA DEL CIELO* OR *SKYLINE*

From Alfau's *Locos* (1936) and Jenny Ballou's *Spanish Prelude* (1937) I now pass on to a consideration of contemporary and postmodern Spanish, Madrid-born director Fernando Colomo's film *La línea del cielo* or *Skyline* released in 1983.[10] Significantly, one of his latest films, released in 2003 and titled *Al sur de Granada* (South of Granada), offers a reconstruction of the time the British Bloomsbury writer and Hispanist Gerald Brenan spent in Andalusia as a young man beginning in 1920. Brenan is known for, among other works, *The Literature of the Spanish People* (1951) and *St. John of the Cross* (1972). As in *La línea del cielo,* Colomo focuses on a transnational subject—a move that allows him to explore constructions of Spain by foreigners and, in Brenan's case, by a person engaged in a project of *transculturation*. By transculturation I mean, following Latina/o studies scholars Frances R. Aparicio and Susana Chávez Silverman's definition, a process of "discursive dialogism in which both dominant and marginalized subjectivities . . . are at once given voice and constantly relativized in an analysis [or, I might add, cultural expression] that attempts to transcend the old binary of self/other."[11] Colomo's earlier film, *La línea del cielo,* explores the failure of precisely this kind of transculturation, though its emphasis on failure might be said to constitute its own attempt at creating a "space for discursive dialogism" about the barricades coded into transnational experience. In its (ironic) contemplation of the sky, *La línea del cielo* returns thematically and aesthetically to some of the concerns of texts such as Alfau's *Locos,* which attempts to deliquesce or liquidate stereotypes in the river Tajo running through Toledo, or Ballou's *Spanish Prelude,* which ultimately seeks to relieve itself of the fetters of representation when irony fails to yield sufficient means of critical self-reflection. One of the last major images the book presents is that of a sky that is simply too big and mutable for words. However, in typically postmodern fashion, even the sky in *La línea del cielo* is already "sentenced." *Línea* in the Spanish title and "line" in the "Skyline" of the English translation carry the connotation that quite literally constraining cultural constructions are misrecognized as vehicles for freedom and originality.

The film *La línea del cielo* addresses the way in which people are trapped by clichés about another—as well as their own—culture. And yet, as part of the process of exploring the effects of "cliché" on people's ability to adapt to new situations, it manages to challenge notions of a fixed or stable "Spanish identity," in this case of a distinctly "Spanish gaze," as well as that of an "American" modernist aesthetic. To summarize briefly, the film is about the misadventures of Gustavo Fernández, a photographer from Spain who, influenced by the U.S. modernist tradition of photography (Stieglitz, Bernice Abbott, etc.), goes to New York City and tries to launch a career with well-known picture magazines such as *Life* by selling this modernist urban aesthetic back to U.S. residents. His ambitions are frustrated, however, because the U.S. magazine agents think his photographs look like material they have seen decades ago. They want something *raro, primitivo,* and "new." Roy Hoffman, a writer who speaks Spanish and befriends Gustavo, explains that these agencies are looking for "typical things, for example, the Alhambra, the Basque revolutionaries, the Galicians, gazpacho soup." In other words, they want evidence of "Spanishness"—of a distinctly "Spanish" gaze from Gustavo. His photographs of buildings in New York are not what they expect or desire; they are caught up in a cliché of what a "Spanish" photographer should have to offer. Gustavo himself is equally blinded by clichés about life in the United States, which he associates with instant success, fame, and fortune. He is very disoriented by New York City itself—millions of people from all over the world struggling to survive in the big city. He meets other Spanish-speaking people—Puerto Ricans, Cubans, and Colombians—in various stages of marginalization and assimilation, further disconcerting him. With the exception of Roy Hoffman, the only company he actively seeks out is that of other Spaniards. He gravitates toward Pat, a woman from Barcelona, on whom he develops a crush. When success with his photographs is not instantly forthcoming, he decides to declare his "love" and return to Spain with her. Because she has to spend all her time working at small jobs to pay the rent and thus has little left over for producing videos (her dream), and because she misses her boyfriend, she has already decided to return, independently of Gustavo. This added disappointment only seems to hasten his departure. Immediately after he leaves, the phone rings in the loft that he rented. The answering machine clicks on; one of the U.S. agents is calling to inform him that *Life* magazine is offering to publish his photographs in an article titled "A European Looks at New York City." It is too late. Having missed his opportunity, Gustavo is bound for the airport in a yellow cab.

The word and the concept *cliché,* derived from the French term used by both English and Spanish speakers, is central to *La línea del cielo.* The film's plot revolves around Gustavo's photographs, which he describes as "of buildings in New York City," "modern," "more modern," "different," and of "buildings, very long, very beautiful." However, the closest one gets to a glimpse of these photographs is a brief glance at a few black-and-white reproductions of photographs of cast-iron architecture in Soho and Tribeca from a coffee-table monograph of work by an unnamed U.S. photographer of the early 1970s. The book is offered to him so that he may explain how his photographs of buildings in New York City are different from those produced by U.S. modernist photographers since the early twentieth century, and especially how they are new. The viewer is made privy to Gustavo's private horror at the unoriginality of his photographs through a voice-over: "Horrified, I realized the extraordinary similarity between those photos and mine." Like Gustavo's photographic prints passed from scene to scene in a concealing manila envelope and never shown to the viewer, the word *cliché*, referring to stereotypes, trite expressions, and to photographic negatives, is almost taboo. *Cliché* is used only once in a crucial scene in which Gustavo's potential agent, Thornton, attempts to answer Gustavo's question of whether he can "make it" in New York City:

> It won't be easy. Personally, I like your pictures, but here there are good photographers from all over the world . . . I can just imagine the reaction I'll get when I show them to editors of magazines here. They'll say they're good but that they already had that fifteen years ago. I mean for us they're a little like a "cliché" or something like that. I'm not saying that, but I imagine that they'll say that because in foreign photographers they are looking for something rare, primitive, or something like that.

Gustavo repeatedly asks for the "honest opinion" of agents, critics, journalists, and dealers, but no one has the heart to directly call his work "cliché" and Gustavo cannot or will not recognize his own problematic relationship as a Spaniard to the U.S. modernist aesthetics he emulates. He refuses (perhaps unconsciously) to supply photographic images of the U.S. modernists' clichéd idea of "Spanishness" as a source of the rare, the primitive, the passionate, and the exotic of which they have made themselves the self-appointed curators to extract, abstract, and translate. However, through his desire for internationalism, fame, fortune, and the "American Dream," he falls into another cliché, that of U.S. modernist views of New York City as the image of that dream: the skyscrapers presumably represented by Gustavo's hidden photographs and named in the dialogue but never really shown until the last frames of the film when an eye-level camera takes a long shot of a brownstone-flanked downtown street at the end of which stand, in a haze, the twin towers of the World Trade Center.

The film itself attempts to "break clichés" at the same time that it "documents" them by creating scenes in which a disjuncture between dialogue and visual image is made apparent. These disjunctures function to frustrate or parody the viewing pleasures of the traditional narrative film in which what is named is shown (if not initially, then eventually) and vice versa. With subtitles in English and Spanish, and the product of a collaboration between Spaniards and U.S. residents, the film is aimed at both "Spanish" and "American" audiences. The title and the setting of the action in New York City initially promise a "Spanish" audience that they will see New York, that is, it plays on the foreign viewer's potential associations of New York with panoramic vistas and skyscrapers. Location and title are designed to elicit a foreign audience's association of the city with excitement, romance, large crowds, and sublimity. For a U.S. audience, the setting and title may seem "cliché," but the story of a "Spanish photographer's adventures" sets in motion the expectation that something will be revealed about "Spanish" photography, Spaniards, and "Spanishness." The film foils these clichéd expectations. With respect to the typically New York (and, synecdochically, "American")—the Statue of Liberty, the Empire State Building, Times Square, and the Twin Towers—the major tourist landmarks of New York City are tantalizingly mentioned in conversation but are either absent from the camera's view or, if shown at all, are filmed through some obstructing fog or haze. Similarly, the desires to learn something concrete about "Spanish" photography or to see signs of "Spanishness" are frustrated or parodied. In one scene, for example, the stereotype of "the Spanish male" as a cavalier or knight always ready to defend his honor and virility is referenced and deflated by a mock umbrella fight between Gustavo and Jaime, the psychoanalyst from Spain. In another scene, Gustavo is being interviewed about the "situation of photography in Spain" on a mock weekly news program that is actually one of Pat's video projects. The disjuncture between what is said and what is seen is most apparent in the video scene. The mock interviewer claims that the subject is the "situation of photography in Spain." Rather than showing photographs by Gustavo or any other Spanish photographer, the background against which Gustavo and the interviewer are seated is a blue wall with three illegible drawings of dancing geometric, whimsical figures on yellowish paper serialized like frames from an animated film. Gustavo is introduced as "from this European country" but appears in a costume different from the subdued, tailored, formal attire that characterized him in previous scenes. He wears dark sunglasses and a sport shirt printed with a pattern suggesting palm leaves. His new clothes, in combination with his thick, dark mustache make him look like the "cliché" image of a Cuban from Florida. The Gypsy music that plays over the scene further exoticizes him. While promising the "Spanish," *Skyline* does not gratify its viewers with a reliable or stable image to accompany its terms.

The film is not entirely effective in denaturalizing nationality because it is so intent on successfully taking clichés or pictures and breaking clichés or aesthetic stereotypes. Gustavo's visible failure as a modernist, international photographer facilitates Colomo's success as a postmodern filmmaker. Gustavo is never seen executing his photographic project of taking pictures in the designated modernist field: the city street and other public spaces of the urban environment. Instead, Colomo's camera captures Gustavo indoors feeding the birds and the cat, doing his English homework, and talking to writers, dealers, and agents. Colomo appropriates for himself—for his own camera—the latest development (vis-à-vis the film's production and release dates) in New York City architecture, the transformation of commercial interiors of derelict buildings in Soho and Tribeca into the late 1970s/early 1980s phenomenon of "loft living."[12] The film's director places his own vision on the cutting edge at the expense of his character, whom he represents as unproductive, lazy, and unaware of the trendy significance of his surroundings—to summarize, an embarrassingly clueless immigrant who, unwittingly rather than defiantly, remains an outsider. In contrast, Colomo establishes himself as a filmmaker from Spain in the know about the latest developments on the New York art scene and thus as successfully "international," unlike Gustavo, who, in his ignorance and lack of initiative, bears the burden of some of the most pervasive Anglo-American stereotypes about Spaniards.

DISORIENTING GUIDES: THE PHOTOGRAPHS OF XURXO LOBATO AND MANUEL SENDÓN

Rivalry between film and photography, film's basis in photography (its moving texture of photographs), is utilized in *La línea del cielo* to denaturalize nationality, but with the Spanish photographer as the butt of its ironic twists. This tactic of enlisting the rivalrous relation between film and photography is turned to a critique of U.S. cultural hegemony by two Spanish photographers whose work views both interiors and landscapes of the region as already shot through with signs of global capital, particularly in the form of the signs and products of U.S. film, TV, and televised sports industries. A film about a Spanish photographer failing in the United States and, moreover, failing to grasp the irony of his own subaltern transnational position deserves to be followed up by a consideration of some photographs by two actual contemporary photographers from La Coruña, Galicia, Spain. Their work toured the United States in 1992 as part of a larger show of Spanish contemporary documentary photography. Unlike Gustavo's photographs of New York skyscrapers, the quintessential icon of U.S. northeastern, urban modernism itself along with the Brooklyn Bridge—just consider the titles of Hart Crane's two books of poetry, *White Buildings* (1926) and *The Bridge* (1930), his Ohio birth notwithstanding—Xurxo Lobato's and Manuel Sendón's photographs symptomatize a diffident awareness of transnational positionality. This awareness can be detected, I argue, in their scenes that denaturalize nationality within the framework of "documenting" a particular place. These scenes pit region against nation and intercept region or the local (relatively speaking) with evidence of the incursions of late-1980s, early-1990s U.S.-dominated transnational capitalism. Before I consider specific photographs by Lobato and Sendón I would like to describe the context in which I saw them in 1992.

From January 17 to March 15, 1992, an exhibition titled *Open Spain/ España Abierta: Contemporary Documentary Photography in Spain,* part of the Quincentennial celebration, was on display at the Museum of Contemporary Photography at Columbia College in Chicago, Illinois. It then toured the United States, Europe, and Latin America. As the exhibition's title suggests, the work of the Spanish photographers chosen for the show was billed as "documentary" photography, a genre dedicated to capturing the "real," in this case the supposed disappearance of "traditional" Spain, "Spanish" customs, and ways of life in the new Spain of industry, technology, "American" influence, and the European Common Market.

The show nostalgically rested on a conceptual opposition of old, "true" Spain with the new, transitional Spain in which Spaniards of the old Spain were tacitly and sometimes overtly associated with manifest destiny's figure of the "doomed Indian" and Spaniards of the new were more or less equated with "Americans," the "us" assumed in the commentary on wall plaques and in the catalog. Many of the photographs were of religious processions, bullfights, and the Fiesta of San Fermín. Presumably they were "documenting" the old, true Spain and, by implication, the *Spanishness* of Spain. These images seemed to have been created and selected with foreign consumption in mind because they resembled and reinforced travelers' ethnographic and tourists' holiday postcard stereotypes. Historically, foreigners and even many Spaniards themselves have treated activities such as bullfights or religious processions as symbols of the supposedly "essential difference" of Spain from Europe and the United States. But bloody bullfights and religious processions are certainly not any more "typical" of Spain than is the legal tradition of *los fueros* (group rights and privileges), with a long history in various regions of Spain; or a legacy of medical studies dating back to the time of the Arabs and the Jews; or disputes over agrarian reform; or the history of discrimination against and attempts to assimilate the Gypsies. Photographs of bullfights and religious processions are not representative of the diversity of Spain or of life as it used to be or still is, either in the countryside, the small villages, the towns, or the big cities. As much as they strive for the status of document, they are products of a conjunction of ethnographic and ethnocentric desires. In this exhibit about Spain for foreign consumption, the two activities that, in the nineteenth century, became an important part of the creation of a national myth for Spaniards and of the definition of the "typically Spanish" for French, British, and Anglo-American travelers were foregrounded both in the gallery and in the catalog as signs of Spain's "distinctiveness." Much of *España Abierta* replicated nineteenth-century modes of thought and representation.

However, not all the photographs in the exhibition were essentializing. Xurxo Lobato and Manuel Sendón have done work that challenges the project of defining or asserting a stable "Spanish" identity and does not participate in unexamined nostalgia. The inclusion of their work in the exhibit suggests that curatorial decisions were informed by postmodern trends in photography, including the questioning of the truth status of the photographic image and, thus, the documentary project of identifying and classifying. In the catalog written by the director of the museum in collaboration with other contributors, Lobato and Sendón, along with Humberto Rivas (who took pseudoethnographic full-frontal photos of his friends), were designated as guides to disorientation, that of the "new" Spain and of the viewer. However, the extent to which Lobato's and Sendón's pictures were allowed to disrupt viewers' expectations was curtailed by the exhibit's layout. Their works were hung on the cramped second level of the museum gallery rather than on the spacious first level, where museumgoers spent most of their time. Not only were they relegated to the second floor, but, when I visited the exhibit, there were no signs to indicate that the show continued upstairs. Furthermore, their photographs were reproduced in the last fourth of the catalog, after numerous photographs of bullfights, religious processions, and ritualistic shows of "macho" strength in small villages. Finally, Manuel Sendón's ironic "landscape" photograph titled *Vigo*, from the series *Paisaxes* or *Landscapes* (Figure 19), showing a fillet of smoked salmon laid out on a fish-shaped cutting board placed in front of a large photomural of river rapids, was reproduced

Figure 19. Manuel Sendón, *Tienda de afumados/Smoked food shop, Vigo*, from the series *Landscapes* (1989–91), chromogenic development print (Ektacolor), 20 × 24 inches. Centro de Estudios Fotográficos de Vigo.

on the cover of the catalog. Appearing without its title as the background for large white letters spelling out the exhibition's title, *Open Spain/España Abierta,* the image of the salmon is emptied of its irony and functions simply as a mouthwatering attention grabber suggesting that Spain has been filleted open for consumption. This presentation has the effect of setting up an equivalence between Spain and a "loose fish," to borrow the term, discussed in Herman Melville's *Moby Dick,* for a whale that is "fair game for anybody who can soonest catch it."[13] The view of Spain as a decontextualized commodity, a fish out of water vis-à-vis Europe, has historical antecedents. The front matter of Melville's novel contains a section titled "Extracts (supplied by a sub-sub-librarian)." That section includes a quotation taken from Edmund Burke's writings figuring Spain as "a great whale stranded on the shores of Europe."[14]

Both Lobato and Sendón chose titles for their photographs that were simultaneously relevant and misleading with respect to the images. The title, as guide to or identifier of the subject of the photograph, raised expectations or associations that were frustrated by the photograph itself. Lobato's pictures, for example, were all from a series labeled *Galicia, Sitio Distinto* or *Galicia, Different Place* (1987–90). The title suggested that the photographs would attest to Galicia's essential difference from the rest of Spain and/or the world and that the photographs would reference things both typically and uniquely Galician. One photograph showed a woman sitting on a sofa, knitting (Figure 20). In front of her on a table was a huge shell mounted on a pedestal and covered with small shells clinging to it like garden snails. Beside her was a modern clothes dryer or washing machine. Another photograph was of an elderly woman and man sitting in a café bar having coffee (Figure 21), the man seemingly startled by the taking of the photograph and the woman with head averted from the camera. Above them on the wall hung caricature-like paintings of fishermen. Yet another photograph showed a man playing with a jackpot machine labeled "Baby Fruits de Lujo" (Figure 22). Beside the machine, hanging from a hook on the wall, was a flayed fish, a hake perhaps. One of the more obviously disorienting photographs was of two young girls dressed in traditional folk costume seated beside a young boy in a T-shirt, sweats, and sneakers (Figure 23). All three were taking a ride on an amusement park whirligig. Behind them in the background was a poster of Superman, who seemed to be watching and cheering them on as they whirled by.

Another such photograph was of children playing in the shadows of a sunny village street. One young boy wore jeans, sunglasses, and a T-shirt that read "Champions . . . fully designed by" (Figure 24). Rather than being given a picture of a unitary or homogeneous way of life, the viewer is met with curious juxtapositions, contradictions, and non sequiturs—a heteroclite, a state in which "things are 'laid,' 'placed,' 'arranged' in sites [or 'from sites'] so very different from one another that it is impossible to find a place of residence for them, to define a *common locus* beneath them all":[15] a woman doing "traditional" work while sitting near a modern appliance—the dryer or washing machine—and an object at once natural and highly artificial (the shell covered with shells); the café where the one indication of what might be considered a typical, regional business—the fishing industry—appears only in a caricature-like sign; a hake "prepared" not as a *plato típico* (a typical dish) but instead as a flayed carcass beside a jackpot advertising candy in English; and the children who are seemingly

Figure 20. Xurxo Lobato, untitled, Vigo from the series *Galicia, Different Place* (1987–90), silver dye bleach print, 11⅞ × 17⅞ inches. Courtesy of the photographer.

Figure 21. Xurxo Lobato, untitled, Vigo from the series *Galicia, Different Place* (1987–90), silver dye bleach print, 17⅞ × 11⅞ inches. Courtesy of the photographer.

at home in an Anglo-Americanized environment. The photographs are not sentimental laments or laments at all. Instead, they are cool interrogations of the possible significations of the word *different* in the general title for the series—*Galicia, Different Place.* The one signification of *different* that is not satisfied by the photographs is the idea of "essential difference." The photographs show things that can be found in Galicia, but that do not distinguish "it" completely and absolutely from anywhere else. In other words, Lobato's photographs and title recruit the notion of difference to split "the typical" from the "the distinctive." Furthermore, as the signs in the photographs themselves do not all point in the same direction—to the same "place," so to speak—the photographs leave the viewer in doubt as to what, in fact, is typically "Galician" or even "Spanish" about these scenes. Significantly, the issue of a fixed "Spanish" identity is displaced by a provincialism that, in turn, is destabilized by isolated pieces of U.S. mass culture and assembly-line machinery.

Figure 22. Xurxo Lobato, untitled, Vigo from the series *Galicia, Different Place* (1987–90), silver dye bleach print, 11⅞ × 17⅞ inches. Courtesy of the photographer.

Figure 23. Xurxo Lobato, untitled, Coia, Vigo, from the series *Galicia, Different Place* (1987–90), silver dye bleach print, 17⅞ × 11⅞ inches. Courtesy of the photographer.

The photographs by Manuel Sendón were from a series titled *Paisaxes* or *Landscapes,* a label that suggested the photographs would be of land, and maybe even of a particular place outdoors, and presumably in Spain. However, the photographs punned on the three conventional designations of the term "landscape"—hence, perhaps, the choice to pluralize the word in the title. These three designations are (1) the lay of the land, (2) a visual representation of land, and (3) a panoramic view, generally of land. The series denaturalized landscape as the unmediated view of land by deliberately (con)fusing these different designations in each of the photographs and, in particular, by documenting not the outdoors, but the use of framed or otherwise bounded images of the outdoors indoors. The possibility of contemplating some picturesque, beautiful, or sublime "natural" domain was exchanged for the experience of landscape as a representation on paper, canvas, or cardboard placed in domestic or commercial spaces. The appearance of landscape merely as a possession within domestic or commercial spaces—someone's house, a bar, a shoe store, a fish market,

Figure 24. Xurxo Lobato, untitled, Muxia, La Coruña, from the series *Galicia, Different Place* (1987–90), silver dye bleach print, 11¾ × 11⅞ inches. Courtesy of the photographer.

a cigarette vending machine (Figure 25)—serves to remind viewers that landscape as a genre is intimately tied to the significations of property, ownership, natural resources, fecundity, and the social and political order under a particular regime or government. It serves to foreground the ideological function of landscape as a genre, to remind viewers of its colonization by individual, communal, regional, national, and imperial interests. It is at this point that the full irony of Sendón's photographs may be appreciated. Playing on viewers' expectations to see "Spanish" landscapes by a "Spanish" photographer, or at least Galician landscapes by a Galician, Sendón had taken photographs of spaces that were hard, if not impossible, to place as even being in Spain. One photograph, for example, showed a group of boys playing *fusbol* in front of a mural of the New York skyline

Figure 25. Manuel Sendón, *Brión,* from the series *Landscapes* (1989–91), chromogenic development print (Ektacolor), 20 × 24 inches. Centro de Estudios Fotográficos de Vigo.

and harbor (Figure 26). Another from the *Paisaxes* series was of a man opening the door of his car, which had across its windshield a cardboard heat shade depicting a surfer riding a big blue wave, an image remindful of the TV series *Hawaii Five-O* or the popular song "Surfing U.S.A." (Figure 27). In these photographs, the outdoors and the indoors, the "natural" and the simulated, the "Spanish" and the "American" are conflated. Landscape exists indoors, as a commodity advertising other commodities. The only "outdoors" photograph was taken in a parking lot, a no-place, a limbo-land of cars, where a product first marketed in California, the heat shade, simultaneously blocks the view through the window and provides the only panorama of nature in the picture. Sendón's *Landscapes* are not about a stable "Spanish" identity or nature; every "place" is either composed of other places or in another place through simulation and circulation.

Figure 26. Manuel Sendón, *O Couto, Ourense,* from the series *Landscapes* (1989–91), chromogenic development print (Ektacolor), 20 × 24 inches. Centro de Estudios Fotográficos de Vigo.

By challenging the project of documenting or defining a stable "Spanish" identity, Lobato and Sendón attempt to resist compromise by the ethnographic fantasies of foreigners, by the ethnocentrism of their fellow Spaniards, or by the somewhat insular nostalgia of photographing scenes that bear no imprint of the consequences of both Anglo-American imperialism and Spaniards' complicity in their own "Americanization." However, although their work challenges the project of defining an essential "Spanish" identity, it may not entirely destabilize the underlying power relations in the formation and maintenance of national identity. The point of view of their cameras places the spectator in a potentially superior position to the objects, spaces, and people thus framed. Cheap oil paintings; homespun doilies; elderly working-class people caught off guard and making grotesque facial expressions mimicked in the caricature-like paintings;

Figure 27. Manuel Sendón, *Praia de Samil/Samil's Beach, Vigo,* from the series *Landscapes* (1989–91), chromogenic development print (Ektacolor), 20 × 24 inches. Centro de Estudios Fotográficos de Vigo.

wrinkled clothes, scraggly hair, and careless paint jobs; and an aging man with 1970s sideburns and a dowdy visor cap contrasted with the "beautiful surfer boy" on the imported heat shade may reinforce an identification of Galicia, and perhaps Spain, with backwardness and inferiority. In a "Spanish" context, these photographs locate Spaniards' own insecurities in the constructed place of "Galicia," potentially providing middle- to upper-middle-class urban Spaniards with a justification for willing complicity with foreign interests in Spain. Similarly, in an American context, these images, while disorienting viewers in terms of place and national identity, may reassure them of their position as tasteful or sophisticated consumers in relation to the people "captured" by the camera.

IMPOSTURING "AMERICAN" IDENTITY: PERFORMING "THE SPANISH" IN KATHY ACKER'S *DON QUIXOTE* AND FELIPE ALFAU'S *CHROMOS*

From the denaturalizations of nationality in the visual work of Colomo, Lobato, and Sendón I would like to return to the question of verbal denaturalizations of nationality, both "American" and "Spanish," this time focusing on one unquestionably postmodern text (Acker's *Don Quixote* [1986]) and on another that, on account of its hybrid, pastiche style, qualifies as a postmodern experiment in narrative and representation (Alfau's *Chromos* [1948; 1990]). Both novels share similar techniques for denaturalizing nationality. Above all, they share a technique of imposture. In an unpublished short story written in 1930 titled "The Impostor," Jewish American modernist writer Nathanael West (Nathan Weinstein by birth), very familiar with and indebted to the Spanish picaresque tradition, offers a kind of dramatically descriptive definition of the act of being an impostor, in this case as a U.S. expatriate in Paris:

> After hiding in my hotel for about a week, not daring to show myself at the *Dome* for fear of making a bad impression, I hit on a great idea. I had come to Paris from a runner's job in Wall Street and still had the clothes I had worn there. Instead of buying a strange outfit and trying to cultivate some new idiosyncrasies, I decided to go in the other direction. "Craziness" through the exaggeration of normality was to be my method. In this land of soft shirts, worn open to the navel and corduroy trousers, I would wear

hard collars and carefully pressed suits of formal, stylish cut, and carry clean gloves and a tightly rolled umbrella. I would have precise, elaborate manners and exhibit pronounced horror at the slightest, *public* breach of conventions.[16]

Neither Acker's *Don Quixote* nor Alfau's *Chromos* symptomizes much fear of making a bad impression. On the contrary, their work would seem to revel in making a bad impression, certainly a disobediently confounding one with regard to the reiteration of nationality, either "American" or "Spanish," not to mention expatriate in a literal as well as a philosophical and political sense. But their techniques of imposture partake, in part, of the contrarian and paradoxical "exaggeration of normality" described in West's story. In West's work, normality always appears as a copied and artificial reality reinforced as natural through repetition in the form of imitation and then pressed to a farcical extreme. Acker's and Alfau's works manifest many moments of contrarian "exaggeration of normality," but mimesis entails more than resemblance and resemblance as farce. It involves the wholesale incorporation of the copied Other into the self, imitation more akin to plagiarism. This incorporation is a mode of mimetic exaggeration that undermines mimesis with an excess mimesis.

Rather than the representation of the Other framed as Other, the Other appears in the guise of the self and vice versa. Acker offers an "American" female knight named Don Quixote, a New York City woman with, among other names, a fictional Spanish man's name. Instead of Spaniards in the United States Alfau presents his readers with "Americaniards" in exile expounding Anglo-Saxon–sounding theories of racial superiority. With regard to nationality and subject positioning, these novels present characters that not only strike poses but that, moreover, usurp by incorporating a pose. A pose does not remain merely external or incidental to their inner selves, hence (im)posture. Rather, it involves an involution of act and identity that implodes the very illusion of interiority that creates "characters" in a conventional sense. Nationality is denaturalized through the defiguration of character away from psychology and even behavior toward rhetoric and slipping sign, like old calendar pictures sliding off the wall. In this respect, the technique of imposture in Acker's *Don Quixote* and Alfau's *Chromos* is not unrelated to the disorienting tactics of Lobato's and Sendón's photographs. Although many of them portray people, none of them are portraits, and most of them actually discourage the viewer from this particular viewing convention by giving equal emphasis to the evidence of the impact of transnational products and media on the environment surrounding any human figure. The same is true of the landscapes, many of which are not landscapes in anything but a doubly or triply removed manner.

In Acker's *Don Quixote* and Alfau's *Chromos,* nationality as an essence or as a fixed, unitary, or "pure" identity, like essence itself, is a construction, a fiction, a collective hallucination—a matter of propaganda and lies in Acker's novel; an issue of illusion and self-deception in Alfau's. In these novels, the denaturalization of nationality does not, as in Alfau's earlier book *Locos* and Ballou's *Spanish Prelude,* depend on the partial presentation of a stereotype that is then redrawn or disfigured, nor on a disjuncture between word and image, as in Colomo's *Skyline* and Lobato's and Sendón's photographs. Instead, *Don Quixote* and *Chromos* rely heavily on quotation, paraphrase, and what Acker bluntly refers to as plagiarism of other people's arguments, which are tossed, turned, incorporated into each other, and bent out of shape in a running commentary among or dialogue between characters. Verbal description evoking visual images is a component of both novels. The visual images offered, however, rarely function to create a tableau that arrests the rather relentless "decentrifugal" flow of their narratives. Attributes that identify characters do not constitute typical physical description. Bodies are redimensualized: these texts refuse to sustain the illusion of three dimensions. Costumes become disguises, voices become language games, and gestures become performances that construct character as only a fleeting and transmuting conjunction of discourses. This flattening of the text shifts the tableau from the virtual dimension beyond the text to its surface, where verbal performance decenters and exceeds the classic *vraisemblance* and central organization of tableau. Despite their deconstruction of character, these texts remain classic novels of ideas much in the tradition and style of Miguel de Cervantes's *Don Quijote* (1605 and 1615). The techniques of intertextuality and appropriation of others' arguments are used to create a debate about national identity. Juxtaposing arguments, these debates are between ideas rather than characters.

Acker's novel continually questions received notions about "American" identity as being synonymous with democracy, freedom, and civil rights, so-called Anglo-Saxon traditions. A substantial part of this questioning involves a deliberate act of plagiarism of a famous, if not *the* famous, Spanish novel *Don Quijote* as well as fragmented references to Spanish history. Her novel is a narrative about a female knight, one of whose names is Don Quixote. This knight, hoping to find love and save the world from its own self-destruction, goes on a jumbled, apocalyptic dream journey through New York City and also, in a scattered way, through U.S. history, accompanied by a pack of dogs. The narrative of this journey functions as a critique of the Cold War and the Star War eras that is informed by, among other things, Cervantes's treatment of *el libre albedrío* (free will) in *The Colloquy of the Dogs* and *Don Quijote,* as well as by Giner de los Ríos's theories about the role of education and the activity of learning for social change. In the novel, one of the main themes of which is the "failure of revolution" in an "America" of hypercapitalism (called "postcapitalism" by Acker) and of military-industrial corporations, Don Quixote, near the end of her dream journey, thinks of Spain, the Spanish Republic of 1931, and Giner de los Ríos, who argued for the importance of an education not dominated by either the church or the government and not serving the interests of national or cultural chauvinism. What seems to appeal to Don Quixote (and perhaps to Acker) about the Spanish Republic of 1931 is the philosophy and tactics of the anarchist leaders who wanted to believe in the value of decentralized political power, the individual, collective action, and nonhierarchical structures. The picture of the anarchists, drawn in a few strokes, is obviously idealized. For a brief section in Acker's text they are conjured up to embody an ideal of egalitarian harmony serving as an antidote to a conception of human beings as essentially unreasonable creatures, unable, therefore to exercise any "free will," and thoroughly selfish (like the dogs that follow Don Quixote only when they are hungry), a view advanced by Thomas Hobbes, who is figured as the Angel of Death presiding over the twentieth century.

Although the French, Italian, and Russian revolutions are all alluded to in the course of the narrative, the location of the allusions to the Spanish Republic, Giner de los Ríos, and so forth, at the conclusion of the novel in a section titled "Don Quixote's Dream" gives them a particular importance. The quotation of Thomas Jefferson's words in the middle of the portion on the Spanish Republic indicates that the allusions are not setting up an argument about the "Spanishness" of the Spanish civil war. Instead, the allusions function as part of an attempt to answer the question about what type of education and culture might provide guarantees against the abuse of authority and the use of force or brutality. An alternative to the "American" Dream of social advancement through material acquisition is modeled on excerpts from the writings of a number of intellectuals in Spain important to the cultural life of the Spanish Republic of 1931. This situation, I argue, provokes the question, "What, after all, is 'American' about that *other* American dream of the right to liberty, equality, and the pursuit of happiness?" Furthermore, to the extent that the presumably "Spanish hero" is transferred with a sex change to a U.S. setting and that Spanish anarchist ideals are shown calling for a cultivation both of localism and internationalism, the question arises as to what was or is particularly "Spanish" about the Spanish Republic. In short, although one of the basic concerns of the novel is with unsettling chauvinist and essentialist conceptions of "American" identity, it provides no reasons to see "Spanish" as a fixed or bounded identity either. Acker's postmodern vision seems to find a glimmer of hope in the possibility of an internationalist and ultimately postnationalist scenario, depending on whether one interprets her stance toward the ideals of the Spanish Republic as skeptically ironic or respectfully committed.

The title of Felipe Alfau's novel *Chromos* references the sentimental and stereotyped calendar-style pictures or stamps of "the typically Spanish": young ladies with high combs and black, mournful eyes; a bullfighter dying in a chapel surrounded by his loyal assistants, and so on. The novel persistently questions foreigners' and, I argue, especially Anglo-Americans' assumptions about the existence of an essential "Spanish" identity radically different from what they would consider to be their own "American" identity. Written in English and set largely in New York City, the book is aimed at an English-speaking public. Questions are suggested through the tertulias (intellectual conversations) among "Americaniards," transplanted Spaniards in varying degrees of assimilation into and resistance toward the dominant Anglo-American culture. These transplanted Spaniards alternately embrace and reject the stereotypes of Spain as the country of the Inquisition, darkness, sadists, "Oriental blood," outlaws, brigands, violent passions (fueled by the imbibing of wine and sherry and the consumption of garlic and peppers), laziness, primitivism, timelessness and/or stagnation, tragedy, mystics, morbidity, and death. Furthermore, a satirical distance from these stereotypes is achieved by having "Spanish" characters placed in Spain as well as some of the "Americaniards" in New York rehearse or play out to an absurd degree the very stereotypes themselves. While the "Spanish" characters in the stories of one Americaniard, Garcia, kill out of jealousy and wounded pride over marital infidelities; conduct torrid adulterous, sadomasochistic, and necrophilic sexual affairs; lose their sanity and have epileptic fits; commit incest and suicide; dance flamenco; and delight in their own martyrdom, the Americaniards torment flies, loiter unproductively in public places, and gravitate toward metaphysical, hair-splitting arguments. The excessiveness of the various characters' behaviors has the effect of turning "attributes" presumed to be innate, constitutional, or dispositional with Spaniards into ludicrous performances of those very attributes. Any conception of an essential "Spanish" identity becomes equated with a staged imposition or "imposture" rather than with an objective description of disposition. Alfau's characters, I contend, are in fact largely a bundle of *assumed* or put-on characteristics. Inasmuch as these characters are deployed to play out these characteristics to their logical extreme, they flash out as inventions of cultural fantasies and the author's imagination.

Anglo-American identity, which canonically has been constructed as "American" identity, is also "impostured" in Alfau's text. The vehicle for the "imposture" is a character referred to as the "Irish Moor" and whose name is Don Pedro Guzman O'Moore Algoracid, truncated by the "American" public to "Pete Guz." He himself uses "American" slang and expounds racial theories to prove the superiority of Spaniards over "Nordics such as Anglo-Saxons, Teutons, Scandinavians, and so forth," thus simultaneously mirroring and inverting Anglo-American claims to racial superiority.[17] The fact that a Spanish-Irish-Moor can sound and act so traditionally "American" suggests that "American identity" is merely about "performance," which may be learned by any immigrant, not about innate qualities or essence. The doubt cast on the existence of a fixed, unitary, and distinctive Spanish identity ultimately functions to subvert sacrosanct and chauvinist notions of "American" identity. Those who pretend without ironic distance to "Spanishness" or "Americanness" are self-deluded impostors for Alfau, to whom identity is vertiginous hybridity and a "wastepaper basket full of discarded roles" (304).

THE LIMITS OF "IMPOSTURE"

Now that I have set up this presumably radical and utopian ideal of the deconstruction of national identity, I may have to take it away in the process of answering these questions: "To what ends has nationality been deconstructed? What is imposed in its place?" In Acker's *Don Quixote* nationality is taken apart to immobilize one of the state's central fictions used to group people together and pit them against each other in either market competition or actual combat. With regard to a definition of "the state," classic Marxist theory describes the state as a state apparatus and mostly focuses on its repressive and often violent functions and institutions: the police, the courts, the prisons, the military, the government, and the administration. However, in his 1970 essay "Ideology and Ideological State Apparatuses," Louis Althusser made a significant addition to this description with his theory of the central role played by ideology. He divided the state apparatus in two—repressive and ideological. He concentrated on ideology or "representations of the imaginary relationship of individuals to their real conditions of existence," though he was careful to show the imbrication of ideological and repressive state apparatuses. Typical ideological state apparatuses were and are institutions of organized religion, education, and mass communication or the media. Furthermore, according to his theory, certain concepts or ideas could in themselves function in this capacity—concepts such as "justice," "duty," "nation," and "nationality." Such concepts were and are used to induce individuals to become exploitable subjects of the state.[18]

Moreover, in Acker's *Don Quixote* nationality is questioned and confounded, not incidentally, through the experiences of a female knight-errant or nomad. In patriarchal systems, women have been assigned the role of mothers designated to stay within national boundaries and to provide the nation-state with worthy sons and daughters. Men, on the other hand, have been expected to go on adventures, to cross national borders, to have international relations. Acker constructs a female knight with multiple names and no fixed nationality, a kind of female pirate knight engaging in a guerrilla war of statelessness against the central fictions of the state-co-opted war machine.[19] First we read, "She had left the only land she had ever known—Spain—and there was no land to which she wanted to go, or to which she knew how to go," and later, "She had never been to Spain."[20] Having no country to which she belongs, in the sense of either ownership or allegiance, she is free, as few women have been, to wander, to "settle into nowhere," and to draw up her will (201). But, as is intimated in the word *nowhere,* this nomadic guerrilla ideal of the deconstruction of nationality has also already been potentially emptied of its revolutionary significances. It has been co-opted by a state apparatus such as the Central Intelligence Agency (CIA) or another espionage agency whose business it is to permeate national boundaries by training personnel to simulate other "national" identities well enough to pass while retaining access to the institutional structures of the "home" land. Furthermore, multinational corporations have already commodified the ideal of a postnationalist scenario. In *Don Quixote* Acker plagiarizes a section of the Caracas Declaration, a 1954 amendment to the Monroe Doctrine: "The interests of these banks and companies are truly global, for the United States controls, or believes it controls . . . the globe. Thus the multinational corporations form an integrated economic system which must be protected: this 'Cold War'" (73). In an essay titled "A Few Notes on Two of My Books," she states outright, "I live in a world which is at least partly defined by the multi-nationals, the CIA, etc."[21]

The solution offered in *Don Quixote* to the co-optation and commodification of the postnationalist ideal by the state and by capitalism is a politics of the individual body—that is, of a decomposing performative body that has nonreproductive sex and dies or becomes a corpse that "speaks directly" on numerous occasions. This is the body disobedient, a body that, Acker seems to suggest, can be neither co-opted by the state, as it is useless for reproducing the social order, nor commodified, as it is excessive in its sexual manifestations and scandalous in its death, a decaying corpse in the marketplace. The fact that her narrative focuses on the quest of one female knight and the disobedience of her one body indicates that what is offered as a possibly viable alternative to the system is an individualistic anarchism. I wish to emphasize the word *individualistic.* The last word in the novel is *me:* "I closed my eyes, head drooping, like a person drunk for so long she no longer knows she's drunk, and then, drunk, awoke to the world which lay before me" (207). Collective action, that ideal that coexisted along with anarchism in the section on the Spanish Republic, has disappeared upon the knight's waking from her dream journey. The last image of the book is of the individual quester. If this is the only "alternative," one wonders to what extent Acker has managed to wander beyond the paradigms of Anglo-American ideology with its stubborn privileging of individual above collective vision and action.

In Alfau's *Chromos* the deconstruction of nationality serves three functions. One is to defy or confound negative stereotyping of Spaniards by reappropriating for his own fiction-making purposes the "great artificial, international stereotype, fed on the things he knew most foreigners thought of his land" (307). The second is, paradoxically, to bring the land that Alfau left, Spain, closer to the place to which he immigrated—New York City. After all, *Chromos* is about what is termed the "Spanish colony" in that city: "everything was quite Spanish; the setting just right to make one forget that one was in New York" (25). Unlike Acker's text, in which desire for a place that does not yet exist is utopian and future-oriented, in *Chromos* virtually all the Americaniards and the narrator betray a nostalgic longing to return to Spain, to "their" country, even if it is not to the Spain of their early youth, but to the one they have imagined, which Alfau's novel suggests are synonymous. This nostalgia, which is intimately connected with the interrogation of nationality as a fixed or essential identity, betokens a counterdesire to hold on to a stable identity, a particular place, the "orienting" fiction of nationality and national pride. It is the remembrance of a world elsewhere that sustains the resistance of immigrants from Spain to assimilation into Anglo-American culture. In fact, Alfau still retains his Spanish citizenship.

The third function of the deconstruction of nationality and the ludic parade of hybridity in Alfau's *Chromos* is to create *disorder*—that "wastepaper basket full of discarded roles"—so as to ultimately affirm another *order,* to indulge in a fatalistic *contemptus mundi.* This *contemptus mundi* operates as a protest against the optimistic idealism of Anglo-American culture and against the "Latin Americanization" of the small colony of Spaniards in New York City. The last lines of *Chromos* read:

> [I]t was for someone else to bring back their true colors [that is, of "chromos in disrepute"] . . . a job for a pen much better than mine, which is rusty, not so much for lack of use but because it is no feather from a soaring wing, work for a pen mightier than the swords of those same conquerors, to span the years and distances, to . . . decide whether my ancestors were

but immigrants disguised as conquerors, or whether all other aliens are but conquerors disguised as immigrants. (348)

In this passage there is a suggestion that the narrative of the conquest of the Americas, central to both Spanish and Anglo-American identities, is nothing but the product of a distorting self-aggrandizement. However, there is also a fear of those "other aliens," which I interpret to mean Latin Americans, and particularly Latinos who challenge Alfau's narrator's discrete sense of himself as a "Spaniard" in New York City. To set himself apart and above the immigrant "hordes," he assumes a fatalistic attitude, an attitude many foreigners, and even Spaniards themselves, have claimed is a defining characteristic of the "Spanish temper."

Closure in both Alfau's and Acker's texts involves a rehearsal of nationality—of ways of thinking and being generally associated with specific national identities. On the one hand, as postmodern texts, both works encourage the view that these "ways of being" are mannerisms, performances open to conscious alteration, not enduring or indelible traits. On the other hand, as conclusions these rehearsals are enacted without any subsequent destabilization and thus mark an end limit. This end limit, in both Acker's and Alfau's texts, serves to define the narrator as a singular ego and to defend that ego—"I," "me," "mine," and "my"—giving finalizing shape to the narrator's hitherto indefinite positioning. Acker's narrator winds up sounding like the typical individualistic "American" adventurer and Alfau's narrator like the typical "Spaniard" concerned with his *sangre pura* (pure-bloodedness) in flight from those Latinos with whom Anglo-American culture might conflate him. Although the end limit would seem to denote deflation in Acker's text and defeat in Alfau's, in each case the punctuating stop of the first-person narration from the tales' vertiginous flows leaves the reader with the conventions of a predictable subjectivity—the equation of subjectivity with exceptionalism, whether heroic or anti-heroic. In Acker's case, nothing could be more culturally prescribed than subjectivity constructed according to the creed of "American" individualism, an awakening to that nationally inflected stance of the "world which lay before *me*" (my emphasis). Similarly, Alfau's text, in its attempt to create closure, falls back on an elegiac mode, a mode of lamentation about something irremediably tarnished: "This is what the possible visions of greatness suggested by the conquistadors had finally come to: rhapsodic, nomadic incidents with hanging tarnished threads of past splendor out of time and out of place. Chromos in disrepute . . . In Spanish I don't have to explain my nation or countrymen. In English, I can't" (348). The expatriated "I" reaches back toward a sustaining fiction and this fiction is nationalistic in the extreme—"conquistadors" and the heroic past of which mere shreds remain. Of course, this passage is full of ironic possibilities, but the very last lines of the novel juxtaposing "my ancestors" against "all other aliens" insinuate a mark of distinction drawn along the line of a highly nationalistic epic, however dilapidated. To stand beyond the reach of one's culture is indeed a quixotic affair, especially at the moment of closure, when the challenge is to make an "end" without naturalizing such conventions.

To stand beyond the reach of one's culture may indeed be impossible. Moreover, as suggested along the way in this chapter, it may be undesirable if it means only one of two things: (1) falling into a self-deception that such a thing has transpired; or (2) being absorbed by the expansionist ambitions or assimilationist demands of another culture. Alfau's stories revolve around characters who tend to fall into one of two categories— those who feel as if they have "lost" their identity, such as Don Fulano, or immigrants who, unmoored from their motherland and, in order to retain some semblance of identity, derive all their sustenance from nostalgic stereotypes about their culture. Nevertheless, a third category exists. To this category belong self-styled hybrids like Don Pedro Guzman O'Moore Algoracid, otherwise known as Pete Guz, the Spanish-Irish-Moor who spouts Anglo-sounding theories of racial superiority. For Pete, however, that racial superiority is of Spaniards over Anglos. In many ways, Pete Guz could be a tailor-made example of Homi Bhabha's concept of "hybridity." Bhabha has argued that hybridity intervenes in the exercise of authority by exposing the impossibility of stable identity, by complicating the identification of authority, and by representing the unpredictability of the location of the guise of authority. Central to this concept of hybridity are mimicry, mockery, or parodic replication of the structures and discourses of power.[22] Regardless of whether one approves of the form this mimicry of the dominant culture takes for Pete Guz, this character represents the paradox of the assumption or creation of an identity that disrupts identity as sanctioned by the dominant culture. This character is hardly without identity, nor does he embrace the stereotypes of his culture. His very persona fragments monolithic notions of a culture on which stereotypes depend.

If both exclusion and forced inclusion are the specters haunting the act of assuming or claiming any identity, Pete Guz's "reverse racism" encompasses both those specters writ large. Although his name, mixed heritage, and the fact that he uses the "master"'s tools to subvert Anglo-American assumptions about cultural and racial superiority bring to mind Bhabha's concept of hybridity, his apparent adherence to theories about the racial superiority of Spaniards over "Nordics such as Anglo-Saxons, Teutons, Scandinavians" does not. If Bhabha's hybridity is ideally supposed to produce new and evolving subject positions, Pete Guz's reverse racism, though performative in the extreme, also marks the limits of the character's ability to symbolize hybridity as a strategy for liberating identity from the twin specters of exclusion and forced inclusion. In Pete Guz's case, the exclusion is obvious—all those people defined as "Nordics." Given Don Pedro Guzman O'Moore Algoracid's mixed heritage, it is unclear whether the focus on Spaniards' superiority excludes or includes the Moors and the Irish. If excluded, the meaning of that exclusion remains ambiguous. Is the character emblematic of self-division and selective identification? If included, is the association of "Moor," "Irish," and "Spanish," compacted in the name itself, a wonderful way of getting back at Anglo-American travelers who went to Spain and described the inhabitants through pejorative comparisons with "Moors" and "the Irish" (historically regarded by many Anglos as the wrong kind of British)? Or is the semantic binding of "Moor" and "Irish" with the "Spanish" in the name of a character who insists on the racial superiority of Spaniards an instance of forced inclusion, a co-optation of the Moorish and the Celtic for the nationalist cause of a unified identity? Worth noting is the similarity between Pete Guz's stance—about the racial superiority of Spaniards in general—and that of a man whom, according to an interview conducted by Ilan Stavans in 1991, Alfau has always admired: "Generalísimo Francisco Franco."[23] The notion of the racial and cultural superiority of Spaniards was evident in much of Franco's discourse, and certainly in Franco's film *Raza* (*Race*). Speaking of forced inclusion, such theories about the racial superiority of Spaniards have been as much a part of the dream of reviving the Spanish Empire as have ideas about Anglo superiority to Anglo-American manifest destiny.

Ironically, despite the dubious qualifications of Don Pedro Guzman O'Moore Algoracid as an example of the utopian hybridity posited by Bhabha and despite Alfau's stated political reactionaryism, of all the works examined in this chapter, *Chromos* is by far the most hybrid, hybridizing one with regard to the issue of Spain in relation to Anglo-American culture and the United States generally. Subtly but continually intermixing English and Spanish, it most radically disorients linguistically constructed identity; it most challengingly denaturalizes nationality; and it most incessantly and perversely plays on fears of internal disintegration, both of self and of empire.

If Alfau's *Chromos* is the most hybridizing of the works discussed, Acker's *Don Quixote* is the most hard-hitting vis-à-vis the "American" scene, which her novel renders altogether alienating, an assault on self-constitution. However, the novel's conclusion is assimilable to the ethos of individualism. Images of the lone individual battling entropic forces—the knight bereft even of her pack of dogs—are only a minor variation on the pioneer, cowboy, and/or free agent unsubordinated to others so dear to "American" mythology. Furthermore, this assent to individualism, however shattered, shields, if not covers for, the existence of a U.S. empire at the same time that the work in question would seem to criticize or rail against this empire. Individualism prevents a clear view of empire because empire has classically been understood to entail the subordination of the self to a larger regime while affording that self the sense that it contains multitudes and is representative of a larger "us" and, furthermore—and here lies its hubris—of "them."

All the works—by Ballou, Alfau, Acker, Colomo, Lobato, and Sendón—more or less successfully de-naturalize nationality. To the extent that "empire" is dependent on nationality in the form of expansionist nationalism, these works chip away at what historically has been the basis of empire since at least the Renaissance. The great paradox is that inasmuch as empire is not dependent on nationality, or rather trades in the denaturalization of nationality—the nationality of the Other—these works are less successful. Their modus operandi presents a self-suspended threat to the imperial project of reconstructing the Other in the image of the Self. Colomo, Lobato, and Sendón all seem to be documenting more than undermining the processes by which Spain and/or "Spaniards" have been colonized, reoriented to the "American." Colomo's *La línea del cielo,* for example, follows the misadventures of a colonized subject. Gustavo appears clueless about the very condition of his mental colonization. The dramatic irony of the film proceeds from the protagonist's lack of insight into his situation. Gustavo's blindness is experienced as audience embarrassment for him. The film compensates for this embarrassing blindness of the Spanish photographer by never allowing viewers to glimpse the photographs he carries in the envelope, photographs that might well glamorize the colonizer, the United States, with its "buildings very tall" that have so impressed him. The film is constructed around a protagonist with no postcolonial sensibility. However, neither does it glamorize the colonizer, refusing as it does to deliver that sought-after Manhattan skyline. *La línea del cielo* puts up a kind of halfhearted resistance to empire that might best be described as a pre-postcolonial protest. One could speculate on the reasons for this pre-postcoloniality. For instance, is this a case of having one's cake and eating it too? A plausible, less ad hominem explanation is that Spaniards, unlike Latinas/os, are not used to thinking of themselves as colonized but are much more likely to proudly, or not so proudly, remember their country's imperial history.[24] As for Ballou, Prospero-like, she renounces her potentially imperializing pen, joyfully letting it slide over the balcony at the symbolically loaded Escorial, monument to the empire of Philip II. The textual gesture, opting for the transcendentalist sublimity of clouds passing over mountaintops, is beautiful, but more idealizingly renunciatory than resistant to the aesthetics of empire.

Finally, Acker and Alfau, through a picaresque aesthetics of obscenity, concoct a protest against the cultural forces that would demand their allegiance. Obscenity, understood to mean being out of the scene, and the picaresque are of a piece in Acker's *Don Quixote* and Alfau's *Chromos*. Traditionally, as a genre, the picaresque novel has been episodic, structureless, filled with dubious or menial characters, relatively unconcerned with character per se, more interested in satirizing national follies, and so on. One of its most salient features is that its antiheroic protagonist goes through a series of bad masters and petty crimes, finally disappearing out of the novel altogether, leaving things "obscenely" unresolved. The picaresque novel as a genre was, by the mid-eighteenth century, associated by both French and British writers with Spain; it was regarded as a Spanish form. In fact, Spanish Jewish *converso* Mateo Alemán's novel *Guzmán de Alfarache* (1599 and 1602) is credited with having begun the vogue for the picaresque novel. Besides the anonymous novel *Vida de Lazarillo de Tormes y de sus for-tunas y adversidades* (1554) and *Guzmán de Alfarache,* the most well known and emulated example of the picaresque was Cervantes's *Don Quijote* (1605). John Dos Passos wittily observed in 1922:

> Spain is the home of that type of novel which the pigeonhole-makers have named the picaresque. These loafers and wanderers of Baroja's, like his artists and grotesque dreamers and fanatics, are all the descendants of the people in the *Quijote* and the *Novelas Ejemplares,* of the rogues and ban-dits of the *Lazarillo de Tormes,* who through *Gil Blas* invaded France and England, where they rollicked through the novel until Mrs. Grundy and George Eliot packed them off to the reform school.[25]

If Cervantes's text was written in critical reaction to the Counter-Reformation, perhaps there is something very fitting in the use of Cervan-tesque texts to throw into question the legitimacy of an Anglo-dominated U.S. culture and empire. Against the imperial reconstruction of the Other in the image of the Self, Acker's *Don Quixote* and Alfau's *Chromos* offer, as postmodern picaresque, a vertiginous mixture of codes, texts poaching off of other texts, intertextuality as deconstruction "ending" in an unre-solving disappearing act—lucidity masquerading as drunkenness in Acker, conquerors disguised as immigrants in Alfau. Both *Don Quixote* and *Chromos*—the latter despite Alfau's apparent fear of "all other aliens"—introduce the postcolonialist suggestion that abjection and marginaliza-tion are themselves disappearing acts, which, in time, might generate the possibility of their return as rejected knowledge and power more than merely *posing* a threat to Anglo-American U.S. empire.

chapter 6

AFTERLIVES OF EMPIRE

RETROSPECTIVE

Spain's Long Shadow is the story of the long-term captivation of Anglo-American culture with figures of Spain. Since the late eighteenth century, Anglo-American identity as "American" has been dependent on Spain. Figures of Spain have been central to the dominant fictions of revolution, manifest destiny, birth/rebirth, and "American" exceptionalism in general. Figures of Spain have been indispensable to the constitution, elaboration, and even, as is evident, for example, in Kathy Acker's *Don Quixote* (1986), to the interrogation of these dominant fictions.

This study has shown that the long-standing fascination with Spain in Anglo-American culture has been far from amorphous. It has had the definite shape and trajectory of a curved path cutting across two centuries of time. "American" dependence on figures of Spain sprang from and manifested itself in a rivalry with morally blackened alien whiteness. It moved on to the initiation of a figurative conquest of the "Other" colonizer of the Americas through the representational mode of a racially stigmatizing Orientalization. This movement culminated in the consolidation of Anglo-American imperial identity around the Spanish-Cuban-American War (1898) with the symbolic conquest of Spain through the knotting together of Black Legend and Orientalist modes and with the literal defeat of Spain in the war.

As Freud and Lacan have pointed out, the life of the symbol depends on the death of the thing. Thus, it should come as no surprise that in the

wake of the Spanish-Cuban-American War during the era of high modernism Spain should have had a totemic afterlife as the "last wonderful
country"—a substitute for a number of vitalizing properties regarded as
lost or unavailable in Anglo-American culture, not the least of which was
the frontier itself. This totemic sacralization also contained within it the
logic of ritual sacrifice, even condemnation, as exemplified by Richard
Wright's *Pagan Spain* (1957). On the whole, the symbolic afterlife of Spain
as totem was expressed in an idealizing appreciative register lasting through
the "descent" of the "sacred bull" of the modernists into the kitsch of the
U.S. tourist industry in the 1960s and 1970s. If the 1960s and 1970s constituted the commodification of the expatriate modernist totemic relation
to Spain, the 1980s and early 1990s witnessed a postmodern resistance,
apparent in certain texts and/or visual works from the United States and
Spain, to more than a century of unproblematized Anglo-American consumptions of Spain. A proto-postmodernist form of this resistance manifested itself during the modernist era itself, judging from Ballou's *Spanish
Prelude* (1937) and Alfau's *Locos* (1936) and *Chromos* (written in 1948; published in 1990). The proto-postmodern and postmodern works I discussed
from the 1980s and early 1990s attempt to denaturalize nationality—both
"Spanish" and "American"—and thus chip away at the basis of empire
(nation writ large). However, in tandem with a chipping away at the basis
of empire or at the representational modes of Anglo-American imperial
ideology, the works of the 1980s and early 1990s can be read as signs of the
pervasiveness of a U.S., and more specifically Anglo-American, empire, as
well as the symbolic afterlife of Spain in the Anglo-American imaginary.
This trend continued into the 1990s and, concluding from the growing
heterogeneity of uses of Spain in Latina/o cultural production, as well as
the three instances of its invocation that I consider in this last chapter,
figures of Spain have significant afterlives.

Some of the works I considered in the preceding chapter, such as Acker's
Don Quixote and Alfau's *Chromos*, do not have widespread appeal. They are
brain food for readers familiar with literary theory and/or accustomed to
reading highly experimental fiction. The nature of their potential audience
is betrayed by their publishers—the Grove and Dalkey Archive presses,
small publishing houses dedicated to the dissemination of experimental
and avant-garde works. These novels, *Don Quixote* and *Chromos,* unfold
conscious from the start of their difficulty and their marginalization from

the dominant culture and its consumers. The opening line of *Chromos* is "the moment one learns English, complications set in"; the opening phrase of *Don Quixote,* "[w]hen she was finally crazy."[1] Furthermore, neither Acker nor Alfau is an Anglo-American. In other words, the long-term fascination with Spain among Anglos in Anglo-American culture would seem to have descended toward the horizon of newer obsessions—Asia, "Hispanics," "illegal" and extraterrestrial aliens, microorganisms and microchips or biological and cybernetic warfare, Muslim "terrorism"—behind which it is sinking, perhaps to have peaked again for a brief ballistic sweep across the hallucinatory skies of the national-imperial imaginary in 1998, the centennial of the Spanish-Cuban-American War. However, the horizon of newer obsessions—particularly Anglo-America's twin obsessions with the rising "brown tide" of Latinas/os in the United States and Muslim "terrorism" both within and beyond national borders—is limned in the shapes and colors of the hitherto unremarked substrata obsession with Spain and Spanish empire, the rival in and for the Americas and for the very status of world empire that the United States has, through various wars and internal colonization, acquired, in effect becoming another "Spain," as Protestant minister and professor of political economy William Graham Sumner warned in his 1899 essay "The Conquest of the United States by Spain."

SPAIN AND POSTCOLONIAL PROSPECTS OF *LATINIDAD*

As I have already suggested in my analysis of Gertrude Stein's, Richard Wright's, Felipe Alfau's, and Kathy Acker's work, non-Anglo U.S. writers, negotiating Anglo-American culture and their location in it vis-à-vis histories of conquest, enslavement, ethnoracial discrimination/management, and empire in the Americas, have redefined what it is to be "American" through simultaneously agonistic and identificatory reworkings of figures of Spain.[2] Performance studies scholar and cultural critic José Esteban Muñoz has elaborated a paradigm of *disidentification* among "queers of color" in relation to "the hegemonic supremacy of the majoritarian public sphere."[3] With the phrase "majoritarian public sphere" he means, it seems to me, the cultural space largely produced for, recognized as "legitimate" by, and imaginatively occupied by white, Anglo-dominant, heteronormative North Americans. Muñoz employs the term "disidentifications" on the part of queers of color to signal a process by which people in this

category consume this majoritarian public sphere not in a passive or obe-
dient way, but rather in a manner marked by a consciousness of their own
marginalization and by a concomitant resistance to being kept in their
marginalized or ghettoized place. *Disidentification* signals a dual activity
of seemingly identifying with the dominant culture through a recycling of
its tropes but performing that recycling with a noticeable (however subtle) difference. This concept is preliminarily useful in thinking through
what non-Anglo writers and artists are doing with Anglo-American figures
of Spain. But, rather than simply adapt the term "disidentification" to the
question of their relation to Spain in the context of Anglo-American hegemony, I would acknowledge its usefulness but talk in terms of simultaneous agonism and identification or a *postcolonial identificatory relation*.
The double dialectics of the triangulation between Anglo-American hegemony, a legacy of Spanish empire, and the purposes of the cultural productions of non-Anglos in relation to these dual legacies makes the term
"disidentification," theorized with one majoritarian culture in mind, trick-
ier to import to the situation with which I am concerned here.

Among non-Anglo writers and artists, such a postcolonial identificatory
version is particularly discernible, though hitherto overlooked, among
African American and Afro-Latina/o as well as Latina/o writers and artists
more generally. For example, Afro-Puerto Rican Cenen and African
American writer and scholar Barbara Smith in "The Blood—Yes, the
Blood: A Conversation" (1983), discussing Afro-Latino identity vis-à-vis
"color, race, and appearance," posit a postcolonial identificatory relation
to nineteenth-century Anglo-American racially stigmatizing Orientalizations of Spain.[4] Cenen remarks:

> Those people who wound up in Puerto Rico got less and less contact with
> the outside world so they had to interact heavily with each other. African,
> Indian, and Spanish who are not white anyway, as far as I'm concerned.
> Except for the North, there are very few places in Spain where the Moors
> had not entered, where the Africans did not go . . . [T]hink how Europe
> doesn't perceive Spain as being part of the European continent, because of
> its mixture with Africa.[5]

Kristal Brent Zook, in her essay "Light-Skinned-ded Naps" (1990), fur-
thers this kind of identification, stating in no uncertain terms that on the

basis of skin color she felt "at home in Spain," a country she includes under the rubric "Latino heritage":

> Due to a complex combination of socio-economic circumstances, I hap-
> pened to find a kind of psychological shelter in Latino heritage and even
> grew to identify more with *it* than with my own culture(s) . . . It wasn't until
> years later that I realized why I had such an obsessive drive to learn Spanish
> and why I felt so at ease, relaxed and at home in Spain, a country whose
> people had the *exact* same skin color as I did: I had simply been searching
> for a kind of psychic shelter, wherever I could find it.[6]

Zook's formulation of her obsession with Spain is radically subversive of the legacy of Anglo-American figurations of Spain and that legacy's assumptions about both normative "Americanness" and "Spanishness." Spain is "home" because it is a space of miscegenation and alterity, not despite what is highlighted as a visible sign of "Otherness." Americanness as "Brady Bunch utopia" is found not in the Anglo-dominated United States, but in Spain.[7] Spain is not presented as the Old World source of pure Hispanicity of which Latinos are regarded as an impure and unfor-tunate derivative, but rather as existing within the continuum of *latinidad.* Zook's formulation—not more than a paragraph long—boldly and com-pletely turns the tables on centuries of imperial ideology, Spanish and Anglo, to yield a postcolonial vision of Spain based on identificatory simili-tudes or equivalences—"the *exact* same skin color as I." This conception of Spain and Spaniards as self-empowering *imago* is strikingly different from that of Poe's "William Wilson" or any of the Anglo-American texts that equate "the Spaniard" with the Anglo on the basis of skin color, but blacken him or her morally, a blackening that, as demonstrated, was stigmatizingly racialized so pervasively, especially from the mid- to late nineteenth century.

Of course, not all non-Anglo writers of the last couple of decades have proposed such a positive postcolonial identificatory relation with Spain. For instance, many of the narrative attempts of Latino/a writers to articu-late a postcolonial visibility for themselves are seriously invested—one might say "dependent"—on figures of Spain, but in a highly ambivalent way. Unlike a majority of Anglo-American works, the works by U.S. Lati-nos ("whether Mexican, Chicano, Caribbean, Central or South Ameri-can")[8] U.S.—particularly by Chicanos, in contradistinction to Mexican

Americans of an older generation), and Puerto Ricans and Cubans of the last three decades—evince a keen awareness of the problematics of both identification with and rejection of Spain, Spaniards, and "Spanish culture." In *Memories of the Alhambra* (1977), Chicano writer Nash Candelaria illustrates the internalized colonialism of the unexamined identification with Spaniards through a Mexican American character, "José," who travels through Spain dreaming, "I am Spanish. A son of conquistadors. Maybe we can get together with the Anglos but with the Indian dogs—never."⁹ Candelaria shows José's self-construction to be a case of misguided identification with the conquerors and self-hating denial of indigenous cultures. Implied in the words "maybe we [the Spanish] can get together with the Anglos" is an equivalency between Anglos and Spaniards as imperialists. The full historical import of this equivalency is precisely what the Anglo-American myth of conquest in terms of anticonquest disguises.

The figure of the Spaniard as a double of the Anglo-American appears in the writings of many other Latino writers. Take, for example, *Cantando Bajito/Singing Softly* (1989) by Carmen de Monteflores and *Silent Dancing* (1990) by Judith Ortiz Cofer, both novels by mainland-based Puerto Ricans. *Cantando Bajito* proffers a verbal description of a Spanish woman named Catalina: "Catalina was a little older than Pilar. Blonde. Pilar hadn't seen a blonde Spaniard before . . . Catalina was very pretty to look at. It made you want to do things for her . . . That day Pilar wished Catalina could be her friend. But she also knew that it was not possible."¹⁰ *Silent Dancing* (1990) also presents a "white," blonde Spaniard:

> Kiki [the mayor's daughter with her "golden hair" and "freckles on her shoulders"] would be a pale fish among the golden tadpoles [the pueblo children] in the water. She came from a Spanish family who believed in keeping the bloodlines pure.¹¹

Both Carmen de Monteflores and Judith Ortiz Cofer imply a similarity between Spaniards and Anglos in a colonial system where skin color not only demarcates but determines class privilege.

If the work of many Latina/o writers evinces a problematic identification with Spaniards (peninsular or creole) and Spain, many of them simultaneously interrogate rejection of their Spanish heritage. The writers interrogate this rejection because they recognize, some more explicitly than others, the material conditions characterizing the putative "double bind" of colonization by both Spaniards and Anglos. However much they decry the evils of the Spanish Conquest of the Americas in 1492 and the colonial system in place until the independence movements of the early nineteenth century, and in some cases beyond the 1820s, they are also aware of the fact that the Americas as a whole have been colonized by the political and economic interest of the Anglo-dominated United States—in other words, by Anglo-American expansionist ambitions concretized as a political-economic empire with military force to maintain this status quo. Judit Moschkovich, a Latina Jewish immigrant from Argentina to the United States writes:

> As to the "historical" accident that both North and South America are not dominated by Latin (i.e. non-Anglo) culture, I don't call the appropriation of Mexican land an accident, but an imperialist/expansionist move by the United States. Latin America is a mixture of Native, Black, Spanish, and sometimes other European cultures, but it is *dominated* by American *mass* culture as Latin American economic systems are dominated by American interests (this applies to most Latin American countries, not all).[12]

Moschkovich defines "American" and "American culture" at the beginning of her essay: "When I say 'American culture' I obviously do not include Afro-American, Native American, Asian American, Chicana, etc. I am speaking of the *Anglo* culture which dominates American society."[13] I wish that rather than inadvertently ceding "American" to the dominant group she had used the terms "Anglo-American" and "Anglo-American culture." As Mexican-cum-Chicano performance artist and cultural critic Guillermo Gómez-Peña inquires rhetorically, is it that "Anglos themselves aren't also an 'ethnic group,' one of the most violent and antisocial tribes on this planet? That the five hundred million Latin American *mestizos* that inhabit the Americas are a 'minority'?"[14] Nevertheless, Moschkovich's point is well taken and is representative of the realizations of many Latinas/os who, though they might designate "the Spaniards" as historical oppressors, would not part with their "Spanish heritage" (whatever that means to them), particularly in the face of the double standard of Anglo-American culture toward those Americans of, among other things, "Spanish" descent.

These Latina/o writers have woven into their tales and attempted to renegotiate the long history of Anglo-American imperial aggression against the "Spanish" Americans, from Anglo "founding father" Benjamin Franklin's 1767 designs to acquire Mexico, then New Spain, as well as Cuba,[15] to Thomas Jefferson's proclamation "that it was best for Spain to rule [Latin America] until 'our [Anglo] population can be sufficiently advanced to gain it from them piece by piece,'"[16] to the Monroe Doctrine of 1823, to the land grabbing by the Anglos in the Mexican-American War (1846–48) and the Spanish-Cuban-American War (1898), to the 1904 Roosevelt corollary to the Monroe Doctrine or the overt U.S. military interventionism of the "big stick policy," to the exploitative "Good Neighbor Policy" of the 1930s transforming Central American and Caribbean countries into "banana republics" overseen by U.S.-backed dictators, to Cold War covert operations of the CIA all over Latin America (1950s onward), to the decades-old U.S. trade embargo against Cuba (begun in 1960 and recently intensified), to the invasion of Nicaragua and Panama during the hypocritical Pax Americana policy of the Reagan–Bush years, to the economic exploitation of Mexico by U.S. corporations sanctioned by the North American Free Trade Agreement, and finally to the violent U.S.–Mexico border enforcement, the demonization of Latino/a immigrants, and the reversal of affirmative action, setting the foreign enemy-within-tone of the late 1990s and early 2000s. Thus, for these Latinos/as, the rejection of their "Spanish" heritage (whether in the guise of language, religion, names, holidays, folklore, and forms, or any combination of these) would be, at best, an act of "independence" haunted by the specter of shame and lingering anxiety about having overassimilated into the dominant Anglo-American culture or, at worst, partial cultural suicide.

Partial cultural suicide for not being able to claim something more than a merely negative connection to Spain is openly acknowledged and dramatized in Edward Rivera's *Family Installments: Memories of Growing up Hispanic* (1982). As mentioned earlier, the Puerto Rican barrio boy protagonist Santos Malánguez is made to feel ashamed of being Puerto Rican and Hispanic/Latino through the history lessons he receives at school that equate southern Europeans, Spaniards in particular, and their descendants (full or partial) with barbarism. Only when he begins to see the pattern between these history lessons and his own depression and cultural dysphoria does he begin to feel better about himself as a Puerto Rican. In a similar vein, Ana Castillo's central protagonist in her novel *Peel My Love Like an Onion* (1999), Carmen la Coja (Carmen the one-legged cripple), who in her very person embodies certain Orientalist stereotypes about "Hispanics" and flamenco dancers, dreams about a connection with southern Spain (Andalusia), and, in this way, buoys herself up against her social and cultural marginalization living in the big, cold city of Chicago.

Southern Spain, and specifically Andalusia, provides a means of connection not just for Castillo but for a number of queer Latino writers whose work demonstrates a strong identification with the culture of *cante jondo,* the often persecuted Gypsies of Andalusia, and, above all, with a figure that they elevate to the status of patron saint of poetry mourning the repression of desire, but also celebrating cultural difference not only within Spain but in the United States as well—Federico García Lorca. For Puerto Rican poet Victor Hernández Cruz, reading Lorca's *Poeta en Nueva York* in his own essay "Writing Migrations," is to find "Hindu rhythms . . . out of place and alive and well in flamenco" or an enabling reconfiguration of geographic and cultural coordinates. Cruz writes of Lorca: "His visit to New York produced a creative tension similar to that felt by contemporary U.S. Latino poets in their own geographic and cultural displacement. Lorca is a point of confluence—there are so many differences that collide within him and that he sings and unifies, even while enjoying the contradictions."[17]

Among the first intellectuals/artists murdered by Franco's Nationalist forces and a gay man, Lorca, is not just a "point of confluence" or another exile among many, but also a political point of affiliation specifically for openly gay Latinos struggling against reactionary politics in the United States, against laws that make the Spanish language illegal, against discrimination directed at people, regardless of ethnicity, on the basis of sexual preference, and against the suppression of difference in the name of cultural unity and national security. Moreover, as a well-known gay Hispanic man who championed the socially marginalized, including women, many gay Latino writers ally with Lorca in their own battles against machismo, homophobia, and misogyny within their own communities and the culture at large. For these writers who claim Lorca as their own, Spain is not solely the country of conquerors or conquistadores, of the Black Legend, myths of *sangre pura,* inquisitorial Catholicism, or of Castile and northern Spain (Galicia, the Basque country, Asturias, etc.). It is, instead, the Spain of the south represented as the site of poetry born of tolerance and, even more, of queer love as a celebration of cultural hybridity. Colombian U.S.-based poet Jaime Manrique's "My Night with/Mi noche con Federico García Lorca," in the 1995 collection of the same title, recounts a "night of love" that "has lasted all my life" in which Lorca and the teller of the tale share caresses, tenderness, and conversation in, the poem emphasizes, "Spanish," or, rather, a Spanish learned from "my grandmother, a Sephardic Jew," a native tongue inherited from another Spain, that of the Jews and Moors.[18] The night of love with Lorca becomes "dark love" on the brink of ending in Cuban American poet Rafael Campo's homage "I am Mrs. Lorca," from *Diva* (1999), and yet Mrs. Lorca declares, "I am married to romance" and, though "our bed [is] as arid as the flat interior of Spain," "I love him just the same."[19] This past-tense invocation of Lorca that promises to extend a queer night of love into the present is sustained in Chicano poet Francisco X. Alarcón's "El otro día me encontré a García Lorca/The Other Day I Ran into García Lorca," from his new and selected poems, *Del otro lado de la noche/From the Other Side of Night* (2002). The past does not merely stalk the present like a legacy one cannot escape or the contemporary gay Chicano poet who calls on Lorca as a recuperable precedent. Instead, the poet of olive-colored guitars that weep and afternoons that dance flamenco physically hails the present, touching queer Latino poetry in an anointing embrace by planting the lips of the poem's "I" with a kiss "like an Andalusian sun."[20]

Alarcón's collection is also partly modeled on the mystical poetry of sixteenth-century poet and Discalced Carmelite reformer from Fontiveros near Ávila, Spain, Saint John of the Cross. Among other things, the title of Alarcón's book of poems is derived from the first two words—*Noche oscura*—of Saint John of the Cross's *Canciones del alma que se goza de haber llegado al alto estado de la perfección que es la unión con Dios, por el camino de la negación espiritual.* In fact, the sixteenth-century Spanish mystics Saint John of the Cross and Saint Teresa of Ávila or Saint Teresa de Jesús have been the sources of inspiration for other Latina/o writers, not only in literary but also in political terms. Their reforming zeal against the corrupt imbrication of the church with the state and their subsequent persecution by the Spanish Inquisition have earned these mystics the position of honorary Latinas/os because the particulars of their trials and tribulations would seem to set them apart from the hegemonic ideology of intolerant Catholic, Castilian Spanish imperialism of their day. Among the Latina/o writers and cultural critics who appropriate Saint Teresa de Cepeda Dávila y Ahumada, Chicana lesbian writer and theorist Gloria Anzaldúa remembers the Spanish saint's body and corpus as part of her own in the poem "Holy Relics" with the refrain, "We are the holy relics, / the scattered bones of a saint, / the best loved bones of Spain. / We seek each other," in the well-known collection of poetry and essays *Borderlands/La Frontera: The New Mestiza* (1987), in which she elaborates her concept of spiritual *mestizaje* that draws on the syncretic, heavily indigenized folk Catholicism of Mexico and the Southwest as well as this persecuted history within Spanish Catholicism.[21]

Perhaps even more surprising than postcolonial identifications with the other Spain, with multicultural Indo-Afro-Arabic-Jewish Andalusia and southern Spain, with García Lorca, and with Spanish sixteenth-century mystics is the inhabitation of the generally heinous, seemingly irrecoverable conquistador figure as a device for counterconquest in, for example, the appropriation of "discovery" for the purpose of celebrating the tropicalization/Caribbeanization of New York in mainland-based Puerto Rican Victor Hernández Cruz's collection of essays and poems, *Panoramas* (1997). In "Mesa Blanca," with lines such as "The Castilians were coming / Out of the mouth of a volcano / falling as ash unto red dirt," the conquistadores become ashes and, the *mestizaje* of colonization, a form of transculturation in which the Taino survive, despite the ashes, as "The past in the smoke of the cigar / Bringing the future-in-formation."[22] In self-termed "Chicago-rriqueño" poet Rane Arroyo's collection *Pale Ramón* (1998), the figure of a reduced conquistador is dispersed like an unburied and dismembered body throughout the volume to speak of the cultural marginalization of Latinas/os, especially Puerto Ricans, within a U.S. culture that by and large still treats them as second-class citizens and subjects of a younger empire than that of Spain. In "An Ordinary Conquistador," the poem's "I" (a poor puertorriqueño poet), waiting for "the dead to whisper" as the "Ashes of a firefly are trapped inside / my stereo's kisses," identifies with the figure of the conquistador now turned into an everyday condition of anticlimax and the deferral of the attainment of one's dreams: "I pushed hard / to get here, to be this lonely / an ordinary conquistador."[23]

From Ana Castillo to Rane Arroyo, Latina/o writers, many of them queer-identified, not only appropriate and revalue Anglo-American Orientalizations of Spain but they have made good on exiled Spanish historian and critic Américo Castro's controversial thesis (pursued across books from the 1948 history of Spain *España en su historia: Cristianos, moros, y judíos,* published in Buenos Aires, to the 1973 study *Españoles al margen*) that the coexistence and cross-influence between Christians, Moors, and Jews was the primary factor in the development of Spanish culture. Speaking of alternative historically informed mappings of a culture's development or composition, Kirsten Silva Gruesz's *Ambassadors of Culture: The Transamerican Origins of Latino Writing* demonstrates the importance of reconstructing a suppressed transnational nineteenth-century literary history between the Americas for a historical understanding of "Latino subjectivity." This 1820s to 1880s literary history includes Spanish-language periodicals; literary exchanges between Latin American and U.S. writers (particularly poets), diplomats, and travelers; the "ambassadorial role" played by writer-translators; the trans-American print trade that took place in New Orleans, the city linking the U.S. South and the northern states with the Mexican Southwest and with South America and the Caribbean, and home to Cuban rebel poets forging Texan-Mexican-Cuban coalitions (an early example of pan-*latinidad*); and the cultural and political work more generally of Mexican and Cuban exiles living in various parts of the United States and in contact with some well-known Anglo U.S. poets such as William Cullen Bryant and Longfellow. Gruesz's study even aspires to "reclaim Spanish as a literary language of the United States."[24] A similar book, though potentially more politically controversial, yet equally necessary, should be written titled *The Transatlantic "Origins" of Latina/o Writing.* The word *origins,* however, probably ought to yield to a term less easily assimilable to notions of historically valued original versus (more contemporary) derivative copy. Moreover, those "origins" with regard to the Spanish peninsula would have to be rigorously reconceptualized as other than Castilian, Catholic, "white," and so on, which is not to say that reconceptualizing them could or should be used to cover over or engage in subtle apologetics for the dynamics of conquest and colonialism, both internal and in relation to the Americas.

Of course, there are many Latinas/os who have attempted to wrestle out of the dual bind of the legacy of Anglo and Spanish cultural colonization by positing a distinct Latina/o culture, different from both the Anglo and the "Spanish." As Moschkovich writes:

It is important, however, to know that the Latin American people residing in the U.S. are not some vague "Spanish" conqueror race, but a multi-racial/cultural people of Native, Black, and European background. Latin American culture is quite different [as well] from Anglo culture in that each country has retained and integrated the indigenous cultures in food, music, literature, etc.[25]

The paradigm for Latina/o identity is thus heterogeneity and alterity in integration, not the homogenization and insistence on common denominators (as defined by the dominant culture, of course) of the U.S. "American," or rather, Anglo-American, model. *Latinidad* is a heterotopia, a Chinese encyclopedia of differently inflected nationalities and ethnicities coming together and mixing in space and time, not the whitewashed "utopia" of conforming sameness. Michel Foucault, in *The Order of Things: An Archaeology of the Human Sciences,* may have inadvertently stumbled upon the cultural logic of *latinidad* in his discussion of Borges's Chinese encyclopedia: "the Chinese encyclopaedia . . . and the taxonomy it proposes, lead . . . to words and categories . . . rooted in a ceremonial space, overburdened with complex figures, with tangled paths, strange places, secret passages, and unexpected communications."[26] The displacement to China of a description that could be interpreted as primarily about Latin(a/o) American identity makes all the sense in the world when one thinks of the tremendous mixture of peoples and cultures in China. Even more apt, somehow, is the conjoining of the "Latin" with the Chinese or, more generally, Asian, in light of transnational migratory patterns and demographic processes in the Americas over the last three centuries—that is, the enormous influx of Asian immigrants and the movement of Latina/o peoples across the Americas, south to north and west to east. What has and will continue to result from these converging processes might begin to be described under the rubric *Latinasia.*

Although *latinidad* is an abstraction embraced by many in the Americas, its definitions are hotly debated. How my distinction would apply to both these debates and cultural production in general is a topic for another study. May the distinction of "Latin" versus Anglo-American cultures on the basis of their embrace or rejection of heterogeneity and alterity in integration suffice for the present one. It is clear that among African Americans and Latinas/os whose work is engaged with representing Spain and Spaniards, Spain may or may not be represented as encompassing this heterogeneity in integration. When the Spanish legacy in the Americas is viewed as the mirror image of Anglo-American imperialism, one of the strategies may be to construct *latinidad* as indigenous rather than hybrid because the very concept of "hybridity" may imply something or someone that is a tool of empire or merely derived and derivative of it rather than a postcolonial, postimperial way of being and thinking.[27] This may explain in part why Chicano poet Jimmy Santiago Baca in canto 21 of "Meditations on the South Valley" calls upon images of what is to be taken as supra-historical *indigenous* nature—"mesquite tree," "Río Grande agua," "black mesas," and "twisting arroyos"—rather than on the legacy of the two empires, Anglo and Spanish, to construct Chicano identity. In contrast to these images of nature, he presents readers with images of a "they" that stand on Plymouth Rock and "stare down on La Raza" or endure the desert sun for the sake of triumph (possibly conquest?), of a "they" celebrating "Columbus Day" or inventing "their own Día de Cortez."[28] Such verses suggest an oppressive equivalency between Anglo and Spanish empire captured in the images of Anglos contemptuously and defiantly staring "down on La Raza" while others, presumably Spaniards as well as those wishing to prove that they can lay claim to either the literal or the symbolic currency of "the blood of the conquerors"—to borrow Anglo New Mexican novelist Harvey Fergusson's title for his 1921 novel about the degeneration of the Spanish landowners in the Southwest—celebrate Columbus Day or invent yet another conquistador holiday, "el Día de Cortez." And yet, in other cases, as I have endeavored to signal, Latinas/os claim Spain as an essential component of their own cultural hybridity, but a hybridity in which Spain and Spanishness are not valued over and above any of the other elements and in which Spain is reconceived in terms of hybridity itself—not merely a static white and/or a Christian Spain, but also an Indo-Afro-Arabic-Jewish one and dynamic, changing even in its own understandings of "it"-self, that is, not culturally monolithic.

NOT ALL HOMECOMINGS ARE THE SAME: SPAIN AS FAMILIAR PAIN

In the 1990s partly because of the continuance of the Black Legend against Spain within the academy and in the popular imagination and partly because of the *New World* rather than transatlantic emphasis of precisely those fields—multicultural literacy, New Americas studies, and so forth—dedicated to serious literary and cultural studies of the work of non-Anglos, scant thought has been given to the complexities of non-Anglo or, for that matter, Anglo representations of Spain.[29] It might seem that in the 1990s Spain disappeared behind the horizon of other obsessions. However, there are a number of films and texts that recycle the tropes and types that I have been outlining in this study. For instance, rather than inventing new figures of Spain, these works produced in the 1990s reprise Spain as a place of danger, hot-blooded, dark-skinned Orientalized types, political and random violence, thievery, persecution, pain, death, loss, grief, tragedy, and the artful ritualization of violent loss—even when the focus of the film or text is on a particular region of the country such as Barcelona (Catalonia), Morón de la Frontera, Seville, and the Costa del Sol (Andalusia), or Mallorca, Formentera, and Ibiza (three of the Spanish Balearic Islands east of Spain), as well as the Canary Islands. The 1990s works that captured my attention are the film *Barcelona* (1994), directed by the Anglo-American Whit Stillman, the short novel *Returning to A* (1995) by the Jewish American Dorien Ross, and the longer novel *State of Emergency* (1996) by self-declared "Spaniard/Spic/Hispanic," Colorado-born, California-based writer Floyd Salas.[30] Each work tells a very different kind of story involving U.S. characters and Spain at the same time that it recycles familiar tropes. The overall question is what to make of this recycling. In part, the recycling of certain kinds of figurations of Spain in the mid-1990s symptomatizes the cycling and continued life of empire, in this case Anglo-American imperial ideology. Such ideology has hardly disappeared. In fact, it is at this moment (the early 2000s), enjoying a disturbing rebirth, with all that implies. As the ideology recycles, so do engagements with it, whatever their angle. But, this is only part of the explanation for the recycling. The rest of the explanation may be deduced from the overall patterns in the recycling of figures of Spain. In the cases I am about to examine, Spain is represented as a return to a familiar pain and yet, significantly, the pain is sought out rather than merely avoided. I read this as an indication that something other than Spain is at stake—a nostalgia for a lost United States, lost to the decenterings of its imperial status, that necessitates a *fort-da* movement away and then back toward the United States with Spain as the place/space to be crossed between those two movements. Of course, such a return to a familiar pain does not necessarily guarantee that one can go home again.

Barcelona (1994) is an art-house comedy of errors.[31] Set in "Barcelona, Spain during the last decade of the Cold War" (the 1980s), it focuses with somewhat deadpan irony on the embarrassingly inadequate behavior of its protagonists Fred and Ted, "emissaries of Anglo-American imperialism, military and commercial."[32] Despite the unflattering presentation of its protagonists, the film figures Barcelona as the place where uptight, straight, and generally uninteresting Anglo-American males go through a trial by fire of insults, two terrorist bombings, romantic deception, and one nearly fatal gunshot wound to the head, to emerge, if not victorious, then desirable. In the end Fred, Ted, and a third Anglo, Dickie Taylor, win the hearts of the trade-fair girls (Montserrat, Greta, and Aurora) away from their rival, the dark-faced Spaniard Ramón. Ramón is characterized as a "pseudo-intellectual" left-wing journalist who displaces his sexual impotence problem onto an obsession with Spain's defeat in the "Spanish-American War," the role the United States may have had in sinking the *Maine,* and the covert activities of the CIA along the lines of Philip Agee's descriptions in *Inside the Company* (1975).

The film concludes by showing that the Barcelona trade-fair girls are not deterred from their romantic choices by Ramón's theories about U.S. foul play to justify the war with Spain in 1898 or his articles on CIA conspiracies to control the governments and markets of other countries. The resolution of the plot's entanglements serves to strongly suggest not only the desirability of the Anglo-American males over the likes of Ramón, but the superiority of the comforting commonsense truthfulness of their version of history and politics over Ramón's unsettling "conspiracy theories." Fred and Ted, "emissaries of Anglo-American imperialism," along with Dickie Taylor, master of corporate management, are vindicated after all. Although a comedy of errors, *Barcelona* is a triumphalist tale that reduces Spain to Barcelona and decontextualizes the city, despite its dangers, into appropriable capital in the form of a reward for perseverance, the trade-fair girls, commodities in an ultimately U.S.-dominated market of international exchange. The importation of the trade-fair girls to the United States, where they are introduced to the "wholesome" pleasure of eating hamburgers in the heartland (somewhere outside of Chicago), would seem to be aimed at allaying anxieties that the globalization of the

U.S. corporate empire will result in the loss of essential "Americanness," those "ideal burgers of memory."

If *Barcelona* is a romantic comedy of errors turned triumphalist, Dorien Ross's *Returning to A* could be described as a fusion of an elegiac tale of grief—"It is, of course, a story about grief"[33]—with a bildungsroman, a novel of development. Like a typical elegy, it attempts to resurrect the dead, or at least to reconnect with them and thus "return" from death to life: "We start with death and move backward into life" (21). Spain is figured as the only place where "a dead man [is] more alive than the living" (30). Briefly, *Returning to A* is the story of a young Jewish American woman, Loren, who travels to Morón de la Frontera, forty miles southeast of Seville in Andalusia, to learn from the Gypsies there how to play the flamenco guitar, traditionally off-limits to women. The narrative shuttles back and forth between the present moment of recollection, presumably in the 1990s, to the early 1960s, when Loren first goes to Andalusia from New York and her brother Aaron leaves for California: "Aaron left for the West Coast. I left for Andalusia. It seemed Aaron was going forward in time and I was going back" (8). Most of the narrative is concerned with the time between the early 1960s and the late 1970s when, as Dorien Ross tells the reader in a prefatory note, "I studied guitar and lived with my Gypsy friends." Early on in that space of time, Loren's brother, with whom she was extremely close, dies from inhaling nitrous oxide gas (22) in a "little cottage . . . built into the edge of a cliff" (146) of the Hollywood Hills. Loren's trips to Spain and her sojourn with the Gypsies at Morón become more than a technical apprenticeship. Learning flamenco guitar and living among the Gypsies, who, unlike Loren's father after Aaron's death (21), presumably do not repress their grief and pain but instead transform them into *cante jondo* ("deep song" to express profound loss), are equated with confronting the alienation and exile from life caused by tragedy and making of grief an art of returning home: "We foreigners had become the wanderers, returning home through the music" (4). Repressing grief is emotional death. Loren's father is aptly named "Mort," to whom Diego, a venerated flamenco guitar teacher among the Gypsies at Morón, is contrasted: "The morning Diego died . . . we Americans living there wept for the father we had never had" (ibid.). Playing flamenco guitar and singing *cante jondo* is being alive, having the courage to face life: "*Cante jondo* flies straight out of sleep into the world without a glance backward. Out of the cradle into the void it flies . . . Take heart! Courage is the key" (105). Morón de la Frontera, Seville, and so forth, Spain itself—with "one foot in the preindustrial world. One foot in the modern" (106)—provides "the bridge," musical, emotional, and philosophical, between the dead and the living. Spain in *Returning to A* functions as a place of "continuity" (5) and thus of integration after shattering devastation.

Spain is also figured as a site for emotional maturation. In the bildungsroman tradition, Loren undergoes a series of initiations, light in comparison to the death of her brother. She gets drunk on too much wine and cognac, flowing freely "like blood and tears" (36), cuts her hand very badly on the whirling blades of an electric fan (28), loses her innocence and four teeth (46–55, 68), gains insight on what it means to be an outsider (54), learns like a Hemingway hero to experience the fiestas as rituals, both "holy and profane," of living life intensely (75), and falls in love with a Gypsy named Manuel, finally allowing herself something akin to the intimacy she had with her brother (163–67). The fusion of elegy and bildungsroman is achieved in the narrative's overall movement of "returning to 'A,'" the significance of which I will discuss later.

Unlike either *Barcelona,* a triumphalist comedy of errors, or *Returning to A,* a fusion of elegy and bildungsroman, Floyd Salas's novel *State of Emergency* is an epic tale of fear—an odyssey of surveillance and paranoia. The novel revisits, in fictionalized form, the year 1968–69 of Richard Nixon's election to the U.S. presidency as well as of student rebellion against the Vietnam War and against what is referred to in Deleuze and Guattarian fashion as "the war machine" of the U.S. military-industrial complex.[34] The novel is divided into eleven episodes about the odyssey of a radical professor Roger Leon his former student turned girlfriend Penelope Lawson, and false friend undercover agent George Leary. This odyssey extends from London to Bilbao and Madrid through some of Spain's Balearic and Canary Islands, to Northern Africa, then to Paris (site of the 1968 student uprising), and finally back to the United States. "[A]lienated from America" (150) like Penny, his girlfriend, Roger is trying to write a novelistic exposé of U.S. government and military endeavors to annihilate not only dissidents like himself, but any dissent at all. He finds himself constantly on the move because he dreads being tailed and arrested by agents of a state-sanctioned terrorism carried out by the U.S. government (with the help of the CIA and the FBI) to sabotage, in the name of a just war of law and order against the "forces of Communism" (18), the civil rights promised to U.S. citizens under "democracy." His more immediate and less heroic reason for fearing arrest is his habit of transporting small amounts of dope across various national borders. In Spain the professor thinks that he is being followed by CIA- and FBI-like agents of Franco's Brigada Social de Investigación, established to arrest, jail, and, it is rumored, torture and kill political opposition. Roger, who believes that Nixon (the U.S. president in 1969) and Franco are coconspirators against all forms of dissent, thinks Franco's regime has defined him as a political dissident:

> [I]t was all related to the State of Emergency decreed by Franco and Nixon's inaugurations and their just finished Chiefs of State meeting . . . Now he knew why Nixon came to Spain right after being President, why there'd been a State of Emergency and why they had tried to harass him [Roger] out of the village and drive him from Spain. (199–200)

With regard to an actual declaration of a state of emergency in 1969 or thereabouts by the Franco regime, Salas, to convey Roger's state of mind, has deliberately exaggerated the involvement of President Nixon with such a declaration. A "state of exception," to be distinguished from the more serious "state of alarm" and "state of war," was declared for two months between January 24 and March 22, 1969, when labor unrest and nationalist agitation occurred in the Basque provinces along with continued student rebellion.[35] This "state of exception" had no direct connection with any visit from President Nixon in the late 1960s. Nevertheless, according to historian Stanley Payne, "the relationship with the United States remained the cornerstone of Spain's foreign policy."[36] The United States in turn was interested in minimizing the chances for social revolution or upheaval during the transition from Franco's regime to a democratic monarchy. From the U.S. point of view, such uprisings would have possibly resulted in a Socialist or Communist government and would have been ideologically and materially inconvenient to the maintenance of U.S. air bases and other investments in Spain. Thus, in 1970 a five-year Agreement of Friendship and Cooperation with the United States was signed between the United States and Spain and Nixon made a brief visit to Madrid during his European tour, a visit followed up by General Vernon A. Walters, deputy chief of the CIA.[37] Although some historians, including Payne, argue that by the late 1960s Franco's regime had grown more moderate, that censorship officially ended in 1966, and that a general liberalization and expansion of the press followed, the regime still disciplined and punished opposition, jailing activists, fining and censoring liberal and leftist papers, and doling out the death penalty to certain Communist leaders and various members of anti-Franco terrorist groups. Rising opposition to the regime by university students, progressive priests, and industrial workers characterized the second half of the 1960s. Those who opposed the regime put their lives and livelihoods at risk, with the harshest treatment reserved for defecting priests and workers.

State of Emergency, despite its historical references, is not a historical novel of social protest. Rather, it reads like a cross between a disturbing memoir of the times disguised as third-person fiction and Pynchonesque parody, along the lines of *Gravity's Rainbow* (1973), of a male protagonist on a mission who cannot achieve the distance on himself that the text maintains. Although the paranoia that Roger feels is never explicitly dismissed as the effect of unfounded conspiracy theory induced by hallucinogens or hallucenogenic cannabis, he allows his every action to be governed by a fear of the government agents who are supposedly dogging him, bugging his rented rooms, tailing him in the streets, and, above all, staring at him in various guises. His 1960s countercultural idealism, manifested by his professed adherence to truth, justice, free love, and hashish, is framed by bitterness and suspicion born out of the fear of being undermined or betrayed by those closest to him—undermined from within by "plants," some of them highly seductive, such as Anne Marie, "the beautiful blonde with the bare brown midriff and the white hot pants swaying back and forth" (79) whom Roger suspects. His state of vigilance comes to parallel, like a mirror reflection, that of a government agent. Roger begins to imitate the at-war mentality of his enemies, from both the United States and Spain. As if acting out a denotation of his first name "Roger," he receives and internalizes messages from a remote source and replies in kind: "*They* were giving him a signal through the invisible wall they had wrapped around him." (330–31). The character "Roger," whose name means "message received and understood," is implicated even on the level of his name in the reduplication of the terroristic effects of the state. Despite the apparent authorial corroboration in the first episode of *State of Emergency* that George Leary does exist independently of Roger's state of mind and that Leary is in fact "a security agent" (18) who goes wherever Roger goes (12), Leary drops out of the narrative after this initial episode to briefly, almost apparitionally, reappear under the alias "Fuzz" (slang for policeman or detective) in the fifth, sixth, tenth, and eleventh episodes, leaving the reader with a lingering uncertainty as to whether Roger is fighting a "real" enemy or merely shadowboxing.

As mentioned earlier, *Barcelona, Returning to A,* and *State of Emergency* all recycle rather familiar types and tropes of Spain—types and tropes that date from particular periods. For example, *Barcelona* recycles the Orientalist version of the tyrannical, simultaneously hypermasculinized and emasculated Spanish male popular in the United States from the mid-nineteenth century onward, and especially during the Spanish-Cuban-American War. That Ramón is characterized by his obsession with that war is not merely a joke on certain Spanish intellectuals but is part and parcel of the presentation of his "type." Type is in a synecdochical relation to trope. *Barcelona* also recycles the centuries-old fantasy of the dangerousness of Spain, even as it would seem to particularize this scene of danger to Barcelona, a move that merely superimposes one fantasy upon another. Associations of Barcelona with bombs, anarchy, and instability have a long history dating back to the late nineteenth century (1892–97) and to the "Semana Trágica" (Tragic week) of 1909. Thievery and sexual infidelity, components of classic associations of Spain and Spaniards with dangerous deception, are thrown in for added effect.[38]

Furthermore, and perhaps most important, for cultivating a certain amount of audience sympathy and even identification for its otherwise embarrassingly inadequate and downright obnoxious protagonist Fred, representative of the U.S. military, *Barcelona* rehearses the associations of Spain with the pain and gore of blood sports, ritual bloodletting—in war, the bullring, and the festivities of Spanish Catholicism. The film cannily picks up and combines the fears and fantasies of nineteenth-century travelers and ethnographers with twentieth-century interests in Spain centering on the Spanish civil war, the "sacrifices" of the battlefield and bullring, and the notion of Spain as tragic. Amid the pyrotechnics of bombs and parties in *Barcelona,* the scene of the Spanish doctor emerging from the operating room after treating Fred's head wound sums up this complicated constellation of associations, cutting in numerous but interrelated directions. Spreading out across the upper half of the doctor's operating gown is a large bloodstain in the shape of the United States. The blood does not belong to a Spaniard who died on the battlefield or to a Spanish bull; it belongs to Fred. This moment in the film does not merely serve to indicate the gravity of the terrorist attack on Fred's person inspired by Ramón's inflammatory journalism. It also has the effect of transferring to the film's representative of the U.S. military the heroism, death-defying dignity, and "tragedy" attributed to soldiers, bullfighters, and sacrificed martyrs. In other words, Fred the Anglo-American military man, not Ramón the Spanish journalist spinning theories about the Spanish-Cuban-American War, gets to be the next closest thing to a war hero in the absence of an actual war. The bloodstain on the surgeon's gown and the black eye patch that appears later over Fred's eye are his "badge[s] of courage."

Returning to A also rehearses associations of Spain with deception and pain (physical and emotional), though in quite a different spirit from *Barcelona*. Unlike Fred, who combatatively resists his environment and triumphs over it despite his injury, Loren is shown welcoming the painful experiences—"I wanted only to do with *cante jondo,* the deep song" (11)— even when she is the butt of the joke, as during her "*bulerías* education" (41). Both Fred and Loren court danger, grief, and pain in Spain, but of different kinds. Fred, ignoring warnings from the U.S. consul that his military uniform may provoke civilian hostility, persists in wearing it. The danger, grief, and pain he courts are at the service of his fundamentally belligerent attitude. Although *Barcelona* cannot be reduced to this one character, the film itself uses the basic association of Spain with pain to vindicate its Anglo-American boys. In contrast, Loren courts danger, grief, and pain from an a priori ethnically inflected identificatory position:

> One day . . . I got up the nerve to ask Diego . . . to teach me . . . the song of weeping, the song of death . . . It felt familiar to me, the old voice wailing like the shofar horn blowing on Yom Kippur. I didn't know then that this form was as serious as the blowing of the horn on the high holiday. I just knew that within the sound I felt suddenly at home. (10)

Loren, the narrator, and presumably Ross herself, who tells readers in her prefatory note, "[t]his novel is based on fact, held by memory, and woven into fantasy," as Jews and Jewish Americans of the Diaspora, identify with the Gypsies of Spain, with their culture, and particularly with their "deep songs" or *cante jondo* (19), full of the pain of a persecuted, dispersed people. *Returning to A* reminds the reader, "It is said that a Jew gains historical context through his or her own personal grief. In this way, I move into history" (85). Effectively, when Loren enters the history of the *cante* among the Gypsies at Morón, she enters as a Jew:

> A Jewess from the United States
> A child called the Fat One
> Gave her heart and her purse
> To a Gypsy with no shame. (55)

Unlike a product of Anglo-American imperialist ideology, *Returning to A* does not enact the dichotomization of Orientalized Otherness and Westernized Sameness. Ross's text, though largely about her friends and teachers among the Gypsies of Morón, is quite free of exoticizing descriptive language about their appearance. When it does resort to physical description, it casts both Loren, Ross's persona, and the Gypsies in the same terms—"my long black hair" (7, 16) and "a tall, lanky, dark Gypsy boy" (45). *Returning to A* suggests an equivalence between the Gypsies and the Jewish Loren, not in "racial" terms, but in cultural and historical ones—as people long acquainted with pain and suffering sharing a common history in Spain, especially in Andalusia. Significantly, Loren finds her "ancient Jewish star" in the Barrio Santa Cruz (173), most likely the famous neighborhood of that name in Seville. Thus, rather than Orientalizing the Gypsies of Spain, the novel presents them as guides to Loren's, and presumably Ross's, self-knowledge or knowledge of themselves as having a particular identity or orientation in the world: "[T]he Gypsies expressed a style, or more to the point, a form that told you they knew who they were" (42). It is a way of orienting and expressing herself that Loren learns concurrently and coextensively with how to play the flamenco guitar: "We foreigners had become the wanderers, returning home through the music" (4).

Returning "to A" is more than beginning "the long road home to the A-chord" on the guitar, or, rather, the "A-chord" is more than just a configuration of the fingers upon the frets (134). That "A-chord" is a mystic symbol for connecting with various other "A"s—Aaron, atonement, and finally, one might argue, America. For Loren, after Aaron's death, a pall falls over the United States, and especially California, the far coast of the country's promise: "In our family Los Angeles equals death. But this thinking leaves so few places one can go" (85). Loren's apprenticeship with the Gypsies, her dedication to learning all the forms and moods of flamenco guitar playing and singing, from deep, unspeakable wailing sorrow to *alegría* (joy), brings her to terms with her own grief for her brother. By playing, she consecrates that grief into an art form that not only gives expression to her grief, but, in expressing it, extends her brother's life beyond the grave: "I [Loren] accept your [Aaron's] presence . . . In death you are becoming what you never succeeded at in life" (147). Giving expression to her sorrow, she gives expression to the sorrow that may have been responsible for her brother's death—possible suicide by nitrous oxide—which she was not able to prevent (146).

Grief is not the only emotion that her apprenticeship with the Gypsies in Spain transmutes. Guilt for not being able to save her brother, for being apart from him, is the other related emotion. The "A-chord" is thus also most symbolic of the work of atonement as reconciliation, bringing together what has been sundered and dispersed, creating a union between herself and the Gypsies, herself and her brother, her various lives—in Andalusia and "America." Her life among the Gypsies in Spain, her intimate involvement with the music of their pain, Spain as pain, all compose her atonement and the long road "home to the A-chord," the goal of atonement—harmony, resolution, accord, traditionally a unity with God, in this book a unity between the living and the dead and consequently the lifting of the curse off of America, formerly a place of death, an "almanac of the dead," as Leslie Marmon Silko suggests in her novel by that title.[39] Ultimately, returning to A or that "A-chord" means the ability, if not exactly to reinfuse "America" with hope, then to go back to the United States enabled, optimistic. *Returning to A* tells readers that "[t]he relationship between music and optimism is not a casual one" (116). The last paragraph of the novel ends with Loren's anticipation of her departure from Spain and her return to the States: "As I turned away from Sevilla I begin to imagine the white walls of my studio, thousands of miles away . . . and now I know it is my turn to play" (175).

Salas's *State of Emergency* recycles the well-worn Anglo-American trope (as old as the Puritans and inherited by them from England) of Spain as primarily an inquisitorial "state of emergency" where an alienated "American" can experience the full brunt of persecution. However, unlike the many Anglo, and even non-Anglo, narratives that present Spain as tyrannical "Other," Salas's novel represents its Spanish scenario as altogether familiar, as parallel to that of the United States. It is precisely this sameness, this mirror-like mimetic relation between the United States and Spain, that defines danger, persecution, and psychic pain as draconian, bilateral, state-sanctioned terrorism. Unlike *Barcelona, State of Emergency* does not locate terrorism in a particular country or city. Terrorism is not merely the punishing gaze of one government on its dissident citizens, but the punishing gaze of two or more governments configured in parallel complicity with each other's intentions and aims—in Salas's novel, Franco's regime and Nixon's administration, Spain and the United States. Significantly, Roger Leon, from whose point of view most of the novel is narrated, is descended from Spaniards and Native Americans (11). In other words, like the writer Floyd Salas, he is a self-declared "Spaniard/Spic/ Hispanic" whose ancestors are neither wholly from Spain or from the Americas and whose "home," if under such continual persecution he may be said to have one, is in the United States. This United States is dominated by Anglos, a hitherto hegemonic and thus unmarked minority of the Americas, the Americas colonized by the Spaniards before the Anglos ever set foot on Plymouth Rock. As the novel tells its readers, using the Spaniards, not the Anglos, to gauge the antiquity of its native ancestors, "The other branches [of Roger Leon's family] have supposedly been in the United States since Ponce de León came" (ibid.). One could make an argument for a connection between *State of Emergency*'s "parallax view" (to borrow the title of the 1974 film) of the late-1960s' diplomatic relationship between Spain and the United States and the sense of being doubly "colonized" and constantly besieged.

Considering *Barcelona, Returning to A* and *State of Emergency* as representative of continuing dependence on figures of Spain and Spaniards in the United States in the mid 1990s, what emerges is the trope of going to Spain as a return to pain. As is evident from *Returning to A,* this association is not always negative, but the opposite—the source of growth and integration, something like growing pains. The dominance of this single trope of Spain as pain coupled with the recession in time of each of the narratives—*Barcelona* to the last decade of the Cold War (the 1980s), *Returning to A* to the 1960s and 1970s, and *State of Emergency* to the late 1960s—strongly suggests that what governs the mid-1990s' lingering U.S. dependence on figures of Spain are modes of nostalgia. Renato Rosaldo, in an article titled "Imperialist Nostalgia" (1989), defines nostalgia in the following manner:

> Far from being eternal, the term *nostalgia* (from the Greek *nostos*, "to return home," and *algia*, "a painful condition") dates from the late seventeenth century when it was coined to describe a medical condition. The term described, for example, a pathological homesickness among Swiss mercenaries who were fighting far from their homeland. (Even in its origins, the term appears to have been associated with processes of domination.)[40]

Rosaldo defines nostalgia as both the painful yearning to return home from somewhere else and a mourning for or longing to return to the traditional/primitive society whose passing/demise one has brought about, unwittingly or intentionally. He views nostalgia as complicitous with processes of domination, the colonizer's desire to see the colonized culture as it was when the colonizer first encountered it—hence, imperialist nostalgia.[41] More recent articles on nostalgia—for instance, Stuart Tannock's "Nostalgia Critique" (1995)—have questioned the blanket association of nostalgia with dominator culture or reactionary forces. Borrowing Raymond Williams's term for nostalgia—a "structure of feeling"[42]—Tannock's article argues that "nostalgia is a valuable way of approaching the past, important to all social groups," and that it can be liberating or merely palliative, progressive or reactionary, remindful or amnesiac, activist or escapist, an inspiration for challenging the status quo or merely a mystification of the processes of domination, a safety valve of misplaced feeling restricting action.[43]

If nostalgia is the mode informing dependence on figures of Spain in *Barcelona, Returning to A,* and *State of Emergency,* I submit that nostalgia in these works manifests itself as a desire to go home (to the United States) through a familiar pain, Spain, located in the past, as Spain so often is in cultural representations. Following both Tannock's and Rosaldo's line of inquiry, the question is the nature of the relation of Anglo-American imperialism and the historical fact of the United States as an empire to the nostalgia of these works. *Barcelona* is a relatively clear case of what I have defined as nostalgia—the desire to go home through a familiar pain located in the past—in the service of Anglo-American imperialism, for all the reasons I have outlined. Despite the aesthetics of embarrassment, the film does set its story in the last decade of the Cold War, reviving the Cold War so as to have a doubly fortifying antagonist—the Cold War and Spain—against which to define self. Moreover, one of the most striking features of the film is that, aside from a shot of Gaudí's Sagrada Familia church and a few glimpses of Art Nouveau architecture, the cinematography reveals nothing else typical or representative of the city. All ambient or stylistic elements are "American" retro: big-band music, conservative men's clothes, clean-shaven faces harking back to the 1940s, trendy women's fashions, makeup and hairstyles of the late 1980s, and a declared preference for dance music of the 1970s over experimental jazz, the very dance music that Stillman would celebrate and yet declare more or less dead in his later 1998 film *The Last Days of Disco*.[44] In other words, *Barcelona,* from its beginning in Barcelona to its conclusion in the U.S. Midwest, is nostalgic above all for Spain inasmuch as it is made to resemble earlier versions of Anglo-American culture, with the ideal of a World War II era of "just" wars, clear enemies, and world gratitude toward the United States lurking just beneath the mid-1990s surface hipness, slickness, and ironic self-deprecation.

Returning to A is a deeply moving work of identification with a particular place (Andalusia and, specifically, Morón de la Frontera) and people (the Gypsies) in Spain of the 1960s and 1970s. The Spanish Gypsies and southern Spain of the 1960s are allotted a chosen part in the shaping of Loren's and Ross's identities as "American" Jews. *Returning to A,* with its book cover involving a scarlet letter "A" framed by actual pictures of Spanish Gypsies Ross knew, would seem to be a refutation of Nathaniel Hawthorne's very Anglo-American office of the Scarlet Letter. A less Anglo-American imperialist novel than *Returning to A* vis-à-vis Gypsies in Spain would be hard to find. However, the epigraph of the book—"I was not stolen by the Gypsies as a child. I stole the Gypsies as my own"—symptomizes a peculiar problem of the book. The novel simultaneously identifies with and appropriates these Gypsies, placing that action sometime in the past, as indicated by the verb "stole." Although *Returning to A* is not an imperial text, the desire to go home through a familiar pain

located in the past does make of the Gypsies a medium, a means in the
past to an end in the future in relation to that past. This "structure of feeling" warrants the question of whether the conventional trope of mourning the passing of a traditional or so-called primitive society is part of
the novel's elegiac stance and whether this kind of mourning approxi-
mates Renato Rosaldo's definition of imperialist nostalgia. His definition
of imperialist nostalgia includes the isolation of a dynamic in which the
narrator/observer mourns the very cultural transformations in which she
or he has participated as a major or minor player.

Returning to A, though not exactly idealizing the Gypsies, does set them
up as the embodiment of timeless naturalized tradition, "as old as the
breezes that pass through the poplars in front of the church" (42): "Just by
smoking a cigarette, the Gypsies expressed a style, or more to the point,
a form that told you they knew who they were" (ibid.). The very next
paragraph recounts how countless foreign adolescents came to Morón de
la Frontera to deal with "[t]he kind of crisis . . . so familiar to adolescents
of other countries . . . unheard of" in Morón:

> [T]hey came, these foreign boys, in their twenties and thirties. They came
> from all over the world. But mainly they came from America and England.
> And by hook or by crook they found Morón. (Ibid.)

The novel never mentions the words *tourist* or *tourism.* It calls the foreigners "wanderers" (94), refers to their "traveling" (4), their "seeking," like
pilgrims, "a home in an unbroken world, one in which Diego's generation
was still firmly rooted" (ibid.). Loren and her friends are scripted as traveling apprentices, not tourists. The decided preference for certain words
to the total exclusion of others indicates that a myth of self-construction
is at work not so very different from the fetishization of "aficionados" in
Hemingway's *The Sun Also Rises.* Like Hemingway's novel, *Returning to A*
implicitly posits the ability to recognize and appreciate the "pure art in its
natural habitat" (71) as one of the distinguishing characteristics between
the true apprentice (aficionado, of course, for Hemingway) and the unmentioned and unmentionable tourist. Like many of the expatriate modernist texts on bullfighting in Spain, *Returning to A* must tautologically
"root" the art of real flamenco guitar playing in the soil to prove it timeless, unspoiled, "authentic":

They [a few foreign boys with talent] were taken into the [Gypsy] family. They were taught the authentic versions, the real material, whose roots extended beyond the town and found their source in the dry soil, the arches of the Roman bridges and stone *verias,* ancient paths. (42)

The emphasis on the timelessness of Gypsy culture in Morón obscures socioeconomic and cultural conflict, both old and new, as manifested in the way that Morón is described upon Loren's first "encounter" with it: "a dream of the past that I had no knowledge of, but I immediately recognized . . . as the missing dimension. It was a more remote past than Eastern Europe, which was too soaked in the blood of my people to walk again in this lifetime" (8). No mention is made of socioeconomic and cultural conflicts in Morón, Andalusia, or Spain as a whole—for instance, the intermittent, violent persecutions of the Gypsies and the Jews in the history of Spain, their forced expulsions, the struggles of Gypsies living in Spain the 1960s and 1970s, or in the 1990s, for that matter. *Returning to A* imagines Morón and its Gypsies as an oasis in time, relatively unbroken and unbloodied by the past and unspoiled by modern technology and the very presence of so many foreigners like the narrator herself. This picture of Morón, though seductive, discourages Ross from seeing herself and her book as agents, however minor, of change and displacement of the very place, people, and art forms she would like to preserve in that inviolate oasis of the past. Concomitantly, the mystification serves as a foil against modern-day Spain:

That modern-day Spain no longer holds the secret power of the *Cante* is a distressing possibility. We have all heard rumors of ruined fiestas, of dishonest *falsetas* being sold in the marketplace, of the *bulerías* being played with thirteen beats instead of twelve. Who will guard the archetypes from these unspeakable violations . . . ? (129)

If it is a distressing possibility that modern-day Spain no longer "holds" the power of the *cante,* it is also an equally unsettling possibility that *Returning to A* unintentionally has the effect of privileging an art form and its purity over the conditions of its producers, the Gypsies, and of appropriating that art form from them. Is it *Returning to A* and not the Gypsies that will "guard the archetypes from these unspeakable violations"?

What if the book further encourages the very touristic consumptions it laments?

Furthermore, one might ask whether the unmentioned and unmentionable tourists are the only source of cultural violation. It so happens that Morón de la Frontera, the town southeast of Seville where most of Ross's story takes place, has been the site of one of the four U.S. air bases in Spain since the bases were established through a pact between Franco and the Truman administration in 1958. The many Anglo adolescents Ross's novel mentions coming to Morón may not have arrived "by hook or by crook" of their own accord or primarily to learn the art of the Gypsies. Many were most likely the children of U.S. military officers or were themselves working for the base. Whether Ross knew of the presence of the U.S. military base, a presence hard to miss in a small town like Morón, cannot be ascertained from her novel. Perhaps she did know and chose to ignore this fact, acknowledgment of which would have precluded a representation of Morón as an oasis in time and space. Whatever the case, though not an imperialist text, its desire to go home through a familiar place of consecrated pain in the past is not entirely free of the shadow of imperialist nostalgia.

Within an odyssey of returning "home," Salas's *State of Emergency* deploys the trope of Spain as a familiar pain and the devices of recession in time and perspective toward a very different end than either Stillman's film or Ross's novel—toward an ending without closure, toward an ending that is just beginning. This inconclusive end is negotiated through the text's distance effect on the main protagonist, Roger Leon, from whose point of view the story is narrated. The reader is never certain whether Leon is really being followed, hounded to death, or is just suffering paranoid delusions from inhaling too much hashish. The most disturbing and disorienting possibility is that he is being followed, and the drugs have simply magnified or expanded legitimate concerns. The distance effect—both temporal and perspectival—plays a paradoxical role. It lends a suspenseful edge both to the mimetic codes of the book (evident in the mention of historical events such as the Kennedy and King assassinations, the Vietnam War, FBI and CIA infiltrations into the student movement, Nixon's inauguration) and to the dynamic of terrorful mimesis. Doubts, fears, and suspicions that state-sanctioned terrorism is undermining the civil rights of citizens, rather than playing themselves out on the page, are gradually internalized by the ever-expectant reader. More than discrediting Roger, the lack of solid evidence produces a festering anxiety denied the catharsis of proof or resolution. A terrorful mimesis rules not only international relations between Spain and the United States but also Roger and, potentially, the reader caught in the text's web of intrigue or, more to the point, spectral hall of mirrors. The description of this text as a spectral hall of mirrors is no mere figure of speech. The effect of the novel as that of a funhouse or nuthouse hall of mirrors is quite literally crystallized in the scene in which Roger joins the French intellectual Pierre in a Paris café:

> Pierre led them down the stairs and out onto the winding street a couple of doors to a cafe. They all walked through to a back room with big, black, soft-leather booths and walls lined with mirrors. Roger, in spite of the pleasure of having James Jones' phone number in his pocket, felt instantaneously uncomfortable. There was almost no place he could look without seeing himself. He noticed, though, that Hans and Beverly both looked full at themselves, then at him before and after they sat down, and a horrible feeling came over him. Everywhere he looked he saw himself reflected in mirrors. He had to stare straight at a person to keep from looking into his own face. He felt as if he were in the nuthouse and everyone was looking at him, watching him, trying to see how he'd react. (317)

This passage is a *mise en abîme*—a recessed replication in miniature—of the form and concerns of the novel as a whole and thus of the psychological effects of state-sanctioned terrorism that invades all spaces of private or intimate communication between people and the very constitution of subjectivity.

Although set some thirty years back in the past (the late 1960s), the novel cannily manipulates the contemporary reader's sense of an enigmatic or elusive legacy (who indeed was responsible for the killing of King and both Kennedy brothers?) to create a textual "state of emergency," a radical uncertainty about so-called American democracy. In this respect, the book is not retro, but entirely postmodern. There is no sure center around which to rally or mourn, only the "symbolic symbols" (395) with which the secret agent Leary, alias Fuzz, obliquely threatens Roger. What remains in this scenario of surveillance and fear is a proliferating network of shadowy signs disappearing the political, as discussed in Jean Baudrillard's *The Transparency of Evil: Essays on Extreme Phenomena* (1993).[45] In such a universe, terrorism, state-sanctioned included, is, as Baudrillard has theorized, not merely a set of particular acts or events, but a hyper-real "state" of fear in which orientation (national, international) through differentiation is impossible and a displacing sameness reigns supreme, threatening to exhaust action and numb passion, to produce a massive burnout. State-sanctioned terrorism in particular strips its citizens of the very features of their citizenship. It strips citizens not merely of rights, but of the very desire to act and of forums in which to constitute themselves, to write and speak out, to be public persons, to do more than chat or chatter through their teeth with their ideas interrupted and reduced to framed sound bites and unintelligible, damning outbursts, or more generally to an ominous silence. It is this enervating nervous exhaustion induced by the disruptions of being tracked and surveyed and the very fear itself of further persecution that Penny expresses on her return "home" from Spain, where she and Roger were never "away," but instead were wandering around small panopticon islands (Mallorca, Formentera, Ibiza, the Canaries, and the Spanish mainland itself) rather than a large country (the United States): "I just want to live a normal life. I can't take this constant suffering" (394). Penny, whose name suggests another famous Penny—Penelope, Odysseus's long-suffering wife—is not alone in her desire for refuge, for the presumed safety of a private life where she imagines she might avoid pain. On more than one occasion, the continually voyaging Roger fantasizes about committing suicide as a solitary way "out" of the unrelenting pressure of his predicament as a persecuted radical:

> He [Roger] stopped at the next landing and looked over the banister. There was room for a body to drop straight down to the white tile floor of the foyer. It would be quick and easy. *Just a few seconds of fear* and one good swan dive. That's all. Then falling, knowing it was too late. The gaping hole had a magnetic pull, like a promise that would end all his troubles. He had to push himself away from the banister and make himself turn to start down the stairs again. (111; my emphasis)

Like the death-wish fantasy picture of nuclear war as lasting "just a few seconds," Roger's picture of suicide presents him with the temptation of exchanging a life of fear for "a few seconds of fear," but he manages to resist and continue his embattled endeavor to write his exposé. He writes so as not to die, so as not to commit suicide, so as not to use "the only weapon left against a totalitarian state when there's no avenue for hope" (277). Writing is Roger's weapon of preference and he writes both to stave off the last resort and, like a true idealist, "make a better world" (366).

To conclude, the nostalgic, elegiac move of *State of Emergency*—its purposely failing revivification of the struggle for agency of the counterculture of the late 1960s and its journey "home" through Franco's Spain as a familiar pain—manages to prevent nostalgia from functioning as the usual antidote to fear of the contemporary scene, in this case, the mid-1990s and the imminent future (the early twenty-first century). Both *Barcelona* and *Returning to A* are ultimately palliative or tranquilizing—the first delivering an "all's well that ends well" finale to its comedy of cultural errors and the second permitting the reader to escape with Loren's *falseta* "out over the darkening earth" (175). *State of Emergency* provides no such cathartic exit from the imperial, border-crossing, globe-trotting, co-opting "state of emergency" that, through nightmarish figurations of Spain, the novel suggests "America" has become. The implication would seem to be that nothing short of a *collective* existential crisis will change the present course of things accelerating, the novel suggests, toward a terrifying sameness. Flying into Kennedy airport on the return trip to the United States, Roger thinks to himself, "He was approaching the fascist fist of the state on Independence Day!" (389). In other words, "Independence Day," the holiday of democracy in the "American" Way and not according to some other country's code for democracy, appears in the same breath, or rather is placed in the same line, so to speak, as "the fascist fist of the state" or totalitarianism. With reference to the function of nostalgia in this novel, Independence Day as the occasion of prospective hope for the continuation of "democracy" within a militantly patriotic retrospective celebration of its supposed founding is transmuted into a completely prospective mirror image of democracy's proverbial Other—of fascism looming fistlike on the horizon. Earlier in the story, Roger had remarked about the United States, "We're still a partial democracy, not a total corporate fascist state yet!" (104). At the novel's conclusion, for Roger, anyway, the "still" has departed and the "yet" has arrived. And, because of the superpower status of the United States, this "now"—the novel's 1969 prefiguring of things to come—is more fearful than Franco's fascism, which Roger has left behind in Spain and its little islands.

Since the publication of Salas's *State of Emergency* (1996), a tremendous amount has happened that would seem to bear out Roger's and Salas's worst nightmares. A little less than a decade later "terrorism," terrorist tactics and massive surveillance of all sorts and from many different directions (paramilitary, governmental, etc.) have become not only the watchwords of the day but pervasive structures of feeling, thought, and action. Under the directive of the Partido Popular, successor to Spain's fourteen-year socialist government (1982–96) and inheritor of a vision of Spain more closely resembling that of the late Franco years, Spain's foreign policy was more or less aligned with U.S. foreign policy. This alignment was consummated during the meeting between George W. Bush, José María Aznar, and Tony Blair in the Azores on March 16, 2003. The transatlantic nature of the alliance was literalized through the use of the Azores as common meeting ground. Although not reflective of the opinions or desires of most of its citizens, Spain became, like England under Tony Blair, a minor satellite to the "planeta americano" (to hark back to Vicente Verdú's phrase from his 1996 essay)—the American planet of U.S. imperialism. How much this state of affairs will change or shift under socialist control remains to be seen, but the new socialist government soon began a more pro-European alignment by Spain with France and Germany to create a multipolar counterweight to the unilateralism of U.S. foreign policy at the beginning of the twenty-first century.

Furthermore, and this may be one of the most significant developments, the status of the United States as an empire is no secret anymore. As late as the 1990s one might find a rather widespread denial of this historical fact, or, if not denial, distaste for it to the point of denial. However, events after 2000—including the U.S. invasion of Afghanistan, the war against Iraq, the heightened embargo with Cuba as a means of gaining potential leverage over the future of the island, the increased involvement in the Middle East, the extension in the Pacific rim of U.S. economic interests at the expense of human rights, and the development and implementation of the definition of the "axis of evil" justifying preventative U.S. military action in Iraq, Iran, and North Korea—have made such a denial much less credible.

The recognition of the United States of America as an empire and not simply some innocently "postcolonial" nation is already beginning to produce other kinds of representations of Spain in relation to the Americas. These other representations both reflect and engender a consciousness of a continuation between Spain and Spaniards and Latinas/os in terms of cultural positioning vis-à-vis a dominant Anglo-American culture, the hegemony of which is nevertheless being challenged by the increasing number and presence of Latinas/os within the geographical borders of the United States. From the evidence of the texts discussed in this chapter's section "Spain and Postcolonial Prospects of *Latinidad*," this consciousness neither defers to nor rejects whatever is deemed to be associated with Spain on account of the historical atrocities of colonization and conquest. Implicit in these representational complications of "Spain" and "Spanish" beyond the binaries of colonizer and colonized, implicit in these shifting elaborations of identity and identification in relation to (re)constructions of history, are changing ideas about and practices of assimilation, transculturation, and resistance. That is to say, some of the more recent representations of Spain and Spaniards found in the writings of Latinas/os and also non-Latinas/os, as we have seen in the case of Dorien Ross's *Returning to A,* suggest more flexible or open-ended approaches to the question of the relation of hitherto marginalized identities to both the concept and the existence of a dominant Anglo-American culture. In the mirror game of *imago*/alter ego between Spain and Anglo-America, an alteration in the representation of one variable or variable complex (in that the idea of "Spain" or of "Anglo-America" is composed of myriad ideas) entails many alterations in the representation of the other. And these alterations are both consequence and cause of new identity formations that are taking place in and beyond the United States.

NOTES

INTRODUCTION

1. There have been innumerable explicit calls for the implementation of paradigms of multiculturalism to the study of American literature and culture. Take, for instance, Timothy Powell's two books *Reconstructing Cultural Identity in a Multicultural Context* and *Ruthless Democracy: A Multicultural Interpretation of the American Renaissance.*

2. From the mid-1990s onward, the U.S. focus on questions of race and ethnicity has widened under initiatives sponsored by centers of transnational and international studies as well as programs in comparative ethnic studies to encompass the Americas in a hemispheric or more global sense. Take, for instance, the promising seminars held at the Brown Center for the Study of Race and Ethnicity in America or the 2001 inauguration of the Institute for the Study of Race and Ethnicity in the Americas at Ohio State University. One open question of many is the extent to which a new hemispheric and globalist emphasis will present a deep-structure challenge to the center-periphery model of U.S./Latin American and Caribbean and U.S./world relations and thus resist or counteract what, given the sources of funding, may result in an "inevitable" NAFTA-ization of American-cum-Americas studies. Most likely, the new initiatives symptomize a complex imbrication of agendas with many possible and somewhat contradictory results.

3. The field of study that has most insisted on the ethnicity of "Anglo" is Latina/o studies. Sometimes, outside of Latina/o studies one may find "Anglo" qualified as ethnic under the big umbrella rubric "Euro-American" or "European-American," though such a rubric assumes a somewhat factitious consensus about what constitutes European.

4. Wertheimer, *Imagined Empires,* 12.

5. See Shields, *Oracles of Empire.*

6. See Werckmeister, *Citadel Culture.*

7. Freud, *Totem and Taboo,* 2.

8. Ginsberg, "Howl," 127.

9. Castillo, *Peel My Love like an Onion*, 49, 168.

10. Dos Passos, "Young Spain," 41.

11. Ibid., 42.

12. Lacan, "The Mirror Stage as Formative of the Function of the I as Revealed in Psychoanalytic Experience," 1–7.

13. Consider, for example, Stanley Williams's treatment of the interests of "Hispanophiles" such as Washington Irving or George Ticknor in the two-volume study *The Spanish Background of American Literature*. Or, for a very contemporary reference to the "Romantic" image of Spain purveyed by the Hispanophiles that managed to fix and limit the critical discourse on their cultural legacy, as well as on the less than damning literary uses and critical handling of Spain and Spanish culture(s), see the opening page of chapter 1 of the curious philosophical-historiographic polemic by Harold Raley, professor of languages at Houston Baptist University, an essay in the guise of a book-length manuscript titled *The Spirit of Spain*. Raley's essay transvalues what he takes to be superficial assessments of the actuality, not the construct, of "Romantic Spain" into a Spanish passion for the "real world" (3), which he calls Spain's "reverse romanticism" (2). In his diminishment of any African influences operating within Hispanic cultures (either Old or New World) and in his zeal to Westernize, Europeanize, Christianize, and, most paradoxically, subject to a chivalric code what he identifies as a Spanish passion for "the real world" and "reality" (3) in the image of the Castilian white knight Don Quijote (6), he does not make this connection. However, his emphasis on such passion reminds me of the valorization of "realness" among African Americans and the identification with this realness that prompted the Andalusian poet from Granada Federico García Lorca to associate the blues and African American spirituals with *duende* (a mysterious or compelling spirit or force of enhancement and engagement). I suggest this connection not to argue that what Raley calls the Spanish passion for reality—for life "without apology" (3)—is the same as realness for African Americans, but rather to demonstrate the ideologically fraught nature of any endeavor to form claims about either cultural uniqueness or affinity, not to mention shared influence. Resistance to notions of cultural hybridity and intracultural difference in favor of hypostasized abstractions that are deployed to incorporate one another (as, for example, when "European" substitutes for "Mediterranean") make tricky the task of even beginning to describe cultural complexity and the relation between the local and the global.

14. Gallop, *Reading Lacan*, 62.

15. Sumner, "The Conquest of the United States by Spain," 139.

16. Although the presence of Spanish missionaries between Florida and what became Virginia hardly receives the attention in historical accounts that the presence of Spanish missionaries all along the West Coast does, the fact is that Spanish Jesuit missionaries had ventured into what later became North Carolina and Virginia even before the Jamestown settlement of 1607. The founding of the first permanent township of the British forced the Spanish missionaries to move back down the coast as far

as Santa Catalina, south of what in 1733 became the British-founded Savannah. See Fernández-Florez, *The Spanish Heritage in the United Sates*, 138.

17. The relative appropriability of the phrase "our America" in contradistinction to "Other America" is quite well illustrated by the very existence of Walter Benn Michaels's *Our America* (1995), rather different in its orientation and claims to, for instance, José David Saldívar's *The Dialectics of Our America* (1991).

18. Gracia, *Hispanic/Latino Identity*, 4.

19. Oboler, *Ethnic Labels, Latino Lives*, 17–43.

20. This fantasy has assumed even greater proportions in the first years of the twenty-first century, despite all the talk of globalization and international cooperation. For an incisive description of the implications of an often isolationist self-referential—solipsistic—insistence on independence coupled with an appetite for interventionism, see Spanish essayist and journalist Vicente Verdú's *El planeta americano*. I take exception to his analysis of the character of U.S. imperialism, however, for it seems to me that he de-talons it, or rather does not see the talons among the feathers.

21. Harrison, *The Pan-American Dream*, 231–72.

22. See the chapter "What Should We Call Ourselves?" in Gracia's *Hispanic/Latino Identity*, 1–26.

23. Oboler, *Ethnic Labels, Latino Lives*, 25.

24. Oboler borrows the phrase "fantasy heritage" from McWilliams, *North from Mexico*.

25. Baca, "Thirteen Mexicans," in *C-Train and Thirteen Mexicans*, 64.

26. For a highly informative, multimedia book on this U.S. imperialist war and its legacy into the contemporary period, see Shaw and Francia, *Vestiges of War*.

27. See Kinder's *Blood Cinema*. Drawing on theories of the relation between violence and reproductions of, as well as challenges to, the dominant social order in, among other works, René Girard's *Violence and the Sacred* (1977) and Tzvetan Todorov's *The Conquest of America: The Question of the Other* (trans. 1984), Kinder offers cultural psychoanalytic readings of the representation of violence and physical and psychic trauma in Franco and post-Franco Spanish film. Her study, like Slotkin's, rests on the fundamental psychoanalytic premise that violence and trauma, encounters with and returns to pain, are implicated in axiomatic questions of identity reconstitution and regeneration where "reconstitution" and "regeneration" imply both reiteration (repetition of existing paradigms) and discontinuity with the previous order of things.

1. THE SHADOW OF THE BLACK LEGEND

1. This "power of blackness" was broodingly and cosmologically explored from an existentialist perspective by Harry Levin in the late 1950s. Quoting Herman Melville, Levin defines it as "a power which 'derives its force from its appeals to that Calvinistic sense of Innate Depravity and Original Sin, from whose visitations, in some shape or other, no deeply thinking mind is always and wholly free'" (Levin, *The Power of Blackness*, 33). His book equates a sensitivity to this "blackness" with a "tragic

view of life" (172). Recent critiques of the black/white binary governing U.S. race relations and much scholarly work on ethnic and racial representations are too numerous to list. For a few examples, see the following handful of insightful essays in *The Latino/a Condition: A Critical Reader,* edited by Richard Delgado and Jean Stefancic: Angel R. Oquendo, "Re-imagining the Latino/a Race"; Juan F. Perea, "The Black/White Binary Paradigm of Race"; Richard Delgado, "The Black/White Binary, *How Does It Work?*"; Elizabeth Martínez, "Beyond Black/White: The Racisms of Our Time"; and Deborah A. Ramirez, "It's Not Just Black and White Anymore."

2. This phenomenon is similar to the strategic use of the "race card" in American politics, which all too often has the effect of naturalizing, rather than counteracting or subverting, various kinds of "branding" typologies. As Ann Seaton, assistant professor of English and associate editor of *Salmagundi,* has remarked, the seeming converse of "branding" the Other is the taxidermic performance of speaking in the place of the other or wearing the Other (conversation, Cambridge, Massachusetts, October 1995).

3. The term *leyenda negra* was coined by Spanish scholar Julián Juderías. His book *La leyenda negra* is a standard work on the subject. Subsequent studies suggest that Juderías's book was first published around 1914. See also Ricardo García Cárcel, *La leyenda negra,* and Miguel Molina Martinez, *La leyenda negra.*

4. Gracia, *Hispanic/Latino Identity,* 12.

5. See Teresa A. Goddu's "Introduction" to *Gothic America,* 1–12.

6. Brown, *Wieland,* 82; hereafter cited in the text.

7. See the chapters "Liberty and the Anglo-Saxons" and "Aryans Follow the Sun" in Reginald Horsman's *Race and Manifest Destiny,* 9–42.

8. See Bradstreet, "The Four Elements," 116.

9. Poe, "Appalachia," 327.

10. As quoted in James Chace and Caleb Carr, *America Invulnerable,* 29.

11. See Barbara Maria Stafford's discussion of the cabinet of curiosities in the chapter "Exhibitionism" of her *Artful Science,* 238–64.

12. Ronald Paulson, *Emblem and Expression,* 22–23.

13. Fliegelman, *Prodigals and Pilgrims,* 238.

14. Christophersen, *The Apparition in the Glass,* 25.

15. Ibid., 38.

16. Steven Watts, *The Romance of Real Life,* 86 and 81.

17. Ibid., 192.

18. Charles Brockden Brown, *Memoirs of Carwin the Biloquist,* in *Wieland and Memoirs of Carwin the Biloquist,* 311–14.

19. *Marranos* is the Spanish term for Jews who converted outwardly to Catholic Christianity but who secretly continued to practice their Jewish faith. For a discussion of eighteenth-century European anti-Semitism, particularly among British and French Enlightenment figures, see Richard H. Popkin, "Medicine, Racism, Anti-Semitism," 423–42.

20. David Lee Clark, *Charles Brockden Brown,* 170.

21. Stafford, *Artful Science,* 10.

22. The role that Carwin plays in the dark chamber of Clara's closet (a metaphor for her mind terrorized and turned around by images suggested to her by the very sound of the voices he ventriloquizes) is remindful of that of the historical figure of the Jesuit priest Athanasius Kircher who, steeped in natural magic or alchemy, was one of the chief innovators of the magic lantern. He was fascinated by the possibilities and effects of projection.

23. It is in Avignon that Major Stuart is stabbed and killed in cold blood by a "swarthy and malignant figure" (275). *Swarthy* and *malignant* are adjectives remindful of those used to describe Carwin, as well as of those employed in the eighteenth century to mark Jews. Just as readers of *Wieland* probably would have known of the recent annexation by the French state of the infamously popish Avignon, they may also have connected, in the manner of conspiracy theorists, the "swarthy" figures from the notoriously large and thriving Jewish community in Avignon (comparable only to Bordeaux) to those by which they "shadowed" Spain as "Oriental."

24. Seelye, "Charles Brockden Brown and Early American Fiction," 183.

25. Steven Watts, *The Romance of Real Life,* 29.

26. Ibid., 176.

27. Ibid., 180.

28. Dayan, "Amorous Bondage: Poe, Ladies, and Slaves," 240. See also her *Fables of the Mind.*

29. Nelson, *The Word in Black and White,* 90, 92, 107.

30. J. Gerald Kennedy and Liliane Wiessberg, "Introduction," in *Romancing the Shadow,* xvii.

31. J. Gerald Kennedy, "'Trust No Man': Poe, Douglass, and the Culture of Slavery," in *Romancing the Shadow,* 234.

32. John Carlos Rowe, "Edgar Allan Poe's Imperial Fantasy and the American Frontier," in *Romancing the Shadow,* 85.

33. Ibid., 100.

34. Leland S. Person, "Poe's Philosophy of Amalgamation: Reading Racism in the Tales," *Romancing the Shadow,* 207.

35. Ibid., 212.

36. Ibid., 220.

37. Edgar Allan Poe, "William Wilson," 627; hereafter cited as "Wilson" in parentheses in the text.

38. Edgar Allan Poe, "The Pit and the Pendulum," 246; hereafter cited as "Pit" in parentheses in the text.

39. Barthes, *The Rustle of Language,* 15–16.

40. Edgar Allan Poe, "Twice-Told Tales," 446; my emphasis.

41. Sigmund Freud, *The Ego and the Id,* 19. Freud uses the analogy of a man on horseback to describe the relation of the ego to the id.

42. Ibid.

43. Basically, the Black Legend is an image, or rather innumerable images, of Spain

and Spaniards as tyrannical, cruel, backward, and intolerant that began circulating in the sixteenth century and that for centuries was especially embellished by its Protestant rivals.

44. Freud, *The Ego and the Id*, 49.

45. Poe, "The Philosophy of Composition," 454.

46. Poe, "The Imp of the Perverse," 281–82; hereafter cited as "Imp" in parentheses in the text.

47. What the narrator wore to the costume ball of the Duke Di Broglio is never described, only that William Wilson the antagonist was wearing a costume "altogether similar" to that of the narrator or William Wilson the protagonist.

48. Poe, "The Philosophy of Composition," 454.

49. Poe, "The Facts in the Case of M. Valdemar," 96; hereafter cited as "Valdemar" in parentheses in the text.

50. Here I borrow Roland Barthes's translated phrase "image-repertoire" to mean, in cultural terms (rather than in the individual terms in which Barthes speaks when addressing images central to his consciousness), the bank, array, or stock of images, associations, and references that circulate and repeat in a given culture and that are available to be called upon or drawn from seemingly at whim, though actually as a matter of code, an internalization of a code through conditioning and an identification with the elements of that code. This concept can be found in several of his books, for instance, *Roland Barthes* (1977), *Image—Music—Text* (1977), *A Lover's Discourse* (1977), and *Camera Lucida* (1980).

51. Barthes, *The Pleasure of the Text*, 43.

52. Nelson, *The Word in Black and White*, 109. Subsequent references are given in the text.

53. Herman Melville, "Benito Cereno," 161; hereafter cited in parentheses in the text.

54. Despite Amasa Delano's Latinate last name (ending in "o"), he is never marked as anything but Yankee, white, and "American"; that is, for Melville's New England audience, as undifferentiated from the Anglo standard.

55. See Robert E. Burkholder, ed., *Critical Essays on Herman Melville's "Benito Cereno."*

56. Barthes, "Diderot, Brecht, Eisenstein," 71.

57. Hugh W. Hetherington, *Melville's Reviewers*, 250.

58. See Eric J. Sundquist's highly informative essay "*Benito Cereno* and New World Slavery," 93–122.

59. Barthes, "Diderot, Brecht, Eisenstein," 70.

60. Ibid., 73.

61. See Sundquist, "*Benito Cereno* and New World Slavery," 98.

62. Karcher, "Darkening Shadows of Doom in 'The Encantadas,' 'Benito Cereno,' and 'The Bell Tower,'" in *Shadow over the Promised Land*, 128.

63. Ibid., 129.

64. Anderson, *Imagined Communities*, 145.

65. Nelson, *The Word in Black and White*, 127.

66. Melville, *Moby Dick,* xv.

67. Ibid., 381; my emphasis.

2. IMPERIAL VISIONS

1. U.S. and British writers never tired of attempting to find reasons for the famous or infamous "Spanish temper." Pridefulness and a cruel streak are invariably cited as part of the "Spanish temper." The Spanish Inquisition and Spaniards' alleged attachment to their bloody religious imagery and to bullfights are treated as evidence and as expressions of this cruelty. Frequently, U.S. and British writers attempted to relate these supposed elements of the "Spanish temper" to the racial and cultural influence of the Arabs and the Moors. These writers, like some of the French writers before them, associate southern Spain (Andalusia) with blood, sensuality, and death. See British writer V. S. Pritchett, *The Spanish Temper* (1954).

2. David Mitchell, in his *Viajeros por España* (originally titled *Here in Spain* [1988]), claims that Spain became part of the Grand Tour in the eighteenth century in the wake of reforms made by the enlightened despot Charles III. (*Viajeros por España,* 25–26). Such may have been the case for British travelers, but not, I would argue, for U.S. ones. As Stanley Williams observes in *The Spanish Background of American Literature,* "for many Spain was rather formidable, a dark enigma . . . Spain was less desirable than England, France, or Italy" (159).

3. On Sicily, see, for example, Bayard Taylor, *The Lands of the Saracens; or, Pictures of Palestine, Asia Minor, Sicily, and Spain.* On Venice, see, for example, William Dean Howells, "The Armenians" and "The Ghetto and the Jews of Venice," in *Venetian Life,* 194–219.

4. The definitional foil for the "European," in nineteenth-century Anglo-American discourse, was often the "Indian." Imaged to embody the primitive or rude arts, barbarism or savagery, and the untrodden wilderness of the Americas, the figure of the Indian, if incarnating power in nineteenth-century visual representation, signified an immanent mystical or spiritual force. The lone Indian in painted frontier landscapes functioned as a quasi-physical reminder or marker of the divine spirit for the viewer's romantic contemplation. For Anglo-American writers such as James Fenimore Cooper and painters such as Thomas Cole and Thomas Moran, the "noble red man" served as a personification of faculties and ideals valued throughout the Romantic period—a poetic sensibility, an intuitive capacity, and a closeness to Nature, if not pristine Nature itself. However, with few exceptions, at least until quite recently, the religious or spiritual traditions of Native Americans were constructed, in Anglo-American discourse, as both pagan and primitive and therefore without legitimate authorization. Anglo-American deauthorization of Native American spiritual traditions supplied a convenient pretext for the expropriation of their sacred lands. See, for example, paintings such as George Catlin's *Buffalo Dance,* Charles Deas's *The Death Struggle* (1845), and Thomas Moran's *The Spirit of the Indian* (1869).

5. See "General Jackson and Mister Adams, 1816–1823" and "Manifest Destiny as National Security," in James Chace and Caleb Carr, *America Invulnerable,* 41-108.

6. Drawings such as Granville Perkins's *The Bivouac of De Soto's Expedition in Florida* and W. L. Shepard's *Burial of De Soto,* and paintings such as John Vanderlyn's *The Return of Columbus* (1842), William Merritt Chase's *Christopher Columbus before the Spanish Council at Salamanca* (late 1870s), and William Keith's *Discovery of San Francisco Bay* (1896), all presented the Spaniard to the Anglo-American public as white and as a conqueror or knightly explorer/adventurer. For a detailed analysis of Vanderlyn's *The Landing of Columbus* (1847) and associated images such as William H. Powell's *Discovery of the Missisipi by De Soto* (1847–55), see Vivien Green Fryd's book on the United States capitol and its artworks, *Art and Empire,* 54–59.

7. I have used the terms "Catholic/Christian" together to suggest that although nineteenth-century Anglo-American discourse disparaged Spaniards as Catholics and false Christians, in certain instances, Spain was a figure for pious identification and self-congratulatory appropriation, as, for example, with the representation of the Spaniards' professed mission to Christianize the Native Americans. This identificatory representation of Spain was not operative among the Puritans. The Puritans usually viewed the Catholicism of the Spaniards as just as much of a threat as the perceived paganism of the Native Americans. Both popery and paganism were considered works of Satan.

8. For an extended discussion of the U.S. quest to find a usable past out of which to create the legends/myths that would reflect growing nationalistic pride and sense of manifest destiny, see, for example, "Search for Symbols," in Daniel J. Boorstin, *The Americans.* Boorstin's book is itself an example of what he describes. Boorstin celebrates the U.S. search for symbols of national purpose or destiny; he seems quite unconcerned with the more problematic, if not harmful, aspects of this quest. Given that he does not mention Anglo-Americans' use of the figure of the *Spanish* conquistador, he does not speculate on the meanings or consequences of their use of that figure, even though he does quote, with great gusto, the well-known U.S. historian George Bancroft: "Annihilate the past of any one leading nation of the world, and our destiny would have been changed. Italy and Spain, in the persons of COLUMBUS and ISABELLA, joined together for the great discovery that opened America to emigration and commerce" (371).

9. Irving, *History of the Life and Voyages of Christopher Columbus,* 441. Charles Gibson writes: "Las Casas's works, convincingly authenticated by the Spanish citizenship and episcopal rank of their author, and seized upon by the enemies of Spain, were reprinted in many translations. The result was the Black Legend of condemnation of Spain. The process began in the sixteenth century, but it gained cumulative power later, when Spanish decline could be more clearly seen" (Gibson, *Spain in America,* 43). Although Gibson overstates the singular responsibility of las Casas's writings for the Black Legend, his observation is valuable inasmuch as it points to the emergence of numerous translations, "enriched" with "eloquent titles and horrifying illustrations," of las Casas's works and to the impact that these translations had on many writers' and historians' assessments of Spanish empire in the Americas.

10. Longfellow, "The Theologian's Tale: Torquemada," in *Selected Poems,* 152.

11. Ibid., 158.

12. See Norman P. Tucker, *Americans in Spain: Patriots, Expatriates, and Early American Hispanists 1780–1850.*

13. Ibid., 16.

14. Lummis, *The Land of Poco Tiempo,* 3.

15. Rana Kabbani makes this argument about European representations of Islam: "The Islamic world was seen as Anti-Europe, and was held in suspicion as such. Christian Europe had entered a confrontation with the Islamic Orient that was cultural, religious, political and military, one that would decide from then on the very nature of the discourse between West and East. Post-Crusader Europe would never wholly emerge from the antagonism its 'Holy Wars' had plunged it into. Its old desire to assert itself against its Islamic rival converted easily into a determination to dominate; this would become the psychological motivations of imperialists from Napoleon onwards" (*Europe's Myths of the Orient,* 5).

16. Harrison, *Spain in Profile,* 194; my emphasis.

17. Dumas, *Adventures in Spain,* 89.

18. See Philippe Jullian, *The Orientalists,* 115.

19. Ibid., 116.

20. Downes, *Spanish Ways and By-Ways,* 34.

21. Howells, *Familiar Spanish Travels,* 128, 181, 263–64.

22. For further information on U.S. artists in Paris, see Michael Andrew Marlais, "Americans and Paris," in *Americans and Paris,* 7–36.

23. See Donald A. Rosenthal, *Orientalism: The Near East in French Painting, 1800–1880,* 138. Richard Ford, the British traveler and amateur, was equally intrigued by Moorish Spain. He spent much time in Seville and Granada, made sketches of what he saw, wrote a *Hand-Book for Travellers in Spain* (1845), and was a friend of several U.S. Hispanophiles who could also be called Orientalists, such as Washington Irving. See Brinsley Ford, *Richard Ford in Spain,* 13, 23.

24. Even a scholarly study such as Allen Josephs's *White Wall of Spain* plays into the stereotypes with chapter titles such as "Culture of Death," "Dancer of Gades," and "Matador" at the same time that it purports to engage critically with them. Josephs's description of the "Hispanophile Imperative," which he obviously shares with Richard Ford, Washington Irving, and others, illustrates the ongoing appeal of Orientalism as a "style of thought" for U.S. and British travelers, scholars included: "The Hispanophile Imperative is the utter inability to avoid writing books about Spain. It flourished in Roman times, during the Romantic period, and again in the twentieth century. What is worst about the Hispanophile Imperative is that it has produced a steady stream of terrible books about Spain—usually the worse the book the more it propagates the superficiality of the stereotype. What is best about it are the superb books that explain Spain's radically different culture, heritage, and history to unenlightened Westerners. The Hispanophile Imperative exists because over the centuries Spain, and particularly Andalucía, has fascinated the travellers who ventured there . . . Andalucía, while not African, is nevertheless the most Oriental land in western Europe" (Josephs, *White Wall of Spain,* 6–8).

25. Downes, *Spanish Ways and By-Ways,* 30.

26. Irving, *The Alhambra,* 14–15.

27. An examination of Washington Irving's letters reveals a network of correspondents that would suggest that Irving functioned as a major contact point between many of the Anglo-Americans who were intrigued enough by Spaniards and/or Native Americans to depict them in their writings: James Fenimore Cooper, Henry R. Schoolcraft, Nathaniel Hawthorne, George Bancroft, Bayard Taylor, Oliver Wendell Holmes, Richard Henry Dana, and George Ticknor. See Washington Irving, *Letters,* vols. 2 and 4.

28. Taylor, "To Washington Irving," in *Lands of the Saracens.*

29. Wharton, *A Backward Glance,* 31.

30. Irving, *The Alhambra,* 80.

31. Emanuel Leutze was born in Germany and lived there for the first nine years of his life. After immigrating to Philadelphia with his parents, he spent many years outside of the United States. Although foreign-born and despite his frequent absence from the United States, Leutze became a favorite portrait and history painter for collectors of the Anglo-American establishment. He was commissioned numerous times by Congress to produce grand-scale history pictures for the Capitol in Washington, DC. One of the commissions resulted in the painting *The Discovery of the Mississippi by De Soto,* now in the rotunda of the Capitol. Other works reimagining Spanish history such as *The Return of Columbus in Chains to Cadiz* and *King Ferdinand Removing the Chains from Columbus* were bought by American collectors in Philadelphia and Connecticut, respectively. See Raymond Louis Stehle, *Emanuel Leutze: 1816–1868,* 309. Examining Randolph Rogers's reliefs, on the Capitol's rotunda doors, of *The Landing of Columbus* and other related scenes, John Vanderlyn's painting of Columbus landing in the New World, and the German-trained Leutze's painting *Westward the Course of Empire Takes Its Way (Westward Ho!),* Vivien Green Fryd argues in *Art and Empire* that time and time again these images and others like them marginalize or push to the literal frames the Native Americans and also represent these marginalized Native Americans as "a threat that . . . must be vanquished" and as "abject creature[s] who will vanish" (161). I agree with her argument, but I would add that in some of these images there are already hints that Spaniards are being figured in relation to the same teleological narrative of threat to be eradicated and, moreover, ontologically doomed subject. This is significant as images of Spanish discoverers and conquerors are often assumed to be triumphant and expressive of a much less equivocal identification of the Anglo viewer with the "white" Spanish subject. I am underscoring the presence of signs that split triumph into triumph and doom, with the latter actually subverting the former.

32. Irving, *The Alhambra,* 130.

33. On the Columbus story, see, for example, Kirkpatrick Sale, *The Conquest of Paradise: Christopher Columbus and the Columbian Legacy,* and Lyle N. McAlister, *Spain and Portugal in the New World, 1492–1700.*

34. See Robert Selph Henry, *The Story of the Mexican War,* and William H. Truettner, "Repainting the Past," 59–63.

35. Hawthorne and Holmes had limited, if any, "experience" with the borderlands, Latin America, or Spain. Whatever they purported to know about Spaniards on the borders, in Latin America, or in Spain probably came from books they read and perhaps images they saw. An examination of the letters of Hawthorne, Simms, and Holmes reveals that all three writers had read the works of Washington Irving, whose representations of Spain were influenced by those produced by the French and the British. These writers knew each other and read each other's work. Hawthorne and Holmes belonged to the Saturday Club in Boston and saw each other regularly there. See Oliver Wendell Holmes, *Life and Letters of Oliver Wendell Holmes,* vol. 1, 244–45. Hawthorne and Irving corresponded, as did Hawthorne and Holmes. See Hawthorne, *The Letters, 1843–1853,* vol. 2, 500. William Gilmore Simms, who had more direct access to the Spanish–Native American legacy in Florida and South Carolina, was a friend of Washington Irving and read Irving's works. A painting titled *Washington Irving and His Literary Friends at Sunnyside* shows Simms seated in the group to the left of Irving, who is the central figure. See Alexander S. Salley, "Biographical Sketch," in Simms, *The Letters of William Gilmore Simms,* vol. 1 (1830–44), cxvi.

36. Hawthorne, *The Scarlet Letter;* hereafter cited in parentheses in the text.

37. Holmes, *Elsie Venner: A Romance of Destiny;* hereafter cited in parentheses in the text. I am indebted to Debbie Lopez for calling my attention to this novel.

38. See Richard Volney Chase, *The American Novel and Its Tradition.* Other critics who have claimed or assumed that the romance is a distinctively "American" literary tradition include Perry Miller, "The Romance and the Novel," in *Nature's Nation,* 241–78, and Joel Porte, *The Romance in America,* ix.

39. Simms, *The Yemassee: A Romance of Carolina,* xxix; hereafter cited in parentheses in the text.

40. Hugh admonishes his brother: "will you never be a freeman, Walter—will you always be a water-carrier for a master? Why do you seek and serve this swaggerer [Gabriel Harrison], as if you had lost every jot of manly independence?" (140).

41. Reginald Horsman, *Race and Manifest Destiny,* 167.

42. Holmes probably refers to the theories of Louis Agassiz, the Swiss-born naturalist who came to the United States in 1846. During Agassiz's tenure at Harvard, he was one of the most respected and widely read proponents of the theory of polygenesis. Horsman explains: "By the 1850s, while still arguing for man's spiritual and moral unity under God, Agassiz maintained that there were essentially different human races. Genesis, he argued, merely described the origin of one race; it gave an account of the 'branches of the white race'" (*Race and Manifest Destiny,* 132). Agassiz argued that empirical proof could be found for the following theories: (1) that not all races were created at the same time; (2) that there were inferior and superior races; and (3) that the "inferior races" might not be capable of improvement or civilization. Many Anglo-Americans seized upon Agassiz's ideas and similar ideas held by other naturalists because they served to give "scientific" legitimization to their romantic racial nationalism.

43. Holmes, *Our Hundred Days in Europe,* 33–4.

44. For comparative purposes, see two other novels by William Gilmore Simms: *Count Julian,* about Moors in medieval Spain, and *The Cassique of Kiawah,* in which the heroine is descended from Moors and Spaniards.

45. Bercovitch, "The Return of Hester Prynne," in *The Rites of Assent,* 194.

46. Ibid., 195.

47. Irving, *Astoria,* 199.

48. A fandango is both a Spanish courtship dance and a type of Spanish folk song. The dance was probably of Moorish origin and was popular in Europe in the eighteenth century. It still exists in the twentieth century as a folk dance in Spain, Portugal, southern France, and Latin America. It is danced to the rhythm, which begins slowly and gradually picks up speed, of castanets, hand clapping, finger snapping, and foot stamping. As it is a courtship dance, it is customarily danced by a man and a woman and is supposed to be an expression of passion. Two men sometimes dance together, however, in a contest of skill. There is reason to question whether all the songs referred to as fandangos in the Spanish Peninsula were or are of Moorish origin. According to Andrés Salom, there are many folkloric songs under that rubric that sound different from those fandango songs, from Andalusia or from the border shared by Castile and the kingdom of Granada, with resonances derived from centuries of contact with the Muslims (*Didáctica del cante jondo,* 62).

49. The "saraband" comes from *sarabande,* a sixteenth-century Spanish court dance of unclear origin, probably Arabic-Moorish, and generally distinguished as wild and licentious in character.

50. James D. Hart, *The Oxford Companion to American Literature,* 339.

51. See Adams, *"Imperialism" and "The Tracks of Our Forefathers": A Paper Read by Charles Francis Adams before the Lexington, Massachusetts Historical Society, Tuesday, December 20, 1898.*

52. Berlant, "The Nationalist Preface," in *The Anatomy of National Fantasy,* 187–88.

53. See Patricia Hills, "Sargent's *El Jaleo,* Bizet's *Carmen,* and the Lure of Spain," 10–11, 52; Charles Merrill Mount, *John Singer Sargent: A Biography;* Stanley Olson, *John Singer Sargent: His Portrait;* and Mary Crawford Volk, "Sargent, Spain, and *El Jaleo,*" in *John Singer Sargent's El Jaleo,* 21–109.

54. Trevor J. Fairbrother, *John Singer Sargent and America,* 51–58; subsequent references are given in the text.

55. Henry James, *The Painter's Eye,* 220–21.

56. Said, *Orientalism,* 103. As Joseph A. Boone has discussed in his excellent article on Orientalism and homoerotic representation, Said never discusses what he only indirectly names. Homoeroticism, gay discourse, and male homosexual practices become in Said's text "queerness," "sexual experience unobtainable in Europe," and "a different type of sexuality." See Boone, "Vacation Cruises; or, The Homoerotics of Orientalism," 89–107.

57. The hand movements and the positioning of the fingers do not have any particular significance or symbolism in the context of flamenco dance, according to Ana María Tenorio Notario, coordinator of the documentation center of the Andalusian

Foundation of Flamenco (letter to author, October 21, 1992). An actual *bailadora* or dancer, Susana Fernández Cortés, declared that in flamenco a dancer's hand gestures have nothing to do with making horns or *los cuernos,* although dancers do in fact have their fingers in that position at some point in the course of their dance, during which they move their hand and fingers in many different ways (letter to author, November 2, 1992).

58. Mount, *John Singer Sargent,* 367.

59. Volk, "Sargent, Spain, and *El Jaleo,"* 190.

60. Andrés Salom argues that Spanish Gypsy *cantaores* (singers) gave the *jondura* (what for an American reader might translate as the kind of "depth" heard in the blues) to the *cante flamenco* and that this *jondura* was an expression of the marginalization, persecution, and sufferings of the Gypsies in their ghettoized condition in Andalusia (*Didáctica del cante jondo,* 30–31). García Lorca and Langston Hughes and certain musicians such as Paco de Lucia and Miles Davis have recognized the sociohistorical and expressive similarities between flamenco and jazz, between *cante jondo* and the blues, and have created works that synthesize the two traditions. On the controversies surrounding the origins of *cante jondo,* as well as for a subcultural interpretation of flamenco song style, see Timothy Mitchell, *Flamenco Deep Song.*

61. Volk, "Sargent, Spain, and *El Jaleo,"* 63–66.

62. ". . . je ne suis pas de ce pays de filous, de marchands d'oranges pourries" (Georges Bizet, *Carmen,* 77).

63. Prosper Mérimée, "Carmen," 36.

64. See, for example, Nigel Glendinning, "Goya and Arriaza's *Profecia del Pirineo,"* 363–66.

65. I am indebted to Margarita Estevez Abe for this idea concerning the appearance of the shadows on the right-hand side of the wall.

3. CONSOLIDATING ANGLO-AMERICAN IMPERIAL IDENTITY AROUND THE SPANISH-AMERICAN WAR

1. I have chosen to retain the nineteenth-century U.S. term "Spanish-American War" because this chapter is about Anglo-American constructions of the war, efforts to create and conscript popular patriotism despite dissensus, and the dissemination of an imperial identity. The war over control of Spain's colonies in the Caribbean should more accurately be termed the Spanish-Cuban-American War. As Doris Sommer has observed, a highly resistant ten-year Cuban slave rebellion had been waged against Spanish rule and had greatly weakened it before the United States declared war on Spain and claimed the credit for having liberated Cuba, Puerto Rico, and other Spanish colonies from the "Spanish tyrant." She likened the U.S. action and the subsequent erasure of the idea of the war as the "Spanish-Cuban-American War" from the historical record to the vainglory of the matador who, having waited for the banderilleros and picador to weaken the bull almost unto death, steps in for the final sword thrust and arrogates *el momento de la verdad* (the moment of truth) to himself (Doris Sommer, conversation, Harvard University, November 8, 1993). Philip S. Foner,

Samuel Flagg Bemis, and other historians have criticized the widespread use of the term "Spanish-American War" for similar reasons.

2. Merish, "Not 'Just a Cigar': Commodity Culture and the Construction of Imperial Manhood," 270–303; subsequent references are given in the text. See also Eve Kosofsky Sedgwick, "Introduction," in *Between Men: English Literature and Male Homosocial Desire*.

3. See Kaplan, "Black and Blue on San Juan Hill," 219–36.

4. Latimer, *Spain in the Nineteenth Century*, 2d ed.; hereafter cited in parentheses in the text.

5. Nixon, *With a Pessimist in Spain*, frontispiece; hereafter cited in parentheses in the text.

6. Goldman, "Patriotism," in *Anarchism and Other Essays*, 133–34.

7. The name was coined by John Hay, U.S. ambassador to Great Britain and in October 1898 U.S. secretary of state.

8. For a discussion of some of the activities of the anti-imperialists, see Nell Irvin Painter, *Standing at Armageddon: The United States, 1877–1919*, 154–58.

9. Banta, *Imaging American Women*, 553.

10. John Hay, *William McKinley's Memorial Address by John Hay, Delivered in the Capitol February 27, 1902, by Invitation of the Congress*.

11. Banta, *Imaging American Women*, 568–69.

12. Luis Fernández-Cifuentes suggested that Columbia's arm in Cox's study be compared to the arm (viewer's left) of Michelangelo's *David* (conversation, Harvard University, April 26, 1996). Such a comparison is an apt one, I think, because it underscores the extent to which the Cox study attempts to authorize iconographically Columbia's role within the rubric of a patriarchal patriotism. "David" is the youth who, according to biblical tradition, was called by God to defend the Israelite nation against Goliath and the other Philistines and to become King David, one of the ur-fathers of his people. If Michelangelo's *David* is a model for the pose of Columbia in Cox's study, then Columbia is like the chosen David doing battle against Goliath-like Spaniards or the Philistine Spanish Empire.

13. Frank Norris's father was a wealthy wholesale jeweler who sent his son to Paris to study painting and later to Harvard, hoping that there he would cultivate his aesthetic judgment and intellect.

14. James, *The Varieties of Religious Experience*. See especially the chapters titled "Saintliness," "The Value of Saintliness," and "Mysticism," 267, 346, 407.

15. William James was quoting the German writer Heine to equate journalists and politicians with the legalism presumed to characterize Jews. See James, *Essays, Comments, and Reviews*, 62.

16. William James, in Henry James, ed., *The Letters of William James*, 1:126, 2:86.

17. Ibid., 2:284.

18. William James, letter to François Pillon, Cambridge, Massachusetts, June 15, 1898, in ibid., 2:74.

19. I thank John Trumpbour for this observation.

20. See George Cotkin, "The Imperial Imperative," in *William James, Public Philosopher,* 127–30, for a discussion of the Mugwump anti-imperialists.

21. R. W. Stallman and E. R. Hagemann, eds., *The War Dispatches of Stephen Crane,* 110; hereafter cited in parentheses in the text.

22. Lawrence I. Berkove, "Introduction," in *Ambrose Bierce: Skepticism and Dissent, Selected Journalism from 1898–1901,* vi.

23. Ibid., vii.

24. Taffy or toffee is a chewy candy made by boiling and pulling sugar or molasses. The word *taffy* has been used colloquially to mean "flattery."

25. Frederic Remington, "Under Which King?" in *The Collected Writings of Frederic Remington,* 361.

26. Remington, "They Bore a Hand," in *Collected Writings,* 407.

27. Remington, "Horses of the Plains," in *Collected Writings,* 21.

28. Colton Reed to Frederic Remington, New York City, May 29, 1909, *Remington Papers,* microfiche, roll NOR. 1, frames unnumbered. At the Remington Art Memorial collection, this particular letter can be identified as FRAM 71.823.89.

29. Draper, *The Rescue of Cuba,* 81. Draper was president of the University of Illinois in 1899. His manifesto/essay is a historical description of the significance of the Spanish-American War for the "progress of the world towards universal liberty" and for the U.S. role in world affairs.

30. Ibid., 16–17.

31. Ibid., 26–27.

32. Adams, "Address by the President," 68.

33. Nell Irvin Painter, in her book *Standing at Armageddon,* describes the situation in Cuba prior to the Spanish-American War: "Between 1868 and 1878 Cubans had challenged Spanish control, waging a guerrilla war and emancipating slaves. As a result of the Ten Years' War, slavery was abolished permanently and American investors bought many sugar plantations from planters bankrupted by the war" (143). When a renewed war for Cuban independence broke out in 1895, "the rebellion entailed losses for Americans as well as Cubans and Spaniards" (ibid.). Painter adds that, as the war dragged on, public opinion, goaded by the yellow press, increasingly favored American intervention to "stop the bloodshed and protect American investments" (144).

34. Adams, "Address by the President," 71–72.

35. Moses, "The Recent War with Spain from an Historical Point of View," 5–7; hereafter cited in parentheses in the text.

36. Lodge, *The War with Spain,* 1.

37. See the phrases "the expulsion of the Moriscos" (256), and the "expulsion of the Jews" (278, 280) in Prescott's *History of the Reign of Ferdinand and Isabella the Catholic;* "Jews . . . ordered to be expelled" (245) and "to convert or expel the Moors" (246) in Dunham's *History of Spain and Portugal,* vol. 2; "expelling the Moors" (166) and "the expulsion of the Jews" (236) in Abbott's *The Romance of Spanish History;* "the expulsion of the Jews" (xxi, 313) in Harrison's *Spain;* and "expelling the Moors from

the land" (99) and "their [the Jews'] final expulsion, in 1492" (290) in Watts's *The Christian Recovery of Spain.*

38. Latimer, *Spain in the Nineteenth Century,* iii; my emphasis.

39. It is possible, of course, that the occurrence of the Greco-Turkish War may have provided an additional "motive" for comparing and even conflating Spaniards with Turks. See Marble, "Gineral Fitzhugh Lee," in *Spanish-American War Songs: A Complete Collection of Newspaper Verse during the Recent War with Spain,* 628, and Bruce, "Letter to the Editor of *The News and Observer*" (Raleigh, North Carolina [May 22, 1898]), quoted in Willard B. Gatewood Jr., *"Smoked Yankees" and the Struggle for Empire: Letters from Negro Soldiers, 1898–1902,* 106. Bruce, an instructor at Shaw University in Raleigh, North Carolina, wrote to the *News and Observer* requesting the recognition of "Negro" patriotism.

40. "Preface," *Cartoons of the Spanish-American War by Bart with Dates of Important Events from "The Minneapolis Journal."*

41. Sidney A. Witherbee, *Spanish-American War Songs,* 27.

42. Banta, *Imaging American Women,* 116.

43. Robert Tomes, *The Bazar Book of Decorum: The Care of the Person, Manners, Etiquette, and Ceremonials,* 25, quoted in ibid.

44. Banta, *Imaging American Women,* 123.

45. Witherbee, *Spanish-American War Songs,* 179; my emphasis.

46. The record of this commemorative medal is Medals, No. QK 331 at the Mariners' Museum, 100 Museum Drive, Newport News, VA 23606-3798. The image of Uncle Sam spanking the Spaniard is on the obverse of the medal and the inscription is on the reverse. This item was found with the gracious assistance of Lois Oglesby.

47. Banta, *Imaging American Women,* 557.

48. The French had adopted the Phrygian cap as a symbol of liberty during the First Republic.

4. SACRED BULLS OF MODERNISM

1. Zimmerman, *Spain and Her People,* 14–15, 297.

2. See Lily Litvak, *A Dream of Arcadia: Anti-Industrialism in Spanish Literature.*

3. Shaw, *The Generation of 1898 in Spain.*

4. See Ángel Capellan, *Hemingway and the Hispanic World.*

5. Castillo-Puche, *Hemingway in Spain: A Personal Reminiscence of Hemingway's Years in Spain.*

6. See Guttmann, *The Wound in the Heart: America and the Spanish Civil War;* Muste, *Say That We Saw Spain Die: Literary Consequences of the Spanish Civil War.*

7. Dos Passos, *Rosinante to the Road Again,* 174.

8. Stevens, "The Idea of Order at Key West," in *The Collected Poems of Wallace Stevens,* 130.

9. Archibald MacLeish, *Conquistador,* in *Collected Poems, 1917–1982* book 15, verses 44–45, 261.

10. Crane, "Ave Maria," stanza 2, verses 1 and 5, of *The Bridge,* in *The Complete Poems and Selected Letters and Prose of Hart Crane,* 48; MacLeish, *Conquistador,* book 1, verses 268 and 271, 180.

11. Freud, *Totem and Taboo,* 146–50.

12. Ibid., 146.

13. Ibid., 153.

14. Wright, *Pagan Spain,* 136; hereafter cited in parentheses in the text.

15. Stein, *Paris France,* 11, 2; hereafter cited in parentheses in the text. And Stein, "What Are Masterpieces?" 156.

16. Stein, "Picasso," in *Picasso: The Complete Writings,* 53; hereafter cited as "Picasso" in parentheses in the text.

17. West, *The Day of the Locust,* in *West: Novels and Other Writings,* 257.

18. Gertrude Stein, *The Autobiography of Alice B. Toklas,* 12; hereafter cited as *Autobiography* in parentheses in the text.

19. Stein, *The Geographical History of America,* 54; hereafter cited as *Geographical History* in parentheses in the text.

20. For a book dedicated solely to Hemingway and the fiestas of San Fermín, see José María Iribarren, *Hemingway y los Sonfermines.*

21. For a classic example of the interest in Hemingway, bullfighting, and his mystical relationship to the corrida or bullfight, see Kenneth Kinnamon, "Hemingway, the Corrida, and Spain" *Texas Studies in Literature and Language 1* (spring 1959): 44–54, reprinted in *Ernest Hemingway's "The Sun Also Rises": A Casebook,* ed. Linda Wagner-Martin.

22. Ernest Hemingway, "A Clean Well-Lighted Place," in *The Snows of Kilimanjaro and Other Stories,* 32–33.

23. Hemingway, *For Whom the Bell Tolls,* 369–70; my emphasis; hereafter cited in parentheses in the text.

24. Ernest Hemingway, *The Sun Also Rises,* 10; hereafter cited in parentheses in the text.

25. Williams, *The Spanish Background of American Literature,* vol. 2, 282.

26. *Anis* is a liqueur made from the berries of the blackthorn tree. Hemingway imagined *anis "del toro."* No such *anis* has ever existed in Spain. Traditionally, the three available *anises* have been *anis Las Cadenas, anis de Chinchon,* and *anis El Mono. "Anis del toro"* or "anise of the bull" works well to enhance the myth Hemingway was elaborating of imbibing and consuming the essence of the Spanish soil.

27. Hemingway, *A Moveable Feast,* 4–5.

28. For a compatible historical-materialist reading of *The Sun Also Rises* as both product and reflection of its socioeconomic environment separating "work from culture" (49) and "pass[ing] off the profane as sacred" (137) according to the logic of the commodity fetish, see Marc D. Baldwin, *Reading "The Sun Also Rises": Hemingway's Political Unconscious.*

29. Barthes, "Wine and Milk," in *Mythologies,* 58.

30. Barthes, "Steak and Chips," in *Mythologies,* 62.

31. Hemingway, "Under the Ridge," in *The Fifth Column and Four Stories of the Spanish Civil War,* 150.

32. Jordan thinks to himself, "[A] stone is a stein is a rock is a boulder is a pebble" (289).

33. Kenneth S. Lynn, *Hemingway,* 415.

34. Ibid., 511.

35. Fabre, *The Unfinished Quest of Richard Wright,* 407–16.

36. Pratt, *Imperial Eyes,* 223.

37. Faith Berry, introduction to *Pagan Spain,* xii; hereafter cited in parentheses in the text.

38. See Joan Dayan, "Gothic Americas," in *Haiti, History, and the Gods,* 187–267.

39. *Elegies to the Spanish Republic* feature looming, black phallic forms on stark white backgrounds. Critics have interpreted these paintings by pointing to Motherwell's revulsion at the events of the Spanish civil war and his desire to express his feelings of hatred and impotence against the Franco regime. I claim that this series as well as other paintings by Motherwell such as *Little Spanish Prison* (1941) and *Spanish Prison* (1943–44) of dark prison cells rendered in a more or less abstract manner have the effect of associating Spain in general, not just the Nationalist Party or Franco's policies, with despair, horror, and death.

40. Fabre, *The Unfinished Quest of Richard Wright,* 414–15.

41. About television in the 1950s, Stephen J. Whitfield writes that it was "an inescapable medium that quickly rivaled the power of movies, radio, and mass-circulation magazines to transmit ideas and images. In 1950, 3.1 million television sets could be found in American homes. By 1955, the figure was already up to 32 million, and ten thousand Americans a day were buying their first TV sets" (*The Culture of the Cold War,* 153).

42. Bercovitch, *The Puritan Origins of the American Self.*

43. This black bull billboard referred to as "el Toro Negro" has become a symbol of Spain, so much so that a new law banning the use of billboards on the highway (because they might fatally distract drivers from the road) has overlooked the Toro Negro, which still stands on hillsides along many a road. Ironically, producers of brandy and sherry such as Domecq, Williams and Hurt, Gonzalez Byass, John Harvey, and Osborne are of British descent. These families came to the peninsula at the beginning of the nineteenth century when the Duke of Wellington ordered an expedition to fight Napoleon, who invaded Spain in 1808.

5. (POST)MODERN DENATURALIZATIONS OF NATIONALITY

1. I am referring to writers such as Cotton Mather, Joel Barlow, Charles Brockden Brown, Washington Irving, Nathaniel Hawthorne, Ernest Hemingway, Richard Wright, and numerous others whom I have examined intensively or mentioned in passing. In the nineteenth century, many Anglo-American painters depicted Spain and Spaniards in an essentializing manner, among them Walter Gay, William Dannat, Mary Cassatt, Frederick Arthur Bridgman, and John Singer Sargent. U.S. films that reinforce the trope of Spain's difference from the rest of Europe and from the United

States as a medieval and/or an Oriental/non-Western country have been numerous. They have contributed to more general but related associations of Spain with "backwardness" or "the past" and with "the irrational" or with "the passions," especially tormented romantic love and the desire for revenge. Examples are *The Siren of Seville* (1924), *Blood and Sand* with Rudolph Valentino (1922) and with Tyrone Power (1941), *El Cid* (1961), and *Man of la Mancha* (1972). Contemporary U.S. photographers Robert Vavra (whose photographs illustrated James Michener's best-selling book *Iberia* as well as another book, *The Sevilla of Carmen,* with comments by Michener) and Loomis Dean (whose work illustrated the book *Hemingway's Spain*) have focused on bullfights, festivals, Holy Week processions, Gypsy caravans, dancers, and peasants to create images that are supposed to serve as evidence of the "typically Spanish," as signifiers of "Spanishness."

2. See Brennan, "The Geography of Enunciation: Hysterical Pastiche in Kathy Acker's Fiction," 243–69.

3. *Random House College Dictionary* (New York: Random House, 1973), 662.

4. The philosopher, essayist, novelist, poet, and playwright Miguel de Unamuno (1864–1936) is probably most famous for the following works: *En torno al casticismo* (1902), *Vida de Don Quijote y Sancho* (1905), *Del sentimiento trágico de la vida en los hombres y en los pueblos* (1913), and *La agonía del cristianismo* (1925). His work has been interpreted both as an expression of and an attempt to define the supposed mysticism of the "Spanish temper," as well as the cultural malaise of Spain. Valle-Inclán (1866–1936) was a major novelist and playwright who in the 1920s and 1930s wrote works of *esperpento* or the grotesque, one of the main techniques of which was the creation of distorted and incongruous images and characters. Many of his novels functioned as critiques of military brutality and governmental corruption in Spain during the nineteenth century.

5. The philosopher and essayist José Ortega y Gasset (1883–1955) was famous for criticizing his own country for its supposed absence of intellectual life and for insisting on its need to overcome its isolation and "Europeanize" its art, philosophy, and culture. He studied philosophy in Germany for many years, where he became further entrenched in Neo-Kantianism, with which he appraised "modern art," claiming that irony is the modern artist's most important tool. Pío Baroja (1872–1956), a major novelist from San Sebastian (in the north of Spain), was prejudiced against Castilian Spain and used mostly French models in his early writing. He subscribed to racial theories that classified the Germans and the English as superior to the Jews and the "Mediterranean races." He considered himself to be a member of the superior races. He sympathized with social outcasts, and particularly with vagrants and tramps, however, and his work demonstrates a major concern with social and moral injustice.

6. Each chapter of *Locos* is a tale that could stand on its own.

7. Felipe Alfau, *Locos: A Comedy of Gestures,* 15; hereafter cited in parentheses in the text.

8. Interestingly, in Spanish the word *chine* means a silk textile of many colors. *Lato* is a synonym for "general" or "wide." The name "Chinelato" suggests both a commodity (silk) for which Europeans traveled to and colonized the East and an

unspecific, unbounded identity, particularly with regard to the category of "race." Racial typing is suggested on two counts by the word *Chinelato* inasmuch as the first half of it refers to a silk of many "colors" and the whole of it is homologous to the term *mulato*.

9. Ballou, *Spanish Prelude*, 9, 12; hereafter cited in parentheses in the text.

10. Fernando Colomo, *Skyline*, 16 mm, La Salamandra production company, Spain, 1983.

11. Aparicio and Chávez-Silverman, eds., *Tropicalizations: Transcultural Representations of Latinidad*, 1.

12. It seems more than coincidental that Colomo made his movie featuring converted lofts a year after Sharon Zukin's book *Loft Living: Culture and Capital in Urban Change* (1982) was published.

13. Melville, *Moby Dick*, 379.

14. Ibid., xv.

15. Michel Foucault, "Preface," in *The Order of Things: An Archaeology of the Human Sciences*, xvii–xviii.

16. West, "The Impostor," 411–12.

17. Alfau, *Chromos*, 141; hereafter cited in parentheses in the text.

18. See Althusser, "Ideology and Ideological State Apparatuses," 36 and 1–60.

19. In *A Thousand Plateaus: Capitalism and Schizophrenia*, Gilles Deleuze and Félix Guattari make a fundamental distinction between "the war machine" and "the state": "it [the war machine] seems to be irreducible to the State apparatus, to be outside its sovereignty and prior to its law: it comes from elsewhere" (352). See "Treatise on Nomadology—The War Machine," in *A Thousand Plateaus*, 351–423. They celebrate the war machine's nomadic tribal irruptions, subversions, intensities, metamorphoses when not allied or co-opted by "the State apparatus." They deplore it when it is. As for a definition of "the war machine," their most direct description of it is, following Thomas Hobbes's declaration, "the State was against war, so war is against the State" (357), "the mode of a social state that wards off and prevents the State" (ibid.).

20. Acker, *Don Quixote*, 125, 201; hereafter cited in parentheses in the text.

21. Acker, "A Few Notes on Two of My Books," 35.

22. See Bhabha, "Signs Taken for Wonders," in *The Location of Culture*, 114–15.

23. Stavans, "Anonymity: An Interview with Felipe Alfau," 148.

24. The idea of "pre-postcoloniality" was suggested to me in a discussion about this film with Luis Fernández-Cifuentes, Harvard University, April 26, 1996.

25. Dos Passos, *Rosinante to the Road Again*, 86–87.

6. AFTERLIVES OF EMPIRE

1. Alfau, *Chromos*, 7; Acker, *Don Quixote*, 9.

2. Here please excuse the awkwardness of language and classificatory terminology. "Non-Anglo" seems like a negative identity, a kind of nonbeing. This is not how I mean it. I say "non-Anglo" U.S. writers and artists as a reminder that Anglo and U.S. cannot be synonymous, however much Anglo-American ideology may claim and exercise cultural hegemony.

3. Muñoz, *Disidentifications: Queers of Color and the Performance of Politics.*

4. Cenen and Smith, "The Blood—Yes, the Blood: A Conversation," 43.

5. Ibid., 44.

6. Zook, "Light Skinned-ded Naps," 92.

7. Ibid.

8. Guillermo Gómez-Peña, "Documented/Undocumented," 133.

9. Candelaria, *Memories of the Alhambra,* 163.

10. Monteflores, *Cantando Bajito/Singing Softly,* 76.

11. Cofer, *Silent Dancing: A Partial Remembrance of a Puerto Rican Childhood,* 148.

12. Moschkovich, "—But I Know You, American Woman," 81.

13. Ibid., 79.

14. Gómez-Peña, "Documented/Undocumented," 132.

15. Rodolfo Acuña, *Occupied America: A History of Chicanos,* 43.

16. Noam Chomsky, "Introduction: World Orders, Old and New," 4.

17. Cruz, "Writing Migrations," in *Panoramas,* 127.

18. Manrique, *My Night with/Mi noche con Federico García Lorca,* 80–83.

19. Campo, *Diva,* 83.

20. Francisco X. Alarcón, *Del otro lado de la noche/From the Other Side of Night: New and Selected Poems,* 39.

21. Anzaldúa, *Borderlands/La Frontera: The New Mestiza,* 176–81.

22. Cruz, *Panoramas,* 47–58.

23. Arroyo, *Pale Ramón: Poems,* 14.

24. Gruesz, *Ambassadors of Culture: The Transamerican Origins of Latino Writing,* xvii.

25. Moschkovich, "—But I Know You, American Woman," 81.

26. Foucault, *The Order of Things,* xix.

27. For critiques of hybridity, see Robert J. C. Young, *Colonial Desire: Hybridity in Theory, Culture and Race,* and Jennifer DeVere Brody, *Impossible Purities: Blackness, Femininity, and Victorian Culture.*

28. Baca, "Meditations on the South Valley," canto 21, verses 40–46, in *Martín and Meditations on the South Valley,* 84.

29. This bias in favor of New World studies over transatlantic studies is being productively challenged by diaspora and globalism studies.

30. With regard to Salas's self-positioning, see Gerald Haslam, "A *MELUS* Interview: Floyd Salas," 97–109. Salas has claimed on numerous occasions, both in interviews like this one and on the Internet (http://www.floydsalas.com/Writerbiography.pdf), that he is descended from Spanish conquistadores Ponce de León and Coronado. In the same breath he indicates that he is aware that such revelations or claims are politically unpopular or "incorrect," as are his Irish and Belgian ancestry and his blood relation to a redheaded Catholic priest. He adds that, in contrast, mention of his five generations of Navajo ancestors has not thus far caused him trouble.

31. This film was written, directed, and produced by Whit Stillman, Harvard college alumnus, former executive director of an international daily news magazine,

freelance writer for publications such as *Harper's* and the *Wall Street Journal,* head of a small firm representing top-rank animation illustrators, and creator of the much-acclaimed film *Metropolitan,* which debuted in 1990.

32. Whit Stillman, quoted in "Claqueta," a pamphlet about his film distributed to moviegoers at Rosales, a Madrid cinemateque showing foreign films in their original language.

33. Ross, *Returning to A,* 19; hereafter cited in parentheses in the text.

34. Salas, *State of Emergency,* 19–21; hereafter cited in parentheses in the text.

35. Stanley G. Payne, *The Franco Regime: 1936–1975,* 511–20.

36. Ibid., 572.

37. Ibid., 573.

38. Published the same year the film *Barcelona* was released—1994 (an offshoot of the 1992 Quincentennial attention paid to Spain)—the collection of short stories *A Cast of Spaniards* by U.S. career foreign service officer and novelist Mark Jacobs also recycles familiar tropes about Spain, mostly Black Legend ones—not especially Orientalized. The stories from this collection are set in Central and South America, not in Spain. However, the very first story is titled "Eusebio's Spaniard," despite its Peruvian setting. Eusebio's Spaniard is depicted as greedy for gold, murderous, fanatic, and droolingly crazy. Spaniards in other stories from this collection do not fare much better. The story "Jumping Jesus" offers an image of Spaniards setting up "Jesus as a kind of slave master, master bleeder, a sucker of human marrow" (154) over Bolivian Indians. The story "Black Moon Rising" presents a "blind and bitter" "transplanted Spaniard, a Catalan" who "never got over his exile in the New World" (164–65). And the last story, "The Nature of Fiction," contains a character with "pale" and "un-healthy" skin and "black eyes" named Pilar, "the daughter . . . of a Spanish spy run afoul of his own government" (197). Jacobs has also written a novel to be published by Simon and Schuster titled biblically and forebodingly *A Handful of Kings* and set in Madrid, where Jacobs served as cultural affairs officer in the U.S. embassy. It concerns a U.S. diplomat named Vicky Sorrell working in Spain who is drawn into underground terrorist and spy networks. As in Stillman's film *Barcelona,* Spain is characterized by tyranny, violence, instability, and deception, a characterization that extends to Central and South American countries in *A Cast of Spaniards.*

39. See Silko, *Almanac of the Dead: A Novel.*

40. Rosaldo, "Imperialist Nostalgia," 108–9.

41. Ibid., 107.

42. The term "structure of feeling" is to be found in Raymond Williams's *Marxism and Literature.*

43. Tannock, "Nostalgia Critique," 453–64.

44. The politics of declaring disco "dead" is particularly suspect considering that it was and still is a largely queer, African American, and Latina/o cultural expression. It is a politics remindful of that of representations depicting "the last Indian" or "the vanished Indian."

45. Baudrillard, *The Transparency of Evil: Essays on Extreme Phenomena,* 75–80.

BIBLIOGRAPHY

Abbott, John S. C. *The Romance of Spanish History.* New York: Harper, 1869.

Acker, Kathy. *Don Quixote.* New York: Grove Press, 1986.

———. "A Few Notes on Two of My Books." *Review of Contemporary Fiction* (fall 1989): 31–36.

Acuña, Rodolfo. *Occupied America: A History of Chicanos.* 4th edition. Reading, MA: Addison-Wesley Longman, 2000.

Adams, Charles Francis. "Address by the President." *Proceedings of the Massachusetts Historical Society* 2d ser. 12 (1899).

———. *"Imperialism" and "The Tracks of Our Forefathers": A Paper Read by Charles Francis Adams before the Lexington, Massachusetts Historical Society, Tuesday, December 20, 1898.* Boston: Dana Estes, 1899.

Alarcón, Francisco X. *Del otro lado de la noche/From the Other Side of Night: New and Selected Poems.* Tucson: University of Arizona Press, 2002.

Alfau, Felipe. *Chromos.* Elmwood Park, IL: Dalkey Archive Press, 1990.

———. *Locos: A Comedy of Gestures.* New York: Vintage International, 1990.

Althusser, Louis. "Ideology and Ideological State Apparatuses." In *Essays on Ideology.* New York: Verso, 1984.

Anderson, Benedict. *Imagined Communities.* New York: Verso, 1991.

Anzaldúa, Gloria. *Borderlands/La Frontera: The New Mestiza.* San Francisco: Aunt Lute Books, 1987.

Aparicio, Frances R., and Susana Chávez-Silverman, eds., *Tropicalizations: Transcultural Representations of Latinidad.* Hanover, NH: University Press of New England, 1997.

Arroyo, Rane. *Pale Ramón: Poems.* Cambridge, MA: Zoland Books, 1998.

Baca, Jimmy Santiago. *C-Train and Thirteen Mexicans.* New York: Grove Press, 2002.

———. *Martín and Meditations on the South Valley.* New York: New Directions, 1987.

Baldwin, Marc D. *Reading "The Sun Also Rises": Hemingway's Political Unconscious.* New York: Peter Lang, 1997.

Ballou, Jenny. *Spanish Prelude.* Boston: Houghton Mifflin, 1937.

Banta, Martha. *Imaging American Women: Ideas and Ideals in Cultural History.* New York: Columbia University Press, 1987.

Barthes, Roland. *Camera lucida: Reflections on Photography.* Trans. Richard Howard. 1st American ed. New York: Hill and Wang, 1981.

———. "Diderot, Brecht, Eisenstein." In *Image—Music—Text,* trans. Stephen Heath. New York: Noonday Press, 1977.

———. *A Lover's Discourse: Fragments.* Trans. Richard Howard. 1st American ed. New York: Hill and Wang, 1978.

———. *Mythologies.* Ed. and trans. Annette Lavers. New York: Noonday Press, 1989.

———. *The Pleasure of the Text.* Trans. Richard Miller. New York: Noonday Press, 1989.

———. *Roland Barthes* Trans. Richard Howard. New York: Hill and Wang, 1977.

———. *The Rustle of Language.* Trans. Richard Howard. Berkeley: University of California Press, 1989.

Baudrillard, Jean. *The Transparency of Evil: Essays on Extreme Phenomena.* Trans. James Benedict. New York: Verso, 1993.

Bednap, Jeffrey, and Raúl Fernández, eds. *José Martí's "Our America": From National to Hemispheric Cultural Studies.* Durham, NC, and London: Duke University Press, 1998.

Bercovitch, Sacvan. *The Puritan Origins of the American Self.* New Haven: Yale University Press, 1975.

———. *The Rites of Assent: Transformations in the Symbolic Construction of America.* New York: Routledge, 1993.

Bergland, Renée L. *The National Uncanny: Indian Ghosts and American Subjects.* Hanover, NH: University Press of New England, 2000.

Berkove, Lawrence I., ed. *Ambrose Bierce: Skepticism and Dissent, Selected Journalism from 1898–1901.* Ann Arbor, MI.: Delmar, 1980.

Berlant, Lauren. *The Anatomy of National Fantasy: Hawthorne, Utopia, and Everyday Life.* Chicago: University of Chicago Press, 1991.

Bhabha, Homi. *The Location of Culture.* London: Routledge, 1994.

Bizet, Georges. *Carmen.* Ed. Nicolas John. London: John Calder, 1982.

Boone, Joseph A. "Vacation Cruises; or, The Homoerotics of Orientalism." *PMLA* 110.1 (January 1995): 89–107.

Boorstin, Daniel J. *The Americans: The National Experience.* New York: Vintage Books, 1965.

Bradstreet, Anne. "The Four Elements." In *The Works of Anne Bradstreet,* ed. John Harvard Ellis. Charlestown, MA: Abram E. Cutter, 1867.

Brennan, Karen. "The Geography of Enunciation: Hysterical Pastiche in Kathy Acker's Fiction." *boundary 2* 21.2 (summer 1994): 243–69.

Brown, Charles Brockden. *Wieland and Memoirs of Carwin the Biloquist.* New York: Penguin, 1991.

————. *Wieland; or, the Transformation: An American Tale*. Garden City, NY: Anchor Press, 1973.

Burkholder, Robert E., ed. *Critical Essays on Herman Melville's "Benito Cereno."* New York: G. K. Hall, 1992.

Campo, Rafael. *Diva*. Durham, NC: Duke University Press, 1999.

Candelaria, Nash. *Memories of the Alhambra*. Palo Alto, CA: Cibola Press, 1977.

Capellan, Ángel. *Hemingway and the Hispanic World*. Ann Arbor, MI: UMI Research Press, 1985.

Cárcel, Ricardo García. *La leyenda negra: historia y opinión*. Madrid: Alianza Editorial, 1992.

Cartoons of the Spanish-American War by Bart with Dates of Important Events from "The Minneapolis Journal." Minneapolis: Journal Printing Company, 1899.

Cartoons of the War of 1898 with Spain from Leading Foreign and American Papers. Chicago: Belford, Middlebrook & Co., 1898.

Castillo, Ana. *Peel My Love like an Onion*. New York: Doubleday, 1999.

Castillo-Puche, José Luis. *Hemingway in Spain: A Personal Reminiscence of Hemingway's Years in Spain*. Trans. Helen R. Lane. Garden City, NY: Doubleday, 1974.

Castro, Américo. *España en su historia: cristianos, moros, y judíos*. Buenos Aires: Editorial Losada, 1948.

————. *Españoles al margen*. 1973. Reprint, Madrid: Ediciones Jucar, 1975.

Cenen, and Barbara Smith. "The Blood—Yes, the Blood: A Conversation." In *Home Girls: A Black Feminist Anthology*, ed. Barbara Smith. New York: Kitchen Table—Women of Color Press, 1983.

Chace, James, and Caleb Carr. *America Invulnerable: The Quest for Absolute Security from 1812 to Star Wars*. New York: Summit Books, 1988.

Chace, Richard Volney. *The American Novel and Its Tradition*. Garden City, NY: Doubleday, 1957.

Chomsky, Noam. "Introduction: World Orders, Old and New." In *Altered States: A Reader in the New World Order*, ed. Phyllis Bennis and Michael Moushabeck. New York: Olive Branch Press, 1993.

Christophersen, Bill. *The Apparition in the Glass: Charles Brockden Brown's American Gothic*. Athens: University of Georgia Press, 1993.

Clark, David Lee. *Charles Brockden Brown: Pioneer Voice of America*. Durham, NC: Duke University Press, 1952.

Cofer, Judith Ortiz. *Silent Dancing: A Partial Remembrance of a Puerto Rican Childhood*. Houston: Arte Público Press, 1990.

Colomo, Fernando. *Skyline*. 16 mm. La Salamandra production company, Spain, 1983.

Conrad, Barnaby, and Loomis Dean. *Hemingway's Spain*. San Francisco: Chronicle Books, 1989.

Cotkin, George. *William James, Public Philosopher*. Baltimore: Johns Hopkins University Press, 1990.

Crane, Hart. *The Complete Poems and Selected Letters and Prose of Hart Crane*. Garden City, NY: Anchor Books, 1966.

Cruz, Victor Hernández. *Panoramas*. Minneapolis: Coffee House Press, 1997.

Dayan, Joan. "Amorous Bondage: Poe, Ladies, and Slaves." *American Literature* 66.2 (June 1994): 239–73.

———. *Fables of the Mind: An Inquiry into Poe's Fiction*. New York: Oxford University Press, 1987.

———. *Haiti, History, and the Gods*. Berkeley: University of California Press, 1995.

Deleuze, Gilles, and Félix Guattari. *A Thousand Plateaus: Capitalism and Schizophrenia*. Trans. Brian Massumi. Minneapolis: University of Minnesota Press, 1987.

Delgado, Richard, and Jean Stefancic, eds. *The Latino/a Condition: A Critical Reader*. New York: New York University Press, 1998.

DeVere Brody, Jennifer. *Impossible Purities: Blackness, Femininity, and Victorian Culture*. Durham, NC: Duke University Press, 1998.

Dos Passos, John. *Rosinante to the Road Again*. New York: George H. Doran, 1922.

———. "Young Spain." In *The Major Nonfictional Prose*, ed. Donald Pizer. Detroit: Wayne State University Press, 1988.

———. *U.S.A.* New York: Harcourt, Brace & Company, 1938.

Downes, William Howe. *Spanish Ways and By-Ways*. Boston: Cupples, Upham, 1883.

Draper, Andrew S. *The Rescue of Cuba: An Episode in the Growth of Free Government*. Boston: Silver, Burdett, 1899.

Dumas, Alexandre. *Adventures in Spain*. Trans. Alma Elizabeth Murch. Philadelphia: Chilton, 1959.

Dunham, Samuel Astley. *History of Spain and Portugal*. 5 vols. New York: Harper, 1854.

Elliott, Emory, ed. *The Columbia Literary History of the United States*. New York: Columbia University Press, 1988.

Fabre, Michel. *The Unfinished Quest of Richard Wright*. Trans. Isabel Barzun. 2d ed. Chicago: University of Illinois Press, 1993.

Fairbrother, Trevor J. *John Singer Sargent and America*. New York: Garland Publishing, 1986.

Fernandez-Florez, Dario. *The Spanish Heritage in the United States,* 2d ed. Madrid: Publicaciones Españolas, 1968.

Fliegelman, Jay. *Prodigals and Pilgrims: The American Revolution against Patriarchal Authority, 1750–1800*. New York: Cambridge University Press, 1982.

Ford, Brinsley. *Richard Ford in Spain*. London: Wildenstein, 1974.

Foucault, Michel. *The Order of Things: An Archaeology of the Human Sciences*. New York: Vintage Books, 1973.

Frank, Waldo. *Virgin Spain; Scenes from the Spiritual Drama of a Great People*. New York: Boni & Liveright, 1926.

Freud, Sigmund. *The Ego and the Id*. New York: W. W. Norton, 1960.

———. *Totem and Taboo: Some Points of Agreement between the Mental Lives of Savages and Neurotics*. New York: W. W. Norton, 1950.

Fryd, Vivien Green. *Art and Empire: The Politics of Ethnicity in the United States Capitol, 1815–1860*. New Haven: Yale University Press, 1992.

Gallop, Jane. *Reading Lacan.* Ithaca, NY: Cornell University Press, 1985.

Gatewood, Willard B., Jr. *"Smoked Yankees" and the Struggle for Empire: Letters from Negro Soldiers, 1898–1902.* Fayetteville: University of Arkansas Press, 1987.

Gibson, Charles. *Spain in America.* New York: Harper & Row, 1966.

Ginsberg, Allen. "Howl." In *Collected Poems, 1947–1980.* New York: Harper & Row, 1988.

Glendinning, Nigel. "Goya and Arriaza's *Profecia del Pirineo.*" *Journal of the Warburg and Courtauld Institutes* 26 (1963): 363–66.

Goddu, Teresa A. *Gothic America: Narrative, History, and Nation.* New York: Columbia University Press, 1997.

Goldman, Emma. *Anarchism and Other Essays.* 1910. Reprint, New York: Dover Publications, 1969.

Gómez-Peña, Guillermo. "Documented/ Undocumented." In *Multi-Cultural Literacy,* ed. Rick Simonson and Scott Walker. Saint Paul, MN: Graywolf Press, 1988.

Gracia, Jorge J. E. *Hispanic/Latino Identity: A Philosophical Perspective.* Malden, MA: Blackwell Publishers, 2000.

Gruesz, Kirsten Silva. *Ambassadors of Culture: The Transamerican Origins of Latino Writing.* Princeton, NJ: Princeton University Press, 2002.

Guttmann, Allen. *The Wound in the Heart: America and the Spanish Civil War.* New York: Free Press of Glencoe, 1962.

Harrison, James Albert. *Spain.* Boston: D. Lothrop, 1882.

———. *Spain in Profile: A Summer among the Olives and Aloes.* Boston: Houghton, Osgood, 1879.

Harrison, Lawrence E. *The Pan-American Dream: Do Latin America's Cultural Values Discourage True Partnership with the United States and Canada?* New York: Basic Books, 1997.

Hart, James D. *The Oxford Companion to American Literature.* 5th ed. New York: Oxford University Press, 1983.

Haslam, Gerald. "A *MELUS* Interview: Floyd Salas." *MELUS: The Journal of the Society for the Study of Multi-Ethnic Literature of the United States,* no. 1 (spring 1993): 97–109.

Hawthorne, Nathaniel. *The Letters, 1843–1853.* 6 vols. Ed. Thomas Woodson, L. Neal Smith, and Norman Holmes Pearson. Columbus: Ohio State University Press, 1984–88.

———. *The Scarlet Letter.* New York: New American Library, 1980.

Hay, John. *William McKinley's Memorial Address by John Hay, Delivered in the Capitol February 27, 1902, by Invitation of the Congress.* Washington, DC: U.S. Government Printing Office, 1902.

Heidegger, Martin. *Being and Time.* Trans. Joan Stambaugh. Albany: State University of New York Press, 1996.

Hemingway, Ernest. *The Fifth Column and Four Stories of the Spanish Civil War.* New York: Charles Scribner's Sons, 1972.

————. *For Whom the Bell Tolls.* 1940. Reprint, New York: Macmillan, 1987.

————. *A Moveable Feast.* 1964. Reprint, New York: Macmillan, 1987.

————. *The Snows of Kilimanjaro and Other Stories.* 1927. Reprint, New York: Macmillan, 1986.

————. *The Sun Also Rises.* 1926. Reprint, New York: Macmillan, 1986.

Henry, Robert Selph. *The Story of the Mexican War.* New York: Da Capo Press, 1950.

Hetherington, Hugh W. *Melville's Reviewers: British and American, 1846–1891.* Chapel Hill: University of North Carolina Press, 1961.

Hills, Patricia. "Sargent's *El Jaleo,* Bizet's *Carmen,* and the Lure of Spain." *Art New England* 13.6 (October/November 1992): 10–11, 52.

Holmes, Oliver Wendell. *Elsie Venner: A Romance of Destiny.* London: Routledge, 1861.

————. *Life and Letters of Oliver Wendell Holmes.* 2 vols. Ed. John Torrey Morse Jr. Boston: Houghton, Mifflin, 1896.

————. *Our Hundred Days in Europe.* Boston: Houghton Mifflin, 1887.

Horsman, Reginald. *Race and Manifest Destiny: The Origins of American Racial Anglo-Saxonism.* Cambridge: Harvard University Press, 1981.

Howells, William Dean. *Familiar Spanish Travels.* New York: Harper & Brothers, 1913.

————. *Venetian Life.* New York: Hurd and Houghton, 1867.

Iribarren, José María. *Hemingway y los Sonfermines.* Pamplona: Editorial Gómez, 1970.

Irving, Washington. *The Alhambra.* Tarrytown, NY: Sleepy Hollow Press, 1982.

————. *Astoria.* New York: The Co-operative Publication Society, n.d.

————. *History of the Life and Voyages of Christopher Columbus.* Ed. John Harmon McElroy. Boston: Twayne Publishers, 1981.

————. *Letters.* 4 vols. Ed. Ralph M. Aderman, Herbert L. Kleinfeld, and Jenifer S. Banks. Boston: Twayne Publishers, 1978–82.

Jacobs, Mark. *A Cast of Spaniards.* Hoboken, NJ: Talisman House, 1994.

James, Henry. *The Painter's Eye: Notes and Essays on the Pictorial Arts.* Ed. John L. Sweeney. London: Rupert Hart-Davis, 1956.

————. ed. *The Letters of William James.* 2 vols. Boston: Little, Brown, 1926.

James, William. *Essays, Comments, and Reviews.* Cambridge: Harvard University Press, 1987.

————. *The Varieties of Religious Experience: A Study in Human Nature.* 1902. Reprint, New York: Viking Penguin, 1982.

John Singer Sargent's El Jaleo. Curated by Mary Crawford Volk. Washington, DC: National Gallery of Art, 1992.

Josephs, Allen. *White Wall of Spain: The Mysteries of Andalusian Culture.* Ames: Iowa State University Press, 1983.

Juderías, Julián. *La leyenda negra: estudios acerca del concepto de España en el extranjero.* 2d ed. Barcelona: Editorial Araluce, 1917.

Jullian, Philippe. *The Orientalists: European Painters of Eastern Scenes.* Trans. Helga and Dinah Harrison. Oxford: Phaidon Press, 1977.

Kabbani, Rana. *Europe's Myths of the Orient.* Bloomington: Indiana University Press, 1986.

Kaplan, Amy. "Black and Blue on San Juan Hill." In *Cultures of United States Imperialism,* ed. Amy Kaplan and Donald Pease. Durham, NC: Duke University Press, 1993.

Karcher, Carolyn L. *Shadow over the Promised Land: Slavery, Race, and Violence in Melville's America.* Baton Rouge: Louisiana State University Press, 1980.

Kennedy, J. Gerald, and Liliane Wiessberg, eds. *Romancing the Shadow: Poe and Race.* New York: Oxford University Press, 2001.

Kinder, Marsha. *Blood Cinema: The Reconstruction of National Identity in Spain.* Berkeley: University of California Press, 1993.

Lacan, Jacques. "The Mirror Stage as Formative of the Function of the I as Revealed in Psychoanalytic Experience." In *Écrits: A Selection,* trans. Alan Sheridan. New York: W. W. Norton, 1977.

Latimer, Elizabeth Wormeley. *Spain in the Nineteenth Century.* 2d ed. Chicago: A. C. McClurg, 1898.

Levin, Harry. *The Power of Blackness: Hawthorne, Poe, and Melville.* London: Faber and Faber, 1958.

Levine, Lawrence W. *Highbrow/Lowbrow: The Emergence of Cultural Hierarchy in America.* Cambridge: Harvard University Press, 1988.

Litvak, Lily. *A Dream of Arcadia: Anti-Industrialism in Spanish Literature.* Austin: University of Texas Press, 1975.

Lodge, Henry Cabot. *The War with Spain.* New York: Harper, 1899.

Longfellow, Henry Wadsworth. *Selected Poems.* Ed. Lawrence Buell. New York: Viking Penguin, 1988.

Lummis, Charles F. *The Land of Poco Tiempo.* Albuquerque: University of New Mexico Press, 1952.

Lynn, Kenneth. *Hemingway.* New York: Ballantine Books, 1988.

MacLeish, Archibald. *Collected Poems, 1917–1982.* Boston: Houghton Mifflin, 1985.

Manrique, Jaime. *My Night with/Mi noche con Federico García Lorca.* Trans. Edith Grossman and Eugene Richie. New York: Painted Leaf Press, 1997.

Marble, Earl. "Gineral Fitzhugh Lee." In *Spanish-American War Songs: A Complete Collection of Newspaper Verse during the Recent War with Spain,* comp. and ed. Sidney A. Witherbee. Detroit: Sidney A. Witherbee, 1898.

Marlais, Michael Andrew. *Americans and Paris.* Waterville, ME: Colby College Museum of Art, 1990.

Martí, José. *José Martí's "Our America": From National to Hemispheric Cultural Studies.* Ed. Jeffrey Belknap and Raúl Fernández. Durham, NC, and London: Duke University Press, 1998.

Martínez, Miguel Molina. *La leyenda negra.* Madrid: NEREA, 1991.

McAlister, Lyle N. *Spain and Portugal in the New World, 1492–1700.* Minneapolis: University of Minnesota Press, 1984.

McWilliams, Carey. *North from Mexico: The Spanish-Speaking People of the United States.* New York: Praeger, 1990.

Melville, Herman. "Benito Cereno." In *Billy Budd and Other Stories*. New York: Viking Penguin, 1986.

———. *Moby Dick*. New York: Nal Penguin, 1980.

Mérimée, Prosper. "Carmen." In *Mérimée*, ed. Alexander Jessup, trans. George Burham Ives. New York: G. P. Putnam's Sons, 1903.

Merish, Lori. "Not 'Just a Cigar': Commodity Culture and the Construction of Imperial Manhood." In *Sentimental Materialism: Gender, Commodity Culture, and Nineteenth-Century American Literature*. Durham, NC: Duke University Press, 2000.

Michaels, Walter Benn. *Our America: Nativism, Modernism, and Pluralism*. Durham, NC: Duke University Press, 1995.

Miller, Perry. *Nature's Nation*. Cambridge: Harvard University Press, 1967.

Mitchell, David. *Viajeros por España: de Borrow a Hemingway*. Trans. Isabel Gómez-Arnau. Madrid: Mondadori, 1989.

Mitchell, Timothy. *Flamenco Deep Song*. New Haven: Yale University Press, 1994.

Monteflores, Carmen de. *Cantando Bajito/Singing Softly*. San Francisco: Spinsters/Aunt Lute, 1989.

Moschkovich, Judit. "—But I Know You, American Woman." In *This Bridge Called My Back: Writings by Radical Women of Color*, ed. Cherríe Moraga and Gloria Anzaldúa. New York: Kitchen Table, 1983.

Moses, Bernard. "The Recent War with Spain from an Historical Point of View." *University Chronicle* 2.6 (1899): 400–420.

Mount, Charles Merrill. *John Singer Sargent: A Biography*. New York: W. W. Norton, 1955.

Muñoz, José Esteban. *Disidentifications: Queers of Color and the Performance of Politics* Minneapolis: University of Minnesota Press, 1999.

Muste, John M. *Say That We Saw Spain Die: Literary Consequences of the Spanish Civil War*. Seattle: University of Washington Press, 1966.

Nelson, Dana. *The Word in Black and White: Reading "Race" in American Literature, 1638–1867*. New York: Oxford University Press, 1992.

Nixon, Mary F. *With a Pessimist in Spain*. Chicago: A. C. McClurg, 1897.

Oboler, Suzanne. *Ethnic Labels, Latino Lives: Identity and the Politics of (Re)Presentation in the United States*. Minneapolis: University of Minnesota Press, 1995.

Olson, Stanley. *John Singer Sargent: His Portrait*. London: Macmillan, 1986.

Open Spain/España Abierta: Contemporary Documentary Photography in Spain. Curated by Denise Miller-Clark. Trans. Lee Fontanella. Chicago: Museum of Contemporary Photography, 1992.

Painter, Nell Irvin. *Standing at Armageddon: The United States, 1877–1919*. New York: W. W. Norton, 1987.

Paulson, Ronald. *Emblem and Expression: Meaning in English Art of the Eighteenth Century*. London: Thames and Hudson, 1975.

Payne, Stanley G. *The Franco Regime: 1936–1975*. Madison: University of Wisconsin Press, 1987.

Poe, Edgar Allan. "Appalachia." In *The Works of Edgar Allan Poe*, vol. 7, ed. Edmund Clarence and George Edward Woodberry. Chicago: Stone & Kimball, 1894.

———. "The Facts in the Case of M. Valdemar." In *Complete Tales and Poems of Edgar Allan Poe*. New York: Vintage Books, 1975.

———. "The Imp of the Perverse." In *Complete Tales and Poems of Edgar Allan Poe*. New York: Vintage Books, 1975.

———. "The Philosophy of Composition." In *The Selected Writings of Edgar Allan Poe*, ed. Edward H. Davidson. Boston: Houghton Mifflin, 1956.

———. "The Pit and the Pendulum." In *Complete Tales and Poems of Edgar Allan Poe*. New York: Vintage Books, 1975.

———. "Twice-Told Tales." In *The Selected Writings of Edgar Allan Poe*, ed. Edward H. Davidson. Boston: Houghton Mifflin, 1956.

———. "William Wilson." In *Complete Tales and Poems of Edgar Allan Poe*. New York: Vintage Books, 1975.

Popkin, Richard H. "Medicine, Racism, Anti-Semitism: A Dimension of Enlightenment Culture." In *The Languages of Psyche: Mind and Body in Enlightenment Thought*, ed. G. S. Rousseau. Berkeley: University of California Press, 1990.

Porte, Joel. *The Romance in America*. Middletown, CT: Wesleyan University Press, 1969.

Powell, Timothy. *Reconstructing Cultural Identity in a Multicultural Context*. New Brunswick, NJ: Rutgers University Press, 1999.

———. *Ruthless Democracy: A Multicultural Interpretation of the American Renaissance*. Princeton, NJ: Princeton University Press, 2000.

Pratt, Mary Louise. *Imperial Eyes: Travel Writing and Transculturation*. New York: Routledge, 1992.

Prescott, William Hickling. *History of the Reign of Ferdinand and Isabella the Catholic*. Philadelphia: J. B. Lippincott, 1892.

Pritchett, V. S. *The Spanish Temper*. London: Hogarth Press, 1984.

Raley, Harold. *The Spirit of Spain*. Houston: Halcyon Press, 2001.

Remington, Frederic. *The Collected Writings of Frederic Remington*. Ed. Peggy Samuels and Harold Samuels. Garden City, NY: Doubleday, 1979.

———. *Remington Papers*. Ogdensburg, NY: Remington Art Memorial, 1956. Microfiche.

Rivera, Edward. *Family Installments: Memories of Growing up Hispanic*. New York: William Morrow & Co., 1982.

Rosaldo, Renato. "Imperialist Nostalgia." *Representations* 26 (spring 1989): 107–22.

Rosenthal, Donald A. *Orientalism: The Near East in French Painting, 1800–1880*. Rochester, NY: Memorial Art Gallery of the University of Rochester, 1982.

Ross, Dorien. *Returning to A*. San Francisco: City Lights Books, 1995.

Said, Edward W. *Orientalism*. New York: Vintage Books, 1978.

Salas, Floyd. *State of Emergency*. Houston: Arte Público Press, 1996.

Saldívar, José David. *The Dialectics of Our America: Genealogy, Cultural Critique, and Literary History*. Durham, NC: Duke University Press, 1991.

Sale, Kirkpatrick. *The Conquest of Paradise: Christopher Columbus and the Columbian Legacy.* New York: Knopf, 1990.

Salom, Andrés. *Didáctica del cante jondo.* Murcia, Spain: Ediciones 1976, 23–27.

Sedgwick , Eve Kosofsky. "Introduction." In *Between Men: English Literature and Male Homosocial Desire.* New York: Columbia University Press, 1985.

Seelye, John. "Charles Brockden Brown and Early American Fiction." In *The Columbia Literary History of the United States,* ed. Emory Elliott. New York: Columbia University Press, 1988.

Shaw, Angel Velasco, and Luis H. Francia, eds. *Vestiges of War: The Philippine-American War and the Aftermath of an Imperial Dream.* New York: New York University Press, 2002.

Shaw, Donald Leslie. *The Generation of 1898 in Spain.* London: E. Benn, 1975.

Shields, David S. *Oracles of Empire: Poetry, Politics, and Commerce in British America, 1690–1750.* Chicago: University of Chicago Press, 1990.

Silko, Leslie Marmon. *Almanac of the Dead: A Novel.* New York: Penguin, 1991.

Simms, William Gilmore. 6 vols. *The Letters of William Gilmore Simms.* Ed. Mary C. Simms Oliphant, Alfred Taylor Odell, and T. C. Duncan Eaves. Columbia: University of South Carolina Press, 1952–82.

———. *The Yemassee: A Romance of Carolina.* New York: Redfield, 1854.

Slotkin, Richard. *Regeneration through Violence: The Mythology of the American Frontier, 1600–1860.* Middletown, CT: Wesleyan University Press, 1973.

Stafford, Barbara Maria. *Artful Science: Enlightenment Entertainments and the Eclipse of Visual Education.* Cambridge: MIT Press, 1994.

Stallman, R. W., and E. R. Hagemann, eds. *The War Dispatches of Stephen Crane.* New York: New York University Press, 1964.

Stavans, Ilan. "Anonymity: An Interview with Felipe Alfau." *Review of Contemporary Fiction* 13.1 (spring 1993): 146–55.

Stehle, Raymond Louis. *Emanuel Leutze: 1816-1868.* Washington, DC: Columbia Historical Society, 1971.

Stein, Gertrude. *The Autobiography of Alice B. Toklas.* 1933. Reprint, New York: Vintage Books, 1961.

———. *The Geographical History of America.* 1936. Reprint, Baltimore: Johns Hopkins University Press, 1973.

———. *Paris France.* 1940. Reprint, New York: Liveright, 1970.

———. *Picasso: The Complete Writings.* Boston: Beacon Press, 1985.

———. "What Are Masterpieces?" In *The Oxford Book of Exile,* ed. John Simpson. New York: Oxford University Press, 1995.

Stevens, Wallace. *The Collected Poems of Wallace Stevens.* New York: Vintage Books, 1982.

Stillman, Whit. *Barcelona.* 16 mm. Castle Rock Entertainment, 1994.

Sumner, William Graham. "The Conquest of the United States by Spain." *Yale Law Journal* 8 (January 1899) 168–93.

Sundquist, Eric J. "*Benito Cereno* and New World Slavery." In *Reconstructing American Literary History,* ed. Sacvan Bercovitch. Cambridge: Harvard University Press, 1986.

Tannock, Stuart. "Nostalgia Critique." *Cultural Studies* 9.3 (October 1995): 453–64.

Taylor, Bayard. *The Lands of the Saracens; or, Pictures of Palestine, Asia Minor, Sicily, and Spain.* New York: G. P. Putnam's Sons, 1855.

Tomes, Robert. *The Bazar Book of Decorum: The Care of the Person, Manners, Etiquette, and Ceremonials.* New York, 1870.

Truettner, William H. "Repainting the Past." In *The West as America: Reinterpreting Images of the Frontier, 1820–1920,* ed. William H. Truettner. Washington, DC: Smithsonian Institution Press, 1991.

Tucker, Norman P. *Americans in Spain: Patriots, Expatriates, and Early American Hispanists 1780-1850.* Boston: Boston Athenaeum, 1980.

Ulsar Pietri, Arturo. "The Other America." Trans. Andrée Conrad. *Review* 14 (spring 1975): 42–47.

Véliz, Claudio. *The New World of the Gothic Fox: Culture and Economy in English and Spanish America.* Berkeley: University of California Press, 1994.

Verdú, Vicente. *El planeta americano.* Barcelona: Editorial Anagrama, 1996.

Volk, Mary Crawford. "Sargent, Spain, and El Jaleo." In *John Singer Sargent's El Jaleo.* Washington, DC: National Gallery of Art, 1992.

Wagner-Martin, Linda, ed. *Ernest Hemingway's "The Sun Also Rises": A Casebook.* New York: Oxford University Press, 2002.

Watts, Henry Edward. *The Christian Recovery of Spain.* New York: G. P. Putnam's Sons, 1894.

Watts, Steven. *The Romance of Real Life: Charles Brockden Brown and the Origins of American Culture.* Baltimore: Johns Hopkins University Press, 1994.

Werckmeister, O. K. *Citadel Culture.* Chicago: University of Chicago Press, 1991.

Wertheimer, Eric. *Imagined Empires: Incas, Aztecs, and the New World of American Literature, 1771–1876.* New York: Cambridge University Press, 1999.

West, Nathanael. *The Day of the Locust.* In *West: Novels and Other Writings,* ed. Sacvan Bercovitch. New York: Literary Classics of the United States, 1997.

———. "The Impostor." In *West: Novels and Other Writings,* ed. Sacvan Bercovitch. New York: Literary Classics of the United States, 1997.

Wharton, Edith. *A Backward Glance.* New York: D. Appleton-Century, 1934.

Whitfield, Stephen J. *The Culture of the Cold War.* Baltimore: Johns Hopkins University Press, 1991.

Whitman, Walt. "Spain, 1873–74." From *Noon to Starry Night,* in *The Complete Poetry and Prose of Walt Whitman,* vol. 1, p. 414. New York: Pellegrini & Cudahy, 1948.

Williams, Raymond. *Marxism and Literature.* Oxford: Oxford University Press, 1977.

Williams, Stanley T. *The Spanish Background of American Literature.* 2 vols. 1955. Reprint, Hamden, CT: Archon Books, 1968.

Witherbee, Sidney A., comp. and ed. *Spanish-American War Songs: A Complete Collection of Newspaper Verse during the Recent War with Spain.* Detroit: Sidney A. Witherbee, 1898.

Wright, Richard. *Pagan Spain.* 1957. Reprint, New York: HarperPerennial, 1995.

Young, Robert J. C. *Colonial Desire: Hybridity in Theory, Culture and Race.* New York: Routledge, 1995.

Zimmerman, Jeremiah, *Spain and Her People*. Philadelphia: George W. Jacobs, 1902.
Zook, Kristal Brent. "Light Skinned-ded Naps." In *Making Face, Making Soul/ Haciendo Caras: Creative and Critical Perspectives by Women of Color,* ed. Gloria Anzaldúa. San Francisco: Aunt Lute Foundation Books, 1990.

INDEX

María DeGuzmán is associate professor of English and director of Latina/o studies at the University of North Carolina, Chapel Hill. She has published essays on Latina/o writers and on the Spanish-Cuban-American War of 1898. She is also a conceptual photographer, and her text-image work has been shown nationally and internationally.